Life's Mysterious Paths

A Woman's Life

D1744756

By Angela Valentine

Author of

The Dark Edge of the Rainbow

The Great thing in this world
Is not so much where we are
But in what direction
We are moving
Oliver Wendell Holmes 1809-1894

I dedicate this book
To my children
Sarah Valentine – Schrider
and
Peter and Amy Valentine
My grand children
Eva and Charlie Valentine

May you remember your Mum and Granny.

Newton Abbot 2018

Prologue

After my husband left me and the children, I found myself in a strange part of England of which I did not know much about. I had lived and worked in London for almost ten years and then lived in Epsom, where my children were born and started school. Innocently, when my ex-husband refused to let me go back to Germany, I moved to Devon and found it to be so completely different from London. I had arrived in deepest beautiful Devonshire where people were still watching propaganda films made in Shepperton Studios in the 40's.

When my children came home one day with their new and curious friends and wanted to know if I or my mother and their relatives in Germany were Nazi's, I was a little speechless and wondered how to answer this especially when I saw their schoolmates beady little eyes watching me like mini hawks. I told them that I was their age when the war happened. I really did not know how to explain to 10 and 11 year old children the horrors of war and decided to write about my life during the War. It is not available in the bookshops in Britain, but my friends and family here and in Germany and New Zealand read the book and found it quite different to what they had imagined and said they could not put it down until they had finished reading it.

It followed that I had to write the rest of my story, since it turned out to be so completely different from what I had always dreamt of doing. I didn't have a lot of choice, since my schooling was so much interrupted because of the war. I went to work just 7 years after the war. There was not enough room at home, there was very little money and my mother had to bring the three of us up by herself, since my father did not return from the War. Nobody could tell whether he was alive or dead. We had lost everything and could not go back home, since it was lost forever to Poland, Russia and the Iron Curtain. So I left and started my working life a month after my 16th Birthday. I was so very homesick but there was little anybody could do. I had to learn to look after myself.

And here begins my second book. I am no good in writing fiction, and so this is all reality. Some of it was super exciting, a lot of it sad and very hard to bear and disappointing, a lot of it surprising and also a lot of it quite wonderful, and all of it a great adventure.

My grandparents' mother's side had large estates in East Prussia and Silesia and as children we used to go and enjoy the country, coming from Berlin where my father had a dental practice until the War started. Mother used to be a Nurse in a large Berlin hospital. I used to love to ride and be with animals. Horses were my Grandfather's passion and life; he used to train and breed them. I suppose it was in my blood. Grandfather took the role of my missing father. I loved him dearly.

When I left school there was not much available as far as jobs were concerned and I decided to go into farming. I became an agricultural apprentice.

I did my exams and went to college afterwards and then started on my journeyman's years. I chose Finland. I did well there and there I learned Finish and decided that I should learn English if I wanted to get on internationally. I came to England, Ireland and back to Germany.

Things had changed and women had a difficult time finding a job in farming. Farming had changed in the three years I was away and I thought I go into farming admin. But I was sent to Basel Badischer Bahnhof to work for the German Railways in Switzerland. In Germany you don't argue with the job centre.

After 5 years of farming and 18 months of learning English, I changed course and worked in signals, but also travelled in my homeland, in what was left after the iron curtain was drawn, for a penny a kilometre.

I went back briefly to England to take the lower Cambridge Certificate in English to get a better job, but stayed and worked for Lufthansa in Old Bond Street London. Here an entirely different life started for me. I travelled the world around the globe several times.

There followed a difficult marriage, a stepson who was a heroin addict and his girlfriend, my gorgeous children and hardships, but also bliss and happiness.

I hope you find it interesting; so much has changed in the time when I left home, so soon after the last War. Modern life has taken over and we live in a completely different world today. Our young people have little idea how their mother's and grandmother's lives' has been lived, since everything changes so quickly, When I think that my mother never had a drivers license but was able to drive a coach and four!

It might be of interest. It was a good life, albeit hard at times. I had to use some rough language and hope to be forgiven for that.
Angela Valentine.

1

Leaving Home

"Take care my little sparrow", Margarete said, hugging her daughter Angela at the railway station. She was leaving to start her second year as an agricultural apprentice in the Upper Palatinate, a train journey away from home. A long way Margarete thought, two hours by train. Her daughter's first year was only a short bike ride away. A choking feeling crept into her heart. Why couldn't the children stay small a little longer? She thought. This dreadful war finished only seven years ago. She hasn't recovered from the trauma. None of us have.

Angela freed herself. Her mother was always so emotional. She had a lump in her throat, and hated it. It was bad enough, feeling sad at leaving home, leaving her sisters and mother. They were all so close, a tight parcel throughout the horrors of the war, and now time and circumstance had broken the string, and she had fallen out. She was in two minds over leaving home. If this new farm was as bad as the first one, she seriously doubted whether she would continue with her choice of career, but it was good to escape from the cramped existence at home.

"Have you got everything?" her mother asked for the umpteenth time. "Yes, the suitcase, the bag and the bike. It's all here. Stop worrying. I'll visit, I'll write."

She looked at her mother. Always there, caring and comforting her three girls, her one and only important thing in life. What will she do, once they are all gone, as surely they will, she thought. Mothering and building a nest for her little ones is what she knows best. And she had had to build so many nests in the past; the family home in Berlin, the cosy temporary nests, three of them in East Prussia, and then the haphazard dozen, no sooner built than destroyed until they found rest in this lovely town, where her mother was born, in another time and another world away, or so it seemed.

They shared their second floor apartment with a pair of bullfinches, a pair of crossbills, a pair of gold and a green finches, and a blue tit, who managed to join them from the outside, finding a way in through the netting of the aviary which they had made their balcony into. The french windows were open throughout the summer and the birds had the freedom of the room to fly about in, and had built their nests among the flower pots and foliage of the balcony. Amazingly, their droppings were only seen on the balcony. It was a truly magical place, especially after Fifi arrived as a blind little baby. Fifi was a red squirrel, which took to their home and the many birds immediately, and was full of mischief. It made its nest behind the books, gnawing all the pages from Schiller's complete works to make a cosy and soft nest for itself, and as they discovered later, several storage chambers too. Fifi ruled their home, and the birds respected Fifi too. Margarete put a nut under her pillow and every morning, at the same time, Fifi would come, tap her lightly on the face so that she would move her head, and then collect the nut. A sweet tame thing.

The train came into the station, and Angela pushed her bike towards the parcel wagon, where the attendant helped her lift it up. Then she returned to her mother who had lifted the heavy suitcase into the carriage. Angela picked up the bag and followed her. Margarete's tears flowed freely. Drat the farewells, she thought. She hated crying, but couldn't help it.

"I'll be home for Christmas" Angela said and hugged her mother again.

"God bless, and write. You must write". The whistle went and Margarete stepped up to the door. Angela pulled down the window and waved, as the train slowly rolled out of the Regensburg station. She waved for as long as she could see her. Bine will be gone next year, she thought. Mother must find something to do, a proper job. They had discussed her going back to nursing. But she needed her papers, and they were all lost in the bombing and during the many moves,   together with everything else they had ever possessed. Margarete had written to the hospital in Berlin, where she had trained, and even there, vital records were lost. Most of the staff gone, no one knew where. So the search went on. Nurses were needed desperately, but she had nothing to prove, that she was a state registered nurse. Still, the authorities were hopeful, and so was Margarete. A warm and loving feeling overtook Angela and she would have liked to have given her mother another hug and said 'thank you'.

She looked out of the window, and watched the buildings slide past. Just over eight years ago, they had skidded into the city from this direction amid a hail of bullets and bombs. They had been shot at by low flying aircraft, the warehouses out there were smouldering and burning, the ships in the docks were lying on their sides, like wounded prehistoric animals. The stench of the burning warehouses had been nauseating. Now, looking out, apart from one or two derelict houses, there was not much evidence of war. The ships in the docks stood upright, beautiful and proud, swanlike, busy cranes loading cargo, there were building sites everywhere. Many people busily moving about dressed in proper clothing, not in rags.

Thinking back to the war and the total collapse, seven years ago, it seemed just like a very bad dream, except that sometimes the reality stood there, big and ugly, confronting her. She could not blot out the memory of the horrors, and then there was this homesickness! They were not at home here, no matter how hard they tried. The sisters had made lots of friends at school. Marie Louise, her best friend, and she had been inseparable, and often a great comfort to one another; she was a refugee from East Prussia, so they had something in common right from the start. Also she was a Protestant.

Marie Louise had been very astonished, when she told her, that she had decided on an agricultural career, with horses. Ise, as everybody called her, wanted to be a lawyer, and kept encouraging her, to do the same. But Angela wanted to be with horses, not to spend her time in offices. A dreadful thought!

"Think of the money" Ise would argue. "There is no money in horses, Ises mother said. machines will take over and horses will belong to yesterday". Angela could not see this at all.

"And what about riding, people will always want to ride, and there are always possibilities in the country, where only horses can be used". Machines are very good in farming, but there is always a need for animals. But Ise was adamant. "You'll regret it one day". But all they truly regretted at that moment was their parting. They promised to write and always be friends, no matter what.

Angela had sometimes wondered, where and when she had made the decision to farm, why this was something she wanted to do. No one in her class chose this career. A few went to university to study law or become doctors, one a dentist. More than half went to be shop assistants or worked in factories. The money there was so fantastic, they laughed at the rest of them for not choosing to earn fortunes. Brigitte became a tailor's apprentice. But the most out of the way, so they all agreed, was Angela with her farming ideas.

When she informed her grandfather of her decision, he nodded:" It's always been in our family, for generationes. Breeding and keeping horses is our life. You are born too late though". He sighed.

But there was Robert, the Russian Prisoner of War from the Caucasus, who had been in East Prussia, and whom she had loved more than her own father. He was a horseman and she wanted to be like him. He seemed to be able to speak to the horses and they understood him. Yes, she wanted to be like Robert. Robert who was shot by his own people and was crudely buried in the forest at Lichtenau after the Russians had overrun it. Robert lived on in her heart. Her soul and his were linked somehow. They had both recognised it then, the man and the child. Would her life be haunted by the events of her childhood?

The train briefly stopped in Regenstauf. She looked over to the right into the beginnings of the Bayerische Wald, the Bavarian Forest, the wooded mountain range bordering onto Czechoslovakia. In home geography she had learned that Regenstauf lay between the Reissberg and the Ottenberg. Really beautiful countryside; her new home now. Would she ever feel truly at home here?

The train moved on, stopping again at Haidhof and Maxhütte. There were many iron ore mines and smelting plants in this area.

At Schwandorf she had to change trains. She heaved the heavy suitcase onto the platform and rushed to get her bike. It was an ancient bike, but she had fitted new brake pads and new tyres and a new bell and polished it as best she could. The dull gleam did not disguise its age and the fact that it was a man's bike. It was a good runner though and all she could afford at the time. It had been her transport, when she got Sunday off every six weeks to race home for a day away from her first farm, and it had not let her down.

Now she struggled down the stairs and up on the other side to reach the platform she needed. A young man, tall and well dressed, wearing glasses, lifted the suitcase.

"Are you running off with some iron ore or something?" he joked. "Which train are you catching?"

"The one to Amberg, over there. I hope I wont miss it" she worried.

"Plenty of time, I have to catch the same train. I live in Amberg." He had only a very small suitcase to carry. He made it look as if her large case was not at all heavy. Securing her little bag on the bike she hurried after him. Down the stairs was no problem, but up the other side was a struggle. It took all her strength to make it look easy. She would not be a helpless, weak girl. He made no remarks.

She deposited her bike in the parcel wagon again and joined the young man in the compartment. He had lifted the heavy suitcase into the net already and now he took her other bag too.

"Where are you going with all this luggage? You planing to stay a while? "

"Yes, I am in my second apprentice ship year" she said proudly. I am an agricultural apprentice". He laughed.

"Fancy that, so am I. I have also just completed my first year, and now I am going home for two days, before I start my second year." He had the appearance of a student of medicine or something like that, but not a farmer. But then she remembered what Ise had said about herself. You are a 'towny', not a country girl.

"Why do you choose to do farming?" she asked. "Is your father a farmer?"

"Oh heavens no, he is a doctor of medicine in Amberg. But I have a sight problem; I am not much good for anything else. And anyway, I love horses!" "A good enough reason, my reason for farming too". They both laughed. She glanced at him shyly as he looked out of the window in silence. He was very handsome, but somehow his eyes lacked life and sparkle. He was tall and his hands were beautifully formed. She always noticed hands and it played a big part in whether or not she liked a person.

She was bursting with questions, but didn't know how to start. Then, after a little while, she said cautiously:

"My name is Geppert, Angela". He stood up immediately, took her hand and bowed slightly and said:

"Behrends, Heiner". He sat down again and they watched the passing countryside through the window. In a minute, they would be in Amberg and he would go, and she would never see him again. He had returned into a shell which she could not penetrate. The train slowed and then stopped. Angela got up, but Heiner stopped her and said:

"We are not quite here yet; this is a little station where the train sometimes stops to wait for the signals. Sure enough the train moved again and she was forced to sit down with the jolt.

Looking out she saw an ancient little town, which reminded her of an overgrown fortified castle.

"Is this Amberg?" she asked delightedly. "What a beautiful place".

Heiner said:"Narrow streets, dark alleys, cramped houses, crumbling walls, damp and wood worm. It may be quaint, but not very comfortable. It will end up as a museum and the inhabitants moving out of town into light spacious new houses." How sad, she thought, but then she never lived in one of those dark cramped houses. Maybe it wasn't as cosy as she always imagined. The train stopped and Heiner was busy lifting her suitcases from the rack. She went to fetch her bike.

"Where to from here" he asked.

"I have to catch the yellow post bus to Hahnbach" she answered.

"No problem, follow me" and he went off carrying her heavy case. She followed with her bike. At the bus station outside the railway station, she found him peering at the destination plates at the front of the waiting busses. He squeezed his eyes together, and walked right past the one saying Hahnbach. Puzzled, she called:

"Isn't this the one?" He came back and squinted at the plate again. He laughed.

"Silly of me" Let's find the driver, so that he can put your bike up". The driver took the bike and hung it on some large hooks at the back of the bus, and shoved her suitcase into the hold also at the back. Heiner gathered his feet together and held out his hand.

"It was a pleasure travelling with you, Fräulein Geppert. Auf wiedersehen". They shook hands:

"Auf wiedersehen, Herr Behrends". She climbed into the bus and waited for it to depart, watching as Heiner, who had returned to the main entrance of the station, shook hands with a tall man, who opened the door of a black mercedes for Heiner to climb in. His face turned to her bus. She gave a futile little wave, and then let her hand sink down. He did not see her. Presently they drove off. Sadly she watched the car disappear.

Gradually the bus filled. The driver came to check the tickets. It was the last ticket in her little booklet. In a way she wished she had two more, for the return journey. Now she had to stay on her new farm at least until she had earned the fare home. But off course, she couldn't leave anyway, because she had already signed the apprentice ship papers at the *Bayerische Staatsministerium für Ernährung, Landwirtschaft und Forsten* (ministry for food, agriculture and forestry), and that was binding. One had to have a very good reason to break the contract, and homesickness was not a good enough reason.

The bus driver now said to her: "I shall call out when we get to the Laubhof". She thanked him and settled into her seat. Suddenly, she felt very much alone. She knew no one, where she was going. She bit back the tears.

*

2

Laubhof

She watched the bus disappear into the direction of Hahnbach. Below her was a flat wide area, backed by thick forest which rose gently up a large hill. In the foreground flowed a river, making a big S, its water still and clear. To the left of the river, directly below her, were some tall elm trees and an ancient tractor toc-toc-tocked its way towards them. One man walked behind the tractor, guiding some machinery, and another man walked away in the direction of the bridge just below.

No one had noticed her. From where she stood on the main road, a steep, unsurfaced road lead down towards the river and the bridge, which crossed it at the lower S-bend and continued along-side it as far as the other bend where the river came in from the right. To the left, at the end of the flat, green expanse, which to her looked like a water meadow, almost meeting the forest, stood some houses, proud, white and clean. The farmhouse, with a little belltower and green shutters on the numerous windows, was joined onto a very long building, which she imagined would house domestic animals, and at the end, turning into a T shape, was another long structure, half brick, half timber. From a building opposite the farmhouse, making it all into an open square without blocking the farmhouse's view, she heard the sounds of a blacksmith. A majestic chestnut tree in the yard partially blocked her view of another long structure with a big arched gateway leading to an area with many giant greenhouses. There were yet more buildings at the back on rising ground, almost hidden by the forest, and an enormous barn way over to the right. She thought it was a beautiful sight, truly magnificent. No little cowfarm here. She heard the sound of peacocks and way over below the green houses she heard turkey cocks hollering aggressively. A large herd of geese was grazing and honking on the water meadow. She could also hear ducks, but for the moment they were invisible.

She looked at her suitcase, wondering how to put it onto the bike and then push it down the steep hill towards the bridge without the large case falling off.

Just then a black car left the farm and jolted up the potholed road towards the little bridge in front of her. It drove up to where she stood and stopped in a cloud of white chalk dust. A man climbed out, and she felt a shock when she saw his face. It was dreadfully disfigured. The man held out his hand and said:

"Laurich". They shook hands. His hands were rough, his handshake firm. So this was her boss.

"Geppert, Angela" she smiled.

"You will like it here. Hard, pleasant work". He seemed a man of few words, around 45 years old, tall and well built. He wore a green jacket and breeches, brown hunting boots and a green hunter's hat adorned with a huge goats beard in a silver holder.

He had lifted her suitcase and bag into the 1936 Mercedes and jumped without another word behind the wheel and drove off, down the main road and turning sharply into a tight V, down the other side and towards the bridge. Angela had turned the bike down the road where he had come up and reached the bridge just before he did and cycled fast, avoiding the many potholes. She should have let him drive in front of her, but in her confusion she hadn't thought of that. She turned her bike into the spacious yard, frightening a turkey cock just as he was showing off his feathers, with purple head and long, floppy nose being jerked in a most undignified manner. She came to a halt by the main entrance to the house.

In a small niche above the door, she noticed a statue of Maria, the holy Mother of God. Huge antlers adorned the top of the door, and a bronze bell inside a skilfully wrought iron bracket hung below the statue.

Several dogs came barking towards her, and one she thought would surely devour her, but just as his ugly teeth came close enough for her to feel truly concerned, a heavy chain jerked him back. Phew! She would have to make friends fast! Herr Laurich climbed out of the car, yelled a command, which made the dog turn immediately back into his hut. He laughed, turning to her:

"Worried a little, hah? Don't! He is there to frighten people. He doesn't bite." Two long haired Dachshounds waddled up on their crooked little legs, their tails working overtime. Just like Grandfather's Hexi she thought. No problems here. She was gently pushed from the back and turning, she came face to face with a beautiful German hunting dog, a wire haired pointer. Some movement at the entrance to the farm caught her eye, and looking up she saw a German shepherd dog galloping towards her. She always imagined wolves to look like that. Growling deeply and showing some teeth, he stopped in front of her and their eyes met, and for several seconds they looked at each other. The dog stopped growling and sat down, slightly moving his tail.

"My compliments!" she heard Herr Laurich behind her.

"She knows how to use a bicycle, and she isn't afraid of dogs. Max here doesn't take to just everybody", and Herr Laurich stroked the Alsatian. She looked around, pleased. One dog on a chain, two dachshounds, one pointer and this Max.

"Are these all the dogs?" she asked. A woman's voice from the entrance door answered:

"Our shepherd has two dogs, but they are rarely on the farm. They go where ever the shepherd is stationed with his flock and cart. "I am Frau Laurich. Welcome." She came down the steps and held out her hand, which Angela took.

"Let me show you to your room, and then I shall take you round the farm. Are you hungry?" She was, but she could wait until meal time.

"No thank you. I had a sandwich on the train".

"Fine. You can meet some of the people at afternoon coffee, and all of them at supper". Frau Laurich led the way up some wide wooden, honey coloured stairs, beautifully polished. Antlers hung on the wall everywhere and also some overdone oil paintings of fallow deer, bellowing and proudly poking their chests into a deep sunset or was it a sunrise? The background on all the paintings was a very romantic alpine scene, somewhere in Bavaria. One in particular caught her eye. It was of a mountain cock in full display. She thought the bird was magnificent. The pictures were all quite beautiful in their own way, framed in heavy gold.

They arrived on the second floor. A long corridor opened up to the left, a shorter one to the right, and many doors indicated the number of rooms. Frau Laurich opened the door opposite the stairs and a light room with two dormer windows opened out in front of her. Blue gingham curtains, three wooden carved beds, beautifully painted in peasant motif, white scrubbed wooden floor. The thick feather beds were covered in the same blue gingham pattern as the curtain. Colourful rag rugs lay on the floor in front of each bed. And, she had to look twice, under each bed was a chamberpot with roses on the outside. She looked at Frau Laurich, but Frau Laurich had gone over to a large carved wardrobe with three doors, painted the same as the beds with matching motives. She opened one door, which offered some shelves and hanging space with four hangers.

"I hope there is enough room here for your things." A boy, about fourteen years old, she guessed, had brought her suitcase up and Frau Laurich put her hand on his shoulder.

"This is my youngest, Stoffel, short for Christoph. The older one, Hermann, who is sixteen,   is at boarding school at Nürnberg. He comes home in the holidays, which starts next week." She turned to go and at the door she stopped, her hand still on her son's shoulder.

"Hang up your things, and then come on down. The other two girls will also arrive this afternoon. The men come in two days time. It is always a little hard for everyone, when the old ones leave, and the new ones come. You'll soon feel at home."

"Thank you, I am sure I will. This is a beautiful place" Angela said. Frau Laurich left, smiling. She was a striking woman with the air of a gipsy, black hair, combed straight back into a big bun which sat low in the nape of her neck. Heavy gold earrings pulled her earlobes down. She wore the traditional farmdress, tight bodice with a wide swinging skirt in green colours trimmed with black, and a white blouse with puffed sleeves, low neckline. Very feminine and very becoming. A green taffeta half apron shimmered in the light and was tied round her waist with the bow at the front. On her feet she wore light black open shoes. A silver pendant was held in place by several short, silver chains in various lengths, fitting tightly around her neck.

Angela sighed. She would truly like such a dress. All country women wore such dresses, summer and winter. She had learned to sew at school, she would save up for some material and ask Frau Laurich for the pattern, and make one in the evenings and Sunday afternoons. She thought, she would need at least two summer ones and two winter ones.

She had almost finished to unpack her suitcase, when the door opened and another young woman came in. Frau Laurich was there again.

"Maria Rössler", she said. "You can show her her space in the wardrobe, Angela, and you can come down together when you are ready." She left again, leaving the two alone.

Maria was a little older than Angela, a lot more sophisticated, and well dressed, new suitcase, almost elegant. And she wore such a dress as Frau Laurich had. Angela said:

"What a lovely dress. Did you make it yourself?"

"Yes. I have work day ones and Sunday ones" Angela was impressed. They shook hands and Angela asked:

"Where do you come from? I am from Regensburg"

"We have a large farm near Rohr in Niederbayern. Haven't you got a farm?" Here we go, Angela thought.

"No, my family and relatives used to live in the east, but that is all gone"

"Ah, refugees." Maria dismissed the subject. There were enough stories about what these refugees lost. The size of their estates were legendary, and the contents astronomical, if one was to believe them. Maria waited for Angela to continue and tell her the size of things they had lost, but Angela quietly unpacked her things. So Maria said:

"Is this where we hang our things?" She opened the second wardrobe door. "Not very spacious, is it?" Angela only shrugged her shoulders and continued to unpack her case. There was plenty of room for her things, even her precious books, which she could never leave behind, and which had made her suitcase so heavy. Maria had a lot of little bottles and make up, face creams and such stuff. Angela only had Nivea. She began to feel a little self conscious. Just then the door opened again and another young woman came in. Frau Laurich smiled at them and said:

"This is Martha Bauer, the last one to join us. At four o clock is afternoon coffee" and she closed the door. Maria and Martha shook hands. Then Martha turned to Angela, and, smiling broadly, shook her hand too. She had a square, red cheeked face, framed with tightly curled hair which seemed untameable, and warm, kind brown eyes, fringed by a thick circle of dark, curled eye lashes. Angela immediately liked her.

"I am from Regensburg, where do you come from?"

"Our farm is near Wald München, right at the Czeck border. But my mother's brother is bishop of Regensburg. We have something in common!" Martha eyes had a happy glint and she added:

"Our farm used to be bigger, but part of it is now on the other side of the border in Czechoslovakia".Angela moved over and opened the third door of the wardrobe.

"Here, this is yours", then she went and sat on the first bed by the door. She did not like to sleep in the middle. First come first served. Maria, seeing her take the first bed, immediately moved over to the window, and took that end bed. That left Martha in the middle. She seemed pleased.

"I slept in the middle at home too, to keep the peace between my sisters." The three of them laughed.

"Not necessary here." Maria said, as she put a photograph of an American soldier onto her bedside table.

"Who is that?" Martha asked. The two of them joined Maria and looked at the foto, and then at Maria.

"I spent a year on an American farm, and I attended highschool there. That's where I met him. His name is Johnny, and he is now in the army, but not, as he hoped, in Germany. He had to go to Korea, and that is where he is now. We thought he would be stationed in Germany and we could be together. We love each other, and we are going to get married. I hope he does not get killed". Martha crossed herself, and Maria did likewise. Then they both looked at Angela.

"Aren't you catholic". Angela shook her head.

"Ah" was all they said.

*

13

The three young women had had afternoon coffee and slices of plaited yeast loaf and jam with the Laurich family. But now Frau Laurich was taking them around the farm. They had left the spacious kitchen, which contained two large tables, one for the men on the left behind the door, the other in the middle of the room for the Laurich family and the girls. A tall backed bench behind the family table devided the room, and behind this bench was the worktable for the kitchen. Opposite the men's table was the fire wood box and a huge wood fire range, a door to the larder, a door into a luxury bathroom, a large window with an enormous, very modern stainless steel sink, a sideboard and dresser with a beautiful display of plates and china, a second large window and the ironing table completed the kitchen.

They walked along the little hall to the back and into the ancient part of the farmhouse. They turned left into the old, dark kitchen with an enormous chimney flue which was still used to smoke sausages and ham. The smell was mouthwatering. A door led into the flour- and bread store. Huge round six pounder rye farmloaves stood on a shelf like so many giant plates.

"We bake every Friday" Frau Laurich pointed out. Turning right, they walked along a dark and very long corridor which led past the wool stockroom, the cellar and further into the feed room which housed several large chests with bran, crushed oats, barley and rolled maize. There was also a large potato steamer in a corner, hissing happily, spreading the comfortable smell of two hundred weight of boiled potatoes. The noise in the distance indicated many pigs. They were shown several large troughs, where the pigs feed was to be mixed, and a row of buckets, which would be used to carry all this lovely slop to the pigs. Frau Laurich lifted the lid of a 20 liter milk churn and pointed to the contents.

"We get this back from the dairy every day." She put her hand in and ate some and invited the three of them to do the same. It was delicious cottage cheese, the sort Angela always had at home with jacket potatoes. A favourite wartime meal. I'll not go hungry here, she grinned to herself. Potatoes boiling over there, cottage cheese here. She remembered her potato stealing sorties after the war.

"Where is the salt?" she grinned, but the other did not get the joke. She must remember, they did not go hungry. Theirs was a different life and very little war.

"We mix this with the pigs feed. It adds to the colour and flavour of the meat. Our pork is highly prized, not too fat, beautiful flavour. The Amberg butchers pay a very good price," Frau Laurich said as she opened the door into the pighouse. The noise was deafening. Maria yelled:

"How many pigs have you got here?"

"A hundred and twenty" Frau Laurich yelled back. They were impressed. There were two rows of large pens either side of the wide corridor, a continuous row of windows giving light. Frau Laurich took them quickly down the gangway and out through a wide double door.

In front of them was the biggest manure pile Angela had ever seen, chickens happily cratching away. Maria and Martha were impressed by the size of it. Proudly Frau Laurich headed them past the pile, which had straight, combed sides and sharp edges, and into the cowhouse, which was joined to the pighouse, but the entrances were separated by the length of the building. It was peaceful here, with the odd cow lowing quietly, all of them munching away on the cud. Angela guessed that there would be about 40 animals, at a quick glance. They came out at the other end and crossed the yard. A steady ching-ching came from the smithy, situated next to the stable, which they now entered. It was because of the many horses that Angela had applied to come here for her second year. She was told that they had stud-horses, but these magnificent stallions were something else. They were so tall! Her face lit up and Frau Laurich said to her:

"You will spend enough time here, don't worry!" The other two looked at her, questioningly. Maria asked:

"Do horses belong to the domestic side of farming on this estate?" Frau Laurich laughed:

"Angela is not a domestic science apprentice, she is one of our agricultural apprentices. She will have to muck in with the domestic side of things of course. She will do one week in three in the kitchen. Every woman needs to know how to housekeep. She'll never make a farmers wife if she doesn't. But mainly she will be outside. The two girls gave each other a meaningful look. Maria said, a little pointedly:

"She isn't built for it!" Frau Laurich led them out of the stable, ignoring what Maria had said.

"That will have to do for now. Let's go in now and prepare supper. They will want some food. Angela, you go up to the beet field and introduce yourself to the Silesian. He is our foreman. Her boss pointed to a field beyond the main road, where she had earlier arrived by bus. The old tractor was busy up there, still toc-toc-tocking away. She looked down at herself. She would have to change, and quickly.

"I'll have to change" she said and raced upstairs. Already it felt, as if she had been here quite a while, and it was a good feeling.

3

The Initiation

The Silesian saw her coming, but did not stop the tractor. He drove right past her and carried on loosening the earth around the growing sugar beets. He had to drive very carefully in the spaces between the rows. The large rear wheels of the tractor just fitted, and the merest diversion would have ruined the plants.

She watched the tractor disappear over the rise, and looked over to the ripening wheat field. Her eyes followed it up the hill, and higher up towards the forest she saw the tall slender rye ears bending with the weight of its fruit. Two more weeks maybe, she guessed and then the rye would be cut. The hay harvest just finished in the last week of June, maybe into July if it had been cold and wet in May; July was a month of relative quiet before the onslaught of the harvest, which usually started with cutting the rye. It had to be cut when it was dead ripe, so that it would not shed too much. It was a time for the farmer to walk the grain fields daily, sometimes more often, feel the grain and test it for moisture and maturity. He would chew it and taste it and worry. He would have to pick the exact day and hour of the day and hope it did not rain. A most stressful and anxious time for the farmer

The tractor appeared again and she walked up to it and as it passed she jumped onto the bar behind the tin bucket seat. She held on to the back of the seat and pulled herself up onto the mudguard of the big wheel and sat down.

"I am Angela, the new apprentice" she yelled. The Silesian nodded. He was about 40 years old, deep lines went down the side of his face. He wore a peaked soldier's cap, and concentrated on the rows of beets before him. The noise of the old Bulldog tractor, a Lanz, was deafening. Everone called it the Bulldog for short. She watched the rows behind her. If he used the wrong slot to hitch the row crop hoe to the tractor, the damage would be dreadful. On her first farm she had to do this job with the horse and the row crop hoe was much smaller. Even then it was a tricky job. She watched intently, as the tractor did five rows at a time. At the end he made a big loop and lined himself up to do the next five rows. Finally they came to the end row and the Silesian pulled a lever which lifted the hoe up into the air. He accelerated and drove quickly to the little field lane. It was so bumpy, she nearly slipped off her perch. She grinned at the foreman, as she held on for dear life. He came to an abrupt halt. In very familiar, broad Silesian dialect he welcomed her. They shook hands.

"Where are you from?" she couldn't resist to ask him, as refugees always enquired of one another. A left over from the war.

"Near Breslau, Trebnitz, we had a farm there. Why?"

"My father comes from Obernigk, and I spent a lot of time in Wohlau", Angela said, remembering the many happy visits to Mönchgut.

"Where in Wohlau exactly?" the Silesian asked.

"Mönchgut, do you know it"

"Know it? My uncle was the brewer there. Have you ever tasted Mönchner beer?"

"I was too small then to be allowed to drink beer. But I know your uncle, he used to give us yeast to lick and malt to chew. I knew his children. We used to play together." Angela said exitedly. Astonished she looked at the Silesian, almost as if he was a relative.

"They were his son's children, who fell in the war. He is bringing them up as his own. I wonder where they are now. I have lost contact with all of them". He looked at her sadly and then added more happily:

"Isn't it a small world?" He put his hand on her shoulder:

"I shall find them one day". He took a deep sigh:

"I am the Silesian around here, but to you, in private I am Herr Kowalski." They shook hands once more. She had made her first good friend, and she felt, that she could come to him if she should ever need help. Just imagine, he has been to Mönchgut. I have to tell mother.

"Hold tight, home we go for supper!" He yanked the gear in and drove off at hair raising speed. He crossed a ditch bridge and turned onto the main road for about a hundred meters and then dipped down the steep slip road towards the bridge, thundered across it with the tractor doing twice the speed it was built for, and then bumped and rattled the last little bit of potholed road to the farm. He never slowed down. She watched the hoe at the back jumping the potholes on its heavy iron wheels, and her head was jerked from side to side. She tightened all her muscles, 'otherwise I shall surely lose my head' she thought. She had a happy feeling in her heart. No careful sissies on this farm.

He slowed down a little as they entered the yard, upsetting the scratching chickens and ruffling the Geese's dignity. A peacock near the front door let down his tail display unceremoniously and angrily stepped aside. The Silesian parked the bulldog by the forge. After unhooking the hoe and pushing it a little to the side, he took her into the stable.

The bulldog continued to toc toc in the background. Later she would learn, that it would only ever be still at night. It would be lit in the morning with a blow torch, at five o clock, and run all day. It was also the motor for many farming machines, and used all the time and everywhere. Amazing!

The Silesian handed her a dung fork and said:

"You can start over there" and he pointed to the white Rottaler stallion. She opened the door to his box and walked in. There was no point to show that she was just a little awed by his size and excited neighing. Robert, her childhood friend in East Prussia always said, show them who is boss. She looked around, came out again and went in search of a wheelbarrow. The Silesian already came around the corner, pushing one.

"You need your own" he said. "You find one just around the corner". Eagerly she mucked out the soiled straw and swept the box, then she went into the next one. Here she found a Rheinland chestnut roan, also, she guessed about 16 hands, maybe more. This stallion was much heavier than the Rottaler. He moved over and would have flattened her against the wall, but she put an arm up and with the entire weight of her body pushed him off and said aloud:

19

"Come on you great ox, what do you think you are doing?" She saw the Silesian and Herr Laurich watching her. They were both laughing. She should have known. She was in for a few initiations.

"That is the first thing he tries with new people. We should have warned you, but you seemed to handle it ok. Let me show you where to put the horse dung. We don't mix it with the rest of the dung.

"I know, you use it to heat the hotbeds in the market garden" she butted in. No need to play totally ignorant. No harm in letting them know she had learned something in her first year.

When the stables were clean and the wheelbarrows put away, the Silesian took her up some very steep steps into the hay loft. Half was piled up to the rafters with golden straw, the other side equally piled with hay. She took a deep breath, enjoying the rich smell of hay and straw. It was soothing and comforting. There were trap doors above the cribs, one for two horses, and she was shown how much to push through each one, and was amazed at the amount. Two cows could feed on one portion! Then there was one larger trap door where she could push the straw down for all the boxes. It was all so well organized, well planned and time saving.

"Don't forget to close all the trap doors when you have finished. We don't want any accidents" the foreman said.

When she climbed down the ladder, she saw the foreman pouring a mixture of oats, barley and rolled maize into special troughs for the stallions. He was using a liter measure for this.

"You use 4 measures of oats, two of barley and two of rolled maize for the stallions, the rest of the workhorses don't get any.

"Why not?"

"They get some first thing in the morning, to sort them out for the day". He looked at her, grinning, and added:

"The stallions have more important things to perform. They have to be in peak condition!" He swaggered, swinging his hips.

Men! She thought. He pointed to the cowhouse.

"We are finished here now, see what you can do in there." She found the dairyman and two women, she had not seen before. They had finished with the mucking out, there was just a little sweeping to do. She got ready to help with the milking. The women giggled, pointing stupidly at her, giving her that sceptical look, because of her 'towny' appearance. She had learned not to get cross about it. They gave her a bucket and a stool and led her to a cow. Watch out, she thought, this cow either kicks, or has sore teats or something. Very likely another initiation. Every new youngster had to suffer it over and over again. She sat down and started to milk. All seemed to go well, the milk jetted nicely into the bucket. She turned and looked triumphantly at the dairyman who was watching. Just then the cow lifted her right hind leg and planted it firmly in the bucket, spilling the lot. He slapped his thighs and fell about laughing. Numerous cats came and made short shrift of the spillage. Then he came over and said quietly:

"With this one, you put your forehead against her flank and keep it there while you milk her. She will be as good as gold. The moment you take your head away, she kicks."

"Are all cows' special characters here?" She asked sarcastically.

"They are all different in their way. But you will soon get to know them." The dairy man was a small, rather ugly man. He was frightfully dirty to look at. His clothes seemed to stand up on their own. The only clean thing on his person were his wellshaped hands, even his fingernails where beautifully clean and well cut. Later she found, that his dairy kitchen, cooler and separator etc. were immaculately clean and without any smell. His pails were scrubbed and his cows washed. In fact everything was impeccable, except himself. He was totally disgusting. Everybody called him Schweizer, because in the olden days, men from Switzerland were hired because of their special knowledge in dairy management. Every respectable farm had their Schweizer and they did nothing else on the farm except look after the milking cows, young cattle, the bull and breeding cattle. Now, anyone doing this kind of work is called a Schweizer.

"How long have you been here on this farm?" She asked him. The answer would determine the amount of respect she would have to give him.

"Seven years" he answered. He knew why she asked and she knew he knew. They grinned at each other.

21

"When you are on dairy duty, it's up at four o clock in the morning, just so that you know" he said and walked away. She had the feeling, that he too could be a friend.

She got herself a new bucket, snuggled her forehead firmly against the side of the cow and continued milking. Some cats were sitting further down against the wall, and every now and then she saw them sitting up, their paws in the air, catching jets of milk which the Schweizer squirted in their direction. She grinned. The people here had endearing habits.

She was steadily filling her bucket. It was most important to have a thick layer of milk foam on top of her bucket, to collect any minute dirt particles that may still find their way into the bucket, and the only way to get the foam was with strong jets, and the only way you got those was with strong arms. She knew that if there was no foam she would be teased no end for being a weak towny. She finished milking and took her bucket to the milk kitchen and poured it into the filter, which would later be checked for dirtcontent. She returned and sat down by the next cow. She was now mightily hungry and with a strange new sense of pleasure, she looked forward to the evening meal.

After her third cow the Schweizer came and said:

"So, how're you doing? Seven more to go before supper." She looked at him, and then down the line. What had he been doing? He was having her on. At most, she worked out, there would be one more to go. Slowly a wide grin spread across her face:

"Nice try, I suppose helping you to clean the dairy is next? I am starving." He grinned back and nodded his head. They walked down to the dairy quietly to finish their work.

Supper was lively, with the leaving lads taking the mickey and teasing the new girls, with a lot of encouragement from Herr Laurich. Frau Laurich took the girls side and told her husband to go easy, but in a way the girls enjoyed the extra attention they got and took advantage. This kind of banter was new to Angela, and she listened and laughed. She felt free and happy. Here she could unfold and be a person in her own right. The door opened and the Silesian came in:

"Ready lads? I haven't got all night!" The men got up from the table and piled outside. The door closed and all was quiet. Frau Laurich moved to the door, and said:

"Time to rest when you have cleared the kitchen. I am in the best room if you still want me." The three of them cleared the table. Angela went over to the sink. It was obvious that she should wash, since she didn't know her way around the kitchen yet. She filled the bowl with very hot water and started to wash. Martha came and dried with Maria putting the leftovers away into the larder and getting things ready for breakfast. Was it only today that they had arrived? All three of them had the feeling that they had been here for weeks.

"Where do you think the men have gone to?" Angela asked.

"To the pub in the next village. Did you get the name of it Maria?" Martha said.

"Kötzersricht" Maria said and Angela laughed.

"What a name."

"You should have gone with them, you are one of them. You shouldn't have to do the dishes. You would never catch any of them helping with the washing up". Angela considered this and then said:

"That's what you get being a woman. It was the same on my first farm. It's expected. Anyway, I like talking with you." They finished cleaning the kitchen and laying the table for breakfast, talking and getting to know each other. They would share their room for the next year and it would be good if they got on well. It was ten o clock when they turned the light off and closed the door behind them. They three of them walked out and across the court, down the road along the river and stopped on the bridge.

"What a beautiful evening" Martha said and sniffed the air. Angela looked around. Not a soul anywhere. The moon was mirroring in the river which flowed quietly under the bridge.

"I am going for a swim, naked. Join me?" Both Maria and Martha shook their heads. Angela went down to the grassy bank and took off her clothes and dived in. The water was refreshing.

"It's lovely, warm and so soft!"

"Can you stand" Maria asked. Carefully Angela put her feet down and found a sandy bottom. She popped her hands out of the water to indicate she wasn't swimming but standing.

"Yes, it's deep though" On her toes she drifted with the current and found it was the same depths all along to the bridge. She swam back against the mild current to where she had dived into the river, and saw Maria also getting into the water. Together they swam up river to the bend and the entrance to the farm. They were a little out of breath when they turned and slowly drifted back. They put their dresses over their wet bodies and went back to the house. As they came past the cowhouse, they saw the Schweizer. "Didn't you go with the lads?" Angela asked, and he answered:

"Much better entertainment closer to home." Martha caught her breath. Maria and Angela said nothing and quietly entered the house, leaving him in the court.

"He's been spying on us, swimming" Maria whispered, when they were halfway up the stairs.

"I suppose it would have involved a wash, going with the lads," Angela remarked.

"What a dirty fellow." Laughing, they went to bed.

4

The new Apprentices

The young men had left the previous day, and today the new apprentices would arrive. There was no work on the fields which was urgent, and everybody helped with the animals to bridge the gap. Angela was in the stable and the cowhouse, Maria and Martha cleaned out the pigs. Frau Laurich fed the poultry.

The girls looked with anticipation towards the arrival of the new apprentices. What would they be like? Already they felt very much at home and wondered how the new lads would fit in. She hoped they would be good friends for the next year. She remembered her male collegue from her first farm. A jealous, miserable and dishonest character, always making her look bad with her boss.

After lunch, Angela and the Silesian went out together to work on the grain barn. It had to be clean for the imminent harvest. Mice and rat holes had to be trapped with poison and then stopped up with soft cement.

The barn was an old structure, mostly timber. The outer walls were solid, rendered brick halfway up. From there to the roof it was timbered. Towards the inner court the red tiled roof had an enormous overhang to shelter the wagons and larger machines. Inside everything was timber. It was like entering a huge wooden cathedral, tall lofty and spacious. A large area in the middle, big enough for the threshing machine, farming implements and tools, divided the barn into three sections. Either side were tool shops, store rooms and the coach house, of the same height as the threshing machine, so that the top of the machine would be level with the roof of the workshops. Here the harvest would be stored until it was going to be threshed, and the empty straw would be put back to be used for bedding. The overflow would go into the other barn.

Angela opened the first door and found the usual tools needed on any farm all the year round. Some would not be used any more. Museums pieces she concluded. Beautiful and interesting things. Many scythes, each with their quiver and sharpening stone, hung neatly on the walls. Wooden rakes and a host of forks were hanging or leaning on the opposite wall. The pitchforks had impressively long shafts, and she wondered how she was going to manage those. A very old wooden plough stood in a corner, covered in dust and cobwebs, its blade shining silver. Not a speck of rust.

The Silesian came over and handed her a brushwood broom:

"You can familiarise yourself by sweeping this clean, the coach house too, and over there the wood working shop. Then you can close the doors tightly and climb up there" and his finger pointed among the rafters and the top floor of the barn. Her eyes searched for a means to get up there and found a vertical ladder, which, once past the roof of the storerooms, went on into the lofty void up a wooden pillar and into the platforms.

"Get the bird droppings off the top floor and whatever else you find up there, little skeletons from the owl,s nest. We don't want that in the grain. He grinned at her as he left. Whistling happily she went to work. She picked up a bucket and crossed over to the yard pump to fetch some water to sprinkle the ground with, so that she wouldn't have to choke in the dust. When she finished the stores she picked up the witches broom, and found an old hoe without a handle to scrape off the bird droppings. Then she went back to the well and pumped some water and tried to drink, but it was difficult to drink and pump at the same time. Each time she stopped, the water stopped too and she had to rush to catch the last drops. She was holding out her hands again in vain, when somebody worked the handle for her. She drank greedily and then looked up. It was the dairyman who looked at her with a friendly grin. His face was so filthy, she wondered what he looked like beneath all that grime. Three days she had been here and had not seen him with a clean face. His stubbles were about four day's growth. Maybe he only washes on Sundays, she thought. She thanked him for the water and went back into the barn and climbed up to the dizzy height of the platform. She started to sweep carefully; the dust was choking. She got rid of piles of old pigeon-, swallow and other bird droppings. She even found the odd dried up mouse carcass and some minute skeletons.

She looked up and felt slightly dizzy. She looked around and could not imagine, that in a very short time, all this would be filled with rye, wheat, oats and barley. But then her thoughts went out to the fields and in her mind she saw the endless stretches of grain weaving gently in the breeze, and worried that the space might not be enough.

Suddenly she heard voices below her and, turning too quickly, she thought she was going to lose her balance, and her palms became sweaty. Steadying herself she saw, who had just entered the barn with Herr Laurich. It was the young man, who had travelled with her in the train as far as Amberg. Heiner Behrends! Her heart made a jump and a strange feeling crept through her body. It was a pleasant feeling. Could he be one of the new apprentices? She sat very still. She did not want them to see her, filthy and covered with dust and spider webs. Another young man joined them. Tall, sinewy and with a shock of blond curly hair. He looked up, saw her immediately, and grinned, but said nothing. No one else looked up. With a bit of luck, she thought, he did not see her very well in this gloomy darkness. They all left again and she continued to clean the platforms and the beams. What a job! And what luck! Heiner here! She had thought she would never see him again. Very quietly she hummed a happy tune.

She heard all the farm noises and voices, but saw no one else enter, and felt a little forgotten. She could do with some company, it wouldn't be quite so boring. The clock on the little tower struck four. Coffee time! She looked around, had she missed anything? She went over to the ladder and started her climb down, quickly swept the rooftops of the toolshops. She would leave the barn floor until after coffee.

Having washed her face and brushed down her trousers and put her fingers through her thick dark golden hair several times, she went in to join them at the coffee table. Everybody was already sitting there, including the new lads. Her heart was beating wildly. Heiner looked at her through his thick glasses, and his face lit up. He got up and turning to Frau Laurich said:

"We have met on the train", then turning to her:

"I never guessed, that you were coming here. What a surprise!" Angela and Heiner shook hands. A little shy, unable to say anything but happy, she shook hands with the other lad. Herr Laurich said:

"That's Shorsch, Shorsch Oberberger from Viechtach". She also shook hands with him and then sat down and poured herself a large cup of coffee from a tall enamelled jug, took a piece of homemade white bread, already prepared with butter and jam and started eating, watching and listening. These would be her working companions for a year. When she finished drinking her coffee, she got up to finish sweeping the barn.

"Angela, you can take those two with you. They can unpack later. What are you doing at the moment?" Herr Laurich had a mischievous glint in his eyes.

"Cleaning the barn ready for the harvest" she answered.

"Well, they can certainly give you a hand and you can get to know each other. Later, you can introduce them to the Silesian. He is at Hermannsricht station, fetching some spare parts with the Lanz bulldog. I shall see you all in half an hour." She went out through the door and crossed the court. Shorsch became very quiet and she sensed his resentment. 'A girl telling him what to do?' Heiner smiled and said seemingly innocent of the sudden tension.

"I should have guessed, that you would come to the Laubhof. Nice to see you again." He looked down at her with a warm smile.

"Since when do we have women doing men's work? You belong into the kitchen!" Shorsch growled in the strongest Bavarian dialect she had ever heard.

"What does Shorsch stand for?" Angela asked, instead of losing her temper. Another threatened male, she thought. Heaven give her patience.

"Anyway" she said before Shorsch could answer, "there are male cooks, aren't there? By your reckoning, should they not be in the kitchen?" Shorsch gave her a very faint grin and then said:

"My name's day is that of Saint Georg". (*The G is pronounced as in 'giving' and the e and o separate. Gaorg).* She was amazed. How could Georg turn into Shorsch. Although she now spoke Bavarian

28

without any foreign accent, there were still areas which made no sense to her. Aloud she said:

"Shorsch doesn't sound like Georg" and Shorsch shrugged his shoulders. Heiner said:

"Shorsch is the French pronunciation of George", and he pronounced it perfectly in French. "It's a leftover from the many times the French invaded our lands, worst of all Napoleon. To speak French was the 'in thing at that time".

"Ah, a scholar!" Shorsch said, grim faced. "What were you doing in the rafters up there just before coffee? Playing monkeys?"

"Scraping the crap off". She tossed him a broom.

"I've done all up there, only the barn floor to do", and she walked away into the stable. She might as well start here. When they have finished being He-Men, they might join her. Through the crack between the stable door and the hinge she peered over into the barn and watched them. Heiner had also found a broom and a shovel, and together they created an enormous cloud of dust. She grabbed a bucket, went to the pump and filled it with water, then went over to the barn and sprinkled the floor liberally with water. She said not a word, and walked off again when she had done. They will come round, she was prepared to be friends. It was those two, who felt uncomfortable, especially Shorsch. She supposed, she had to become one of the lads. They wouldn't meet her half way. She grabbed the handles of the laden wheelbarrow and pushed it towards the enormous manure heap.

She looked around. Nobody about. Good. It wouldn't do to see her struggle and fail, balancing the full load up to the top by way of this narrow board. She lined herself up and ran, to manage enough momentum to get to the top. 'They' could afford to be seen to struggle, even miss, but if it happened to her, they'd never stop laughing. She made it, just, tipped her load and directed the wheelbarrow down the narrow board. As she turned back into the court, she saw the two of them still sweeping.

Later Herr Laurich came into the stable, with both of them in tow.

"Who can ride?" he asked the three of them. Shorsch and Angela said they could. Herr Laurich looked at her sceptically, and Shorsch sighed, pained, but said nothing.

"You can work together then you two. The stallions are going swimming today. When you have done the stables, you ride them into the water. We have our natural horsepool here on this farm", and he pointed up the river, past the pig's meadow and orchard.

"The river has a shallow entry there", and turning to Angela he said: "Shorsch will show you what to do. Heiner, you help the Schweizer." When they were on their own, Shorsch said:

"Can you ride bareback? How are you going to get up there?" he sneered.

"Same as you. I doubt whether even you get up there without stirrups or a legup. It's a long way up. I am going to put on my swim suit. Any objections?" He shook his head.

"Don't be all day" he said weakly.

Her heart was beating wildly. They would all be watching. If she made a mistake, or showed a weakness... She had ridden before, but never brutes like these. 'Don't show it. Just get up there with dignity and stay on'. She came down stairs, with a frock apron over her swim suit and crossed to the stables. Shorsch was already in his underpants. A big safety pin secured the front. She kept a straight face and went over to the tackle.

"Any idea which tackle they use when they take the horses swimming?" She asked over her shoulder. He came and stood behind her and rummaged through the bridles and reines. There was only one set of bridles for each horse among the riding tackle.

"When did you arrive?"

"Two days ago, it seems an age. It's great here. You'll love it". She said.

"We start with the Norikers, you take the Chestnut and I take the Bay." Shorsch looked at her, and she felt his face grow softer, as their eyes held each other steadily.

"Laurich could have waited until tomorrow to take these bloody horses for a swim. I haven't even had a chance to unpack the trunks". Angela grinned at him:

"You want to borrow my apron?" He laughed out loud and went to get his horse ready. Angela found she wasn't tall enough to reach. She grabbed the chestnut above the nose and tried to get his head down, but that only excited him and he started dancing.

"Here, let me", Shorsch had come round and took the reins out of her hand, with his free hand he grabbed the mane just below the ears and then slid his arm over, held the head-gear and fed in the bit. His strong skilled hands knew exactly what to do. When all was secured, he threw the rein over the horses head and held out one hand. Without hesitation, Angela stepped onto it and swung herself up. Holding the reins tightly and gripping with her knees, she found the back of the horse extremely wide. A damned elephant couldn't be worse. Her apron, which she had forgotten to take off in the hurry, hindered her and she hastily undid the buttons in the front and let it fly loose. She ducked as she headed for the door. The stallion sensed freedom and was about to take off. She tightened the reins with gentle force. The stallion responded and danced where she guided him. Shorsch came up behind her, and he cantered the heavy horse past her up to the pigs meadow. The Chestnut followed, and at the end of the meadow Shorsch splashed into the water and soon only the horses head and Shorsch from the waist up was visible. Before she knew what happened, she too was up to her waist in water. Never had she felt so happy and so full of life, confident and unafraid as at this moment.

She saw Herr and Frau Laurich walk up the little path by the river and stop to watch them.

"Up to the bend by those trees yonder and then you turn around" Herr Laurich yelled, and Shorsch and Angela disappeared up the river, her heart exploding with happiness.

*

Three days later the harvest had started. The evening before the big day, the three of them and the Silesian had gone up to the rye field with a scythe each and started to cut the edge, wide enough to use the bulldog with the binder. The girls and Frau Laurich would come later, when they had cleared the supper things, and bind the corn into sheaves by hand. This was slow work, but had to be done to avoid loss of valuable grain.

Angela had trouble with the scythe. She had never done this work before, and she stabbed her blade constantly into the earth. She was deflated and frustrated. Heiner too had difficulty. Shorsch and the Silesian worked ahead and soon disappeared over the rise.

I will not be beaten, she thought. All you need is a rythm. She gripped her scythe firmly by the handle and moved it round to her right, and then with a strong and deliberate movement brought it round to her left in a wide circle, making sure the tip of her blade faced slightly up. It worked. Without stopping she struck again, taking a measured step, and again. She realized, that she was moving slowly away from Heiner. Don't stop, she thought, you got the rythm. Every time she hit the earth, she took a new grip, and forced herself back into the rythm, taking a step for the new strike. Her arms began to ache, but she continued. Soon she too had the rise behind her. The girls had come and she could see them binding the sheaves and putting them into stooks at the very edge of the field.

She still had a third to go, when Shorsch and the Silesian came to the end of the field. Her row might not be so evenly cut as theirs, but her cut grain lay neatly to one side, easily gathered with a sickel and bound. As they came up to her level, binding theirs into sheaves and stooking it, she continued to cut, without looking up. She wanted them to think that this was the most normal task she was performing, and that there was nothing to it. When she came to the end, she turned and helped with the binding and stooking.

This beautiful summer day came to an end. It must be after ten o clock at least, she thought. Heiner passed her, grinning. She now bound his and hers at the same time, so when he caught up they could work together, until they met up with the women.

She took a deep breath. The air was so sweet. There was an earthy smell and the scent of freshly cut corn mingled deliciously. The sky showed off with a range of colours from deepest blue to pale blue-green-yellow-pink and finally purple-red and orange at the horizon. She took another deep breath, and another. Actually she wanted to burst out into a happy squeal, but what would they have thought of her.

Heiner was suddenly beside her, working quietly. Every time they came together to build a stook, he looked at her, and their hands were sometimes touching. A strange feeling came over her. She thought she would do anything for him. Strange, to feel that for another person, a person she hardly knew. It was a new feeling, and she kept it to herself.

5

First Love

The sky was illuminated with merciless silvery azure. The horseflies buzzed, so that the horses threw their heads wildly and swished their tails. The heat was oppressive and the air sticky. The day before they had finished stooking the grain, and because of the dry atmosphere, they were loading today. The men had taken their shirts off, and the sweat was running down their chests, making clean lines where it had washed down the dust. The sun was burning their skin and the flies were making them short tempered.

When they cut the corn with the binder, they had to leave three islands of corn standing, because the scout, who walked before the blades, had discovered newly born fawns. Angela looked with wonderment at the little things and would have loved to hold one, but she was told, that if she had touched it, the mother would abandon it. They were so graceful and beautiful, and their brown velvet eyes looked at her with trust.

"It doesn't pay to be careless at this stage. There wouldn't be anything to hunt later on", her boss said, bringing her back to cruel reality. Now the islands were empty, the mothers had taken their young into the forest for safety and Herr Laurich was cutting the remaining corn by hand.

Angela's blouse was sticking to her, and bits of straw had got caught in it, making her feel very uncomfortable. She was walking along the wagon, picking up the sheaves and reaching them up to Shorsch, who was at the top, loading it. It was an expert's job, and Shorsch, who had done this since he was a boy on his fathers farm, knew how to load straight and high. It was now so high, that the fork, even though it had a very long handle, could hardly reach it. Young Stoffel Laurich was leading the horses from stook to stook. They had three wagons working in rotation, one to be unloaded, the other on the way up, and one being loaded. It all worked like clockwork. Martha was also loading, and the Silesian was on the top of the other wagon. Hermann, Heiner and Maria were with the third wagon. Angela's throat was dry, and just then Shorsch, from his lofty height said:

"Isn't it bread time?" Bread time was always looked forward to on a thirst making job like this. Frau Laurich would bring two big pitchers with cider and a basket of big round slices of rye bread, spread with butter and homemade liverwurst. They would all retire to a big tree at the edge of the field and sit in its shade and drink and eat and make jokes. Didn't time drag, when you waited for a drink!

"Maybe she'd sends it up with the next empty wagon" Angela called up hopefully.

"She better hurry, because we are going down to unload at the end of this row" Shorsch said.

They finished loading and Stoffel and Angela heaved up the long cross beam, which had been trailing behind the wagon while it was loaded. Shorsch grabbed it and laid it over the top. Angela went to the front and threw up the rope in a high arch over the protruding end and lashed it down hard. Shorsch slid down over the side of the wagon, grabbed the rope from her, and with a masculine strong tug, pulled it down another half meter, wound it round securely and stood up, wiping the sweat from his face, his blue eyes shining at her like stars from his brown and dirty face. He was very handsome and he knew it. He looked around and said:

"Ah, drink," and walked over to the Linden tree. The empty wagon had arrived, and with it Frau Laurich with the refreshments. Everybody gathered. Gratefully they rested in the shade, letting the pitchers go from hand to hand. They all drank directly from the enamelled tin jug, long and greedily. When they caught their breath, they ate of the bread, but Angela found it too hot to eat. The cool cider went from mouth to mouth and when it was her turn, she felt she'll never get enough. Nobody spoke. They were all chewing and enjoying the hint of cool breeze. Then, after Shorsch had handed the pitcher back to Angela, he squeezed her upper arm. Startled she looked at him, and he, grinning and giving a meaningful look all round said:

"There is quite a bit of muscle developing here. A pity there is so little in other vital spots". Angela felt the heat in her face, and she looked down. Hopefully, with all this sunburn they would not notice how her face changed colour. She was always teased about her breasts. They were hardly noticeable. Maria and Martha had beautiful breasts, and needed bras, Angela did not. She was lean and sinewy, which was just as well, since she was doing a man's job. She pulled herself together, and, with an effort, grinned at Shorsch and pushed her right elbow into his chest, and said:

"And if you don't watch out, you can wear the bras I don't need". Herr Laurich roared with laughter and slapped her so hard on the shoulder, that she nearly dropped the jug.

"That's telling him". Martha giggled and nearly choked on her bread. The Silesian, who had quietly chewed on his bread, grumbled:

"Leave the girl alone, she is doing a good job".

"I didn't mean she wasn't doing a good job, it's just, well, look at Martha!"

"Shorsch, you mind your own business", Martha said in the deepest Bavarian accent, looking down extremely embarrassed. Martha was a true farm girl, down to earth, but very coy in a charming way.

"Haven't you got anything better to talk about?" Frau Laurich said. Just then Heiner and Maria arrived with their empty wagon.

"You unloaded that fast. Here sit down. "Frau Laurich handed them some bread and the pitcher. Heiner sat down near Angela, so close, that if she moved, she would just touch him, and she wanted to reach out and do just that. Her heart beat wildly. Why did this happen, every time Heiner was near her? She did not understand it. It was a totally new emotion to her.

"Ah, look at the sweet pair" Shorsch said and then added with a theatrical sigh:

"Young love!" Angela got up and pulled her blouse out from her skirt and started to shake all the loose bits of straw all over Shorsch.

"If you don't stop all your stupid teasing, you'll get worse than this. Now lets take this load down" and she walked crossly off towards their full load and hooked the horses back into harness. They had left them half loose for grazing. Shorsch caught up with her and took the reins. Slowly she walked behind Shorsch, ready to steady the load, should it tilt too much, and to work the backbrake on the steep road towards the bridge.

Back in the barn Angela climbed up the steep ladder onto the already stacked corn and Shorsch tossed her the sheaves, two or three at a time. They dropped down so fast she thought he might want to bury her. It wasn't easy to lay them properly with the speed he tossed them. He always had to prove he was such a man!

"Oih!" she yelled,"Steady on, a man you may be, a gentleman you are not. You wouldn't dare tossing them like this to the Silesian. He'd soon sort you out". She coughed, and wondered what he would answer to that. But the bundles kept raining on to her in very quick succession. Oh, what's the point, she thought, trying to keep up. She worked hard, totally ignoring him. Suddenly he was beside her, pulling her over and holding her in his arms, kissing her. They were buried deeply in the straw. It was so totally unexpected. She struggled to keep him off, and when she freed her mouth she said:

"Shorsch, you are presumptuous. Get off." But he pressed down even harder. She grabbed his golden curly hair with both hands and pulled him off her face, and then her racing brain remembered something her grandfather had told her, among other good bits of advice. He had told her, that, if ever she was in trouble, (hadn't really told her what kind of trouble) she should know, that a hard kick with a knee into a certain place, could hurt a man very much, and get her out of trouble. This bit of knowledge had settled into her unconscious mind, and now she suddenly remembered what her grandfather had told her that day. She struggled and suddenly she felt the way free for her knee to do some damage. She brought it up hard and with a moan Shorsch rolled off her. She sat up beside him and looked at him, as he lay moaning in the straw. She was furious and her first reaction was to run and tell somebody about it. But then she told herself she must not act as a 'silly' girl, but as an equal. That was the only way she would survive this apprenticeship.

"Shorsch, you damned idiot! What do you mean by that? You really are stupit and this..," and she put her hand face up, "proves it. As far as I am concerned, a beautiful body isn't everything. Do you understand?" She wasn't cross any more, although she was still shaking.

"And, while I am still in the mood, let me tell you, that you do not take advantage of the fact that I am a girl. In fact, as far as the apprenticeship is concerned, Heiner and I are a year ahead of you, and you can show proper respect. I respect, that you have many more skills because you grew up on a farm, but officially it doesn't count."

She left him lying there and jumped onto the wagon and tossed the remaining sheaves into his direction. Then she took the reins and drove the wagon from the barn.

"Hey, wait!" she heard Shorsch and grinned. She reined in the horses, tied down the reins and walked back into the barn. She climbed up the ladder to the nearest beam, balanced across and then with a yell, she jumped down and helped Shorsch stack the sheaves. Afterwards they slid down to the ground, hopped onto the wagon and Shorsch drove his fork deep into the wooden floor of the wagon and told her to hold on tight. He clicked the horses into a fast canter, and steadying himself on the fork and using his knees as shock absorbers he raced down the bumpy, potholed road to the wooden bridge and thundered across it. Hurriedly she too drove her fork into the floor and practised not to fall over. It looked as if she was doing a wild Indian dance, but Shorsch's feet stood firm on the ground. When he slowed down up the hill, they grinned at each other, but said not a word. They met Martha and the Silesian on the way, but Shorsch was busy again playing the charioteer.

"Draufgänger" (suicidal idiot!) she heard the Silesian yell, as they passed them. Well, she enjoyed being a "Draufgänger". It was the spice of life, and probably one of the many reasons, why she was here and not in an office or a factory somewhere.

Last thing that evening, as she left the kitchen after helping the girls with the dishes, she had just one wish. To have a swim. Just as she went through the front door, Maria came out of the kitchen after her and said:

"What about a swim?"

"I was just going down to the river" Angela answered, and then added:

"Let's ask Martha, she might want to come".

"Unless you manage to teach her to swim" Maria answered.

"Oh, is that it? Come on, between us we can teach her to swim?

"You have to get her into the water first", Maria laughed.

"Oh, let's try". They went back into the kitchen.

"Do we go naked or do we have to put something on" Angela whispered.

"I think we better get the trunks. You know the men, especially the Schweizer."

"And Shorsch" Angela said, remembering the afternoon. They collected the protesting Martha, went for their costumes in the washhouse and sauntered towards the river. They went towards the 'horsepool'.

"It has a shallow entry for you Martha. Just play around and get used to the water. You do that for a bit until you want to learn to swim" Maria offered helpfully. Maria and Angela floated with the current down river, and intended to turn around by the bridge and swim back. As they neared the bridge, they saw the men, and it was soon apparent, that they had all gone in naked. The men created a fuss worse than a bunch of old spinsters. The Schweizer sat on the bridge, his feet just above the water, enjoying every minute of it, provoking both the young men and the girls. Maria swam up to the bridge and splashed some water into the direction of the dairyman, who instantly became quiet, jumped up and stood back, a very worried look on his face. Everybody roared with laughter and the teasing was totally directed at the Schweizer.

"What you don't realize, if splashed with water, he instantly turns into a cow", Heiner said.

"With only one teat" Shorsch roared.

Unnoticed Maria and Angela swam back up river and left the men and their rough jokes. Their voices became faint as they swam round the bend in the river. Maria started to giggle:

"I wouldn't be at all surprised if the Schweizer would turn into something when splashed with water."

"Yeah, he would turn clean" Angela giggled.

The water was warm and refreshing after the oppressive heat, and soothing on the many scratches the straw had left on their bodies. The giant harvest moon reflected in the water, making a golden glittering lane for them to swim in. The moonlight was so bright, that the stars were only visible at the opposite send of the sky. The forest stood in deepest indigo in the background, and the peacocks emitted drowsy noises from among the tall branches.

Just as they reached the upper bend in the river, Heiner and Shorsch had caught up with them on the road. The dairy man was not with them. When the two came out of the water Martha and the men were sitting on the grassy side by the river. They dried themselves, and then Shorsch put his arms around both Martha and Maria and the three walked off, leaving Heiner and Angela to follow on their own.

Angela was nervously quiet. Strange, this feeling, every time Heiner was near. Just seeing him made her insides well up in turmoil. It made her knees go soft and her heart pound.

Heiner walked quietly next to her. Did he feel the same? She wondered, and quietly she glanced up at him. Their eyes met. She heard Heiner say:

"You are very special to me". She waited for more, but that was all he said. She didn't know what to answer. She wanted to say so much, she wanted to touch his hand. How could she tell him she felt the same? The others had reached the front door and waited for them to catch up. Very quickly, afraid she might miss the chance, she touched his hand and she felt him respond with a quick squeeze. Nobody had noticed anything. They said good night and went upstairs.

She wanted to tell somebody how she felt, but thought they might laugh at her. Maria and Martha fell into bed and seemed already asleep, and she realized, that probably she might never sleep again. She didn't want to sleep. All she wanted to do, was to think of Heiner. She was in love. Would she want to marry him? Spend a whole life with him? The way she felt at this moment, she was convinced that she could spend three lifetimes with him. Would three lifetimes be enough? Would she still feel the same tomorrow?

*

6

The call from Korea

There was a loud and urgent knock on the door and the three women woke up with a start.

"Yes, what is it" Angela said, being nearest to the door. It couldn't be the morning, it seemed as if she had only just gone to bed, and she was dead tired. Her limbs felt like lead.

"Maria, quick, come to the telephone. The exchange announced a telephone call from Korea. It will be through in about 10 minutes." Frau Laurich, dressed in a regal nightdress, had turned the light on and the three women blinked, trying to adjust to the brightness.

"Korea!" Maria shot out of bed, followed by the other two.

"A call from Korea! Goodness!" Martha said. Excitedly, all three of them followed Frau Laurich down stairs in their nighties.

"It's a miracle I heard the phone. I was just going to the privy, when it rang. If I hadn't, we would never have heard it" Frau Laurich said as she lead the way, and then added: "Why can't they ring at normal times? Telephoning in the middle of the night!" The clock in the hall said one thirty. When they came into the 'best room', which housed the telephone, Herr Laurich, also in his pyjamas, was bent over the table, studying Stoffel's school atlas. Importantly his right fore finger pointed repeatedly to a spot on the map. They all bent over to have a look. It was a map of the world, spread over two pages and his finger totally blotted out Korea. Then he moved his finger right across both pages, finishing up in the middle of Europe.

"From here to here. Amazing! All that way!" They were busy looking at the countries the call would pass to reach the Laubhof. Quite amazing. The door opened and Stoffel and Hermann came in.

"You should be in bed" Herr Laurich thundered and his finger pointed to the door.

"It's the holidays" and both boys looked at their mother, pleadingly.

"Show them the map, father" she said instead, and happily his finger plopped down on Korea again, and all heads were bent over the little atlas.

"They are ahead of us with the time. Probably their lunchtime tomorrow now" Hermann said.

"What are you talking about", Frau Laurich looked at him and then her face lit up. "Off course, I had quite forgotten. The earth is round", and everybody laughed.

"Fascinating" was all Martha said. Suddenly the telephone brought their heads up with a start and all eyes were turned at the little black wonder. With great dignity Frau Laurich lifted the receiver.

"Gut Laubhof, Bavaria, Chermany" she said and then she listened intently. She looked at Maria, nodded her head, and then said:

"Von moment bitte" and handed the receiver to Maria. Totally absorbed they all listened, but nothing happened. Suddenly Maria burst into English which nobody understood except for the odd word here and there, which they had picked up from the occupying Americans. Angela felt a great desire to be able to speak English. Martha's brown eyes gazed through her thick lashes in wonderment. She whispered into Angela's ear:

"What's she saying?" But Angela shrugged her shoulders and upturned her hands.

"No idea". However, judging by Maria's happy expression, all was well.

Angela had spent years as a child, teaching an American to speak German, and had only picked up a very few words of English herself. Why had nobody thought of teaching her? Her mother and her grandfather spoke English. Why couldn't she? Why hadn't they sent her to a school where she could learn? She resolved there and then to learn English and other languages as soon as she was through with her apprenticeship.

Just then the door opened and Heiner and Shorsch came in. All fingers went to their lips saying: "Shhh" Maria was still speaking on the phone. Martha started to giggle uncontrollably, and in the end left the room. She went into the kitchen followed by Angela who also caught the giggle bug. It all started when the men came in, wearing only their pyjama bottoms, sleep in their eyes, tousled hair, young stubble in their faces, and looking around, she was suddenly aware that they were all in their nighties. Martha and Frau Laurich, in spite of the hot summer, in long, sleeveless flannel nighties, buttoned up to the neck. Maria wore a cotton creation, rather pretty with frills, and obviously American. Angela wore one she had made herself at school, nearly three years ago and getting a little small now, but with pretty embroidery and a low neckline. But the men, in their crazily striped thick, crumpled pyjamas, looking stupidly at what was going on, creased her, and she collapsed with Martha on the kitchen sofa, laughing until the tears rolled down their faces, and looking at each other and started all over again, until they were limbless.

Heiner spoke English rather well, (he would) and told her the next day, what the conversation had been all about. Johnny had been wounded slightly, and was in a hospital, but would transfer to Tokyo tomorrow, well today, and he would ring again from there. She wasn't really listening to his words. Maria had told them the news when they had gone back to bed. She wasn't interested in Johnny or Tokyo, just that Heiner stood there and spoke with her. It was the start of the day they were getting the horses ready. Shorsch joined them in the stable:

"What was so funny last night?" he demanded to know bad temperedly.

"I suppose it was the way we all stood around in our night attire?" Heiner grinned, showing two handsome dimples. He was taller than Shorsch, who, looking at them both, slowly joined in their laughter.

"I suppose... did you see the boss?" he slapped his thighs and the rest got drowned in his laughter.

"He is a bit slow off the mark" Heiner said.

"What was that?" Shorsch asked, still laughing.

"He said you are a little slow" Angela said with a little twinkle.

"No, I wasn't really awake last night, I guess." He drowned what he said in a big yawn.

"Don't we have to work today? If not, why didn't anybody bother to tell me? I could have turned another round in bed." The Silesian stood in the door with his fists resting on his hips, his chin up agressively.

"We were just discussing the telephone call last night" Angela said, hoping to get the Silesian into a better mood. Except for time to sleep and time to eat and church on Sunday, there was never time to just stand around, as far as the Silesian was concerned. And since he didn't sleep in the house, he would not have known about the call.

"What telephone call"

"Last night, 1.30 it was. From Korea. Maria spoke English." Shorsch said. He was still impressed. The Silesian stopped, looked at them, lifted his cap by the peak and scratched his head.

"From Korea, eh? All that way! And they could hear each other clearly?" He shook his head in disbelief.

"Yes, apparently every word" Shorsch said, and then added:

"In our village, only the Bürgermeister has a *Sprechapparat*. (Speaking apparatus). The villagers use it sometimes in an emergency. But the first thing I do, when I take over our farm, is to install this vital appliance. Maybe I can persuade the farmer (meaning his father) to do it sooner than that." Shorsch was very seriously making plans for the future.

"We have to keep up with the times", he added. They had harnessed the three wagons with teams of two horses on each, and Shorsch and Angela were in the first one, the Silesian and Heiner with the day-hands in the second and third.

"All the way from Korea, hah? The Silesian mused, and turning to Shorsch he said:

"Shorsch, I need the bulldog (meaning the old workhorse tractor) up there today." His head motioned in the direction of their destination. "You let Angela take the wagon and you bring up the rear with the tractor. Hook the "canon chassis" onto it. There is heavy equipment which we have to load from the forest barn. For the moment park it at the top end of the wheat field."

The "canon chassis" was a leftover from the war, without the canon. Refugees had brought it to the farm, drawn by a string of horses, carrying their meagre possessions, and Herr Laurich had acquired it by barter. He then converted the thing into a wagon and it

43

turned into the best trailer he had on the farm. The large and sturdy rubber tyres rested in excellent ball bearings and gave a smooth ride.

Shorsch handed her the reins and with a grimace jumped off the wagon. Angela flicked the reins and they moved out of the farm. The next weeks would be very busy, just bringing every thing safely under cover. Harvest time was after all, what farming was all about she was constantly told.

She had driven her fork into the floor of the wagon and stood up. There was much improvement in her balance, her feet stood firmly on the ground with her knees making all the bumby adjustments. Good training for the coming winters skiing. The convoy of harvest wagons moved onto the mainroad and continued along it for about a mile, before they turned right and up a steep lane and through mature, tall and majestic pine-and broadleafed forest. She could see luscious raspberries glowing brightly in the sunshine and promised herself a Sunday afternoon visit to this spot. Forest strawberries displayed their fruits on sunny banks vying with the bushy whortleberry. As they came to the end of the forest, she could see the golden stooks in the distance.

A man came out of the thicket and stood in her way. Over his shoulder, barrel down, hung a hunter's shotgun.

"Is Laurich with you?" He roared. She was just going to say no, that he wasn't, when she heard the engine of the Mercedes.

"There he his now" she said instead. However the man had already seen him and walked towards him, waving his arms.

"Moser! What's to hunt? " Laurich asked boisterously.

"Cursed wild boar! Ploughed up the maize field! Just on my way home. Sat up all night! Hoped I might catch you." He slapped Herr Laurich on the shoulder.

"Join me tonight? Got to make an end to this vermin, not to mention the feast we'd have afterwards, eh?" another slap.

"And the feast the mosquitos will make of us!" Herr Laurich said.

"I take it that means yes?" Herr Moser roared again. He never seemed to say anything in a normal voice.

"All right, we'll man our lookout posts until midnight. We have a harvest to get in." Herr Laurich had caught the hunting fever, however he also realised that he couldn't stay up all night. Not like

Moser, who was semi retired, since his son already ran the farm. Moser and Laurich parted.

"We will man three lookout posts tonight. *Waidmanns Heil"* (greeting among hunters) Herr Laurich called as he went back to his car.

"Wüah!" Angela swished the reins and her team moved on. Steadily they arrived at the field. Would she be allowed to join the men at the hunt? She used to go with her Grandfather, who had been an ardent hunter in his time, and who had taught her a great deal about hunting. Not that she had ever shot anything that was alive, only cardboard targets. He had impressed on her the fact that culling rather than killing for sheer sport was a hunter's job. It was necessary to hunt, but more importantly to preserve the wild animals for their and our own sake, and for proper growth of the forests. "It's an everlasting cycle, which man must not disturb" her grandfather used to say.

"The wildlife needs the forest as the forest needs the wildlife, and man cannot exist without either. Nature doesn't need man, but man needs nature. For every tree you cut down, you have to plant a new one, for every animal you shoot you have to make sure of new stock" Her Grandfather never tired to stress these points. Would wild pigs, who damaded the crop also have to be preserved? Where would one draw the line? The pigs were an awful nuicance especially in the maize fields.

At the eleven o clock "Brotzeit" she sat near Herr Laurich and at a convenient moment asked:

"Can I come hunting too?"

"Try and get out of it. We need everybody, and that includes you". He laughed loudly, and for a moment Angela thought he was teasing her.

"Do you know anything about hunting?" Shyly she said:"yes".

"Good job. Can you hold a rifle?" She wasn't about to tell him, that she never shot at anything live, only clay pigeons so she said:

"I need a lot more practice, but I am not bad".

"Not to worry. You stick to me tonight. I'll teach you" he said and the Silesian laughed.

"Better to give her blanks to start with".

45

"Did you learn with blanks?" Angela snapped, trying not to sound too cross.

"You pull the short one takling her." Heiner said and added: "You'll see. She'll shoot something tonight"

With a lot of teasing and laughter the day came to an end, and at nine o clock they took their positions on the hides. Heiner, who could not use a rifle, because of his poor eye sight, just went along and sat with the Silesian. Shorsch took a stand to himself and Angela climbed up into the tree stand with Herr Laurich. At the end of the steep ladder was a tiny roofed hut, with windows on three sides which were now open, a bench and millions of mosquitos. The heat and the humming insects were unbearable and she thought longingly of a swim in the river. The two sat very quietly, and listened intently. They could not speak or make any sound. Their guns were loaded and at the ready. Herr Laurich had explained the gun to her before they came out, and pointed out how to fix her sights and now they waited. Time dragged and for the hundredth time she wished she was back at the farm in the river. The mosquitos were driving her insane.

Suddenly she heard something; leaves rustling, but no, there was more. Distinctly she heard peaceful snorting and twigs snapping. Forgotten were the damned insects, all her nerves and senses worked overtime. She even opened her eyes wider in order to see better. And then she saw a dark shadowy shape. She nudged Herr Laurich and gently pointed into the direction. He peered and then gestured for her to aim. She looked at him, not sure what he meant. He nodded vigorously and almost impatiently, and she aimed and squeezed, and the shape dropped and stayed put. She put the gun down, and started to shake. She tried to control herself and hoped Herr Laurich did not notice. She didn't want anybody to know that this was probably her first kill, if it stayed put. She had slaughtered chickens and ducks before, but this was different.

Another shot rang out, and then all was still, even the mosquitos seemed to have vanished. They sat, listening with every fibre in their bodies.

"Time to go home" Herr Laurich suddenly said which had made her start. She hurried down the ladder, and Herr Laurich whistled shrilly with the aid of two fingers, and soon Shorsch joined them. Angela and Herr Laurich examined the animal.

"Prime beast! A boar!" and he slapped Angela on the shoulder. She nearly fell over. Shorsch bent down and then turned to Herr Laurich and said:

"Good shot".

"Not me, her" he answered. Shorsch said nothing, and Angela felt the resentment, it was so obvious. Poor Shorsch.

Suddenly the headlights of a car silhouetted the ancient trees and brought Heiner and the Silesian into view. The car stopped and Moser got out.

"Got one" he shouted.

"So have we" Herr Laurich yelled back and then slapped Angela again on the shoulder, so hard, she made several involuntary steps towards Herr Moser.

"Meet Diane the huntress" he roared. Heiner steadied her and quietly said:

"Are the mosquitos giving you trouble?" She nodded her head, but in spite of everything she felt elated and surprised that she enjoyed the night's hunting. Was the shaking-bit part of it? Was it the excitement? She pretended that shooting the boar was nothing special. People did it all the time when they owned or worked land with wild pigs on it, didn't they?

As soon as she got back she went swimming, and Shorsch joined her.

"What made you want to take up farming?" he asked her as they swam side by side up river.

"I like the countryside, I don't like to be cooped up indoors, I like horses, why do you ask?"

"Because women belong into the house. They upset everything when they meddle in men's business. What if all women wanted to do what you are doing?" he asked indignantly.

"They probably will in the future. Its men like you who drive them from the role they held since time began, away from the blasted kitchen sink which embodies all that a woman stands for in life. Cleaning, washing, bearing children year in year out, pouring the water down the drain and with it their life, their thoughts, their ambitions, their hopes, their dreams and possibilities of what their lives could be." Angela was treading water by his side.

"Who is looking after the children then when you women are out replacing us?" He sounded genuinely concerned.

"What about recognizing the work a woman does in the home as equal to that a man does outside? What about a pension in her own right at the end of it all? After all, she produces the next generation and that is the most important work. Take my mother for instance. She has spent her best years bringing up her children single handedly, while my father played at beeing lost in the war when he wasn't, and then, when he could hide no longer, divorced her. He is going to get a lovely pension. Mother does not. Women have been pushed around, used cruelly for far too long."Her anger grew. "Men are still making the rules without consulting the women, without giving them a thought." Shorsch opened his mouth to say something, but she cut him short:

"Take your mother for instance. What happened on your farm during the war while your father was prepared to give up his life in Stalingrad for the glory of the Fatherland? You are glad he made it back. Thousands didn't make it. Did anybody appreciate the fact that your mother coped all those years and ran the farm as it was always run?" She looked at Shorsch and realized that he didn't understand or didn't want to know. "Think of all the women who coped in the war, did men's jobs and then when the men returned were expected to return to the role of the meak little woman. Did you ever give your mother the credit due to her? Did you think she did a damn good job? Did your father admit that he was grateful? Or are you too scared to admit that she is as capable as any man, as capable as you and your father?" Angela got out of the river, too worked up and far too tired to keep a cool head. She didn't want a row with Shorsch. Men, with their bloody attitude! She walked away, leaving him in the river. Wet and still dripping she went upstairs and very quietly sneaked into her room. Martha and Maria were fast asleep. She hung her swimsuit on a hook at the door and naked, slid into bed, her thoughts turning round like windmills.

Before her mother got married and before her father knew whom she was going to marry, he had given her some advice on how to be a good wife. Mother had taken it to heart. Her husband's word was law, even when he demanded that her first born, a son, should be brought up by her mother in law. And when in 1950 he was finally found by the Red Cross living in hiding with his mother, not his wife, claimed that the separation had been too long. It may have been a long time, but four children is a good reason to return and face ones responsibilities!

Margarete had shown Angela her father's little gem of advice, and Angela was quite indignant. It read:

5. May 1932.

"Never sulk. The next morning must not know of that which happened yesterday. It is up to the wife to overcome ill feeling and discord. Never raise your voice, never act vehemently. You dispose too much of yourself, gain nothing, and gamble away all sympathies. Hold your tongue in time, leave the room quietly and serenely. Return soon and settle down to embroider or do some other womanly activity. Be silent but do not brood or look sullen. This is prudent advice of a man who draws the woman in the light she should be seen, and how she will always be loved, attractive and dear to the man, no matter whether it thunders or rains, which it will in any marriage."

Her first thought, after she had read this precious advice, was: 'Poor grandmother!' but then grandmother knew no better and was trained in the art of being an obedient wife, her master being her husband and her subjects her servants, her domain the household. She had died before the end of the First World War which marked the end of genteel living.

When her mother had shown her those lines, Angela was only fourteen years old, but she knew, that, if this was what she had to be like to be a good wife, she would never marry. She needed her personal freedom and no matter what, she felt equal to any man. Her reasoning was as good as theirs, and in many ways, she was more capable than they were. She could cook, sew, bake, preserve all manner of food; she knew about home nursing and child care, anything the men here couldn't do. She had looked at her mother and asked: "Are you telling me I should heed these lines? Is that advice also meant for me? It sounds all very oldfashioned, ignorant and mean". And her mother had smiled and said: "Any man who demands this of you is not worthy of you".

No, she would not marry if it meant for her to become her husbands slave.

She was tossing and turning, but eventually she fell asleep.

Shorsch battled with conflicting thoughts as he dried himself.

Angela was a disturbing girl, different from the girls he knew at home, pretty too, but who ever heard of a woman doing men's work. Her question; 'who did all the work at your farm while your father was away' echoed in his mind. Who indeed, and he did take it totally for granted. Angela was right. But then it was something that mothers and wives and sisters always did when their menfolk went to war, the world over. How else could one defend one's country? His grandmother coped while his grandfather fought in the First World War, and he told him that his father fought with the Austrian Kaiser in Italy whenever that was. So his great grandmother must have managed on her own too, and his own mother did so well with her polish farm hands, that the farm suffered no loss. When his father came back, his mother handed over the reines quietly and retired back into the house and he wondered for the first time what her feelings must have been like. He had never heard his father utter words of appreciation or thanks. But then, off course, his mother had only done her duty, what was expected and no more.

Grudgingly he admitted to himself, that women were capable and he was going to pay more attention to his mother. A strange thought crossed his mind. There should'nt be any more wars. That would keep the women at home and in their place. But for Angela it was too late. It was too late for everyone, he could see this now. He too belonged to the new generation. Angela was a strange young woman, spoke Bavarian like a native, but one could tell that she was a Prussian, every bit of her. He couldn't really say she was proud or stuck up, but there was something different about her. As he slowly crossed the yard, he realized, that he was strangely attracted to her. Her genuine happiness and her enthusiasm for the work here was infectious. Darkly, he wondered how a young woman like that could be attracted to a shortsighted scholar like Heiner.

He also wondered for the first time what she must have gone through during the war. Why did she and all these other refugees have to come to Bavaria? And why did the Bavarians have to share everything? He had never given it a thought. After the war they had arrived in millions along with the Americans, and suddenly the peaceful Bavaria was overrun by people from the East, together with occupaying armies, cars and planes and women who would not knuckle down! Almost all farms in Bavaria had to give up one or two rooms to families from Silesia, East Prussia, Poland, the Ukraine, and the Balkan States along the Danube, Estonia, Latvia and Lithuania and even from Russia. And for the first time he imagined what it would be like if he had to leave his farm and his homeland and find a new life somewhere else with nothing in his pockets. Having had to leave everything behind for the new owners who got it all for free. All the generations of hard work on the land. His land. Well it would never happen, of that he was sure.

*

7

Cycling to Koefering

It was before sunrise on a Sunday morning in the summer of 1953. The sleepy dairy man crossed the yard to start milking, inadvertantly kicking a bucket as he entered the gloomy cow house. Although there were milking machines on the market, they were still far too expensive so soon after the war and they still milked by hand. When it was Angela's turn, every two weeks for one week, she had to milk seven cows before breakfast, sharing the work with the Schweizer. It was an occupation which she found comforting and peaceful. She aimed jets of Milk at the cats who waited eagerly along the wall opposite, expertly opening their mouths to catch the the stream of warm milk, their little tongues licking any droplets from their long whiskers which had not found their mark.

Angela shivered in the early dawn, as she got ready to cycle to Köfering in Lower Bavaria, some 130 km distance. Since she started her agricultural apprentice ship, she had to attend college 4 times a year for a residential week, and her college was at Köfering. When she had absolved her three years, she would have to become a fulltime residential student there. She was now nearly completing her second year.

Her first farm had been a small place not far from Regensburg; four cows, two dreadful old nags, a team of oxen, chickens and four pigs. A big market garden, where the farmer's wife grew asparagus and other choice vegetables for the best hotels in Regensburg, mostly still occupied by the Americans. The farmer and his son grew potatoes, wheat, barley, oats and rye, sugar beets and maize.

A refugee family with nine children, occupied half the farmhouse, which irritated the farmer's wife dreadfully and the maid and Angela seemed to be on the receiving end of all her frustrations. Angela's contract was binding, she could not change to go to another farm, until her year was up. The maid left around Christmas time, pleading homesickness.

When her year was over, she left there with such joy, to go to this magnificent, solitary farm in the Upper Palatinate.

Herr Laurich came out of the front door, sniffed the air and decided what sort of weather it was going to be that day. It promised to be a clear, blue and warm summers day.

"You'll get wet today, there'll be heavy rain in the afternoon". He was never wrong. She wondered how he did it. He looked up into the air, watched the clouds, felt the breeze and made a decision.

"I have the triangular army tent section, with the pointed bit at the back and the wide bit over the handle bars, I should be alright." Angela was busy fastening the Rucksack onto the luggage rack at the back.

"Put your gumboots on to keep your feet dry", he added.She I didn't want to wear her gumboots, they didn't go with her bike. They were horrid smelly things, used to muck out the pigs, the cows and the horses. There was so much mucking out to do. Sometimes she thought that farming evolved around the mucking out, stacking the pile, loading it and spreading it on the fields. But even that was healthy, reassuring and fruitful.

She had a new pair of green shoes, elegant, with crepe soles, her first new pair after the war *and* bought with her own money, by herself. But Herr Laurich was right. She would put her beautiful shoes into her Rucksack to keep them nice.

The farmer came over. He put his large, gnarled hand on her bicycle's shiny, chestnut brown leather saddle.

"Give your bike a rub down when you get home tonight. Stop it from rusting". He stood back and they both looked at the bicycle. Herr Laurich's face had once been smashed in by a horse, as it kicked out and caught him fully in the face. When she first arrived at the farm, she found it very difficult to read his expression, to see his moods, but now, she could read how he felt in the way he spoke, and she watched for the tell tale change of colour in his face. He was a kind and fair man, a lot of fun and a good laugh, but when roused, his temper was something to behold.

"A good buy." He meant the cycle, which had been delivered only three weeks earlier. She had chosen it from a catalogue, payed a deposit of which grandfather had paid half, and after six more monthly instalments, it would be hers for ever. It was a mountain-touring cycle, sky blue and silver-chrome, three gears, back pedal brake, shock absorber in the saddleshaft, airpump, leather toolbag with all necessary tools and repair kit under the saddle. Five year guarantee for the gears, but 25 year guarantee for the frame! It was a perfect dream, admired by all with a certain envy. Even the girls and the young men from the villages around came to look at it and discuss the bicycle on Sunday afternoons, seriously considering such a purchase themselves. Every speck of dirt and dust was immediately and carefully polished away by anyone who spotted it first.

Frau Laurich appeard in the courtyard with a big parcel of packed lunch and a beerbottle of milk.

"Give Fräulein Becher this and my regards". She handed Angela a second parcel which smelled deliciously of Speck. Fräulein Becher, the head mistress at college, and Frau Laurich graduated together before the war and stayed friends.

A last check, hand shaking, good wishes and Angela kicked her bike off the stand and swung herself into the saddle. It was sheer pleasure riding this bike.

"See you in a week!" In fast gear she peddled down the road to Amberg with the iron foundary belching black smoke day and night, 365 days a year, on the horizon to the right. Every night the sky above the foundary was crimson.

Amberg was a beautiful medieval town, still totally surrounded by a thick wall. It was the *Kreisstadt*, county town, and Angela had come here to the market, showing off the horses which were for sale.

It was still only five o clock in the morning and she planned to be in Schwandorf by ten. There were mountains, which would be too steep to peddle up, and she would have to push, making up for time on the way down on the other side. She should be home by two, she calculated, and have the afternoon and evening with mother and her sisters, and continue the next morning early, to be in Köfering by eight.

It had not been easy to leave home two years ago, but there was little else for her to do at the time, and since she had come to the Laubhof, she had never regretted having made the decision to become a graduate farmer, specializing in horses. It was a great career and hers would be a wonderful life. People always have and always would need horses.

The road between Amberg and Schwandorf lead through endless forests. It was so quiet, no traffic at all. A deer was peacefully grazing in a clearing, a shaft of sunshine finding it's way through the thick forest, highlighting the colour on it's back and the dewdrops on some blades of grass. Her fawn standing on her inside, almost completely hidden from the road. The wild flowers shone brilliantly among the tall grasses.

Effortlessly and silently she cruised past, enjoying the scene, the forest, the bicycle, the trip, life.

Clouds gathered indigo, purple and black as she came out of the forest. She stopped briefly. The land spread wide into the distance below her, the Naab river making a silver band right through to the horizon, where the purple clouds met the earth. She dicended fast into the Naab valley. Just before Burg Lengenfeld it started to pour. She found a barn by the road and pushed the bike inside, sat in the hay and had an early lunch.

When she had finished eating, she rested contentedly, waiting for the rain to ease, hopefully stop. At midday she decided to cycle on in the rain. Water soon collected in a puddle on her tent cape, where it was spread between the handle bars, but it kept her knees dry. Soon however it dripped down in streams and straight into her boots, which she had to empty regularly to ease the weight. Then the water ran down her neck and eventually she was wet, even underneath her tent covering. She entered the Regen valley, and cycled along this peaceful river. Nature here was undisturbed, the road not surfaced and there were many potholes to be avoided, full to the brim with rainwater, and she hated her beautiful bicycle getting all muddy. However, she could wipe it afterwards.

Gallingkofen. Now it would be downhill all the way to Stadt am Hof, which was the town at the other end of the Steinerne Brücke. She had to cross this bridge, because they still had not been able to finish rebuilding the Nibelungen Brücke, which had been a motorway bridge across the Danube before the War. Some panic stricken idiot had blasted the 'Steinerne Brücke' in the last minutes of the war, and blown away an eight hundred year old arch, just by the 'Brückentor'. A miracle that the Bridge Gate had not been too damaged by this stupid blunder.

It was still raining heavily, and she slithered on the cobbles, trying to avoid the tramlines.

She cycled up the Maximilian Strasse and stopped at the Parkhotel, wondering wether Arnold was at home. Arnold had come into their lives 7 years earlier, buying grandfather's entire works of Shakespeare in both languages, one page in German and the other page in English. 1945/46 one sold anything for food, and Arnold became a family friend.

She looked down at herself, decided against looking him up, hopped back onto the wet saddle and made it for home. She pushed her bike in to the stairwell, down the five steps to the cellar ante room and then bounded up stairs, two at a time. It was three o clock. Timing wasn't bad.

Mother and the sisters had been waiting, and as she entered she was surrounded, all her wet things torn off her, an old American dressing gown thrown over her shoulder and then they dragged her into the livingroom. Her sisters *always* complained about the farm smells, which seemed to linger on her. They wrinkled their noses and squeezed their nostrils. They also called her *'Bauerntrampe'l*, which translates as clumsy peasant. She decided to ignore their ignorant prattle.

The table was laid, a fresh strawberry cake, a cherry cake, whipped cream, good china and real coffee filled the room with a delicious aroma. The sun had found a hole in the purple clouds and sparkled on the beautiful silver on the table. She counted the cups and saucers. There were seven of them. She looked up inquiringly at her mother who said:

"Grandfather and Tata are coming too". Angela still looked at her, surprised. She laughed.

"Things are alright at the moment, I think Tata's good influence on father is finally paying off".

Tata was Edith Kilian, who had married grandfather in 1949, and after she had got used to suddenly being Frau Baronin von Stuckrad, had turned out to be a lady. It took her nearly three years, working out the various family connections, and her exact status, which was very important to her, and exactly what her husband's daughter with her children were doing there, living so close to grandfather, when it would have been so much more convenient, had they lived at the other side of the moon. She soon realized grandfather's stressed and mixed up feelings, sorted them, out and put things right. She was a fair and unbiased lady.

Grandfather and Angela had always had a special relationship. Angela believed it was their mutual love for horses, a kindred spirit which was special to them and which they both recognised. But there was also the fact, that she would not be intimidated by him, even answered back on several occasions. Her mother was horrified and told her to show respect. Grandfather and Angela respected each other, and Tata welcomed her visits, because it put grandfather into a good mood.

"Ah, Angela, time for a game of cards?" his face would light up as soon as she entered. He hardly ever heard her knock, he was getting deaf. Strangely though, he could hear things he wasn't supposed to hear.

Angela hoped very much, that mother and her father had put their differences aside and were to be friends again, like they were after the trial when he had been accused by the Nazies.

It was a truly happy and united coffee round that afternoon, grandfather, Tata, both in love and happy with each other's company, happy also to be in his daughter's sitting room, mother beaming, her eyes sparkling like the silver on the table. Her sisters Bine and Tissy looking in wonderment at grandfather, not believing what they saw, still a little suspicious. His strictness, supervising their homework, did not go down well with either of them.

Bit by bit the cakes disappeared, the cream also vanished. Mother went to make some more coffee and grandfather lit a cigar. They sat and talked and talked, and nobody wanted to break up the round. When it became dark outside, mother and Angela lit a candle and then sneaked into the kitchen and made smorgesbrod, laying it out on three large platters. They put smoked ham, Cervelat, Salami, soft cheese and Emmentaler, Rocquefort and Bierwurst on ryebread, wheat bread and Pumpernickel. They also sliced some rolls and made 'small bites', then garnished the platters with tomatoes, gherkins, parsely and bits of apples. The platters looked appetising. From the larder they got some home made sloe wine and took everything into the sitting room. A chorus of "Ah" greeted them as they entered, and Bine and Tissy quickly took the coffee things out and laid a new table. The get together continued happily and harmoniously until bedtime.

They discussed mothers new job, which she had had difficulty in getting. She was a state registered nurse, but all papers verifying this fact had been lost, burnt, disappeared in the war, along with a lot of other important papers. She had to locate fellow nurses, professors and examiners, which had been time consuming and difficult. But she had located enough witnesses to get new papers, and anyway, nurses were in great demand.

Bine was leaving school soon and decided to become a nanny. She would like to work with children. She also planned to go to England and work in a home for children with learning difficulties near Birmingham.

Angela looked at her mother and said: "I meant to ask you for a very long time. Have you ever found out anything of the people in Lichtenau?" I wondered constantly what became of all the people we came to love in Lichtenau in East Prussia. Slowly mother got up and went over to a small Rokoko chest of drawers. She came back and handed her a letter.

"I received this two years ago. I didn't want to tell you until you were older. I think now you are ready to read this. It is from the two ladies who lived in the top flat of the schoolhouse in Lichtenau, the two who knitted the pretty cardigans you had for Easter, remember? " Angela remembered.

"Miss Schorn and Miss ..." She couldn't remember her name and looked at the end of the letter.

"Miss Hegarn". Mother nodded.

"Read the letter. It is very sad, I must warn you. At the time I tried to find people who were in Lichtenau and who could maybe tell

me what became of everybody. This is her second letter to me."
Angela took the letter and went into her corner of the room, which
still had her desk and things and her bed. She sat down on her bed
and started to read. It was dated Berlin, April 1949.

Dear Frau Geppert.

Thank you for taking all this trouble and for the parcel with the
warm clothes, the coffee, the milkpowder and the dried potatoes. We
have no food here other than the strict rations which the planes fly in
day and night. Day and night, day and night every three minutes.
Thank your American friend, who was able to smuggle this parcel
onto one of the planes. These planes and the men who fly them are a
true modern day miracle.

Now to answer your questions. I am afraid, there is nothing but
sadness and despair to report. Our escape from deportation or even
death was ironic.

The Russians arrived 4 months after your departure. We stayed,
simply because we had nothing to lose or gain. There was nowhere
for us to go in Berlin or anywhere else. All we had was in our attic
room.

A week after the Russians arrived here, they herded all the
villagers into the little square by the church, and there they waited
until everybody, even the farmers and labourers from the
neighbourhood, farmer Graf and the Kramps and everybody, were
gathered. They were freezing in the icy cold. Our warm clothing had
been taken away. I saw no sign of the Russian or Polish prisoners
from the moment the Soviets arrived. There was a whisper, that they
might have been shot for having worked on the farms.

The villagers were separated into groups, farmer Graf, the
Bürgermeister, the vicar, the teachers and all landowners in fact,
were led away. I can still see Frau Kramp with the new born baby
and all her boys walking away. She was crying so.

The Russians had separated the men from the women, but they
left together, that same day. The last we saw of them was the column
they formed, slowly walking down the Mehlsacker road. We never
saw them again. It was said, that they had been sent to Siberia.

All the land was taken over by Russian farmers. We watched the
beautiful, fruitful land perish around us in the two years we had to

live there. All machinery, ploughs, wagons, threshing machines, everything, was sent to Russia in 1945. The new farmers had no tools to work with. All was left to total ruin. Little Mother Poschman and her sister died of starvation.

In the spring of 1947, with the melting snow, a mass grave was found in the forest just outside of Lichtenau. It was rumoured that the bodies belonged to the Polish and Russian POW's, and that would explain why we were not permitted to gather wood, mushrooms and berries in the forest.

Fräulein Schorn and I went regularly to the Kommandantur and applied to be let out and go to the West. Fräulein Schorns body was violated several times, and I made her stay in our attic room. I was miraculously spared this terrible ordeal. In the end it was quite easy, for all German speaking people, who had not been killed or deported, to get exit papers.

Frau Geppert, when we left Lichtenau, a handful of German speaking people, nobody who lived there while you were here, remained. We were not allowed to take anything with us, and on the train to freedom, our clothes were stolen from our bodies. We arrived at Frankfurt an der Oder, near-naked, starved and frozen.

Frau Geppert, the Russians are subhuman. To call them animals, is an insult to the animal kingdom. We are cold and starving now, but we are free. Thank you again for the parcel, and I look forward to a possible reunion in the future.

Very respectfully yours

Dorothea Hegarn

After all that Angela had heard in the years since the war, the news this letter contained, did not shock her. It really only confirmed what she had known in her heart already. It helped, to know for sure. She folded the letter and returned to the table.

Grandfather now turned to her and said:

"Put it behind you. You have started a new life." and then he asked:

"And what of your plans, after you come out of Agricultural College?"

He was right. She had finished grieving, although her feeling for Robert, the Russian POW from the Caucasus, was different. It helped to know, that he lay in that beautiful forest, where the fairies lived and where they picked berries. It was a good place. She and her family had survived and they had to get on with life. She looked at grandfather. He too had survived. She took a deep breath. Glad and proud to be asked, she answered:

"I have five practical years after that, and some of that I can take abroad. I have chosen Finland, the nearest country to East Prussia I can find, where I am permitted to go. After that I shall also go to England, because I think I would like to learn that language. Then I will be back and prepare myself here for my Masters. I have already started to save money for my fare to Finland." Grandfather smiled contentedly:

"Good, you have your future sorted out. Very good. I shall advance the fare money for you and Bine, should you both find that you have not saved enough and also need some travel money and I shall help you too. You shall pay me back when you can afford it.

Angela looked at her grandfather and their eyes met. He gave her an encouraging and reassuring twinkle. She loved this man. She got up and put her arms around him.

"Thank you grandfather, thank you for everything.

*

8

What about equal pay

Angela was cutting the lucerne in the top field, which was the first task of the day during the green season. The fresh green feed had to be in before the milking started. She always looked forward to her turn. The cows tranquilly chewed away while being milked, and the smell of warm milk mingled with that of alfalfa or meadow grass was comfortable and reassuring.

Bouncing along the rough and bumpy lane to the meadow in the tractor was enjoyable too. She imagined herself on the back of a camel, riding through the desert to a dig in Egypt. Had she been born a little earlier or later, so that the war hadn't interfered with her life, she would have tried to walk in the footsteps of Howard Carter, Arthur Evans or Heinrich Schliemann. Her most favourite book, *'Götter, Gräber und Gelehrte'* (Gods, Tombs and Scholars) a novel of archaeology, was always part of her luggage. She couldn'd remember how many times she had read it. How she longed to see all these ancient places! This was her private dream. Would she ever find somebody to share it with her? Heiner maybe and she smiled happily.

She looked up towards the farm. Heiner would join her a little later and help to load up the fodder. She was cutting the last row for the daily ration. Some of the lucerne would be cut and dried for winter feed. Herr Laurich held, that cattle cannot graze on permanent grazing fields because they would feed on their own waste and that would desease the stock with all sorts of worms and intestinal parasites. Quite apart from that they were relying on the organic furtilizer.

At the end of the row she lifted the silver blade and hooked it securely to the tractor. Still no sign of Heiner!

The quiet before the day started was precious to her. Dawn was still half an hour away; the cutting started at four in the morning. There was the jubilant cry of the blackbird which sounded up from the orchard. Then the sparrows started, the titmouse and finches, and soon there was a joyful chorus filling the air. With the first rays of the still hidden sun, the bees arrived, and her heart could have burst for the beauty all around her. She sighed deeply and happily.

The sky was spreading with pink and she climbed up into the tractor, backed it towards the wagon and hooked it up. No time to waste; she had to be home and milking before the sun was up. She would have to start loading on her own. She lined up the tractor between two rows and stopped after about 10 yards, took the fork and went to the end of the row. Pushing the fork up the row, stabbing it every now and then, she filled the fork and then heaved it up into the wagon. She went back and forked up the other row, then climbed into the tractor and drove on another ten yards.

Heiner probably couldn't get out of bed. Men! They could never get up in the morning, and when they were up, they were grumpy and unfriendly until after breakfast, although she couldn't truthfully say that about Heiner.

He joined her when she had half loaded the wagon and apologised:

"I didn't hear the knock on the door until I heard the Schweizer yell: "Aren't you supposed to be cutting fodder? That made me move, I can tell you. Aw, did he smell!,and that first thing in the morning!"

Angela laughed: "Yak! Serves you right for oversleeping, leaving me to cope. You owe me one!"

"Anything" Heiner said, and he put out a hand as if to touch her.

"Come on, we are late as it is", Angela said quickly. Heiner chucked his bike on the back and she jumped up on the tractor, and very slowly drove down one row, Heiner keeping up and loading, then up the other row until all was done. Heiner grabbed the handle behind her and swung himself up on the bar at the back of the tractor. They returned to the farm. There she drove right into the feed bay, climbed out of her seat, up and over into the wagon and started unloading. The Schweizer grumbled something about being late. She growled back:

"Don't make such a big deal out of it. We'll soon catch up and you'll have your breakfast on time." Then she wrinkled her nose, and despite herself said: "What about a wash and a shave!" the dairyman pretended he hadn't heard.

The cows were eagerly mooing and swishing their tails, impatient for their feed. They stood on clean golden straw, and the cats sat along the wall, waiting for the milking to begin.

She parked the empty wagon under the overhang and the tractor outside the smithy. Coming in through the dairy kitchen, she strapped a stool round her waist, grabbed a bucket and settled down. Rythmically the milk swished into her bucket, filling slowly and forming a thick layer of foam on the top. The last jets of milk she aimed at the cats who had waited patiently and now their little mouths opened eagerly to catch the milk. All she had to do was aim and they would catch with hardly any milk wasted.

It was the end of August and a Saturday, and they all had the afternoon off. 'Zirkus Krone' had come to Hermannsricht, and their colourful and exiting posters were stuck to almost every tree along the roads, up on barn doors, at the station. In fact there wasn't a spot where there wasn't a poster. And in Poppenricht was Kirmess, the annual church-fair. There would be lots of church fairs from now on, and they would have a dance every Saturday in the neighbouring villages. Today, they had planned to go to the Circus in the afternoon and after milking and mucking out they would go dancing in the evening. However Herr Laurich had already warned them, that they might have to work the next day, Sunday, because the last of the harvest grain had to be brought in. She sighed. Didn't every silvercloud have a black lining? They worked steadily through the morning. The afternoon would be fun. Tomorrow was a long time away.

They hurried with lunch, and Angela helped Maria and Martha in the kitchen, so that they could all be off together. Angela had her own bike and so did the men, Maria and Martha borrowed Frau Laurich's and Stoffel's. The Laurich's would go in the car. Going to the circus had become a big affair. Herr Laurich had suggested that they should all go in the tractor with the guncarriage, decked out with rows of benches but the young folk decided on the bikes. They travelled on the trailer all week toing and froing, and the bikes were so much faster and smarter.

"Four years ago, this circus came to Regensburg and for the entire fortnight their roller-skating act joined my class at school", Angela said.

"Would they still be with the circus? We might get free tickets." Martha said.

"I don't know, but their parents were juggling cyclists. When they were in Regensburg that time, we all got a free ticket for a weekday afternoon performance". Angela said, and then continued:

"The Severin sisters, that was what they were called, had to join the nearest school where ever they stopped. I thought they were lucky, travelling all the time, new schools and new friends. Their dream however was to live somewhere permanently and they always looked forward to go to their winter quarters, where they stayed in one place for six months."

"I wonder whether they remember you." Maria looked sceptical.

"Well, they see so many people. I know now why they didn't like travelling so much". Angela wiped the lunchplates and added laughingly:

"There were some young men who used part of our gym to train every afternoon. I was a member of the youth gym club. We had to train for the district championships every afternoon, straight after school. They wanted a human ball, and after watching me do my routine on the mat, they asked me to help out. I had to roll up backwards, with my head through my knees holding onto my ankles, and they threw me around catching me by the waist. They made a pyramid of men and they would toss me all the way up to the top on one side, hold me up high and then toss me down again on the other, or they lay on the floor with their feet up in the air, tossing and catching me with their feet. I thought the whole thing was brilliant, and two days before they had to leave I went home and announced to my mother, that I would go with the circus. Mother just looked at me for a second or two and then slapped my face hard. Well I didn't argue after that. I never mentioned it since. I could run off with them now!" She laughed when she saw Martha's and Maria's horrified faces.

"You are nuts, you know!" Maria said and then inquisitively asked:

"Can you still put your head through your legs?"

"Oh, I don't know! I haven't tried it since." Angela hung the teatowel on the rail above the range and took her apron off. They had got dressed into their Sunday best just before lunch, and now they were ready to go. A quick glance into the mirror.

"I wish I could do something with this awful hair of mine," Martha sighed.

"Look at it!" and her hands tried in vain to get the crazy curls under control.

"My head looks twice the size!" she groaned.

"It's part of you," Maria said and Angela added:

"You've got the eyebrows, the lashes and the shape of the face to go with it. Do you want to change the lot?

Laughing happily, the three women came out of the house to find the men getting the bikes ready. Heiner was pumping air into Angela's rear tyre, Shorsch was busy with Maria's and an extraordinalrily clean and hardly recognizeable Schweizer was busy on Martha's bike. Never before had she seen him so clean and his clothes so neat. She kept looking at him in disbelief. He was a most handsome man and she could not understand why he loved to be so dirty most of the time.

"Ready?" Shorsch had one leg on the pedal ready to push off.

"Ready" Martha said and pushed herself off. They peddled down the lane, and put their bikes into mountain gear to get up the hill to the main road, laughing and flirting. The girls wore their tight bodiced, wide skirted Dirndl dresses, low necked, with puffy sleeved white blouses. Frau Laurich had loaned Angela one of her old ones, and she felt so beautiful in it, even though she didn't fill it in the breast department.

It was only five kilometres to the circus and involuntarily they raced. Shorsch stayed in first place, with Maria and Angela battling for second, the Schweizer and Martha keeping up and Heiner bringing up the rear.

They swarmed into Hermansricht and came to a halt by a cluster of oaktrees near the entrance to the circus field, where they chained their bikes together. Almost simultaniously they sniffed the air.

"Smell the lions!" the Schweizer said.

"And the elephants" Maria added. "I love elephants!"

"It smells of proper circus" Heiner smiled down at Angela and put his arm very lightly over her shoulder.

"What about your friends?" Shorsch asked, hoping that they might all get in free.

"I haven't seen them in four years. They might not even be here, and anyway it feels like begging. I would much rather buy the tickets and then look them up", Angela said.

"She is right", Heiner said, and gently steered her towards the ticket seller's tent. Heiner had invited Angela, Shorsch took Maria and the Schweizer had asked Martha. It was an unwritten law, that the men 'invited' the girls; when they went to functions together. They had a bigger wage packet which the girls thought an injustice. It would have been an insult to the men, had the girls insisted to pay for themselves, or worse still, offer to invite the men, or pay for a beer, never mind the insult to the women. The girls often discussed this, but only in secret and wondered what could be done about it. A typical argument would go like this:

"We should get the same pay as the men, especially you, Angela. You do the same work, and yet you get paid the same as we do. I can understand why we get less, we do womens work." That would be Maria's comment, and Angela would argue:

"That is the wrong attitude. Women work as hard, if not harder than the men. And why should it be up to the women to wake the men in the morning? And look at you! When the men put their feet under the table for the evening meal, that's their day done. But you have to finish in the kitchen, put away the foodstuffs, wash up, sweep and get things ready for the morning. That adds an extra hour and a half at least. In a week that is ten and a half extra hours approximately, *and* you get paid less".

"Angela is right, even though it is a Prussian attitude." Martha would add. But that is as far as it went, and approaching voices or foodsteps would silence them instantly and they would talk about something totally different.

9

When the Circus came

The seats were crude wooden benches which ascendedgradually up towards the back, and the ramps for access were wide 'chickenladders'. Their tickets took them to the centre of the ascent from where they had a good view. They could see the elephants dance with the indian girls, the beautiful white horses doing Lippizzaner tricks, the jugglers, the seals playing ball, the clowns squirting water everywhere and using each other as human canon balls. There was a woman with extraordinary dogs who could do almost human tasks, including riding a bycicle. There were chimpanzees teaching other monkeys to write in a classroom situation. Now they were waiting for the flying humans, and while they were erecting the safety net, a beautiful young girl danced on a high wire with an exotic parasol.

When the flyers came in, she recognized two of the three men who, four years ago had tossed her about, and a young woman, beautiful to look at, who obviously had taken the spot she could have filled, had her mother let her go. She pointed the men out to Maria who sat next to her.

"That woman could be me!" she sighed dramatically and Maria gave her a kick in the ribs:

"You daft thing" she whispered. Giggling quietly they watched as the flyers climbed up and up and up. While their eyes followed them up, they almost missed the Severin sisters. They were wearing two wheeled rollerskates and were sliding along the tightrope. She recognized them immediately and clapped enthusiastically when they had reached their little platforms at the end of the rope. At one time they raced towards each other and one sister jumped over the other one who ducked very low, never stopping. Brilliant. Angela clapped and so did all her friends. One of the sisters looked down and Angela waved a little. The sisters finished their act and the flyers started, with a safety net, summersaulting, twisting and turning. It was a daring, difficult and thrilling act. Then they announced that for this tripple summersault and twist they would remove the net. And to make it even more thrilling, two people would do this simultaneously, crossing in mid air. The audience caught their breath. Their hands sweated, their eyes were glued to the top of the tent. Angela could barely breathe, and the idea sneaked back into her mind, that it could be her up there. It made her grin. Ninety nine percent she knew, that she could not do it. The one percent told her that with daily training and common sense, she might have done it, but...

The 'Flying Humans' performance was nailbitingly thrilling, especially without the net. She thought it was unnecessary to remove it though, since all eyes were on the flyers, not on the net and one forgot it wasn't there. Accidents could happen, and that would be fatal without the net. But the public love a bloody spectacle. Heiner leaned down to her and whispered:

"Aren't people bloodthirsty?" Strange, that he should say that at this precise moment. She looked up and their eyes met. 'What is it about him that makes me feel this way?' she worried. 'Do I love this man?' The thought frightened her. 'I am too young!'

Heiner too had strange feelings. He wanted to kiss her, but never found the right moment. 'I am going to kiss her tonight' he determined. His hand was cautiously searching for hers, and just as she felt his hand on hers, there was a light tap on her shoulder and she looked round.

"Regensburg, 1948, Von der Tann Schule". It was one of the Severin sisters. Angela got up to shake hands and said:

"How did you know I was here?"

"You waved, I saw you. Come to our caravan after the show" she said, and as Angela started to introduce her friends, the bench and footrest on which they sat gave a little jerk, which made her sit down with a bump. There was another shudder and shrieks, and then the entire section of seats in her area sank about a meter down. Nobody moved, and the shrieks stopped. The Severin Sister had nimbly jumped back onto the 'chickenladder' and helplessly watched, as jerkingly bit by bit the benches disappeard ever downward, gently, with the audience falling off as if in slow motion. Since they didn't seriously crash, the people stopped to panic and even laughed and shrieked nervously, and in the end thought it was part of the act, but it wasn't. A section, about 10 meters by 10 had become dislodged. The last yard ended with a hard bump and fear that other benches, which were still up might come down on top of them.

Suddenly three clowns appeared and helped them out from under the remaining seats, other circus people appeared and the tent errection team appeared with props to stop any more benches from collapsing. The danger passed, and everybody laughed. Now they had time to remember other peoples faces, as they came down, how they tried in vain to find something to hang on to, and having found it, letting go instantly when they saw what it was, apologizing, giggling, and not trying to laugh at somebody who dropped his dentures. The 'Laubhofers' looked around for the Laurichs, and to see whether the performance would continue, when the Severin sisters came up to Angela, laughing and apologizing. She was missing Heiner, and looking around, saw him without his spectacles. She watched him a few seconds and realized that he was totally lost. Instantly she ran and searched for his glasses, hoping that they had not come to any harm by the many people milling around. Then she noticed one of the clowns, holding a pair of glasses in his hand and looking around.

"May I have these please, I know to whom they belong", she said to the clown, who handed them to her.

She walked over to Heiner and quietly handed them to him, glad she could help.

One of the Severin Sisters giggled:

"Give them 20 minutes and everybody will be able to return to their seats, the show will continue." the other one added:

"This has never happened before!" Then focussing on Angela she said:

"I don't remember your name, but you used to have thick long plaits, and I wrote a verse into your friendship book. You haven't altered your hairstyle around your face, except that you cut off those gorgeous plaits. I always wanted hair like that.

71

"Incredible how you remembered, and from up there!" Angela was astonished. She introduced her friends properly this time and slowly they wandered across the meadow towards the animal enclosure.

"You know, you look so much alike, I can never keep you apart. Who is who?"

"Waldtraut and Irmela" and they pointed each other out. But it made no difference, they had no distinguishing marks. In the lions tent they met the two flyers, still in their glittering blue and silver flying costumes, who didn't recognize her, but remembered when the sisters called them over.

"Alberto and Alessandro" one of the sisters said and before Angela could say anything, Alessandro said dramatically in a faked Italian accent, pointing at her:

"Angela! The act should have been Alberto! Alessandro! and Angela!" Angela was embarrassed. She'd never live that one down. She had told the girls, and they promised to keep quiet, she never imagined that she would ever run into those two again. Shorsch was quick off the mark:

"What act" and he gave the Schweizer a very meaningful look. Alberto saw Angela's pink face, realized her embarrassment and quickly said:

"A very old joke we shared many years ago. Let me show you the lions".

The day at the circus was talked about and laughed about for many weeks after. The entire contingent from the Waldhof received an invitation to see, at their convenience the whole performance again, free, and from the front row. This time they all travelled on the guncarriage, and at the invitation for anyone brave enaugh to come into the ring to do some trick on horseback, Shorsch, who always thought himself to be an ace rider, volunteered. Athletically he jumped over the wooden wall into the arena. He had to wear a harness, onto which a long rope was hooked, which disappeared into the lofty heights of the circus tent. He was told he had to wear it while he cantered around the arena, standing on the horses back. Insurance regulation, they explained.

"No problem!" he said, and there wasn't until he was lifted up into the air, off the horse, floating flailing with arms and legs and the audience laughing deliriously. The Laubhofers looked on in horror. Angela felt, that Shorsch would blame her for that, that she had arranged this, and she also felt, that he was sick with embarrassment. But nobody in the group had any idea that this would happen.

"Oh dear!" Maria said and looked at Martha.

"He volunteered!" Martha giggled. But to everybody's surprise, they saw him laughing helplessly up there, as he was being hoisted up and down, everybody yelling:

"Swing man! More swing! You'll never get back on the horse this way!" But his heroic struggle was in vain, the horse cantered sedately on without him. When he finally came down and joined them at the ringside, sweating profusely, he laughed so much, that the tears ran down his golden cheeks. His hair was full of sawdust, where he had been lowered just a little bit too low and dragged along the floor. The clowns asked for another 'volunteer' and dozens of young men got up. Five more were chosen, and the laughter never stopped. There was no doubt in anybody's mind, that that had been the best part of the show.

The day before the circus left, Alberto, Alessandro and the Severin Sisters came to visit the Waldhof. They had been invited, but their life being unpredictable, they couldn't make a proper date. They found everybody spread far and wide with just Maria at home preparing the evening meal. Angela and the men were loading oats. When she drove into the court with a wagon load, she saw a truck depart in the opposite direction towards the main road. She stopped in the barn and walked into the kitchen for a slice of bread and a cup of coffee:

"Who was that in the truck?" she asked Maria.

"You just missed the circus. They are leaving tonight. Here is their winter quarter address. Irmela was sorry to have missed Shorsch. If you ask me, that's the only reason they came out". Angela laughed:

"They didn't come to carry me off then? Another dream shattered. You tell Shorsch tonight that Irmela was sorry to have missed him. Maybe he'll join the circus clowns."

"He'd not leave his farm for anyone, nor will he bring home a woman who is not a country ...

...woman with a dowry! Angela finished the sentence.

"I was only joking!"

Maria looked at her and with a hint of contempt explained:

"He couldn't show his face in his community with a circus wench as his wife!" Angela looked at Maria and said:

"Nothing has changed since the middleages. Love is not important among the farming community, money and size of the manure pile is what counts!"

Her temper was welling up inside her. It seemed to her that, ambition, willingness to do hard work and dedication all meant nothing if one didn't have the proper dowry, money and position. You had to be a landowning member of the young farmers. Without it there was no entry anywhere. She left her coffee unfinished and went back to the barn to unload the wagon. Maria watched her leave the kitchen, but did not understand Angela's sudden burst of temper and then thought; she is a towney, she doesn't understand, that a man with a farm thinks of the farm's wellfare first, and any bride he brings home, has to have the ability to further the farm with a wealthy dowry, be healthy and bear sons. But she'll learn.

That was the end of the circus, but the telling went on and on. Every Faire they went to, the story was retold, and Shorsch was a local hero.

"Heaven knows why" Maria said.

Martha had, on that day they first visited the circus, discovered the Schweizer. At first nobody noticed, until it seemed there was a new face at the table at meal times, and then it dawned on them, that the Schweizer was clean and shaven every time. Even his clothes were clean. Then they tried to figure out why! Everybody watched everybody, and finally realised that Martha's large brown eyes met the Schweizer's often and everytime they met, she would blush and look away. Somehow, her beautiful dignity allowed nobody to tease her, or the Schweizer in her presence.

To see the Schweizer clean and handsome was such a marvel in itself. Maria caught Angela in the stable and said:

"I hope nobody says anything. He might just revert to his unwashed days to spite us".

"Has Martha said anything?" Angela asked, but Maria shook her head.

"No. If she wants to talk about it, I think she will tell us. Anyway he is at least ten years older than she is. And what has he got? Nothing!"

"Oh for heavens sake, don't start on that again. They are only looking at each other. Anyway you don't know anything about the Schweizer. He might have the biggest estate you have ever seen, and so that he would be loved for himself only and not for his wealth, he is in disguise!" Maria looked at Angela full of scepticism.

"No room for fairy tales here. Martha has got to marry into a farm. She can't look at a dairyman with no home to his name?" and before Angela could say anything, Maria had gone back to the house. This rich farmer's daughter with her rigid ideas was getting on her nerves. She told herself to ignore Maria.

She stretched herself to reach the back of the stallion she was grooming, when suddenly his head went up and he started to dance and neigh exitedly, tail switching. She stepped aside cautiously and spoke quietly to calm him. All four stallions moved around nervously, dancing, neighing and pounding their feet, and Angela moved aside, out of the way of their large iron shod hooves. Hastily she stepped out of the box to see what was happening.

Herr Laurich came into the stable with a tall man.

"Angela, this is Herr Bauer. He has a mare in season. Get the Noriker Chesnut ready. Where is Shorsch?

"He is in the smithy with the Silesian." Angela went into the tackroom to fetch the bridle and lines to lead the stallion.

Outside two men were holding a lovely mare which had arrived in a horsebox. She was stepping out excitedly, tail held high, dancing, neighing, and obviously very much in season. Where horses were concerned, Herr Laurich was unpredictable, he allowed no room for mistakes, and Angela had never been present when horses mated.

Shorsch came round the corner and Angela was relieved.

"Shorsch", she hissed, "this is the first time for me. What do I do?" And Shorsch said:

"Stick closely to me and be alert." He took the lines from her and went into the box of the Chesnut Noriker and put the bridle on with a line extending on either side; he tossed one to her.

"Hold him tight, but at the same time give him room to move, and don't worry."

The stallion reared and had to be held down to fit through the stable door. Once outside in the yard within sight of the mare, she had to hang onto the line with all her weight to keep him in check, listening all the while in case Shorsch was giving her directions. But he said nothing, so she just handled the situation instinctively and hoped for the best. The stallion was suddenly quite calm, as he came up behind the mare, who was held in an openended enclosure. She was moving this way and that, her head turning to look at her lover, tail held high, invitingly. He gently nudged her and licked her hind legs, probably because he enjoyed the salt on her. Then, as the stallion continued to nibble and sniff at her, she kicked him impatiently, and he moved back, neighing. Suddenly he extended his enormous penis very slowly and hesitatingly, almost reluctantly. But then, in spite of himself, he was up, rearing on his hind legs. Instinctively Angela loosened the line, looking on in astonishment. He took two steps and entered deeply into the mare. With gentle force he came to rest on the mares back and buried his teeth into her mane, foam dribbling out of his mouth. It was a passionate embrace.

Herr Laurich was making crude remarks and the farmer laughed satisfied. Angela thought, as the stallion slid down slowly and reluctantly, that if this was anywhere near what humans did.... well, she didn't know what to think.

Shorsch grinned at her as they took the stallion back and then said:

"Want a go yourself, I am free and available". She kicked him lightly on the shin and laughed:

"I'll remember that, should I ever be desperate, but I am not sure you are my type". She tossed him her line and went out of the stable where she joined Herr Bauer and Herr Laurich who were going into the Office and watched with interest as they wrote out the breeding certificates. Everybody was convinced that the mare was served properly, that she was well in season, even though she had spend nearly 3 hours on the road, coming up from lower Bavaria

*.

10

Maria and Martha had finished the washing up and polished the cooking range, swept and washed the kitchen floor after lunch, and now prepared to muck out the pig house. As soon as the great doors opened, the pigs got excited, they knew what time it was. Freedom in the orchard for the afternoon. They lined up happily snorting behind their individual pen doors, and like children after school, galloped across the hundred meters to the orchard and fallen apples, pears and plums waiting to be guzzeld up. In the shade of the big barn near the river there were mudholes to wallow in and then the afternoon snooze in the dappled shade of the fruit trees. It's good to be a pig, for a while anyway.

The two young women sauntered back to the pig barn and shifted the heavy, juicy muck and forked it into the barrow. The ground rose steeply up to the pig barn and so was almost level with the manure pile, making it much easier to wheel the barrow across the level plank. It still remained a balancing act with the odd mishap.

The day before, a sow had farrowed and the piglets had to be separated, because she would not let anyone near while they were there. She had sixteen of them, cute little babies. The young women cleaned the sty quickly and let the piglets back in. They watched the happy mother present her teats. Like worms in a can the babies shoved and pushed for position, making her huge belly wobble like a giant jelly pudding. Since she didn't have enough teats one or the other was pushed aside and slithered to the outer edge. The winner got a few sucks until he was ousted. Maria said:

"We have to watch this lot. There might be some that need extra help." Maria picked up a tiny one and a furious snort from the sow made her put it back fast.

Martha went out through the feed store room to have a look at the clocktower:" I'll wash and change and lay the coffee table. It's nearly four o clock".

Maria nodded. It was her week of outdoor duty, where she was responsible for the pigs and foul. It was Martha's week in the house, but they helped each other with the tasks where two people were needed. It all worked out very well.

Maria went over to the potato boiler and emtied the previously boiled potatos into a mixing trough and prepared the fodder for the evening feed. Boiled potatoes, cottage cheese and milled grain which she pounded up with a long handled crossed knife and then mixed it with a shovel. She filled dozens of buckets and carried them down the middle gangway and filled the troughs either side, ready for the pigs when they came in from their afternoon outing. At least three mixes were needed.

When the boiler was empty, she went over to the big barn and filled the feed barrow with raw potatoes, took them over to the washer and then tipped the lot into the boiler for the next day. Soon, when the potatoes were harvested, the boiler would go 24 hours a day until the potato silos were full for the winter.

Two more loads and that job was also done. She checked the feed boxes and found them nearly empty. The men would have to drop over some more sacks of wheat pollard and bran. She went over to the remaining sacks and lugged them onto the lifting device and pressed the button. The bags rose slowly. Climbing a few steps up to the platform above the mill she opened them and dropped the starting leaver and the machine came to live with a deafening whining, clanking noise. She emptied the sacks into a large funnel at the top and made sure the crushed grain fell straight into the feed box.

She checked on the time. Coffee! She stopped in the "Old Kitchen" and washed herself by the pump over the stone sink. She reeked of pig sty and fodder, but there was no time to change, except to take off her stinking apron, which she hung on a hook by the door. She had to go straight back afterwards and drive the pigs back into the pens. They always went back into their own compartments. She would then help Martha with the evening meal.

She leaned against the ancient, open fire place and pulled a letter from her skirt pocket. Johnny had written and she felt that the long distance was separating them. She didn't like the way he described the women in Tokyo. What was going on? In his words they were 'exotic flowers with skin like pure silk and delicate like eggshells'. He had been home since he had left the hospital, but was now back and was stationed in Japan. She put the letter back again and sighed. Maybe this separation would be good after all. If he couldn't be faithful now... She hurried on, feeling sad and anxious, and collided with the dairyman who was also on his way to the coffee table.

"Tomorrow we have a bunch of prisoners come to the farm to help repair the old greenhouses and build a row of new ones. I overheard Herr Laurich just now. He was talking to the Silesian. They are petty criminalsand thieves, trustworthy, allowed to earn some money before they are released. So you had better lock up your jewels" he laughed and they entered the kitchen, the last two to join the rest. Happy laughter, teasing and chatting filled the room. Large steaming jugs of coffee and piled high on large plates in the middle of the table, home baked slices of white bread spread with home made butter and jam. Everybody was talking about the prisoners.

"Do they have guards with them" Martha asked. Everybody laughed and Herr Laurich said: "Until they are released they are under guard."

"They are skilled craftsmen, they learned their trade in prison." the Silesian said. It is a way for them to earn some money for a new start when they come out. They are very willing and cheap." No one had ever been near real criminals. What sort of people where they. How many? It was the afternoon coffee table topic and everybody seemed to be talking all at the same time.

Angela's thoughts went back to the time in East Prussia, when she made friends with Robert. He too was a prisoner, but of a different kind. He was no criminal and he had no guard. A great sadness swept over her. Her life turned out to be quite happy, but there was that in her childhood, this blackness which would not go away. It all happened not all that long ago, just a handful of years, and yet nobody spoke about it. Bavarians did not experience the horrors of bombing, of killing or being killed. They did not have to leave their homes, losing all their possessions, seeing dead people almost every day, some just left in the street, because there were not enough stretchers or coffins or men to take them away immediately. She couldn't speak about it, because here, nobody, except the Silesian, had experienced the same. The war horrors had passed them by, and when the Americans came, the Bavarians welcomed them with white sheets and white eggs, fresh chickens and juicy hams.

When the bedraggled, starving and sick refugees came down the country roads, hoping for a barn and maybe some food, the doors were closed. Angela took a deep breath and got up and left the room. She could not put it behind her, she could not forget, and yet she had to get on with life. This had to be locked up in her heart. As she walked over to the stable she wondered if she would have to carry this load throughout her life, forever and wherever she would live. When she had children, what would she tell them? Would she tell them anything at all? Would they ask questions? Should she even get married? It all seemed insurmountable. Would the pain ever leave her? Would she ever be able to make up for her lost childhood? Best to get on with her work. Don't stop and think. The Silesian caught up with her:

"A bit melancholic? What's up?" He had a sensitive soul and she felt he too carried a load around with him. He missed his people and his home.

"Those prisoners tomorrow, they reminded me of a friend I had in East Prussia, a Russian prisoner of war. I am sure I mentioned him before. He taught me about horses when I was very little. He is dead now. Executed." She looked at him, and saw understanding in his eyes. He sighed:

"South Germans, Bavarians in particular will have to face all this sometime. The people here must first of all realize what actually happened in the land which is also their land. They did not experience, they did not see, they don't know, they can't feel. Austria and Bavaria have hatched this egg, and now they pretend they are as clean as the driven snow, innocent of everything and as usually blaming the Prussians, not guilty of anything. But the day will come, when they have to wake up. Then they will want their independence from the rest of Germany. The Austrians already have it, but the Bavarians will want it too. Keep your own council and get on with life. Be happy". He slapped her on her shoulder and tossed her the manure fork and left. There was so much to get on with, but the lump in her throat and the gloom in her heart continued.

81

It was September now and the prisoners were getting on well with the greenhouses. Tons of metal strips had to be soldered together to make the framework to hold all that glass, which was stacked along the garden wall. The men were all well behaved and very polite. So polite, that Maria thought one in particular, Joseph, shouldn't have been there at all. She was caught chatting to him several times and was duly teased. There was an air about them, which made Martha and Angela very suspicious.

Joseph was tall and handsome, about 32 years old, and said he was caught trying to crack open a safe. His very first offence. Said he was led astray by a friend. They had come back from America where they had been Prisoners of War and found that everything and everyone they ever knew had gone, destroyed and dead or missing. Joseph found work with the Americans because he could speak English and then robbed them because, he said, they robbed him of his home, his family and his future. His friend, who was also involved but not caught, never came to see him in prison. He had vanished without a trace. This was not difficult in the chaos which Germany was still in.

His circle of listeners felt sorry for him and thought he had had nothing but bad luck. He had a northern cultured accent. But stealing from the Americans sounded so stupid. They were the best employers, Angela knew from the lodgers who shared their home in Regensburg. Anybody who found work with the Amis was grateful and guarded this job very carefully. The "Amis" were regarded as liberators, not the enemy.

Maria was smitten. She did not listen to Martha and Angela. She promised Joseph a job on her parent's farm in lower Bavaria as soon as he got out.

Shorsch teased her and told her she would get her fingers burnt, and the Dairyman said: "and her heart broken". "You got it all wrong" she protested. "There is nothing going on. Who do you think I am?" They all giggled and Maria went pink in the face. Angela grinned: "Don't be so obvious then. And be careful, he may not be telling the truth". Maria gave her a dark look and turned away.

Martha said to Angela:" Johnny apparently has a Japanese girlfriend. Maria is already heartbroken." "Well, she should keep away from this Joseph, her father won't allow it anyway, and have you seen the malicious look on the other inmates faces? They are crooked through and through, all of them," Angela said worriedly. "Still, nothing to do with me", Angela continued. "By the way, we have to get the spices ready for butchering day, which is only a week away. I sorted out the old sow with Maria today. I give you a list tonight" and Angela went to the office to sort the spices before going to the stables.

*

11

Sausage Making

Angela came into the kitchen and handed over the list needed for the day when the sow was to be butchered. Tins and jars were in the larder, but more might be needed and new rubber bands had to be bought, herbs and spices had to be checked, in order for the work to go smoothly on slaughter day. An appointment had to be made for the butcher and meat inspector. Martha was responsible not to feed the pig the night before. All the knives had to be sharpened and laid out. The laundry kitchen was also the slaughter house, and the big copper cauldron had to be cleaned. The salt barrel had to be in perfect condition. Angela was responsible to see that all the details were attended to.

A week later the day had come. Angela was worried. This was her first pig. She had learned to slaughter chickens and ducks, geese and turkeys, and after the first bout of soft knees and shaky hands, she managed well. But to watch while the life of a pig is snuffed out, an intelligent and friendly animal..., she hated the thought.

At five in the morning she filled the big cauldron with water and lit the fire underneath. The butcher arrived at six and with a slaughter gun the pig was killed and immediately the aorta severed and the blood collected in a big bucket. "Just keep stirring it. It must not klot," the butcher shouted as he held down the pig,"or else it is no good for black pudding".

Slowly the pig stopped moving. "Don't worry my dear", the butcher said kindly, "the pig is dead, this is only the nervous system which takes a while to stop".

This is enough to make me into a vegetarian, Angela thought, and bravely she collected and stirred the blood with her arm up to her elbow in the bucket. Horrible. Warm! Her mind and body went through a process of disgust, revulsion, shock and a weird kind of fear. But this was part of farming too. That's why the pigs were bred and raised. Did pigs think? Did they know? Angela was sure, this pig knew. It sensed something horrible, because normally pigs went where they were herded, this one refused and squealed terribly. She shut down her thoughts. This is part of farming. Later when she was through with her apprenticeship, she would concentrate on horses. Her first and only interest. Her life was horses. The blood had turned into deep red foam, and the butcher said: "That'll do, help me with this."

The pig was thrown into a wooden tub and the first lot of boiling water poured over it to get the bristles off, which were collected and cleaned and finally sold to a brush factory.

Clean and hosed down, the butcher put hooks through the hind legs and pulled the pig up. Quick as lightning the guts, stomach and bladder were removed and turned inside out to be cleaned and left in a bucket of water to be used as sausage skins later. The second lot of water was almost boiling again and the first bits of meat chucked into it. The trotters, the ears, the head, after the brain has been removed, and other bits and pieces along with salt, spices, onions, vegetables and herbs were left to boil.

The lungs, heart, brain and liver, from which the gallbladder had been carefully removed and chucked away, and the tongue were put into another bucket of cold water, to be turned into sausages later. The fillets were taken out and put aside, for smoking with the rest of the smoke meat.

The carcass was hosed down well with cold water and left hanging until cold and inspected. In the afternoon the carcass was sectioned into salt meat, smoke meat, sausage meat, roasts, which is tinned or bottled. The fat is separated and heated until it is as clear as water and the crackling a lovely brown. A little salt is added and then poured into claypots, ready for the use in the kitchen and as spread on bread or for cooking. Some fatty bits are put aside for the black pudding. The mincer takes all the meat which is no good for salting or smoking, and mixed with onions, herbs, garlic, salt and pepper, is turned into delicious salami, ready for smoking.

Now the cooked meat in the copper kettle was ready to be put through the mincer along with onions, bellypork, raw liver, pepper, majoram, salt and nutmeg, some broth, mixed well and put into the large intestine, tied well and boiled slowly to be smoked lightly later. Homemade farmers liversausage, absolutely delicious.

Blackpudding next. Angela fished dark looking meat from the kettle, together with lung and spleen put it through the mincer, onions and fat diced neatly, salt , pepper, nutmeg, thyme and majoram well mixed, and then the warmed up blood with a little broth added carefully to keep the consistency thick, is squeezed into the remaining large intestine, not too full, tied and thrown into the kettle to boil for three quarters of an hour. Phew!

Martha and Maria joined her to help with the bottling and to fill the brawn into the bladder and stomach. That too was put aside to be smoked, two to three days should do it.

There was still the aspic and masses of 'Bratwurst' to be done.

At about 3 in the afternoon Herr Laurich and the men arrived happily with a crate of beer, and Frau Laurich joined with a basket of freshly baked bread rolls, and everybody gathered around the cauldron and started fishing for bits of meat before it was all used up. A barrel of Sauerkraut was opened and eaten raw with fingers. Boiled belly pork and fresh bread with a measure of beer, what could be more delicious.

The butchers reward was a neat cut of meat to take home. The meat inspector never takes meat, because it could be construed as bribery.

Angela thought that her first experience of pigs slaughter wasn't too bad after all. The actual killing was very quick and she was convinced that the pig felt nothing. There was no time to be squeamish, the butcher gave urgent instructions and all she could do was follow them and not to think too much. The day came to an end and she had not cut herself, when everybody forecast that she would. She had learned how to sharpen knives, almost as good as the butcher himself.

That day Martha was kissed for the first time by the dairyman. "Amazing" Maria exclaimed. "How the man changed in those few months, since we arrived". And Martha was seen to be blushing all the time.

12

Preparing to leave Germany

Martha came into the kitchen, looking flushed and embarrassed but with a happy smile on her face. Maria said:

"What do you know about the Schweizer? Do you know where he comes from? You need to meet someone with a farm, you can't fall for a farm hand." But Martha just gave her a very mysterious grin and said nothing. She picked up the bucket with the chicken feed and then said over her shoulder:

"You can talk. What about you and Joseph! But Maria dismissed it and said:

"I just offered him a job on the farm. He is a good worker and father would have a lot of work for him. He needs a new start and that is all. I have no feelings for him". Martha left to feed the poultry and waterfowl, and as she crossed over to the pens, she ran into Angela who was coming out of the stables, carrying a broken fork.

"Tell me, what you think of the Schweizer? " It was a straightforward question and Angela felt touched that Martha thought to ask her such a private question. She had to work with the man a lot and even when he was filthy, she found him a pleasant and intelligent man to talk to and to work with, although the way he kept himself, no personal hygiene at all, was very disturbing. How can anyone let himself go to this can extent, she always wondered. Now that he had cleaned himself up he was really quite unrecognisable from the man he had been before. He mixed with the rest of the men, whereas before he kept to himself and the cows. What was it that had made him neglect himself, and would he go back to his old ways once he got Martha where he wanted her?

Angela said:" I have always found him a good workmate. He is intelligent and has a pleasant character, but I can't understand why he never washed and changed his clothes. Would he go back to his old ways? I could not live with that". Martha nodded and sighed deeply.

"I know what you mean. I am thinking exactly the same thing."

"Take it easy and see what happens. He is a nice man on the whole". Angela put an arm around Martha's shoulder and walked with her a little. "Find out about his family and where he comes from. I don't think he is Bavarian". Martha nodded and continued to the poultry run. Angela went into the smithy, where she had intended to go to repair the broken fork.

A strange feeling came over her. Somehow all this did not affect her. She did not want to get involved, not with Martha and the dairyman, not with Maria and the convict, and stranger still, not with herself and Heiner. Especially herself. Why did she want to bind herself to a man? She had no intention to settle down. She did not even intend to stay in Bavaria. What did she want? She was not sure. However, she was overcome with a very strong emotion whenever she saw him. Could she even bear not being near Heiner? This feeling was surely a delusion that she would die if she could never see him again. Her common sense told her this would not be so. She would not make her life in Bavaria. This was not her home. This was not delusory this was for real. She was going to see the world. Could she escape the blackness that crowded her life?

It was getting into autumn and then winter, and come next summer she would be leaving and going to another farm and other people. She would concentrate on her studies; she had to write her official diary and notebook, which would be judged as part of her exam at the end of her apprenticeship for her entry into agricultural college. She wasn't going to marry a farmer and become a housewife and that would be that. She had plans. She would stay aloof and work hard and the first thing she would do once the harvesting was done, is to sit down and start writing her apprentice book.

The maize was ripe for cutting and shredding into the silo, which was a concrete hole in the ground, about five meters deep and two across. There were three of them to be filled. All the men, except Heiner, cut and drove the corn home and Angela stood on the wagon and threw the corn into the shredder. The huge blades rotated so fast, one could not see them and the bunch of long stalk with the cobs still attached would go through in a split second. Shrmmm and they were blown into the silo.

On the third and final day of cutting Angela lost her footing and fell off the wagon. She felt excruciating pain and lay still, winded. She had missed the chute of the terrible machine by inches, which kept roaring above her. She was in too much pain to think what might have happened. She heard the machine come to a stop and Heiner lifting her up and carrying her down towards the house.

Frau Laurich came rushing out and helping to carry her in and they put her gently onto the sofa in the kitchen. Every move caused her terrible pain. She could not speak, and kept holding her side. An hour later Herr Laurich came into the kitchen with his brother in law, who was a doctor of medicine in Nuremberg and staying with his sister for a week's hunting holiday. So lucky for Angela, because he immediately examined her and ordered her to be put to bed. A urine sample showed injury to the kidney. There was a lot of blood in the urine.

She could not move at all and had to be cared for, which she felt was a terrible burden on her colleagues at this time of the year. But Frau Laurich would not send her to hospital. And she could not go home, because she could not be moved other than by ambulance. The weeks went by and there was still blood in her urine. The doctor had said she could not get up until that stopped.

Heiner was supplying her with books and she read all day and half the night.

Six weeks and the bleeding had stopped, but not the pain. She got up and dragged herself to work. She felt well, except for the terrible pain in her side, which made her walk bent over. It was the potato harvest and she gritted her teeth.

The weeks passed and on the first of Advent, the pain had suddenly gone. Frau Laurich came to see her in the stable and announced that since she had been in bed all those weeks she could not go home for Christmas. The men did not get their time off to go home whilst she was ill and so they were going to have some days off during the holiday.

She smiled, biting back the tears and again gritted her teeth. This is life, hard and unforgiving. So, she would be here and it would probably be a very nice family Christmas. It was her first away from home. She suddenly realized, that there would be many more, more than she had ever had at home with her family. The lump in her throat became so large, she could not even swallow her spit.

Suddenly Martha came in and said: "I am stopping too, Maria is going home, and Johnny is coming to Germany from Tokyo. She is over the moon, and so we will have a wonderful time here. You'll see." Angela looked at her and put out a hand, took Martha's and squeezed it. Martha said: "The Schweitzer's family is from Chechoslovakia and they have lost their land. They had to flee when the communists came and their land was taken, the communists killed his father, and his mother died on the treck. He has an older brother who works on a farm in the Hanover area. They have been paid compensation by the German government, but they shared it between them and so there is not enough for them to start their own farm. They thought they work and get some more money together and then buy something small each or one big farm together. Just imagine, their farm was only about 20Kilometers distant from ours. Our farm is right on the border in the Bavarian Forest, and his in the same forest on the other side." She stood in wonderment. Her round face shone and her frizzy curls stood out like a large dark halo, which the setting sun was illuminating. .

Angela looked at her with warm affection. She put an arm around her shoulder and said: "Aren't you going to inherit your farm? " Martha nodded. "Does the Schweitzer know that?" and Martha shook her head. Angela gave her a squeeze and said:" Keep it to yourself and watch what happens. I think eventually you will be very happy. He might make a good husband and farmer" They both laughed and went their way.

It had started to snow in November and the trees in the nearby forest began to get their thick winter coat of snow, every sound was muffled and there was such stillness all around. There was a shining brightness even when it got dark.

If it snowed even more they would have to get the skis down from the loft. Hey would have to be taken to the forest animals. There were special feeding stations in the forest, and when the animals found no more food in the thick snow, they automatically came to these spots to be fed. She would have to speak to Herr Laurich and also get the sledge out from the carriage shed. She went to have a look. They never checked these tools until they were needed, and she had better make sure they were in working order.

While she was in the shed she discovered a strange device with hooks and turning handle and made a mental note to ask what it was for.

As she came into the kitchen for her afternoon coffee, she found Frau Laurich with a huge basket of wool in many colours and several sets of knitting needles.

"It is time to start knitting and after Christmas we are going to make ropes," she said and Angela asked:

"What are we knitting?"

"Well, don't you need socks and mittens? And wouldn't you want to knit something for your people at home?" Angela thought; I hate knitting, I hate sitting down and sew and knit and stuff like that. Aloud she said:

"What a good idea, and once the thought took hold of her she got even a little excited. All the women caught the bug and in the afternoon they sat together in the kitchen and started to knit socks, mittens, scarves, Maria even knitted a sweater. She was the fastest knitter. Angela could knit a pair of socks in 3 days and she was very proud. She would knit socks and mittens and scarves for her family at home and for herself. Martha, Maria and Frau Laurich were also baking Christmas cookies and she began to look forward to Christmas with a happy heart. She would send a parcel home, filled with goodies. Sadly she thought she would like to see their faces when they unpacked the parcel. It was the first Christmas that she provided something for the family. She felt proud.

Later, after supper when everybody sat around the kitchen table, Herr Laurich said: "While the women sit and knit, you men can knot the binder cord together which we collected after threshing and wind it up into football size balls. In the new year we make ropes."

Suddenly Angela knew as if by instinct, that the wooden devices in the shed were precisely for that purpose. She had a practical and artistic mind, and could work out how it was going to be done, and also thought of other things one might fashion with those rope making devices and all the different lengths one could make. It was so simple, one just placed them further apart and it only took two people to make the ropes. She thought of all the things a farmer can do, all the things she has learned, almost anything from woodworking, forging iron into useful everyday things, repairing equipment and creating wrought iron things like that candlestick she made one Sunday afternoon and the fire hook and tongues she made for her mother, shoe repair, and building work; in fact anything at all. Even plumbing and roofing! Ha! She would never be a helpless little woman.

*

Christmas came and went, a pile of ropes had been made and Angela could smell spring in the air. The snow was melting in patches and where the grey grass came through the first snowdrops and March Cups showed their buds, and on the warm sunny banks of the road the Colt's Foot shone like little suns, and she could feel the first warmth of the sun on her back. She stretched her arms out as if to embrace somebody and smiled contentedly. She went into the stable to saddle one of the stallion to give him his usual exercise. Today she had the great pleasure of taking them out and into the far forest. She had got so used to their elephants backs. Shorsch was already busy saddling one of the other stallions. Good, they would have a good ride together and work the stallions into a sweat. Usually they chose a ploughed field to make it really hard for them, but sometimes, when work was not pressing, they took the horses into the forest for pleasure rides. The stallions were so tall, that the stirrups dangled in front of her face. She had got herself a stool, climbed up and onto the dividing wall to get into the saddle that way. Heaven help her should she ever come off, she would have to walk all the way home. Even Shorsch could not get up by himself, so he could not help her back into the saddle.

They galloped off up the hill and were swallowed up by the forest. She had to duck and cuddle up to the horse's neck to avoid the lower branches. They never wore helmets. The horses slow and lazy gallop was difficult to adjust to, the rhythm was not what her body wanted to do; she had ridden hunters and they took smaller quicker steps, but were not all that much faster than the brutes she was riding at the Laubhof. However, these working animals would not jump fences. The other thing was the widths of their backs, she found it difficult to rise in the stirrups, and had to use her knees.

After about three kilometres they came out of the forest and onto the open meadow and there they let the horses go. No fences or walls or any other obstacles. She felt the joy of the horse as it suddenly propelled itself into a full gallop. She hoped she would not fall off and put the thought right out of her mind. They were just about to enter the top forest when she heard a yell and reined in her stallion with a lot of brrrr brrrr, just as she would when he was pulling a wagon and after about a hundred meters came to a stop and turned round. She saw Shorsch on the ground and the horse had turned and disappeared back to the farm. That horse was always reluctant to leave his oats and would be in the stable eating hey when they got back, she thought. Drat! Shorsch's nose was bleeding, but he sat up and grinned. He was holding his hand, and Angela could tell that the arm must be broken, since it looked so unnatural. She felt a slight turn in her stomach. "Pull your self together," she thought as she slid off the horse and tied him to a tree. She didn't really know what to do, but thought it would be best to secure his arm to his body to stop it from dangling. She undid a stirrup and used the strap like a belt around Shorsch's body and her cardigan as a sling for support.

"This might hurt", she said as she gently took and turned his arm into a natural position and then took her cardigan and laid the arm into it and tied the sleeves around the neck. Then she took the stirrup strap and put it around the middle and fastened it, putting it over the cardigan just under the arm and tightening it securely.

Then she gave him a leg up and admired his bravery, because he did not complain about the obvious pain. He just looked at her, and then very gently touched her hand with his good one. She smiled: "I would have been shedding tears of pain right, left and centre, if it had been me"

As soon as Shorsch's stallion thundered into the yard without his rider and disappeared into the stable, Herr Laurich knew something had happened and got into his 1936 Mercedes and drove into the forest to see if he could help. He met them halfway home. They helped Shorsch into the car and then he gave Angela a leg up and drove off to Amberg's hospital.

Angela came back, unsaddled both horses and mucked out the stables on her own, fed them and then went in to have some coffee. No one had realized what was going on and when she came in by herself, Maria said: "Where is Shorsch?"

"I hope he is in hospital" she answered, "he broke his arm whilst we were riding." They all talked at once and then Frau Laurich came in and said:

"He is alright, the boss rang earlier. He has broken his arm below the elbow and it is now in plaster" Then she came over to Angela and put a hand on her shoulder:" The doctor said, well done about the first aid. Because it was securely strapped, it did not do any more damage and caused less pain." Angela felt a hot flush spread over her face and neck and she grinned. "It seemed common sense to do that," she said shyly. She felt everybody's eyes on her and felt terribly embarrassed. As if to her rescue, Herr Laurich and Shorsch came in and the attention shifted from her to them. She slipped out quickly and no one noticed.

She busied herself cleaning the saddles and thought that now for a few weeks she would have to do the lion's share in the stable and with the tractor. She wondered whether she was going to get temporary help. The Silesian came in and said: "I have already spoken to the gardener, and he said his son would be glad to step in and help, since there is as yet not a lot of work in the garden, and what has to be done in the green houses, he would get his wife to help. So there you are, Hans is your helper. Shorsch is not going home, he can do light work. There is plenty of it".

Angela grinned. Farming! You can't even put your feet up when you have a broken arm.

She was ploughing the far field with the tractor and Heiner was up there with the team of horses to do the difficult parts to where she could not manoeuvre the tractor. Every time she came over the brow and saw him, she felt sorry because she knew he could hear her but not see her. Everything was a struggle for him. She was even a bit worried, because she saw danger for him in the work he did. But ultimately it had nothing to do with her. She had distanced herself from Heiner, but stayed good mates and a friendship developed, which was calm and solid.

She gave a little chuckle when she remembered one Sunday afternoon, soon after Christmas when the snow was so high that nothing could be done outside. She found herself alone in the kitchen using the sewing machine to make herself a dirndl dress, Shorsch came in and started to talk. He said he had realized that she had cooled towards Heiner and he wanted her to come to the cinema with him. They were showing the Coronation of the English Queen in the Amberg's 'Illuminated Play House. 'She said she would come and when Martha and Maria came in she said:

"Shorsch wants to go to the cinema to see the coronation, do you want to come?" And so the entire staff went to the cinema. She saw the dismay on Schorsch's face, and grinned. During the show he tried to put his arm around her, but she told him not to.

She was impressed by the pomp and ceremony of the coronation and was determined to see this place for herself one day. One day! She wasn't sure when that would be, but already she had made inquiries about places abroad for her journeyman years, and England was not on the list. Still, that was two years away from now. Finland was on the top of her list and she had already made enquiries.

She turned the tractor and when she came back over the brow, she saw Herr Laurich, who had come up with the elevenses. At the end of the field she turned for the next row and then stopped the tractor and hopped off. She was very hungry and thirsty.

Herr Laurich looked approvingly at the field and said:

"This will be for maize this year, even though the wild boar will take their share. We will have to watch it. But there will be some good hunting and meat for the table." Angela took a large slice of bread, spread with home made liver sausage and a good amount of sweet home made mustard and then took a long drink from the cider jug.

Suddenly she felt a jab at her heart. She would not mind staying here forever. This beautiful land, good and friendly people, good work and everything she did was appreciated. Here she could do anything and never make mistakes. She had not been criticised. And yet, a year was all she got. Then she had to find yet another farm always a little different and always more to learn. She had to fight her emotions. She wanted to travel, wanted to see the world and also wanted to be secure, somewhere which she could call home. A bolthole, somewhere where she could go and keep some things. She didn't want to have to carry everything she owned around with her from place to place.

Bine, her second sister would leave home in August as well and her mother would be leaving to find a job somewhere and there would not be a home for them anymore. Mother would take the little one, Tissi with her. Tissi still had three years at school and then she too would leave. She would have to find her own place, heaven knows where. But she would not get married to find it.

*

Laubhof 1952

Cleaning out the pigs 1953

Fishing on Päjänne Järvi 1955

Cleaning the beets 1955

Logging in Finland 1956

Defrosting by the fire 1956

My pots 1957

Asikkala

Angela and Hanni, a new friend, who like herself had decided to spend a year or so in Finland as part of her yourneyman's time, got off the train and looked around to orientate themselves. They had travelled for four days on the train from Regensburg to Helsinki via Hamburg, Grossenbrode, Gedser and Stockholm. From there they travelled to Turku Abo by boat and onto Helsinki by train. In Hamburg they had several hours to wait and walked into the city and also to the harbour to see the ocean going boats, which mostly went across the Atlantic to America. They were fascinated by their size and dreamed of one day going themselves across the sea, not just the overnight trip from Stockholm to Abo, but to the other side of the world.

With shocked horror they saw that Hamburg was still a place of rubble, empty, roofless shells of houses towered above them. Some rebuilding had taken place, but on the whole it gave the impression as if the war had only stopped yesterday and not ten years ago. They both stared and felt as if the ten years since the war had not been. Angela thought she could even smell the burning. Will she ever be free from the horror of her childhood?

When Angela finalized her trip to Finland, she enquired in the *Mittel Bayrische Zeitung* if there was anybody else from the area, who would also be travelling to Finland, and Hanni had replied. She was a tall young woman, a little older than Angela, and a refugee from Silesia, which was now Poland. She was a domestic science student, the same as Martha and Maria had been on the Laubhof. Hanni's placement would be in Tampere, nearer the coast, and Angela had to go somewhere north of Lahti. There would be a train for Hanni, but not for Angela. Angela felt forlorn. She saw Hanni onto her train and waved goodbye as the train slowly left the station. They promised to write. They had become very close in the four days it took them to come this far. They had not given the parting time much thought, and now it had all happened rather quickly.

On her own and not able to speak a word of Finnish, she felt a little frightened. What had she done? Still, now there was no turning back. After all she had known all that before and had bravely put all the warnings aside. Hanni was in the same boat and she wouldn't do less than Hanni. She thought, that she should have learned by now, that it would never turn out the way one imagined it would be like in reality. This now was real, and she had to master it.

She went to the bus station, and saw the sign: *Linjaautoasema*, and worked it out. So, that was not so difficult, and if everything else was so easy, she would manage well. Next she bravely went up to the first person near her and asked: "Do you speak German?" and to her surprise the answer came in perfect German: "Yes, what can I do for you?" Angela held up her bit of paper with the address of the place, where she had to get to. It said: Asikkala.

*

It was the eleventh of May 1955 when she started on her journey, just 10 years after the war, almost to the day

She had looked forward to it so much. In her mind she was returning as closely as it was possible to the place were, as a child, she was so happy for one short year. East Prussia was below Finland, and although she could not go there now, because it had been swallowed up by Soviet Russia since then, Finland was close.

However, when the day came for her departure, she felt very reluctant, even something like fear.

She had completed her apprentice years, the last farm was on the Danube in Schwaben, friends of the Laurichs and it was also a wonderful year. She then went to Almesbach to get her Dairy certificate, and then it was time to start college. She boarded in because her home in Regensburg did not exist anymore; her mother had moved to find work as a housekeeper near Salzburg for the time being. Her mother's papers still had not come through, and she could not yet resume her work as a state registered nurse. The records and people who could vouch for her had mostly disappeared in the war.

At college she had met a young farmer, whom she had met in her first year as an apprentice, and he had fallen in love with her and had proposed marriage, and even said she need not bring a dowry, because she was a refugee, and he knew she had nothing. She was touched and felt oddly honoured, but she did not love him. His family were warm and loving, but there was nothing she could do. In the end he understood, and they promised to stay friends.

Now it was Spring, her mother had briefly returned to Regensburg, because she had finally been offered a job as a nurse in a hospital on the borders between Germany and Switzerland, a town called Lörrach on the outskirts of Basel. Angela was going to Finland, Bine to England and Tissi with mother to a new life in the three border country: Germany, France and Switzerland.

Angela had also met a young man, Friedrich, and became good friends. For a month before her departure, whilst she stayed with her family at her grandfather's apartment, Angela, Bine and Friedrich's brother and friends had cycled everywhere, hiked across country and even went climbing amongst the rocks above the Danube. She had not had a holiday since she was three years old, and this was a time of wonderment to her. No work, no war, no worries, just to be free, and every morning she would say, what am I doing today? The answer was always: meet Friedrich and friends. He too was between colleges and they sang songs as they walked, sang as they cycled, learned new songs. His father spoke Russian and they sang those beautiful Russian songs the Cossacks sang, learning the words parrot fashion, not knowing what they meant. Listening to their voices and loving it. Thinking, that nothing sounded so good, so sweet.

They had promised each other to stay friends whilst she went to Finland and he completed his studies at college. She had even forgotten the five years of her journeyman's years and what she wanted to do afterwards. In time she would know what to do.

They had all been at the station to wave her goodbye, Friedrich and his brothers, her mother and sisters, and even her grandfather and fourth wife had come.

"You don't speak a word of Finnish" mother kept repeating. "How will you manage?" But Angela reassured her:"Muttilein, (little mummy) I will be fine. To start with there is always sign language, and I was quick to learn all these different dialects in all the places were we have lived all my life, I am sure I will learn Finish as well. "

"But you don't even know what sort of language it is! I have heard that it is not like Russian, or Swedish or any other language around. Somebody told me it is related to Hungarian, and that is a very difficult language."

"Oh Mum, don't worry!" She put her arms around her mother and again, as so many times before, she realized that her mother was lost and worried and lonely and reluctant to let any of her children go. Her security was to have her children around her and to look after them.

Bine was leaving for England three days after Angela's departure, and mother went to the furthest end of Germany, right onto the Swiss border, with only her youngest, Tissi to look after. She hadn't been a Nurse for close to twenty years and worried whether she would still able to do it. She suddenly realized, that just like herself, her mother did not have a home anymore. Everything was strange, and yet again for the umpteenth time she had to make a new start. All around them there lived people who had lived there all their lives, had relatives and friends and where 'at home'. Angela wondered what that must feel like, to belong.

Strong, brave mother, vulnerable and frightened. She was so courageous during the war, and now? Angela looked at her beloved mother and felt a terrible pain inside her. Life, she thought is cruel, nothing stays, nothing is forever, and it is so painful. She hugged her mother again and whispered:" Be brave, you always showed us that life goes on and turns out all right. I love you" She saw tears flood her mother's eyes and her own throat ached.

Little Tissi, thirteen now and very spoilt, held on to mother's hand. Angela bent down and hugged her baby sister, the one she had mothered all those years ago when they were still children at home. It didn't matter then, that they had lost everything, that they were homeless, that a war raged, that mother had to fight for the four of them to survive. They were one tight unit and nothing could tear them apart.

"It is up to you now to look after mum," Angela said to Tissi. "Be good and don't make mum sad. You know what I mean." And then she whispered into her ear:

"No lipstick, and no nail varnish, and no parading in front of American soldiers, promise?" She expected Tissi's defiant: "You are not my mother, you can't tell me anything!" but it did not come instead Tissi hugged her and started to cry.

"Must you go? You have already been away four years, but you were always just a train journey away. Now you go so far. Will I ever see you again?"

"Angela squeezed her tightly and whispered: I'll be back and we will always be very close in our hearts. No matter what happens to the four of us! But we will have to go out into the world and earn our living, learn, and become good people. Only too soon it will be your turn too. And we always have to look after our little mum. I will write at least once a week, and I expect you write to me too. *Ich hab dich so lieb, mein Kleines.* (I love you so much, little one)"

The train rolled into the station, brakes screeching, and everybody helped with their heavy suitcases, which had clothes for a whole year, winter clothes which they were told to bring because it would be very cold, and some books and things. And then Hanni joined them in the compartment, they turned down the window and everybody except Hanni and Angela, left the train and gathered outside. Last things were said and tears flowed, and then the two mothers held hands just as if they had known each other for a long time and not just met at the station for the first time.

*

The young man stopped in front of a very old fashioned bus and amongst other names it said Lahti. Then he told her that in Lahti she must get off and find another bus to Asikkala. The bus driver helped her with her suitcases and showed her to her seat. It was hard and lumpy. She had no idea how long the trip would be. She was hungry and tired. She had bought a bottle of milk and a roll and decided to eat that now. And then the bus slowly drove out of Helsinki. Half an hour later the surfaced road came to an end and the bus sank into mire, which made the wheels disappear and stirred the mud like so much porridge. The bus swerved and meandered and Angela became car sick and needed to vomit. She managed to slide open the window to try and get some fresh air, and then she vomited and to her total embarrassment and horror the wind carried it to the window behind her and oozed slowly downwards.

Feeling very tired and close to death, she arrived in Lahti several hours later. Some passengers who had been travelling with her felt sorry and helped her off the bus and one of them took her to her home, which was near by, and gave her some strong coffee and slices of hard black bread, butter and cheese. Then she learned that the bus which would have taken her to Asikkala had left because her bus had arrived late in Lahti. Her host rang the people in Asikkala and told them that Angela would be arriving the next day. She was shown into the guest room and the lady let her go to bed right away. Gratefully she sank into the feather bed and was very soon asleep. Her last thought was, that if all Finns were as nice as the people she had met so far, she had nothing to fear.

The next day her host took her to the bus stop and put her on the bus to Asikkala and told her it would take about 3hours before she got there, and her new boss, Mauno Kettonnen would be there to pick her up. Angela gratefully shook hands with her host and promised to visit should she come to Lahti. And then the bus left.

Herra Kettonnen was a handsome man, about 45 years old and, as she soon found out, loved to drink a lot of 'pilsneri', which made him a difficult boss to work for. They travelled in his old pre-war Citroen through endless forest and along a lake, which seemed to stretch past the horizon on one side and more forest on the other. She saw nothing but pines and birches of incredible size. Enormous trunks and so tall, she could hardly believe her eyes. The road was not surfaced, very muddy, and pitted with potholes. Suddenly there was a little clearing and there was a small collection of wooden houses, painted in the typical reddy brown colour. The village here was called Toppola.

A round little woman with a headscarf came out of the door and stared. Behind her, like a row of organ pipes, stared 5 children. Angela smiled and walked towards them with her hand held out to shake the woman's hand. But she turned round and shoved the children back into the house and closed the door. Strange, she thought. Herra Kettonnen gave her an embarrassed grin and opened the door. An old woman came smiling towards her. Isoäiti, (grandmother) she was told by Herra Kettonnen. Angela shook her hand and smiled back. She beckoned her to follow her and they entered a very narrow room, which seemed to be a box room with a bed in it. She was made to understand that this was her room. There was no room for the suitcase and no wardrobe or chest of draws, no shelves, nothing. The door was closed and she was on her own. She sat down on the bed. It was so hard, she lifted up the mattress to see if it was a concrete base. It wasn't, it was wooden. A lump began to form in her throat. She bit back the tears and opened her suitcase. She took out some working clothes and changed. Her dirty things she put into a bag. She would find out about washing those in due course. Then she shoved her case under the bed and found that it fitted to within a tiny margin. That problem was solved. The way she felt at the moment, she didn't want to unpack anyway. She didn't want to stay, and whilst her things were still in her suitcase, she was ready to leave at any moment, except that she had to earn the money for the journey back first.

She went out to meet her new family and to get to know them. Grandmother was there, waiting for her in the little hallway, which was strewn with rag rugs, covering the polished wooden floorboards. The children were peering through a door at her, giggling, with the eldest shouting something.

Grandmother took her from room to room and spoke constantly. Angela understood nothing, but from the gestures she realised that things were explained to her. Was she here on this remote farm to be employed as a domestic servant? Could this be? She would have to speak to Herra Kettonnen. Deep shock set in. A year to sweep and clean, wash and iron, baby-sit! O horror. Politely she followed Grandmother as she explained and pointed. Rag rugs everywhere. Pictures on the wall of people in strange clothes! One in particular took her attention. A most beautiful person, features so pure and clean, angelic. Was it male or female? She looked at the picture so long, that Grandmother touched her arm to bring her back to reality. She said something and pointed through the window. Angela followed her pointing finger, but saw nothing other than a lilac arbour and an old man, bent over sitting on a bench holding a tin with shaking hands which collected a long string of slime constantly running from his nose.

They left the room and went into the kitchen. Rag rugs seemed to be strewn throughout the house. In the middle of the kitchen stood a large table, two benches either side with room for four people on each and a chair on either end. A large wood fired stove and piles of wood in one corner and a big copper kettle humming away, spreading a wonderful aroma of coffee.

Grandmother went over and took two saucers and cups from a shelf above the sink and poured the boiling hot coffee into the cups. Then she placed a bowl with sugar cubes onto the table in front of her. She pointed to the cubes and said something, but Angela shook her head. She did not take sugar in coffee. Grandmother smiled, took the cup off her saucer and poured some coffee into the saucer, then took two sugar cubes and placed them into her mouth under her top lip in front of her teeth. Then she sucked and slurped the coffee happily from the saucer through the cubes and grinned triumphantly. Angela found the coffee far too hot to drink and blew into her cup. Grandmother pointed to the saucer and said something. Angela understood, that it would cool the coffee, and did the same. They grinned at each other and a sort of friendship was formed.

After the coffee, Grandmother took her out of the house to the various outhouses. First they came to the weaving house, which housed two looms. Rag rugs were in progress on one and what she later learned, a Ryyü Matto on the other. She had learned to weave at the college and was interested. Patterns were woven into the mat with long loops of wool, which were later cut, so that a thick long pile was achieved. Well, she thought, if I stay, I might learn how to do that.

Next came several small houses; the laundry house, drying house, etc. One housed a wood fired copper kettle as they used at home and another a huge wooden contraption with enormous boulders in a sledge-box on top. She didn't even attempt to find out what it was.

The clearing, which surrounded the house seemed to be bog land and at the edge of the forest. Where are the fields, she wondered. Toppola is situated on a peninsula, water on three sides, forest and huge, enormously large, strangely rounded boulders strewn haphazardly around. Later she learned that they were the remains of the ice age, which covered this area under several kilometres of ice.

Looking down towards the lake she discovered a little log cabin. She pointed to it and grandmother took her by the arm and led her to the last little cabin just across from the house. They entered a black sauna. The smell was delicious, tar, wood and a strange, pleasant aroma, which reminded her of her birch shampoo, and there was a hint of smoked ham. So this is the famous sauna. Grandmother pointed to the cabin by the lake and said: Ranta Sauna.

There was only one little house left to inspect, grandmother's cottage. It was charming. It had two rooms, one bedroom and one sitting room. Grandmother said something and pointed into the sitting room, but Angela had no idea what she said. She shrugged her shoulders and grandmother smiled. She was a sweet, friendly and somewhat mysterious lady.

14

Vähä Äiniö

The next day was a Sunday and they all piled into the old Citroen and drove to church. A beautiful wooden building painted in bright colours. It was Remembrance Day for the fallen soldiers, and the Unknown Soldier. It was a beautiful service and she heard the National Anthem of Suomi for the first time: Sibelius's Finlandia! She had not heard his music before and was moved. She felt her heart expand and suddenly wished she could fly. She took a deep breath and listened. Yes! His music described the lakes, the forests and the sun, the sun that seems to shine forever. Could she imagine the snowstorms? Could she see the Northern Lights? She heard the ice crack across the lake with a tremendous thunder, just as she heard it when she first arrived.

In the afternoon Herra Kettonnen translated his wife's wishes. She was to take the children into the forest and pick flowers and not return for three hours. She took the two smallest by the hand, the toddler could only just have learned to walk, she thought he was maybe eighteen months and the other little boy three years, the little girl, was maybe six and the oldest seven or eight years old. The boy shouted at her incessantly, angry bullying words. She tried to ignore him and talked to the little girl, who was friendly. The baby cried, so she picked him up and murmured little words to calm him down. There was still a lot of snow where the sun did not reach, but there were also a lot of periwinkles and cotton grass. The little girl made it known to her that her name was Päivi, and Angela repeated it carefully. Päivi beamed and pointed to the shouting brother and said: Juha. She said it again and Angela repeated that name and smiled at Juha, who angrily screamed at her. Pävi did not take any notice of Juha and pointed to the little brother and said: Matti. Angela put down the toddler knelt down and looked at the little boy and said:

hello Matti. He turned to Päivi as if for protection and gave Angela a timid smile. Angela pointed to the toddler and asked: What is his name? And Päivi said: Ilkka.

Angela picked up the baby and said: Juha, Päivi, Matti and Ilkka. What lovely names and the little girl jumped happily ahead and started to pick some flowers.

When they got back Angela went over to Herra Kettonnen and asked in German what it was that Juha was shouting about. It turned out that he was cross with her for not being able to speak Suomen, and whilst she talked with Herra Kettonnen, Juha kept shouting and shouting some more and nobody told him to stop. Angela finally got cross and asked what he was shouting now. Herra Kettonnen said: He is telling you to shut up. Angela was speechless. No manners at all! She got up and went to her room. She sat on her bed and thought, should I cry or laugh? There was a little tap on the door and Päivi came in. She walked up to her and put her arms around Angela. She picked her up onto her lap and there they sat quietly. She fell in love with the little girl.

That Sunday night she wrote her first letter home.

Dear Mother, dear Tissi

I am sure you would want to know all about the trip. Well, we had a compartment all to ourselves from Nürnberg to Hamburg. There were three of us. A young woman, who like us travelled for the first time away from Germany, but she only went as far as Denmark, where she had found a farm near Copenhagen. We went to sleep on the benches in turn, since only two could sleep at a time. In Hamburg we had a lot of time and did some sightseeing. Terrible, the destruction! We bought some rusks, because we did not feel too good and didn't want anything to eat really, but felt we had to eat something. We did not like Hamburg at all. It is a terrible town.

At midday our train left for Grossenbrode-Gedser. It was beautiful weather, whereas in Hamburg it rained dreadfully. We had no seats all the way to Copenhagen, and sat on our suitcases. In Grossenbrode the train had to wait one hour, because the ferry had not arrived. At Copenhagen the ferry waited for us to take us to Malmö. The sea was very rough. We got to know a man from

112

Norway and a German man. They were very friendly and shared their food with us. They also shared our compartment. We slept sitting up but comfortably the night through to Stockholm. Our two friends made sure no one entered our compartment. They were like two busy fathers watching over their precious girls. They knew their way around Stockholm and gave us a little sightseeing tour. It was very early in the morning. We had to say goodbye. They were both going to a European meeting in Uppsala. We were sad to see them go, their train left at 10.30. We went and had coffee and a piece of cake, put our luggage into a lockup and went into Stockholm. They were building an underground or something, because I have never seen such a deep hole anywhere. There is also a lot of water everywhere. It is the Venice of the North, we were told. Swedish is not so difficult, if one tries very hard, one can understand. It is a kind of German. At lunchtime we afforded ourselves a real big lunch. We were hungry!!

In the evening we went back to the station and sat down to wait. We went to sleep. I woke suddenly, because Hannchen snored loudly and my head was resting on her shoulder. It was also high time to grab a taxi and go to the harbour. In Sweden a taxi is not free, it is unmarried. Where it says 'free' in Germany it says 'unmarried' here. Funny isn't it?

We had to wait another two hours before the boat left. We went to our cabin and went to sleep. Next morning the boat docked at quarter to eight. The sea was very rough and the waves sprayed right over the boat. We were getting more and more disheartened. The trip from Turku Abo on the train was not nice. There were some Finns on the train and I could swear they were drunk. When they found out we were German, they became very friendly and kept saying: "Hitler, gut!" We kept saying: "Nix gut". But they insisted they knew better. We wished our two gentlemen were here to protect us. Then they made us sing Lilli Marleen. I knew some words, Hannchen knew some, but we didn't know all of them. When did I last sing Lilli Marleen?!

Looking at the countryside there were only those strange round rocks, huge! And then only forest, old log cabins and more forest. Thick impenetrable forest! How did they get the railway into that?

Then we came to Porkkala, occupied by the Russians. The train stopped and soldiers came in, dressed in white sheepskin coats and hats with the red star on the front of the cap. They were friendly, even though they were carrying guns and revolvers and jackboots. They studied our papers. Do you remember when we were evacuated to East Prussia? Well it was just like that, only this time they were friendly and not Polish. Then the windows were closed with shutters from the outside and the lights came on. Our Finnish companions made rude signs once the soldiers had left and said: "Nix gut".

We got to Helsinki and now things became serious. Hannchen left and I was on my own. Eventually I found the bus. The one to Sysmää had already left, but somebody with perfect German helped and I got onto another bus. I got terribly carsick and in Lahti a lady took me in, because my bus to Asikkala had already left. The bus I was travelling in had to work its way through thick porridge like mud, all the windows were smeared with it, and soon my sick, which was trickling slowly down the window, was not visible anymore. The lady warned me that her husband was a big man. When he entered the room I couldn't believe my eyes. He was a giant without a neck and his shoulders were at least a meter wide and he puffed and huffed and sweated because he had just come out of the sauna. There is still a lot of snow and so much mud, just like in the film "Der Deutsche Landser" .

I have a lumpy sofa-camp-bed in the office. No drawers or wardrobe or anything. Pretty awful really. But I think I will get used to it. It is still very cold and Rouva Kettonnen is just like your sister, Tante Putt, short and fat with a bosom larger than Tante Putt's. I never thought that would be possible.

Soon we will go fishing, the boss said. I will be ok. I will like it.

Please, please write soon and give my love and greetings to everyone, Günter, grandfather, Tata and the two misses, Tissi and yourself and big hug and kisses.

Yours always Ange.

*

Monday seemed to be washday. Rouva Kettonnen picked up a large basket with dirty washing and pointed to a second one and

114

made signs to Angela to pick it up. Angela picked up the basket and followed her. When they came into the washhouse, Rouva Kettonnen talked and talked and pointed and rotated her round little body like a top. And then she suddenly stopped. Angela looked at her for a long time, and then said in her own language: "Give me strength". Rouva Kettonnen said something and Angela repeated:" Give me strength". Her boss actually smiled, lifted her shoulders and left.

Angela lit the fire and prepared to spend the day doing the washing. Diplomatically the thought, well, I have to learn that too, being a woman. She had helped on the farms where she spent her apprentice years every now and then, only because she was female. The male students were never asked to help the women with their work. But this was new territory. She was transported one hundred years into the past.

She was imagining what was going round in Rouva Kettonnen's head. Isolated as she was. Had she ever lived anywhere but here? Could she imagine that there was a world out there away from this forest? Could she imagine that there were people who could not understand Finnish? Her mother seemed to have a better understanding of what it would be like to come here, learning what it is like to live with other people. Well, that would be a mystery for the time being. She would have to learn this language quickly if she was going to find out about these people.

She found baby clothes amongst the washing and wondered.

Päivi came and helped, and Angela learned her first words. They had a great time working together. Angela lifted up some nappies and tiny vests and looked at the little girl questioningly. Päivi smiled and held up her arms as if she was holding a baby. But Angela had not seen a baby in the house nor had she heard one crying. Angela guessed that there must be a baby in the house, new born judging from the size of the little clothes and that would account for the size of Rouva Kettonnen's breasts.

When it came to rinsing the load, Päivi took her to a utensil shed and pointed to a cart. Picking up the cart handle she was directed by the little girl to put the wet washing onto it. It was a huge basket on wheels, which they pulled down to the lake, where she realised the washing was going to be rinsed. In front of the Ranta Sauna there was a long wooden walkway into the lake and there was a small patch of water already free of ice. It was hard work to wring out all the water, which was icy cold, but it would drip on the way back up. Angela's hands were blue with cold and quite numb. Päivi took her to the drying house, where lots of wooden poles where suspended from the ceiling. Angela draped the washing over the poles and Päivi opened some little windows and that was that. By three in the afternoon, with a small break for lunch, the washing was hanging up and fluttering madly in the draught, which came through the little openings. Angela was so cold, she thought her bones would freeze.

She was then asked to sweep last year's rotten leaves in the yard. Päivi came and helped to put the leaves into old potato sacks before they were blown away again. This little girl's energy never flagged. She talked and pointed to things and said words. Angela learned fast. She remembered words and asked Päivi what it meant. It was difficult for the little girl to explain. She would have to ask Herra Kettonnen later. Gratefully she was getting warm sweeping the yard. She worked hard and in the end had to unbutton the top of her jacket.

She was thinking of home. Where and how was Bine, her mother and Tissi? And Friedrich? She counted the days left before she could leave here. Was it only three days since her arrival? She shuddered; there were still three hundred and sixty-two days left. Oh God!

Her bed was hard and her back was aching. She had never suffered from back pain and this was something she had not anticipated. There was a tap early in the morning and grandmother asked her to come with her. They went into the drying house and grandmother showed her how to fold the washing in a special manner. When everything was folded, she was taken to the mangle house.

There was that wooden contraption almost filling the room and on top of it sat a huge wooden box resting on three very smooth logs-cum rolling pins and in it sat the biggest rocks she had ever seen anywhere indoors. The mangle house must surely have been built around this mangle, because it never came in through the door.

The long box with the rocks was tipped up, and grandmother now picked up the first rolling pin. She wound a sheet carefully around it and replaced it well under the box. Grandmother pointed out that

Angela was to pick up the handle of the sledge and pull it down and towards her and back again, to and fro until the sheet seemed smooth. While labouring thus, she imagined herself in ancient Egypt, pulling rocks for the construction of the Pyramids. Maybe in a previous life she had done just that! She learned that for the finer ironing there were little Victorian irons on the stove in the kitchen.

By eight thirty she was done and with a full basket of neatly folded washing she went and claimed her breakfast. Everybody else had already eaten. The pot with the fish soup, fish boiled in Milk, was on the stove, but there were no bits of fish left in the pot. She ladled out the soup which at least tasted of fish, quite delicious, and she ate black bread with that until she was satisfied.

Then Herra Kettonnen had taken her aside and told her how much she would earn a month. This was quite a shock because she had been led to believe that her salary would be the same as a journeyman's at home and now she was offered less than she had earned as an apprentice. She would have to write to the Ministry of Agriculture in Munich, who had arranged this place for her. After all, her grandfather had advanced her part of the fare to Finland and she would have to pay it back before she could save for the fare home, or at least for the fare to anywhere, away from here. Tonight she would write a letter home and to the Ministry. The money she still had saved would not last all that long. She would have to earn a proper salary.

On the 17th of May the ice on the lake burst open with tremendous booming cracks and the ice was melting fast. On the side where Vähä Äinö stood, which she had learned was the name of the farm; the lake was totally free of ice in a matter of two days. When she first arrived she felt a great disappointment, going down to the lake and finding it frozen, when fourteen days earlier she had already been swimming in the Danube. She loved to swim. The melting of the ice happened so fast, and the only explanation she could find, was that the daylight lasted for close to 22 hours and still the nights became shorter all the time.

Two days later, after supper Herra Kettonnen told her to come down to the lake with him. It was already coming up to nine thirty and still the sun was shining in the deepest red, and the lake was red in the evening light. A lake of deep red wine, so beautiful. She was told to row the boat out into the lake. It was a large Suomen fishing boat and looked like a small version of a Viking boat, wooden with long slender oars. She had not rowed a boat before, but told herself, this is the first decent job so far and rowed with great concentration. It wasn't that difficult and she learned fast. Herra Kettonnen sat at the opposite end of the boat with a large pile of nets in front of him. Under his seat was a box with bottles of 'pilsneri', and he took a bottle, expertly knocked off the top on the side of the boat and drank. He did not speak with Angela.

When they were about 1 km out Herra Kettonnen stood up and put out the nets. About ten nets, each about ten to fifteen metres long and attached to one another. They had floaters on the top so that the long line was quite visible. The difficulty was to keep the boat steady by using the oars. Herra Kettonnen was anything but sober.

The next morning at five thirty there was a tap on her door and Herra Kettonnen told her to come with him. She quickly slipped into her clothes and came out. Together they went down to the lake and she took up her position by the oars and he sat on his seat at the other end. She rowed him out to the nets, which he pulled in and there were quite a number of fish in it. With a good load and the odd cry of joy from Herra Kettonnen, when they landed a particularly good specimen

of salmon, they rowed back. At the landing place by the sauna. Herra Kettonnen got a children's zinc bathtub and emptied the fish into it. It was nearly full. He then gave her a hunting knife and told her to clean them on the edge of the water. After delightedly handling some of the fish and pointing things out to her, which didn't mean a lot to her, he disappeared up the hill towards the house. It was six in the morning. Angela spent the next two hours cleaning the fish. This would be her daily routine throughout the summer, until the lake froze over again, and her food from now on would be fish for breakfast, lunch and supper, every day except Sunday when Rouva Kettonnen would break out some very precious strips of salted pork. But at this moment she was still ignorant of this fact. At eight o clock, Angela went up to the house, carrying the cleaned and gutted fish and sat down to a lonely breakfast.

From a little hill behind Vähä Ainiö she had a beautiful view of the lake. It was littered with hundreds of little islands; most of them covered with forest, some with just enormously huge, smoothe round boulders. The several kilometre thick layer of ice, moving south thousands of years ago, must have shaped these perfectly rounded rocks. The "Päyänne Järvi" is the largest lake in Finland. She began to fall in love with this country. Rouva Kettonnen could take a jump.

On the 19th of May was a local holiday; the church celebrated 800 years of existence. The weather was terrible.

They rowed out to the lake in a heavy storm, so bad that the boat was in danger of tipping over, especially since Herra Kettonnen was already worse for drink, first thing in the morning! They caught very few fish, and Angela was glad to be back on terra firma, completely drenched and felt extremely cold. She had not got the appropriate clothing for this sort of work, and felt very uncomfortable, cleaning the fish. Rouva Kettonnen would not be happy with the catch.

When she got back, she was told that they would travel to church after lunch, and Angela was to come too. She went to her room to change and also to use the bathroom.

Just as she wanted to enter the loo, which was a tiny extension with a wooden two-seater, where the waste fell into a closed box, probably a compost loo, Päivi and Matti came and took her hand and led her out of the house and across the yard to an old and broken down little shed. Päivi opened the door and pointed to an ancient wooden contraption. The smell was biting her nose. Angela laughed. An old two seater, never used nowadays. But she soon realized that she was not to use the indoor loo anymore. She was to use this one. And not only that, the adults were too cowardly to tell her themselves. Grandmother made a protest and also started to use the outdoor loo. She also took Angela by the hand and led her to her little cottage and pointed to her sitting room. It had been emptied of her personal things and grandmother made it clear to her that she should get her suitcase and move in. Angela felt so grateful to this old woman, she put her arms around her and hugged her. Grandmother smiled and helped her move in. Her daughter, Rouva Kettonnen stood in the doorway of the house, arms folded across her ample bosom, and frowned. Juha, her eldest stood by her side and shouted furiously. What a family, Angela thought. Päivi was her first visitor and made herself comfortable on her granny's sofa, which was left in the room for Angela to use.

Things were looking up. They all drove to church, about an hours drive away. Distances don't seem to matter here. Villagers live miles apart, and even where the church was situated, only a small number of red coloured houses with white window frames could be seen. Angela was aware, that people stared and asked a lot of questions. Rouva Kettonnen didn't take her eyes of her while she answered their questions. What a strange lot they are, she thought. She made out one word, which was repeated often: Saxalainen, what ever that meant.

After church Herra Kettonnen drove to a house and through the back door he received three crates of Pilsner, which he put into the boot of the car. When they got home, she was told to take the rest of the afternoon off. The first free time since her arrival! She went to her room and tried to make it more homely. She unpacked a few things and put them on the shelf. Päivi was always there. She too began to use the outdoor loo. It wasn't so bad, Angela had used loos like that often in the past. It is part of farming, rustic. But she hated the flies, which attacked her from below.

Grandmother came and invited her over to the house for afternoon coffee and cake. Everybody was there, slurping their coffee through sugar cubes from the saucer. They tried to be friendly. Angela felt a change. Later Herra Kettonnen took her to the lake, but abandoned the fishing because the lake was too wild. She stood by the Ranta Sauna and looked out over the churning waters, and could not believe the huge waves, which were lashing and foaming over the catwalk and almost hit the Ranta Sauna. This was untamed oceanic uproar.

After supper, when all the dishes were washed, Angela went to her room and sat by the window. The little girl came in with some children's books and pulled the other chair over and sat beside her. They looked at the book and Angela began to read. Such long words and so many double vowels and consonants, and nothing made any sense.

Päivi giggled and said the word the way it should be pronounced. Angela repeated it and so they spent the evening. The door was open to the little hall, and when grandmother came in she left her door open as well, and every now and then corrected both of them. This way Angela made her first progress in learning the Suomen kieli.

The trees were getting green and Angela was directed into a new method of cleaning. Every morning when she came back with the cleaned fishes, and had had her breakfast, she had to go and cut branches from a tree lining the road, strip the bottom leaves and only leave the top ones to make a nice bunch, and then sweep the wooden floors of all the rooms. A new bunch for every room and that way the dust was kept in the leaves and didn't settle on the furniture.

'I have become a domestic servant!' she thought. That would never do. When it came to count her time as a trainee student, this time would not count. She had written to the Min. of Ag. and waited for their reply.

The reply, when it came, was not addressed to her, but to the Kettonnen's. A man, maybe fifteen years older than herself, came to the house one morning, when she returned with the cleaned fishes, and went in to breakfast with her. She hoped somebody would introduce her. In the end, she held out her hand and said: Angela, and he smiled and shook her hand saying: Markku. He then spoke in very halting German that she was to go with him after breakfast.

"Where are we going?" she asked

"I will introduce you to our farm" he said, "I am the foreman".

So, now life will become real, I shall do proper work and maybe be paid with real money. She had, after all, a work permit which permitted her to do real work for real money.

The actual farm was less than a kilometre away down the road, which seemed to come from nowhere and go to nowhere, with nothing but water and forest. The forest was so thick and the trees had such dimensions, that she often stood in awe at the edge of the forest and thought: "This is the fairytale forest of the Grimm's tales, where wolves and bears roam".

They travelled to the farm on a little ancient tractor. There were 12 cows and 2 horses, some pigs and a few chickens, two strange looking houses, which had front doors on the upper floor as well as

121

on the ground, but no steps leading up to them. She looked at Markku enquiringly and he explained, that in winter the snow would cover the ground up to the upper front door and they would then only use that door. They would have to use skis in order to be able to move about. But nowadays they don't built houses like this anymore. These are old-fashioned farm workers houses.

She helped with the milking and feeding the animals, tended to the horses and helped feeding the pigs. She was introduced to Markku's wife and the other farm workers. She soon found, that the farm was relatively small; there were not many acres, mostly hey meadows and forestry work. She spent a lot of time preparing the fields and sewing seeds for turnips, wheat and barley and a small field with oats, and one with potatoes. It all grew tremendously fast, twice as quickly as at home. It was amazing. The grass on the sunny sides was getting ready for haymaking, almost the same time as at home, and jet only a short time ago, these meadows were still covered in snow. Although the sun shone for so many hours a day, it remained the land of the long shadows. And even though the sun also shone in the north, it had not sufficient warmth to melt the snow in some parts.

Over night a most terrible plague came over the countryside. Zillions of mosquitoes! They were everywhere, which made it difficult to breathe without getting some of these pesky things down your throat. She could hardly breathe. She was attacked and bitten and thought she must go mad or die or both. The only place where they left her in peace was in the boat when she went out fishing. Cleaning the fish on the beach, she cried and the bites itched and she thought that if she did not concentrate and kept her mind together, she would loose it and go crazy.

The plantain leaves grew everywhere and here in the constant daylight grew to huge proportions. She plucked fists full and rubbed them onto her bites until her skin turned green and the agony was eased. Bravely she continued cleaning the fish. Every now and then she wiped the swarms of her arms and legs, and then wiped the bloody, messy contents of her hand on the grass beside her. It became worst in bed, their whining noise stopped her from sleeping at night. Why did they not have mosquito nets? When she thought she could not stand it any longer and go crazy after all, they disappeared to a large extend. They were still in the forests, but not any worse than at home. And her remedy with the plantain was very effective.

When it was time to weed the beets, a job with a hoe where she had to destroy most of the little plants and only leave one every fifteen centimetres, to give them room to grow, she found herself all on her own. Not a house or person to be seen all day and every day until she had done the entire field. She remembered doing the same job at home with five people going up and down the rows together, chatting and laughing and having good-natured competitions. She recited poems to pass the time. Trying to remember 'Schiller's Glocke', which told of the French Revolution and was pages long and a nightmare to learn and then recite in front of the class.

On the third day Päivi arrived and crawled up and down the furrows with her talking and teaching her to count and learn more vocabulary. She was learning fast and could already form crude sentences. Angela taught Päivi some German and shared the joy this little girl showed when she realized she too could speak in a different, foreign language. They became inseparable.

There had been some difficulty with having a bath. Angela had so far only been able to keep herself clean with water from an outside tap and a bowl in her room. Not very satisfactory, and she ached to be able to submerge herself in water. She realized that there were no bathrooms here. She contemplated to go down to the lake and have a dip in the ice-cold water, but decided against it. Then, three weeks into her stay, grandmother came and invited her into the sauna. She had seen the family disappear into this sooty little hut, but had no idea what happened inside. Grandmother made it clear that they all went in naked. Angela felt terribly embarrassed and fished out her bathing suit and put it on.

Inside the sauna were two platforms and the family were sitting on the top platform. Herra Kettonnen had taken the position above the heated stones and every now and then ladled some more water over them and the searing hot air hit her in the face. The family laughed when she entered, wearing her swimsuit, but she took her position next to Päivi and sat down. She was given a bunch of birch twigs to whip herself with and enjoyed the fragrance the leaves emitted. Alas, the heat shrunk her bathing suit so, that it exposed her breasts, and no matter how hard she pulled, they stayed exposed. She gave in and took off her suit and somehow became one of them. They started to chat and include her in the conversation and encouraged her to speak Finnish and helped her patiently and praised her efforts. From that moment on she was treated with respect and was included in everything they did. Being naked was no great deal and soon she forgot to feel embarrassed.

She noticed that it took all morning to heat the Sauna. Herra Kettonnen and Grandmother busied themselves with adding more logs to the fire, and then when the stones are heated they went in and out of the Sauna until the stones were too cold and did not steam anymore, maybe three hours later. She also learned that the Sauna is the hub of everything social that goes on, especially in winter; children are made and babies are born there, when one is sick, one sits in the Sauna and sweats it out. In fact the Sauna is the cosiest, happiest place for a Finnish family.

There was one mystery left for her to find out. It was the old man she saw around the place, always just out of sight, as if in hiding. He was never there at mealtimes, did not join them in the sauna and she could not even find out where he slept. But he was always there just out of sight.

One Sunday afternoon, enjoying her free time, she saw him from her window sitting quietly all by himself in the lilac arbour. The lilac was in full bloom and she could smell its scent in her room. She decided to go over and introduce herself. She knew enough Finnish to be able to speak with him. As she approached him, he turned away and hid his face. He was holding an old tin. She sat down beside him and started to talk, and to her surprise he answered in good German. He was grandfather, Rouva Kettonnen's father and grandmother's husband. But because he had a terribly runny nose and dribbling mouth, which never stopped oozing slime, which he caught in his tin, he kept to himself. She asked him if he was hiding only because she had arrived, and he said yes, he did not want to offend her. She felt awful and said:

"You don't have to hide from me! I would like you to pretend that I am not a stranger." He laughed and turned towards her. Just then Päivi arrived and went over to Iso Äiti at least that is what she thought the little girl called him. She leant against his knee and he stroked her hair. He has Parkinson's disease, she thought, because he never stopped shaking.

*

15

Tuomela Järvenpää

It was the middle of June on a Saturday afternoon, a month since her arrival, and Herra Kettonen had gone down to the Ranta Sauna to light up the stones. It too was a black Sauna, where the open fire's smoke finds its own way out. There is no chimney, only a little hole at the opposite side from the fire. Above the fire, Herra Kettonen had hung some pork ring sausages and they were cooking in the searing heat and dripping fat into the stones, which evaporated with a hiss, leaving a wonderfully delicious aroma. There was a crate of beer on the shady side of the Sauna and when Angela arrived with the grandparents and the children, Rouva and Herra Kettonen were sitting on the bench in front of the Sauna, naked, and enjoying the sunshine. The Sauna was not yet hot enough. Rouva Kettonen was holding the baby on her lap, and Angela saw it for the first time. She guessed it was about three months old and very sweet. She asked if she could hold it and graciously Rouva Kettonen handed it to her. And then she said very slowly in Finnish:

"Call me Mirja", and Herra Kettonen continued:

"And I am Mauno". Angela acknowledged the honour given to her graciously and, after handing back the baby, proceeded to undress herself and the children. Twenty minutes later Mauno opened the door and invited everybody into the Sauna. After about half an hour sitting and laughing and pouring more water over the stones and hitting each other with the birch branches, Mauno got up, left the Sauna, ran down the catwalk and jumped head first into the lake. Angela got up and followed and after her Juha and Päivi. She was surprised how warm the water was and how well the children could swim. It was total heaven, clear, soft and sweet. She swam out and dived. The water was crystal clear. She could see right down to the bottom of the lake. It was strewn with big boulders and smaller stones and they seemed so close and colourful, green and golden as the sun broke through the water, but she could not get to the bottom. No matter how hard she tried, the pressure on her head and in her ears became unbearable.

She asked Mauno how deep the lake was and he said: "Oh, maybe 25 to 30 meters?" She had never dived that deep. The Danube was maybe 6 meters at most where she used to swim, and the little Vils at the Laubhof never deeper than up to her neck. She would spend every free moment in the lake, swimming. What wonderful bliss.

Oh yes, this was alright!

She also discovered, that she did not need shampoo to wash her long hair, which she wore in a ponytail. Her dark blond hair shone with golden and copper highlights, and flowed like silk, something she had never noticed before. Her body felt healthy and strong and she was aware, for the first time in her life, that she was beautiful, not that she gave it much thought, it just made her happy.

As she climbed out of the lake for the umpteenth time that afternoon to return to the Sauna, Mirja came up behind her and touched her back and said in very bad German. :

"Such muscles! Like man!" Angela felt slightly embarrassed but also proud. This underfed, starving war-child, hounded refugee, homesick for a homeland forever lost, this 19 year old girl was she! Had the War ended only ten years ago? Ten years! Like a flash those years came back into her memory, as they always did. She would never forget, even a day of those years of horror, starvation, loss, sadness and death. Would that awful wound ever heal? Did her contemporaries ever talk about it? All the people who suffered the same! Would they ever have the courage to talk it off their chests?

The fishing trips at dawn and dusk became such a routine, part of her life and she even looked forward to it every day. At dawn the lake was calm, and as they put out from the jetty, they were the reason for the first ripples on the water. Like putting out into a mirror! The grandiose beauty took her breath away, and the chorus of the birds turned into a crescendo. She would dip the oars gently into the liquid crystal and then let them drip before putting them in again, watching the drips as they made rings onto the virgin stillness of the water. It was fascinatingly beautiful. Sadly her mind went back to the days on the Wannsee in Berlin with her father and mother and Bine, before Tissi was born. Peaceful happy days!

The only thing, which disturbed this idyll, was cleaning the fish afterwards. There were so many varieties, some very beautiful, some had such stubborn scales, hard and with hooks embedded in the skin of the fish. These scales looked like tiny hands with their finger's bent as if to make a fist, which clung like claws to the fish. They were so difficult to remove; she had to have two knives, one which she stabbed into the tail section of the fish to hold him fast onto the board and the other to scrape away the obstinate scales. The slimy, slippery fish made the knives difficult to hold and she ended up with her fingers cut to bits. There were huge salmon and trout in wonderful colours, there were Stickle Backs and enormous wells, roach, perch and zander, but one in particular took her attention, because she had never seen the like anywhere. It was horrendously fascinating and Mauno explained that it was a survivor from the dinosaurs and the ice age. Mauno called it salvelinus.

In the end all fish usually ended up in the same pot, except the salmon, which was smoked or cooked in the forest near the Ranta Sauna. (Beach Sauna). A hole was dug and the fish was salted, buttered and covered with herbs and then wrapped in wet newspaper. Many layers of it and then put into the hole and covered first with a layer of earth and then with large pieces of birch wood which were then lit and the fire kept burning for an hour or two and when the ashes where cooling down, the fish was dug out and the remaining newspaper carefully removed and there was the most delicious meal, smoke flavoured, eaten with green salad from the garden and the meadows, black slices of homemade bread and butter. Sometimes they were barbequed and sometimes fried in homemade butter.

For breakfast soup was always served. The fish, which was not worth baking, frying or smoking, and all the heads, were thrown into a large pot with milk, bay leaves and juniper berries, herbs, salt, pepper and sugar, and boiled. Angela got to enjoy this meal, once she got used to the staring eyes, which leered at her from the pot as she ladled out her soup, carefully avoiding the heads. The Kettonnens, all of them, sucked the fish heads dry, and put them on a side plate. Angela thought it was disgusting, but having been offered a head every morning since her arrival, and had been assured that that was the healthiest part, finally gave in. When in Rome... and she was surprised how full of flavour they were.

She also found that sugar was added to most foods. Sweet spinach, sweet potatoes, carrots and beans, sweet cabbage etc. It took away the harshness of the salted pork and went well with the fish.

One stormy and very wet morning they came back from the lake and Mirja was in a state. She screamed and shouted at Angela. She could not work out what the trouble was. Mauno disappeared so quickly and the shouting was now directed only at her. Mauno had helped her clean the fish because it was freezing cold and rained heavily, and she had not got a protective coat with her. She was hungry and cold and very wet and did not know what the shouting was all about. Juha and Matti were standing beside their mother in the kitchen, and Angela did not like the malicious grin on their faces. Apart from that, they were picking their noses and eating the long, fat extractions. Disgusting! Grandfather was sitting on the bench near the range holding his tin under his nose. She was going to be sick. All the friendly behaviour of the past weeks lay in ruins. Shattered, she turned round and left the room, not before she dumped the full tub of cleaned fish at Rouva Kettonnen's feet. As she left, she heard grandfather speaking sharply with his daughter. She went to her room in grandmother's little cottage and sat on the bed. I need to get away. This is unbearable. She would not call them by their Christian names again. She would be as formal as she was when she first arrived. She changed into dry, warm clothes, and did not come out of her room that day to go back into the house. She was very angry and hungry.

It rained and rained and the water ran in streams down to the lake, turning the path into oozing mud. In the afternoon grandmother came and brought her some food and a mug of the disgusting homemade beer, the look of it reminded her of grey milk. The men on the farm drank it all day and smelled of it even worse.

Grandmother seemed to apologize to her for her daughter's behaviour. Angela understood that she was jealous, thought there was something going on between her and her husband. At first she thought she had misunderstood, and asked again, but grandmother explained the same again. Angela was embarrassed and felt her face turn red. Then she became angry. She had not the words in finish to tell them all what she thought. And that cowardly Herra Kettonnen! What did Rouva Kettonnen think? Did she really think she found her husband in any way attractive? He was a drunken middle-aged man! She would have to have a word with him and then she would try and find another place in Finland. She was not staying here.

There was no regular work for her on the farm. She was not asked to go there every day; the farmhands coped without her. She had looked forward to be away from the house. There was nothing much to do in the house either, except fishing, cleaning, washing and wielding the heavy boulders instead of using an electric iron. She wondered why she was here? She felt terribly lonely and her treatment had so deteriorated. The children were in her room all the time, and made her life hell. It seemed that Rouva Kettonnen put the children in charge to watch her every move, except when they went out fishing. The weather didn't improve and she could not take the children out to play. Little Päivi tried to cheer her up, but the three boys were bogy-eating devils. Determined to change things for her, she picked up Päivi and put her on her lap, ignoring the boys and started to read a story from a book left there by the little girl. Regardless of the boy's behaviour, she read on and gradually they became quiet and began to listen. She did not really understand everything she was reading, but that did not matter at this stage. As a German she could read quite easily, even though the words were very long but were pronounced the same way as German words. Not like French or English or the Latin languages. So she read on and found that the children understood her pronunciation which encouraged her to continue. She read the illustrations for herself. Angela decided not to give up, and was encouraged by the children, who were quietly listening. She could learn something from all this. Words embedded themselves in her brain, she would find out later what they meant.

*

Some weeks had passed and Rouva Kettonnen had calmed down. Angela had, on her own, found work to do around the place. If they don't know what to do with me, I shall help myself. They watched her from a distance, but let her get on. She mended fences, and worked in the garden. She helped grandmother and she mended the washhouse. She chopped wood and stacked it as they did in Bavaria, something they had not seen here.

While she was making herself work hard to pass the time, she wondered what had happened to all her friends at home and why Hannchen had not answered her letters. She felt so lonely and forsaken. And there were no more letters from Friedrich. Angela was too proud to ask why he had not written. If he does not want to write, so be it. Quietly she grieved.

Then one day Rouva Kettonnen came up to her and shyly asked her to make some clothes for the children. She gave her the material and some patterns and showed her an ancient sewing machine, which was operated by hand. She spent a fortnight creating children's clothing, something she had never done. She had made things for herself, and could sew well, but the pleasure to make things for children had escaped her. They were as always hanging around, but behaving themselves, because by now Angela had learned Finnish well enough to tell them off and also to ask them to do things. Juha shouting "be quiet" in the beginning of her stay, she now used against him, and the result was amazing. He stopped shouting. The children showed respect, and Päivi was still her champion. To make two dresses for the little girl and a petticoat to go with it, gave her immense pleasure. The little girl danced and turned and let the wide skirt twist and ran towards and away from the mirror. She turned and turned and then quickly sat down, with the skirt making a wide circle around her. Angela laughed and laughed. The boys too looked more shyly at themselves. She had made blue trousers with pockets and shoulder straps and shirts for them. Grandmother sat down beside her and did the buttonholes and buttons. She was chatting constantly and Angela tried out her Finnish. She was learning fast, and the family were quite astonished. Angela understood far more of the conversations around her, and things said to her. But she could not yet form proper sentences. She remembered the Russian prisoners of war. She now spoke Finish the way they spoke German. The Kettonens could understand what she wanted to say. Proper sentences would not yet form themselves on her tongue and it frustrated her. She found that the children understood her far better than the adults did, and Päivi was often her interpreter. Even Juha prided himself in doing this service for Angela now. They were using the "beautiful room" or sitting room in which hung the picture of the beautiful person, which impressed her on her first day at Vähä Äiniö. She pointed to it as asked: Who is that? And Päivi answered: Iso Äiti, grandfather. Unbelievable! What happens to people when they get old?

When she had finished with the sewing machine, she was asked to rip all the remaining bits of material into strips and knot them together with a weavers knot and wind them up onto a flat piece of wood.

Grandmother took her into the weaving house and showed her what the cloth strips were all about. She climbed into one of the looms and started to weave the strips of material into an already existing rag rug. She explained that this was an ongoing thing and this way they did not have to worry about bits of material lying about and having to be stored. The looms were the same size as the one she had used on the farm in Bavaria and at Agricultural College. They both had five foot pedals, but only two pedals were used in either loom. The second loom was used to weave Rüyümatto's. It was tight weaving for about five rows with thick wool and then a row of long loops which were threaded on a round stick with different coloured wool to make a certain pattern. These loops would then be cut open to turn into thick pile. The bigger the loops were the longer and thicker the pile. Sometimes the lengths of the loops differed, so that the pattern on the rug was more accentuated. Angela asked grandmother if she would teach her to weave these carpets. Grandmother smiled and said she would.

It was the middle of July and two more fields were ready for haying. Markku came to fetch her and for the next three days she brought in the hay. The winters are very long and the fodder for the animals has to last from September to May. Tired and scratched but happy and relaxed they went to swim in the lake's black and red-golden waters, and then to bed. She did not draw the curtains because the spectacle of the midnight light was not to be missed. She watched until she fell asleep. To see the sunlight at midnight glowing on the lake, the black forest and the majestic shapes of the giant trees, it would be imprinted into her brain, never to be forgotten.

On the 27th of July she took the bus to Lahti, the nearest town, because she had to see the dentist. As she left the surgery and wandered down the street, feeling lonely and homesick, and wondering where to find some lunch, she saw two pairs of Bavarian shoes walking in front of her, and as her eyes worked their way up the legs she saw that they disappeared in Lederhosen. Before she knew it she exclaimed loudly: 'Lederhosen!' The two young men in those Lederhosen turned round and smiled. They greeted her like an old friend. The hours before the bus went passed to quickly. They were on their way to Lappland. Angela asked if they returned the same way, and if they did, would they visit her at Toppola. How she wished she could go with them. They promised to visit and she stepped into the bus to go home.

She did not tell the Kettonnen's about the boys. If they turned up they would have to put them up. Angela did not care what they thought. Finland had certain rules of hospitality, and Angela would put them to it.

Then a letter arrived inviting her along with all other students from Germany to visit Tampere. A date was set for the 5th of August. Angela leapt with joy. Away from here, a holiday! Meeting with friends. She could not wait. The day arrived and she travelled to Tampere and met with Hannchen and many other students she had not met before. They talked about their places and it seemed that Angela had really found the worst of all places. Everybody praised their families and how wonderful everything was. One young woman especially talked about the farm near Helsinki where she worked and mentioned that two places were free to be filled, and if Angela wanted, she would speak with Rouva af Heurlin, the name of her boss. Angela assured Helga, the name of the young woman, that she would be very interested and would come as soon as she was invited to come.

The students spent four days in Tampere, visiting the noodle factory and the crisp bread factory and then they went swimming in the lake. She met a young man, Gerhard Pohl, and forgot all about Friedrich.

On the way back to Toppola, she was full of optimism and very happy. Hannchen explained that she was the laziest letter writer, and was also in trouble with her family at home, because she had not written. She promised to write, but Angela did not believe her, but it didn't matter, they were still friends.

Two days after her return Hans and Günter turned up fresh from Lapland and Rouva Kettonnen was sweetness herself. The young men helped around the place and then spend a lot of the time swimming in the lake with Angela. They dived from the high rocks and swam well into the night. The young men slept on the farm and stayed a week. What a wonderful week. The Kettonnen's were friendly and offered meals, and Hans and Günter worked during the day. They enjoyed their stay and in the evenings Angela acted as interpreter. They exchanged addresses when they left, and Angela felt terribly lonely after their departure. Rouva Kettonnen returned to her former unfriendliness, but Angela did not care. There was excitement in the air, she felt it.

Sure enough on the 20th of August a letter arrived from Rouva af Heurlin to invite her to come to Tuomela to join her household as an agricultural student as soon as she was able to. There was a letter included for Rouva Kettonnen and Angela handed the letter to her. Without a word Rouva Kettonnen turned and left the room. In the evening the family politely knocked on her door in the cottage and piled into her room. In Finish and with a broad smile, and Angela could smell the beer, Herra Ketonnen said that it would be for the best. When winter came in October she would not be able continue to live in the cottage. It was only used in the summer months and there was no room in the house. He admitted that he had been asking at the agency to find her another place for the winter, but had not yet been able to secure one.

So they were relieved! They were very happy with the arrangement. What strange people they were. Why could they not have discussed it with her! Herra Kettonnen had sufficient German to tell her this, surely. It was decided that she could start in Tuomela on the first of September. Herra Kettonnen used the telephone and arranged it all, and after a big farewell party at the Ranta Sauna and gifts she was taken to the bus station and travelled south.

Her new address was just outside Helsinki, about 20 kilometres away. Hämeenkylä was in deep countryside, surrounded by ancient forest, but close enough to be able to go into Helsinki regularly by bus, which passed the house. To her surprise Hannchen had also been invited to spend the long winter months at Tuomela.

16

The Ski Jump

Tuomela was a modern, stone-built house, large with all comforts of modern bathroom facilities and an indoor sauna. There was also an outdoor sauna of the rural ,Finnish sort, like the one she had loved at Toppola, but no lake, which was just as well since it would be frozen with a thick layer of ice in a very short time. She was one of four Students; Hannchen was the domestic queen and Angela shared the work between household and outdoor. She found herself mostly outdoors with the two male students, Helmut and Eberhard, also from Germany, Lasse Sampo who was the foreman, Eemeli, a farmhand and Jorma Ruinio, the son of the forester.

Her bosses were both professors at Helsinki University and away from home some days in the week. They spoke English, German, Finnish and Swedish. How well they spoke it she couldn't judge at the time, except when they explained something to her in German. Angela chuckled secretly, at the sweet mistakes, like the one she always made, even though Angela corrected it a few times: "Would she please stand the children to bed." Rouva af Heurlin was amazed to find that Angela had learned so much Finnish at Toppola. Hannchen and the men had learned hardly any, and that might have been because they had been placed at more sophisticated situations, where German was spoken, and therefore they did not have to bother to learn the local language.

Every morning, Angela went out to the farm, which was two hundred metres down the lane. The first job was to clean the cowshed and then to milk the cows. It was all done with milking machines. By seven in the morning the milk lorry would come and collect the churns. After that she could go home to have breakfast, and then she would go back to the farm and do the work as it was allocated. It was September and the potatoes, beets and swedes had to be harvested. It was getting dark and darker with the days shortening fast and by three in the afternoon some electric lights lit up the farm.

The last days in September a mountain of large cranberries were delivered by the forest women, and Hanchen and Angela were directed to take them up to the loft and empty them on to the floor. They weren't bottled or juiced or done anything to, just left there. Two days later they were deep-frozen and could be used anytime. So convenient!

Two days into October, the snow came and within a few days she could not walk outside anymore without having to put on skis. She was given some from the household stock and the children of the house taught her. As soon as they can walk, they have to learn to ski. They were so accomplished, and Angela, who had not really skied properly before, was now taught to ski by the children on Sunday afternoons. Strangely, Helmut and Eberhard did not take part in these lessons. They were not interested and worked their way from the house to the farm awkwardly and precariously on the skis. They did not mind when they were laughed at. The children did not really understand, why people of their age could not ski properly. Angela tried hard and made progress. Every morning she put on the skis to go down to the farm and found it exhilarating and such fun to slide at such speed down the lane on established ski spoors. It was like sliding along greased rails. As she arrived, the skis were un-clicked und planted outside the door. They were cross-country skis, only fastened on the front of the boot. She calculated in her mind how much it would cost to get her own skis. Her next trip into Helsinki would be to a ski shop and get boots and skis that would be her own. Her income had improved tremendously. She was now getting a proper wage.

The boots had square shaped toecaps and in the sole four holes which fitted onto pins on the skis. The sole had a wide rim onto which the fastening clip was pressed, so the heel was free for the skier to take long strides when sliding along. In Finland she found that skis were not a luxury item, and therefore they were cheap in comparison to home. She could so easily afford them. She realized though that cross country skis had their limits. It was no good to

137

slalom with these skis as she had tried on borrowed skis in Bavaria on occasions; the ski would unclick itself and continue on without her and she would have to balance on one ski to catch up with the runaway. Often she lay helpless in the snow, laughing so much and sinking ever deeper into this white softness.

There was a mountain of beets to be cleared of the leaves, and the farmhands and students sat on low stools with a big knife and cut the beets clean. The frost had made the leaves mushy and slimy and she got terribly cold. She soon got the hang of it and held the beet in her left hand and with the right she held the knife and chopped off the offending dark and slimy leaves. She wore everything she had and even cut an old pullover so that she could pull it over her bottom to keep her buttocks warm, but the cold crept in and settled in her bones. She had never in her life been so deeply cold. Even though the doors to the beet cellar were closed and a sawdust stove was burning, it did not warm the room. It took however only a week, and this job was done.

In early November it was decided to go with the local children to a ski-jump. They were only going to watch the youngsters jump. They skied through dense forest, trees laden with snow, crossed a small lake and came to a wooden structure. A ladder was quickly climbed by the little boys. They lined up at the very top and slid down with a wishshshsh...

It looked so easy. Effortlessly, these boys came flying down the shoot and then take off and soar down the hill and land gently and elegantly at the bottom and since they could not turn on these skis, let them run out to a stop, making a V as they slowed down. The jump ended on a lake and there was an abrupt change from coming down the hill to the flat of the lake, which made the knees shoot up and that had to be compensated for by the rest of the body. No sooner where they down when they rushed up the steep hill again and climbed the ladder to the top of the jump. They had an admiring audience, with the German students looking on and cheering. The little chaps were eager to show off.

Angela was watching for a while. Because it seemed to be so easy, Angela decided to have a go herself. She climbed up the wooden steps and when she stood at the top, she could not believe how high it all was. She had been watching from the bottom of the jump, the half way mark. Now, from this height she saw the entire drop and her courage faded.

Two boys had climbed up after her, grinned at her encouragingly and got ready to jump. She watched carefully, and saw them depart. She also noticed that as soon as they launched themselves into the air, they leant forward, their bodies almost the same angle as the skis, and the skis were held apart, like narrow platforms riding on air. By the third time she had watched these boys jump, she also noticed that their hands were flat against their bodies.

Eberhard called from below: "If you are going to jump, jump. Otherwise come on down. You best come down anyway, you might break your neck".

Shaking like a leaf, she climbed up to the launching platform and before she could do anything or change her mind, she started to slide down. As she gathered speed and came close to be launched into the air, she remembered:"Lean forward, hands tucked in" but she was already flying through the air. The ground came rushing up and she landed, leaning forward and adjusting her body with her knees.

Good God! She had done it! It was wonderful and so easy. The most difficult bit was getting from the slope of the hill onto the flat lake. She walked back up the hill and took off her skis and climbed back up the ladder to the top.

Eberhard shouted after her:" Beginner's luck" She heard but didn't listen. The second time went ok, a little wobbly, and instead of concentrating on all the tricks she had learned, she became overconfident and when she landed the third time she fell and rolled down the hill, on and on, turning and turning until she came to a halt in a heap of skis and limbs. She lay there, unable to work our where her arms and legs where. She felt no pain, and started to giggle. Eberhard had rushed up to her and undid her skis, and slowly she remembered where her arms and legs were. She could not stop laughing. This was wonderful. You could not even get hurt; the snow was so deep and soft. But she had to admit, that the trees could be a danger.

Eberhard was for going home. It was only 3 in the afternoon, and she was not yet ready. "You go" she said. He had been standing around and was getting very cold. Angela had been up and down the ski jump, she was actually too hot.

"I come back with the boys", she said. That afternoon she learned to ski-jump and would be at the jump with the children as often as she found the time. It was a cross-country walk which took about three-quarters of an hour, and she got faster and faster, trying to keep up with the youngsters. She learned to take long strides and use her arms, pushing herself along with the sticks. The children enjoyed her company and she was happy to be taught, and they were proud to teach her. What a life! She enjoyed the work, the freedom, the snow, the icy cold, the warmth of the house, the warmth of the people, her room, the food, and the children. It was all such a wonderful adventure, and such a complete change from Toppola. Although she enjoyed the lake and rowing the boat, the rest was like a black memory. And she was paid proper wages. She could now begin to save and pay back the money her grandfather had lent her.

By the beginning of December, in deepest darkest winter, most the German agricultural students departed for home. The winter was too cold for them. Angela was surprised. She had agreed to spend a year at least, but she would not go home now. Miss all this fun? The first Christmas in her life where she was not in Germany and even that was a new adventure.

Helmut and Eberhard were packing their suitcases and Hannchen and Angela promised to come to the docks in Helsinki and see them off. As they arrived some more male students arrived. They said that in the winter when everything was covered in snow there would not be a lot for them to do, but at home there would be. Angela thought again that being a woman had its advantages. Hannchen was domestic queen and Angela half and half. There was plenty to do in the house and just as much with the animals. And then there was the work in the forest. Wood for the household and the sauna had to be fetched almost daily with the horses and sledges.

At the dock they met up with some young people they had not met before. However, Gerhard, she had met in Tampere in the summer, and here he was again. They had exchanged addresses and promised to write. Angela had waited, she didn't want to seem forward and be the first to write, but Gerhard had not written. Now here he was again. He came over to her and put an arm around her shoulders:

"Are you staying out the winter?" He asked her. She said yes she would. She would stay the year and maybe even longer if possible. She was happy to be here. Gerhard told her he would stay until May and then head home via Lapland and Sweden. Would she mind if he came to visit. It is not so far to ski across the country. Maybe they could also meet on days off in Helsinki. Happily she agreed.

The leaving students boarded the ship to Stockholm and the rest waved them good bye. They all went to a cafe and had a lovely afternoon before they boarded the bus to go to their various families.

For Christmas she would have her own little tree and she sat down in the evening to draw and cut out some nativity figures, get some moss and have her own little crib. Hannchen happily joined Angela, because Hannchen like Angela stayed out the winter and they shared a room. They drew Mary and Joseph, and little Jesus, Angela made a crib from a matchbox and glued matches together to make the legs, shepherds and a couple of sheep, and lastly the three wise men. They were very pleased with their efforts. They had a trip to Helsinki and did some window-shopping, got some tinsel, baubles and candles and a few other little things, including cards to send home. When the children came to see what they had done, they begged to put it up so that everyone could see it. So it was all rearranged in the best room.

December was very dark and cold. Midday was no lighter than dusk or dawn. But by some miraculous turn of nature, the nights were on average lighter than daytime. Somehow the clouds covered the sky during the day and made everything look gloomy and dark, visibility was limited and usually snowstorms raged, creating huge drifts, sending the snow in hard little semolina typed grains sideways into people's faces. The contours of the countryside seemed to be flattened out. Little hills disappeared; trees and buildings in valleys were only visible by the tips of the branches and the rooftops. It was all quite amazing. She remembered the wooden buildings in Toppola, where the entrances were on the first floor and steps led to the veranda. In the winter off course the snow would cover the lower part of the house. Amazing!

At night however, the clouds vanished and the stars shone brilliantly and the moon was so bright that it cast a shadow on the indigo-blue snow and you could see for miles. Angela preferred to be out in the evening. Nights however where much colder. Visits to the postoffice and to friends were mostly done in the evening. There was one occurrence, which she would not forget so easily.

It had stormed all day, but Hannchen and Angela had finished the Christmas cards and letters and if they should arrive home with their families and friends in time for Christmas, they would have to be posted soon. Hannchen was not a skier, she preferred to be housebound, be safe in the warmth. Angela understood, and made ready to go to the postoffice by herself. She had gone many times before and knew the way. There was a loipe and she slid along the grooves effortlessly. Her best ally in this frozen north was her total ignorance of any possible dangers. She was conscious of the friendly people, the extraordinary way they naturally coped with all this mass of snow and cold, and the magical beauty of the country.

That evening when she returned from the cow-house, the thermometer outside the door showed 38 degrees below zero. Her breath froze to the eyelashes and the minute hairs around her face. When she arrived her face looked like father frost with particles of ice hanging off her face. The good thing was there was no wind and therefore the cold was not biting.

She planted her skis with all the others outside the door. As she entered, the heat of the house momentarily took her breath away, and left her face bathed in dewdrops of melted ice. She shed several layers of clothing and went in to supper. During the meal she announced that she would go to the postoffice that night, a trip of about four kilometres. She collected all the mail, also from the af Heurlins, put on her layers again and wound her scarf round her face covering her nose and mouth and leaving her eyes free. The woollen front of it would soon be as hard as wood from her frozen breath.

The trip would not take too long, since the route was flat and the loipe stretching out in front of her like two distinctly dark rows. She enjoyed the rhythmic movement. She was fairly flying along, the swish-swish of the skis accelerated each and every move.

Part of the way was parallel with the road, but whereas the road wound itself around the countryside, the loipe went straight as an arrow. There was only one farm between Tuomela and the postoffice. All the obstacles were buried beneath the snow. She marvelled at the stars. The sky was deepest indigo, almost black, with just a hint of blue where the moonlight illuminated it, and the stars shone brightly like diamonds, the northern star was almost overhead. She had learned to work out where exactly it was by measuring five equal distances from the square, which makes up Ursa Major. Hanging strangely on the southern horizon was Orion with his brightly shining silvery sword. There were no artificial lights to mar this amazing spectacle. A green and yellow Aurora Borealis flickered across the sky, undulating and moving like a gigantic curtain and then disappearing totally and magically breaking out again. How wonderful is that! She thought.

As she neared the post she had become so warm that she had to open her anorak at the neck. She took off her skis and went inside. There was always a friendly welcome and everybody wanted to know newsy gossip. Angela was not a gossip, but she answered their questions. The postoffice was a general store, post office, travel agent, fashion shop, emergency doctor and chemist, all rolled into one.

She had met the young people, teenage children of the postmaster, at the ski jump. They had become good friends and Angela kept improving her Finish. They all sat down to chat. Maitti, the young girl had been sitting in the weaving frame, weaving rag rugs. She climbed out of that and went over to the stove and picked up the ever-bubbling copper kettle with coffee and poured. They were all slurping it lazily through sugar cubes from the saucers, and chatting happily.

She sorted her mail and paid for it, and then left around nine o-clock in brilliant moonshine. Maitti's father warned her and said she should hurry, because he detected clouds on the horizon. Long, rhythmic strides carried her along. Slowly the clouds covered up the moon and the stars and it became quite dark. She stopped suddenly, because somehow she had lost the loipe. She found herself going up hill, which was strange and worried her. Tying to penetrate the blackness she could make out the giant trees in the distance, and decided to continue up a little and then fork right, and get home that way. She knew the forest well. They had done a lot of logging there.

She moved along quickly, puffing, since she had to work hard with the sticks to stop her from sliding backwards. She was looking out for the right fork. But it didn't come. Then she heard dogs howling. They sounded eerily sad, probably the cold got to them. They could be the Ruinio's dogs. Their house was over to the left a little. She must be further from home than she thought. They would worry at home. She headed towards the howling dogs. She would ask the Ruinio's to ring home and tell them that she would be a little late. Suddenly she recognized a huge stack of felled trees, which they had got ready in the autumn to push down a short shoot and then to be loaded onto sledges. She was a long way from home and not anywhere near the Ruinio's house.

Relieved, that she recognized the way home, she shot down the hill alongside the timber shoot. At the bottom she turned to the right, she hastened along, wondering about the dogs. She reached the end of the forest and swish-swished along, as if the devil was behind her, trying to make up the time. A little way across the fields and she could see the lights of the house. The dogs had followed her steadily. As she neared the house, the door was flung open and everybody talked at once. She flicked off the clips of the skis, planted them firmly into the snow and galloped down the snow steps to the front door and into the house. The door was shut quickly.

"You should have been home long ago, where you lost?" "Yes, a little" she admitted sheepishly. Rouva af Heurlin put an arm around her shoulders and told her how lucky she had been. They gathered around the open fire and Hannchen came in with a steaming hot coffee and handed it to her.

Rouva af Heurlin said:" Let me tell you of an old legend. In the weeks, when the sun is sleeping, and the days are black, a person is protected by a magic, which Ilmarinnen, the forest spirit granted tens

144

of thousands of years ago, to innocent people, who are in danger, which is not of their own making. The wolves are Manala's wolves. Manala, the spirit of the frozen sea in the North, and Ilmarinnen hate each other. Manala gets annoyed with Ilmarinnen's interference. He sends his wolves to teach the people a lesson." She continued: "These spirits are as old as the rocks in Suomi, and they are of the oldest geological formations known. That would make them one thousand four hundred million years old", she was told by the lady professor. "You have seen the spirit's magic tonight. We have never experienced it, and frankly we thought it was just a beautiful fairy tale, taken from the Kalewala".

Herra af Heurlin said: "There were warnings on the radio. The thermometer dropped to 42 degrees below zero. When it gets that cold, the wolves come down south for food."

Angela shuddered. It couldn't have been. It's impossible! Wolves! They only happen in Grimm's fairy tales.

They went upstairs to the window, and they saw strange green lights shining, in pairs of two in the inky darkness. Rouva af Heurlin turned off the light and there, in the snow, where a short while ago, she had planted her skis, were five grey shapes, howling and prowling and looking in through the window.

*

Christmas came and both Hannchen and Angela received a parcel from home, filled with traditional Christmas cookies. Weihnachtsplätzchen! There were some warm socks and mittens and an almighty scarf. Angela had knitted for herself a warm cap with a hole through which her ponytail fitted, but soon found that the icy wind penetrated right through the knitting. The woolly hat was useless and she often borrowed Lasse Sampo's hat. To her surprise, Lasse the foreman had given her a Christmas present, and when she unwrapped it she found it was a warm Finnish sheepskin hat with flaps, that could cover her neck, ears and forehead. She would not be cold again.

In February she learned that mother had finally been offered a job in the District Hospital in Lörrach, just outside Basel, the tight corner where Germany, France and Switzerland come together. She had

145

been working for an agency to look after sick people at their home and it was mostly night duty. The pay would be a lot better now and Mother moved with all her furniture into a slightly bigger flat in the Basler Strasse in Lörrach, such a long way away from Berlin and "Heimat". She suddenly realized that in spite of everything, her family was still hoping to return home one day to Berlin or Silesia. It would probably never be possible. Would the iron curtain ever come down?

Her thoughts were with her mother, wishing her well and hoping that this would not be too difficult for her. Everything was new; of her tight little family only little Tissi was left. Life could be harsh. Her mother wrote that this was her 23rd move in her life. Of those 23 moves, Angela remembered 11, until she left home to go to her first farm. The war had caused most of those moves and for her mother the First World War caused the other moves. She hoped that the work in the hospital, after all those years away, would not be too hard for her mother. Her mother was now 49 years old.

*

She could detect that the days were getting longer. There was a strange light around midday in the sky. People seemed to treat this like a sunny day. It lasted a few hours and grew rapidly every day. The time in the sauna was a new and exhilarating experience. Instead of diving into the lake, as she had done in Toppola, or into a big wooden barrel, which was filled with ice-cold water up to the neck, they just opened the door and dived into a huge snowdrift at 40 degrees below zero, rolled around in it naked, and then rushed back into the hot sauna. The prickling feeling was like peppermint melting on her skin. She couldn't get enough of it. She could not feel the cold when she rushed out of the hot sauna.

In February she experienced another Aurora Borealis. It seemed to illuminate the space beyond the stars, beyond the moon in viridian and yellow, pale orange, red and purple. They were shapes, moving and undulating as if somebody waved a space sized silk scarf in wondrous colours between heaven and earth. Nobody could explain what created this. Herra af Heurlin said it was Space Dust illuminated by the sun.

There were daily trips into the forest with the horses and sledges to fetch wood for the various households. The only fuel to keep the house warm and the kitchen stove lit for cooking and baking.

Angela also travelled to Helsinki once a week on her day off to make arrangements for her journey to England. She was determined to learn English and found a travel agent who would take some money each week towards her ticket. It was great fun to work out the route she would take. She didn't want to leave before she had been to Lappland and the patient lady in the shop offered her various prices and routes.

As she wandered down the Mannerheim Street, a passerby told her to rub her nose. She thought maybe she had a bogey and fished for her handkerchief, feeling very embarrassed. But as she wanted to wipe her nose, she could not feel it. In the shop window she discovered a white point in her face. She remembered! Gently she began to rub it until the blood returned. She went into the nearest department store to warm up. Whilst she was there she succumbed to a temptation, which she had fought against for quite some time. She went and bought a Finnish hunting knife and a pair of reindeer skin slippers, boots with upturned toes in the traditional Saami colours. She had to take something back from Finland, and these seemed to be the most useful items to have. For once she did not mind the money she spent.

17

Sibelius House

It had been a cold day and they worked hard in the forest, had a sauna afterwards and a good supper. Hannchen and Angela sat in their room and talked and made plans for the Spring, which was now evident with the extra daylight. When they left here, what would they like to do? Would they stay together and travel together? Hannchen could not be persuaded to travel to Lappland with her and she was also not interested to come to England. She insisted, that all she wanted to do was to go home after this. Hannchen had a home to go to. Her father had returned from the war and they were given a little compensation from the government to start a smallholding. It was a small farm, and therefore Hannchen felt she was needed at home. Angela did not have a place to go to. Her father never returned, and her mother now lived in a very small flat, big enough to visit but not to stay. She would have to build her life away from home. She would find a farm in England and continue her studies.

With all this talking, they felt hungry. It was very late and they sneaked downstairs into the kitchen to get some yoghurt, which was made new every day and stood on the back of the range in dozens of little bowls to mature. They thought they would have some bread and prepared two large sandwiches. They had just finished making them and wiping the kitchen top, when they heard steps. Like lightning they lifted their skirts and shoved their sandwiches into the top of their woollen stockings. As the door opened and Rouva af Heurlin came in, they picked up their yoghurt and said good night and went upstairs into their room, where they collapsed onto their beds, buried their faces in the pillows and succumbed to fits of giggles. Why were they hiding the fact that they had made sandwiches? It was silly really, because they never had the feeling, that the food they were eating was counted. It was a generous household. Angela felt just a little ashamed and realized, that her behaviour was childish, and hoped Rouva af Heurlin had not noticed. At the same time, both girls could not stop giggling.

By the first of March the Communist Party who were also the Union bosses announced a general strike. Suddenly Finland lay paralysed. No electricity, no public transport, no milk Lorries, no mail, no telephone, no oil for heating, no newspapers, no shopping. Nothing functioned. They had to rely entirely on self-sufficiency.

This meant they had to go out even further into the forest every day and bring home more wood than ever. Angela found herself on the sledge, driving the horses through snow which reached up to the horses belly and made it very difficult for them to walk, and the hard, icy crust of the snow cut the horses legs so badly they bled. The snowplough had cleared the road up to the forest. However since there was no more fuel, the tractor could not be used. Angela put rags around the horse's legs, but they lasted only a short time. Lasse Sampo had a bucket with some kind of salve ointment, which he smeared thickly onto the horse's legs. The bucket was hanging on the side of the sledge, so that the horses could be attended to constantly.

Day in day out they laboured. There were some workers on the farm, who were members of the Communist Party, and at first they refused to come out and help, which made work in the cow house and stable even harder. Angela hated Communism, it was Russian and they had been the enemy since she could remember. And anyway, the communist way of life did not function the way it should. If Finland became a communist country in the next election, she would leave the next day. Rouva af Heurlin thought, that even if the communists win, there would still be a large number of non-communists.

In order to buy the Finn's good will, the Russians had made a big gesture and finally vacated Porkkala in February. They had all gone to watch them leave. They were wearing beautifully cut smart long sheepskin coats which flowed like a skirt from the waist down, partly covering their long highly polished black boots. White sheepskin hats with their flaps tied up and a red star adorning the middle flap

149

above the eyes. They marched smartly onto waiting ships, which would take them over the Baltic to St. Petersburg. (Most Finns did not call it Leningrad) The Finish people stood watching quietly. As the last ship left, the roar of victory was great, and even though it was freezing cold, people had taken off their gloves and clapped. After that the communists worked hard to convince the Finns that Communism was best. Money changed hands and the unions were busy.

Working all day in the forest was hard and very cold work. They arrived in the morning and had to find mounds hidden in the deep snow and start digging. For that they used huge wooden shovels. By the time the pile of wood was sufficiently exposed, they stood up to the waist in a snow hole. From the body heat the snow dampend their trousers, which froze almost immediately and made their clothing quite stiff. Lasse Sampo would light a roaring fire of birch wood, which burned even when frozen and wet, and they all sat around the comforting heat on a snow bench and "defrosted". After a week the communist workers joined them, because they too needed wood, which Lasse had let them know they wouldn't get if they didn't help to get it out of the forest.

The af Heulins were at home since there was nothing working in Helsinki and there was no diesel for the cars. The work in the house was done by Mrs. af Heurlin and Hannchen was sent to help Angela and the men.

Everyday Angela and Hannchen suffered with cold feet. They hurt and in order to keep them warm they hopped around and stamped their feet. Then one day, as they all relaxed by the great fire, Angela said: "It is not so cold today", and Lasse looked at her and said: "It is colder today than it has been previously" and Angela replied: "But my feet aren't cold today". Lasse dropped his cigarette into the fire and come over and demanded she take off her boots.

"What, in this cold?" Lasse urged and started to undo her laces. When finally her feet appeared, she was appalled at the sight of them. They were totally white, and very thin. They looked like skeletons. Before she knew what was going on, the communist farmhand, whose name was Eemeli, and who had something of a far eastern Russian look about him, had emptied the sledge and Lasse had started to rub her feet gently with snow. Then they bundled her onto the sledge, Lasse continued to rub her feet, as the horses pulled the sledge as best they could. Hannchen sat behind Angela to support her. When they got home to his house, he shouted to his wife to bring a bowl with warm water, which came almost immediately, and now the torture began. Her feet returned to life and in no time her toes looked like short frankfurters, and her feet turned an angry red. They became swollen and hot. She was in total agony. Her feet itched so much, that she thought she would go mad. There was no relief and she just had to bear it. Two hours of agony and her feet slowly returned to normal, but she was left with chilblains. Lasse explained that if she had not mentioned that her feet did not feel cold, she would have lost her toes by the evening.

Two days later the thermometer showed 48 degrees below freezing. Since there was no wind, the cold did not feel so severe. It would have been impossible to go outside if there had been wind in this cold. She arrived at the cow house, and as she entered she saw that frozen breath phenomenon again, only this time it really looked like thick lace. Frozen air or frozen breath. It was quite unbelievable. Lasse said: "This is the coldest winter I can remember." The electric bulb turned the frozen lace into a myriad of rainbow crystals and as she entered it fell about like stardust.

Angela's daily task was to take the milk for the house back with her, carrying it on her back. Since the communist farmhands were back Angela and Hannchen were more in the house, and Angela's feet had to heal. She was helping Hannchen with baking bread and making the yoghurt. They also made their own butter and cheese, but when work got too much outside, then Lasse would come and pick her up with the sledge. She would take her skis and fasten them on the back of the sledge, in case she needed them and off they went into the forest. The most important winter job she found was forest work. But March is also the time when the sun is beginning to be active in the sky. The sky was blue and the snow reflected the light so brilliantly, they couldn't be outside without sunglasses. A different kind of fun time began. The snow was now not a hazard, but fun. The shadows were enormously long. She was in "The land of the long shadows" again. When she was a young girl, one of the first books she read had that title. It was about a doctor's family who spent two years working in Spitzbergen. She had devoured the book and always thought that one day she would go there. She had changed her mind. There was too much darkness in the winter even though there were heavenly colours in the sky and she enjoyed the snow and the ski jumping and lived it as the experience she gathered and the adventure it was supposed to be; she realized she was a child of the sun.

This spring of 1956 the newspapers were full of Grace Kelly and her fiancé from Monaco, Prince Rainier. She was such a beautiful woman and everyone wanted to have the same hairstyle, the same clothes and shoes. She was on all the covers of magazines, the covers of the writing paper pads she bought, cups and plates and calendars. It seemed that no one else existed but Grace Kelly and Prince Rainer. The funny thing was, Angela and Hannchen had never heard of her, had never seen a film in which she had acted. Exactly how big this principality of Monaco was, she didn't know either. Her Grandfather was a regular visitor to Monaco and stayed there with friends before the Second World War. That was all she knew about Monaco. She wasn't even quite sure where in the Mediterranean this place was.

Rouva af Heurlin said she was a film star from Hollywood and very famous. That she had had an affair with Frank Sinatra. Angela and Hannchen had not even heard of him either. Where had they been all their lives?

They all went to the cinema, because suddenly films in which she starred were running in all the theatres in Helsinki. They were in English with Finnish subtitles, and she thought what a wonderful country America was. Nothing was real where she had spent her life so far. In America one ought to be. Hannchen was far more down to earth. She told Angela, that it was a dream world. A world that everyone would like to live in, but it did not exist. That is why people go to the cinema, to get away from everyday drudgery. It made sense, but Angela had not been to the cinema to see American films. In Amberg and Heidelberg, she had seen 'Heimatfilme', films which were made in Germany about the romantic mountains and the people who lived there. This was different, and very new. Every weekend the young people went to Helsinki to see a film. One which really impressed her was "High Society!" And afterwards they would talk about it, as if it all had been for real. They would laugh and cry and even be a little afraid; there seemed to be an awful lot of murder cases in America, "Dial M for murder" was especially sinister. Her first Westerns upset her. She found herself siding against the Indians. It was Hannchen who said, that the Indians were not the badies; the intruders were the badies, the people from Europe, who took the land away from the Indians. Angela felt ignorant and uninformed. What did she know about anything? She knew Geography and History, but the importance of what happened after Columbus discovered America, she had no idea. She had learned about the Spanish and how they had killed all the natives in Middle and South America. But the Americans would never do such a thing? Or would they? As a child, when the Americans came to Bavaria, she learned about the Black Americans. She had always wondered how these Africans got to America in the first place, but did not bother to get to the bottom of it. And why, as American soldiers, they were second class soldiers? She noticed that but left it at that. Was it because she was so young and had herself been through a horrendous war, and was now just busy to live her life? Could the good, righteous Americans, who saved Europe from the Nazis, have such a gruesome and black past? Then she learned of the Ku Klux Klan and could not believe that the occupying forces of Germany, who supposedly found such horrendous death camps in her country, could behave similarity in their own country? It was all very puzzling and so difficult to understand. So two faced and untrustworthy.

One Sunday afternoon Gerhard and a friend arrived on skis. Their farm was about 15 km distant from their own place. Angela and Hannchen were very pleased and invited them in for coffee and cake. They were both from North Germany. Gerhard was tall and handsome and smoked a pipe. She had almost forgotten him, since he hadn't been in touch since Christmas. They enquired about the ski jump, because that was the reason in the first place why they came.

Angela was a little disappointed, but they went to the ski jump and Angela did a little showing off. She just could not help it. Gerhard and his friend were simply too tall and lanky to be able to do it. Stiff and awkward they fell off the jump into the deep snow just below the wooden structure and that was that. They tried a few times, even though Angela gave instruction, when it came to launch themselves, they just fell off the jump and the snow hole became deeper and deeper. The children who had come along with them laughed and Gerhard gave up and lit a pipe.

They met up in Helsinki again as they had done before Christmas and went to concerts and the cinema, and did a lot of sight seeing.

Then came the cross-country marathon, which started several kilometres outside Helsinki and finished on the outskirts of the city. They put their names down and paid a little fee. Angela had no idea what was expected of her, but Gerhard explained, that all she had to do was ski across the countryside like mad, just like she does when she skied to the jump or to the post office, and just keep going. It would be easy. Just don't let anybody overtake you. Angela grinned:" I'll try", she said.

Gerhard and Angela arrived in good time for the marathon and enjoyed the camaraderie of the other skiers. She was nervous and excited, but at the same time very confident. She was fast and strong. It was very cold, but the sun shone and the sky was blue. She had her sunglasses on, because the light was blinding. She looked around and found that there were people of all ages. Some looked really professional and were wearing neat ski suits. She didn't have any of that, just her normal warm things she wore in the forest.

"Well", she thought, "I am here for my pleasure. It doesn't matter if I am not amongst the first to arrive." But she was ambitious.

And then they were off. Hundreds of them and she realized that, since she was placed in the middle somewhere, she had to overtake a lot of people. She had to be careful not to get tangled up in the melee with the other skis and sticks. Her confidence left her. What a fool she was to think she could even vaguely compete with the native Finns. They had a certain stride, and a very strong push with the arms and sticks. She concentrated on somebody in front of her and followed him push by push, not losing him. That's good, she thought, but very soon her chest hurt from breathing the icy air. Never mind, just carry on, carry on, carry on. She got very hot, but did not stop. She must not stop. If she did she would never catch up. She did not look where Gerhard was. She just concentrated on the feet in front of her. Slide – slide – slide. Right foot and left arm forward, left foot and right arm forward. A steady rhythm! Then she got into a sort of trance, where everything happened automatically, and a surge of strength and happiness overcame her. I can do anything, she felt as if wings had grown on her back. She left the spoor behind the man and overtook him. She glanced sideways at him. He was at least 50. Don't be too proud, one day you will be fifty. But now is my time. It is so easy! She slid along effortlessly. They passed a place where they handed out drinks, but she did not stop, she feared she would never get back into the rhythm again. She was getting hot and felt she had to take off her gloves, but very soon put them on again without slowing her pace, because her hands were so cold in such a short time. She pulled back her sleeves and felt happy. The bit of exposed skin between her elbow and the ends of her gloves gave her enough cooling down to continue comfortably. She did not look left or right, just straight ahead. She loved doing this. Her first competition where she could show her newly learned skill on skis. There were difficult uphill areas where she had to spread her ski to stop her from sliding back. She concentrated hard not to step on top of her skis. It was hard and tiring. She remembered her cycling days in Bavaria. When it goes up, it must come down. And when the downhill came, she flew straight down, regardless. It was great. Everybody around her was doing the same thing. Determination was on all the faces. She wondered how fast she was going. The birch trees flew past her on either side. She was going really fast, she wished to know how fast. But she also realized that she was not overtaking anybody, that they were all going more or less the same speed. The professionals way ahead and the rest doing what they could.

The outskirts of Helsinki were in sight. There were skiers in front of her and she realised that no matter how hard she tried, she could not get any closer. But as Gerhard had said, don't let anyone pass you. But they had overtaken her and she could do nothing to stop it. However the man she had overtaken was way behind. She found another person she could follow and keep up with. She was now getting tired, breathless but she forced herself to breathe steadily and not to pant.

The first houses, all traffic was stopped. People cheering. Somehow she could not believe that she was actually here, and that some of the cheers were meant for her. It gave her extra strength to overcome her tiredness. She was so full of happiness and joy. She wished her family were here to cheer her. She was having such fun.

Then suddenly, there were no more skiers in front of her and as she looked about her, she realised that she had come through the finish. Slowly she came to a halt. Now she heard herself breathe, more like gasping for breath. Somebody came up to her with a hot drink. Gratefully she took it and carefully sipped it. It was very hot. She pulled down her sleeves again and when she pulled them over her metal watch, she felt something soft and not very nice. When she looked, she saw that her metal strap had frozen the sweaty skin of her wrist and she had pulled all the skin off. The woman who handed her the drink saw what had happened and guided her to the first aid tent. She was told off for having pulled her sleeves up to expose her arms. The first aid person shook her head and bandaged her wrist. It is deceptive, when there is no wind. It seems to be warmer than it actually is.

Then the list of the first fifty was put up. Her number was not there but it came up with the next 50. She was below the hundred out of hundreds! Where was Gerhard? She looked around. Then she spotted him coming up the hill. He was gasping and between gasps said: "I should give up smoking my pipe. Did you win?" Angela looked at him, was he joking? "No, off course not, I was in with the first hundred, and I am happy". She jumped into the air. She felt strong, happy and that life was wonderful. Gerhard was stuffing his pipe. She said, didn't you say you should give up smoking the pipe? He grinned at her and coming close to her ear he said: "tomorrow I shall stop smoking". His breath stank of stale tobacco. She turned away.

The strike had long finished and everything was back to normal. She had taken a lot of money to the travel agent. Her trip was now paid for to Rovaniemi, Kilpisjärvi and Hammerfest, down to Oslo. She had to save up for the rest of the journey. Bine, her sister had managed to get her a place at the children's home where she worked. She was determined to learn English, and did not mind what sort of work she did to learn it. She had agreed to stay with the af Heurlins until the end of May. Now this time was approaching and she had not saved all the money she needed. She spoke to Lasse Sampo about it and he said: "My cousin is expecting a baby, and I am sure she would like to have you for a few of months." Angela went to Rouva af Heurlin and asked if she could leave a little earlier, and explained why. Rouva af Heurlin was very nice about it and even said she would miss her. Before she got ready to leave, her boss had helped her to compose the job application for the Children's home in England. Angela's English was terrible. She new a few words but could not form sentences. Rouva af Heurlin promised to forward any mail that might arrive from England, plus the working permit, which she needed to work there.

On the first of May everyone in Suomi got ready to celebrate spring. This is a genuine Spring holiday. Nothing to do with work, like in Germany it is called "Spring Bank Holiday" "Tag der Arbeit". But in medieval times it was a Spring Festival, and here it was still celebrated as such. Angela had no idea what to be expect. All the Students young and old put on their students caps, spring clothing, even though it was still bitterly cold, but sunshine and spring air was overpowering after this long and dark winter. There was laughter and happiness, craziness and games. Students filled the streets, wandering about arms entwined in wonderful friendship and camaraderie, shouting to others and singing, meeting old friends. The cafés were open and people sat outside, there were Summer picnics in the parks, people sitting on blankets as if it was truly warm. And nobody seemed to be cold, untouched by the icy winds. Angela watched happily with Gerhard as they walked through town, down Mannerheimintie into Alexanderinkatu and up to the Cathedral, where they bought a sausage and roll and sat on the steps and ate it. The happy mood was so infectious and by the time they got home in the afternoon, they had driven out the winter mood.

There was a farewell party, Hannchen stayed two more weeks before she left to go back home. Gerhard came over and invited her to stay at his house in Schleswig Holstein, in a place called Sörup. She agreed and thought it was not so far from Esbjerg, from where she would embark to go to Harwich. Wasn't life fantastic?

Lasse Sampo came and picked her up to take her to Hämeenkyrö near Järvenpää.

The family was young and they were managing an estate in a birch forest. Angela thought it was very beautiful. Spring was heavily in the air, quite wonderful after that endless and dark winter. She was so aware of the light, the sunshine. It was brighter than she could remember.

They had a small farm, a big garden and a lot of forest work. Her boss's name was Sirkku Linnainmaa, and her work included everything, which happens on a mall farm. Children, cooking, working in the stables and milking. One of her daily tasks was to get the horse before a small cart and take logs and milk, water and eggs to a big house, hidden in the birch forest. The name of the villa was called "Ainola".

For two weeks she had been delivering the items daily and never seen anybody. Then her curiosity got the better of her and she asked Sirkku who lived there.

Sirkku smiled and said:" Our very own Jean Sibelius. He is very old, and not very well. We look after him". Angela was dumbfounded. The one who wrote this wonderful music? It occupied her thoughts all day. She would like to speak with him, but would she dare? Then one day, the housekeeper opened the door and asked for some extra eggs. "Did they have any, and if so could she bring them the next day." Angela took the opportunity to ask if it would be possible to see Herra Sibelius one day. She was a German student on the farm and would like to visit. But she did not want to intrude.

Just as the housekeeper wanted to say something, a voice behind her said:" who is it?" The housekeeper told him that it was the girl from the farm who delivers the wood and the milk. He came up behind her and asked Angela to come in. Shyly she entered. What was she to talk about, she had been too forward, and she was not prepared. But she needn't have worried. He was a man of middle height with serious, sculptured features and a huge forehead with no hair at all on his head. They went into the good room, and she noticed that it was all natural wood and rag rugs, a big fireplace in the middle of the room where her huge birch wood logs burned. It

158

was very cosy. He sat down and asked her to sit opposite him on a rocking chair. He asked all the questions and almost immediately asked her where she was from.

"I am from Germany, born in Berlin, but after the war I grew up in Bavaria". This was the standard sentence she had ready when people asked this question.

"I know Berlin well, I have spent quite a lot of time there, and Vienna, my second home", he said and then he spoke to her in German. Almost fluent with a very pleasant accent. He complemented her on her Finnish and said that it is not often that foreigners learn the "Suomenkieli, (Finnish language) they learn Swedish instead, because Finnish is such a difficult language to learn. She explained how it came about without offering her a choice as to which language to choose. She told him of her first placement and said, although it was hard, she would not miss it for the world, because she learnt so much, and she meant not only the language. Having been placed so deeply into the wild remote Finnish countryside, gave her memories she would treasure for ever.

Then he asked her if she played an instrument and she explained that all she ever learnt was the recorder and that not very well. No time no money no room for a piano. He only said: "I understand! The war! You were a child during the war?" And then he asked her to tell him her story how she ended up in Regensburg from Berlin.

The housekeeper brought coffee and some biscuits. They talked for a long time and Angela never felt embarrassed or lost for words. She thought what a great and wonderful man he was. She got up and said she really had to go back to work. They would wonder where she had got to. And he said: "You must come again before you leave". She felt great joy. He likes me, he likes my company. She felt proud. He made her feel completely at ease, as only great men can.

Angela only learned about his music since she had come to Finland, and a better description by music of a country she could not imagine. Listening to it she could see and feel the raging icy winter storms, the deep orange red midsummer night sun glistening on the water, the cracking cold when trees can sound like thunder in the extreme cold, the boom of the ice when it breaks asunder in the

159

spring, the dancing northern lights displaying unearthly colours in space, and the soft, quiet and gentle summer with the still waters lapping against the shores of the lake by the sauna. Even the humming of the awful mosquitos she could hear in the music. The huge black green Finish firs dotted with the spring green of the gentle giant birch trees with the snow white bark, and whose leaves turn to bright gold in autumn. Where the light reflects off the thousands of lakes and makes it a land of light, just like in the winter in the dead of dark night the light of the moon and brilliant stars reflect off the snow, giving light where there shouldn't be any.

His music is an ode to Finland, his beloved land.

Sirkku's family planned a trip to Lappland to see the midnight sun, and Angela was invited. She got the feeling that the trip was in her honour. They set off in the middle of June in a VW camper van and a tent. The children and the new baby came along and Angela had a lot to do. The journey took them past lakes and through endless forests, until they got to the polar circle and the forests receded.

When they finally got to Karigasniemi where the sun is mirroring in the river Tenojoki at midnight in the dead North, they found lots of people had the same idea. Hundreds were gathered on the hill to watch the spectacle. It is not just a bright glow, as she had observed in the South of Finland, but the sun full and glowing. A solid red ball, it descends as if to set, and then it swims along the horizon on top of the water for an hour and then it rises again. What a sight! Looking south all is deep purple darkness except on the sky high above their heads, where the glow is just like a fire reflection she used to observe during the war when the cities burned. This was a fantastic farewell performance of a country so pure and so wild, were the elements were untamed and yet could be very mild and gentle. Angela said her quiet farewells and promised to come back, one day.

18

Gerhard

The af Heurlins with the children, Lasse Sampo and his wife and the Linnainmaas came to see her off at Helsinki airport. She felt very sad, but of the students who arrived the year before, she was the last to leave. She had become so fond of the land and its people. Now in the middle of their short and exciting summer, she had to leave. She had already shipped her enormous suitcase to Gerhard's address in Schleswig Holstein. On this trip she just had a few things in a rucksack and a duffel bag, because she wanted to be free for the adventure. She stepped into the small aircraft and took her seat. Through the little window she saw her friends waving. She felt sad. It had been a most wonderful time, but the sad thing was, that she could not stay. Life was going on elsewhere too and it would then be just ordinary here. She had to finish her years and then take her masters. The plane taxied off and she lost sight of them. Next stop Rovaniemi. She did not take her eyes of the window. Glistening lakes and endless forest made the most incredible patterns. How was it all formed?

In Rovaniemi she stayed in the youth hostel for two nights while she explored the town. Wooden houses and birch trees, a church. Like all Finnish people the faith up here was also Lutheran. It was a small town in the forest of pines and birches. Dreamy and quiet and the sun reflected on the water of the river. None of the roads were surfaced. In the long winters the roads would be surfaced with a layer of hard snow; there would not be potholes or dust.

The Samis wore the traditional clothing mostly red, yellow, green and the main colour blue, very colourful, woven trimmings bordering their wide skirts, the shoulders and fronts of the men's tunics, and women's jackets. They wore fur boots with upturned toes, decorated in blue, red, yellow and green. She supposed they dressed so colourfully, because in the winter the countryside lacks all colour whatsoever. She thought it beautiful and nearly bought a skirt in the small tourist shop, but then changed her mind. Where would she wear it, and she didn't really have the money to spend. She saw some tents on the outskirts of the little town. But they also seemed to live in the town. She could not quite work it out.

She checked her next page on her ticket booklet. A bus ride to Kilpisjärvi, the three-country corner. The mountains here where bare and it was obvious that they were shaped by something massive into strange, smooth forms. Again she stayed in the youth hostel and went with a lot of young people to the spot where one can be in three countries all at the same time. One foot in Norway, one in Sweden and a hand in Finland. The actual spot was in the lake because the border ran right through it. There was still snow on top of the mountains and the birch trees were stunted and short. She was well into the Arctic Circle and the midgets were a plague. A young man near her said: "When you look at the top of the mountain over there, imagine two to three kilometres of ice on top of it." No she could not imagine it. She looked up into the sky and then realised that it would not seem to be so high because where she stood now would also be hundreds of meters higher. That sort of weight would shape a mountain. She wondered if people lived on earth at the time and thought there must have been, but way in the south in Africa. It was all amazing.

She was glad to be back in the bus to escape the mosquitoes, which took her to Hammerfest. It was a long and tiring journey but the country was breathtakingly beautiful. Water, mountains, reflections, colourful sky, sun golden, orange silver and blue and so much green! Yet she felt strangely uncomfortable. The sun rose to about 10 o clock in the sky and skimmed along to three and then slowly went down again and floated along on the horizon until it rose again. It never came up any higher even though it was summer. Hammerfest was a small and very colourful fishing town right by the water in a lovely bay. The houses reflected in the still water of the sea, the sky was blue and the clouds dramatic. It all seemed pristinely clean. But it also reeked of fish. The houses were built for a long, dark winter, when everything was covered in snow it would probably be quite cosy and the bay out to sea frozen with a thick layer of ice. She imagined the people now with little huts over ice holes fishing through the ice. The town was built on a small strip of land between the mountain behind the town and the sea. The bay was full of fishing vessels and there were factories at the waterfront, probably to process all the fish. There were also lots of places where the fish was hung up to dry. Stockfish she thought. It was an interesting, sparkling and cold place at the edge of her world.

She had visited and fulfilled a wish, to visit to most northern town in Europe, and she supposed the birch trees got the very end bit of the Golf Stream which made them the most northern trees, and tourists admired their resilience which made them survive the dreadful winter. She would not return to this cold starkly amazing place.

With a different bus she travelled to Tromsö on winding roads through the mountains. The bus found roads around mountains and mostly along water, Fjords most likely. It was amazing, the clear water and the reflections again, but already the sun started to disappear at midnight and the feeling of being at the edge did not leave her. She spent two more nights in the youth hostel. She bought herself a ticket to go on a boat trip along a fjord, something she thought one should do in Norway. It was overwhelming in an eerie sort of way. She looked up to the tops of the mountains and imagined that they would go down under the water as deep as they were high above the water, or maybe even deeper. The water was so crystal clear and the reflections so pure, the sky in the water and the clouds. She was totally awed. Little houses looked as if they were glued onto the mountain sides and she wondered how people got to them. Flags were flying, probably announcing, we are home!

Her next ticket was a flight to Oslo. She did some sightseeing, and bought herself her first, most ridiculous pair of high heeled shoes she had ever owned in her life. It must have been the influence of all the Grace Kelly pictures she had seen. She simply had to have an elegant pair of heels, and had to wear them right away and found herself teetering about with her rucksack, determined to master an elegant walk. She visited the Viking museum and spent almost an entire day there. After half an hour the shoes ended up in the rucksack.

However, she got bored travelling on her own and without waiting for the day of her departure on the ticket, she went to the station on the spur of the moment and asked to alter the ticket for that day and got onto the next train. It was a long journey, and when she arrived in Flensburg, she rang Gerhard to say she would be on the next train to Sörup. He was at the station to pick her up. Her suitcase had been there a week already and they had such a lot to talk about. Gerhard had made a similar trip on his way home, except that he travelled through Sweden instead of Norway. She thought it would have been nice if she had had a travelling companion. It is always nice to share beautiful moments.

She spent ten wonderful days in Sörup and they went sailing in his boat on the Schlei. They cycled through Schleswig Holstein, she mowed his lawn whilst he had to help his father one day. And then she suddenly realized that his parents thought she might become his fiancé. She felt embarrassed. She had not given it a thought. They were the best of friends, pals even, but that was all. She wondered if Gerhard had such thoughts as well. Oh dear, did I give the wrong signals? On the day of her departure, they promised to write. They were such lovely honest people. He took her to the station, and there for the first time since she knew him, he kissed her on the mouth. He took his pipe out long enough to do that. She did not like the kiss. It tasted of stale pipe. What a pity. Very embarrassed, she departed for Esbjerg.

She boarded the ship and found her cabin. She had very little money but Gerhard had given her a big bag of apples, and his mother had sneaked some sandwiches and a bottle of lemonade into it. She could not afford to go into the dining room for supper, so she sat happily on deck and munched apples. Soon the North Sea turned violent and the ship rolled about and the passengers were hanging around being sick. She was glad not to have had any dinner, because now she saw this expensive dinner splashed almost everywhere she walked. She felt sorry for the limp forms hanging over the rail making dreadful noises every time the ship sank back into a trough.

Thick fog was closing in and the foghorn on their ship made eerie mournful sounds with regular intervals.

There was a young man, who kept watching her. She had a book and was reading, but at the same time watched him. She took a sandwich and the bottle of lemonade and had a late little meal and then went to bed. She could not sleep, the ship was rolling around and the foghorn blew constantly. Every minute the boom sounded from her ship and was answered by a muffled boom from a ferry hidden in the dense fog. They did not make any headway, just rode the waves, and at dawn, when she could not stand it in her cabin anymore, she went out on deck and could not even see the length of the ship, the fog was so thick.

Then she saw the young man again. Tall, blond, blue eyes, broad shoulders, very handsome! As he spotted her looking at him, he smiled and came over. He spoke English and she was so embarrassed not to be able to answer, but not even understanding one word he said. She could feel herself blush, and lifted her shoulders as if to say:" sorry!" He said something in German, she could tell it was meant to be German, but she could not understand what it was he wanted to say. Soon they found a way of communicating and laughed a lot when they understood what the other was trying to say. It was such fun. They discussed the delay; the ship was already six hours late. He lived in London, and his father was a dentist. She explained that her father too had been a dentist. They had something in common. He told her that he had been visiting friends in Copenhagen. He worked in Africa in Tanganyika and so did they. He was home on a three month leave. She understood the gist of what he said and thought with a little concentration English wasn't that difficult. The trouble was, she could not tell him of her adventure. She could not speak English and he did not understand German. When they finally arrived in Harwich, he helped her with her heavy suitcase.

On entering the train carriage, she was shocked. Never, not even after the war in Germany had she seen such filthy trains. The littler on the floor was horrendous. Orange peels, fag ends and ash, paper and paper cups, bags of half eaten crisps, eggshells and apple cores, empty cigarette packets, chocolate wrappers. Just terrible! And then

165

she thought, this sort of litter would not have been possible in Germany after the war, because all these items on the floor would not have been available. And now they were still far too precious to be thrown out. The young man apologized to her about the filth.

Looking out of the window every thing was black. The houses, the cars, everything! Why was everything so black? She asked her companion and was told that it was soot from the many chimneys. Every house had a coal fire in every room to keep warm and the smoke turned everything black. Unbelievable! Didn't they have central heating? Her companion, whose name was Mike, explained it to her with the help of little drawings. They were very neat and the stroke of his automatic pencil was very assured. His handwriting was pleasing too. His hands were well shaped. He had a deep voice, and it sounded as if it came from a sound chamber. She admired him, and quickly looked away.

When they arrived at the station in London he invited her to have a cup of tea and a sandwich. She had heard of this famous cup of tea.

They walked over to a strange stand in the middle of the station, which looked a bit like a tall music hall organ, very high up and the bar was about where her face was. The back of it was tall mirrors and lights, which reflected everything.

The female looked down to them from her dizzy height and said: "What yer havin' ducky?" at least that is what Angela thought she heard. The sandwich, which Mike ordered was pure white bread and there was something soapy inside, which had the same shape as the bread. The bread had no proper crust. It looked as if it was steamed, not baked. She wondered what the soapy bit was, it had a pleasant taste, but the bread was awful, stodgy even. She had never in her life seen bread like it. It was also perfectly square. Bread is not square? The cup of tea went down well, in fact the whole lot was satisfying, even though it was a very strange combination.

Then she said she would have to go to Paddington Station to continue her trip to Kidderminster. Mike offered to find out about the train and also said he would ring up to say she was delayed. It turned out that they were informed when they came to pick her up the day before, and she was not on the train. At the time she should have arrived, she had still been on board the ship.

There were nearly five hours before her train left and Mike hailed a taxi. She had heard a lot about the uniqueness of English taxis and that they drive right into the station, and that everybody drives on the wrong side of the road. They had done in Sweden, but there the steering wheel was on the same side as in Germany. It was strange and exciting. Her big suitcase was secured on an open space next to the driver and then Mike ordered the taxi to take them to the Houses of Parliament, Big Ben, Trafalgar Square and Buckingham Palace and a lot more wonderful sights. However, the blackness of all the buildings was overpowering. England seemed to be black. She had been spoilt by the clean purity of Finland, the clean houses, the pure white snow, the birch green in the spring and the fact that the snow never got dirty no matter how long it lay there. Hardly any dust in the houses. Here, there was litter everywhere on the street, wherever she looked.

With twenty minutes to spare, they arrived at Paddington Station and Mike carried her suitcase to her seat. It was the same story. Filthy dirty compartment. The upholstery was beautiful, thick lush pile reminded of elegant times past, but where her head would rest, was a thick layer of grease. She could not imagine how it would get there, except that the men's hair was dreadfully greasy. Mike's hair was blond, clean and shiny waves curled over his forehead. She said goodbye to Mike and thought: " I shall never see him again". She waved and thought what a pity. I like him. I like him very much.

She sat bolt upright in her seat, careful not to touch the filthy bit behind her and finally, very tired arrived at Kidderminster, where a member of staff from the children's home came to pick her up in a jeep.

When she got to 'Sunfield', a Rudolf Steiner home for children with learning difficulties and some severely mentally handicapped, her sister Sabine was waiting. As soon as the jeep stopped, she came flying down the steps and they hugged. It was wonderful to be together again.

Bine took her straight to her room. There were a couple long wooden huts with a corridor all the way through, which divided the rooms either side. A bed, a wardrobe, a table and chair made up her room, and a communal bathroom and loo in the centre of the corridor completed her new home. There were some sandwiches and a thermos on her table. The bread was brown and looked delicious and nourishing. It was a long time since she had something decent to eat. Bine sat down and wanted to know about her trip. Angela had bought her a little souvenir from Helsinki, a silver Kalewala necklace and broach. Bine was pleased with her gift and they chatted late into the night, whilst Angela unpacked. She had found a second wind and didn't feel tired any more. She told Bine about Mike and that it was such a pity, that she would never see him again. The young people crowded in at the door, wanting to have a look at the "new one."

Two weeks into her stay, a letter arrived for her from Africa. It was a flimsy blue affair, which she had to open carefully so as not to tear into the writing. It was from Mike. His name was Michael Malone and he was in Africa. She had to ask Bine to translate, because Bine had learned English whilst she had learned Finnish. It turned out that he had copied her address from her label on the suitcase and he explained that he worked in Africa for the British and American Tobacco Company and had been to Denmark to visit friends who were also working in Africa and on his way home was where we met. He told her how much he wanted to meet her again and he would be very pleased if she would answer this letter.

Bine helped her to answer it, but Angela felt she could not really tell Mike what she wanted to say in case Bine would laugh. She would have to learn pretty quickly to speak English. Waiting between letters was endless, and she felt so sorry that he was such a long way away. When on earth would she see him again? She should be realistic, probably never. In a letter she got two months later he included a photo of himself. She framed it and put it on a shelf above her bed, and went out to a local photographer and had one taken of herself and sent it to Africa.

Every morning, the staff of the children's home assembled after breakfast to discuss the world situation. What was on everybody's mind was the conflict over the Suez Canal. The British are bombing Cairo; Britain withdraws troops from the Suez Canal Zone. Colonel Gamal Abdul Nasser elected as the new president of Egypt, and nationalizes the Canal. Israeli forces invade Egypt, and the English and the French occupy the Suez Canal. Every morning a new bit of news would be added and Angela took note for the first time since the WWII of politics and what was going on in the world. She couldn't imagine why they bombed Cairo! This is a precious town, stacked with antiquities, treasures from the Pharaoh tombs. Why bomb? She had not heard that there was a war? What was everybody after?

In Russia, the Premier Nikita Khrushchev denounces Joseph Stalin two years after his death. Wow, that is good, and about time. Why did they have to wait for that killing machine to die a natural death?

And then closer to her former home Regensburg, just along the Danube into Hungary the Hungarians are rising against the Communists, and the Russian tanks drive in to crush and kill. So Khrushchev isn't much good either. He too is a Communist bully.

Just four years earlier the Berliners tried the same and were driven back. That was the 17th June 1953, when the workers on the project of the Stalin Allee demanded democratic freedoms. A peaceful demonstration always ended in a bloodbath, when the red army moves in for the kill.

So life started in England, a complete change from what she had been doing these last five years.

Mr. Braithwaite's turn to read the news and he says that the United Nations call for a cease-fire in Egypt will send in their emergency forces to enforce it.

And France gives independence to Morocco and Tunisia.

169

19

England and Ireland

She worked six days in a row and had one day off. It was always the same day, a day in the week and in the beginning Bine had the same day and they went off for the day hitch hiking to see the countryside around them. They even managed to go all the way to Aberystwyth in a day and back out on the various milk Lorries and home as best they could. They earned thirty shillings a week pocket money and Angela had to be very careful with her money. She would have to save in order to find her fare to her next destination. Very few weeks into her stay at Sunfield, she realized, that this was not for her. It was a beautiful place and the people were nice and the days away when they travelled were full of adventure, but the work was not satisfying. She missed the animals and the freedom of the farms, the open air and even the hard work.

She was amazed to see the children and their various handicaps. Some seemed not to be on this earth, it was as if their physical bodies were here, but their spirits dwelt elsewhere. Some little ones with downs syndrome, had so much love to give, she could only return their love. She got used to these children and their habits. They spent their life there until they became teenagers and then they went to a different home. Here only the babies and children up to 15 were accepted. Whilst she was there, a cardboard box arrived with a baby inside. It was shipped by air from Africa, where the parents of the child lived and worked, to join two, who already lived here and had arrived in the same way as this one did. Angela thought that if parents can only have children, who are handicapped, than they should stop after the second and have no more. All three seemed to be just twisted bodies, unaware of anything that was going on around them. It was so sad. But since it was a Rudolf Steiner home, she learned that, no matter how handicapped these children were, their souls and spirits were unaffected, and that they had chosen this life whilst still in the spiritual world, in order to learn or experience something which would help them in their next incarnation and wipe out something which had happened in the previous one. It was all very interesting, and she watched with amazement how some of the children could learn to play the recorder a little, and were made to realize what a terrific achievement it was for them. She watched the little plays they performed on stage, and their pride, when they did well.

Two months into her stay, Bine returned to Germany. Angela felt terribly lonely and out of place. A Swiss girl who had just arrived attached herself to Angela and they went off together on their days off. Angela had learned a lot of English by now and could speak it fairly well. She was proud to be able to write to Mike without her sister's help. She learnt so quickly and efficiently because the staff at the home forbade everybody to speak in their native language among each other. Only English was allowed. Barbara, the Swiss girl, was homesick, and cried a lot. She was only seventeen years old. Angela mothered her a little and they had some wonderful trips, hitch hiking. Bine had showed her around, and now Angela showed Barbara around. Angela was now 20 years old.

In September, Angela had a week's holiday and decided to tramp down to Cornwall. She had her old Rucksack and one third of the old army tent, which she still used as a raincoat, by sticking her head through the window slit when it rained, and that covered her and her Rucksack adequately. She almost immediately had a lift from a lorry. The driver opened the door and said: "Where do you want to get to?" and she answered: "I want to get to Cornwall eventually, Lands End maybe?"

"Hop in, I am going to Falmouth", he grinned and she could see he had no top teeth at all. When he spoke he put his lower teeth onto his top lip to produce the f's and th's. She was fascinated by the way he spoke. He was very friendly and started to ask a lot of questions, and she found for the first time that the English have a weird fascination about the Germans and especially about the Nazis. He wanted to know about her experiences during the war. Nobody had ever asked her these questions. She found the English were strangely ignorant about what had happened, judging by the things her lorry driver came out with as fact. And he called the Germans Huns. She tried to explain, that the Huns where a race, who lived thousands of miles to the East of Europe, and where not even European and that one of their leaders was Ghengis Khan, and later his sons continued to raid and invaded Europe, and if the Germans and their eastern allies of the times had not stopped the invasion in the thirteenth Century, Britain as he knows it today, would not exist.

"Well," he said: "good thing we are all friends now". He invited her to supper in a lorry driver's café, and they had fish and chips. This was her first taste of this truly English food, and she liked it. When they were back in the lorry, he indicated the bed behind him and said: You go and have a good night, I wake you when we are in Falmouth". It was now night anyway, and she said: "What about you, don't you have to sleep?" and he said: "Not today, I have to be in Falmouth in the morning, but then I can sleep for two days"

She made herself comfortable and slept until dawn, when a bump woke her up. She opened the curtain into the driver's cabin, and saw that there was an accident in front of them, and the bump was her driver having to stop suddenly. On the roundabout ahead two cars had collided and the car in front of the lorry had stopped suddenly which made her driver step hard on the brakes. The accident was not a bad one, there was very little traffic on the road, and a police station couldn't have been far away, because already an English Bobby on a bike arrived, parked his bike on a lamppost and walked over to sort things out. In no time they were on their way again and still had two hours to go before they got to Falmouth. Just before they got there, he invited her again for a meal and they had bacon and eggs, fried bread and beans, a big pot of tea, toast and marmalade. He said: "You have been good company, and the long trip wasn't boring. It is quite lonely on these long trips." Angela was embarrassed but very grateful. She went over to the stand and bought a packet of Senior Service, because she had seen him smoke these cigarettes. He showed such pleasure over her little gift. They said their good byes and he pointed her onto the right road to Penzance, because she wanted to visit St. Michaels Mount.

She got there in no time at all, and walked over the causeway to the castle. The tide was way out, and she paid her one and six pence to get in and spent three hours walking through the castle and the gardens, all of which was much neglected. There was a hot dog stand and she bought her self a hot dog and a cup of tea for lunch and then took the little boat back to the dry land, because the tide had come back and the cause way had disappeared. She paid "thru pence" for the trip.

After standing on the road to Lands End for an hour with out seeing even one car, she went over to the other side and started to walk back to Marazion. There were no cars. She kept walking and at four in the afternoon, somebody stopped and gave her a lift as far as Truro. She asked if there was a Youth Hostel, and he pointed it out to her. Her Youth Hostel pass from Finland was still valid, and she had a comfortable night.

The signpost said St. Austell and she placed herself on a spot where it would be easy for a car to stop and started thumbing. But there were so few cars, maybe one in fifteen minutes. She started to walk and pick blackberries in the hedges. They were big, juicy and sweet. She was glad it did not rain.

She heard the car long before it came around the corner and she turned to get ready to thumb. The car stopped immediately when she was spotted. An elderly couple occupied the car. She asked where they were going and they answered: "Kingsbridge". She got her map out to see where it was and said; yes she would like to come if it was all right.

"It would be a pleasure," the man said, and Angela dropped her rucksack onto the back seat and sat down beside it. Then came the questions, how far had she come, where had she stayed the night. What had she seen so far, had she been to Lostwithiel? No she hadn't. "May we invite you? We were going to have lunch there, and it would make us happy." She was amazed at how generous and friendly the English were to a complete stranger.

They were telling her now about their lives, and that they had spent a lifetime in India, in the British Army, he had the rank of colonel, and had only recently retired to Kingsbridge, and they were now getting to know their own country in their retirement. They had spent most of their lives in India, their children went to boarding school in England, but had returned to India, and would probably live there until they retired. For Angela this was a life she could not imagine. "Why could you not retire in India?" she asked.

"Everybody comes home when they retire. You can't mix with the natives. Most of our acquaintances from India now live in Devon. We have so many friends here." Angela wondered about the children. Did the parents know them at all? Was it important to know your children when you are in the army? She remembered to have heard the saying about the British: "To keep a stiff upper lip" Does that mean to have no emotions? To feel love but not show it?

The lady turned round in the car and looked at her:" You have an accent my dear, where are you from?" And Angela said: "I am from Germany, born in Berlin".

The colonel laughed and his wife said:" Good heavens, from Germany!" as if this was something extraordinary. And then she said something even stranger: "Do you know, we have never been abroad."

Angela was dumfounded. Where was India if not abroad? The English are a strange lot. There was certain arrogance, not offensive though. There was also ignorance about Europe, as if it was further away than India, a mysterious place where they spoke a truly foreign language and where only barbarians live. They knew everything about their colonies, and yet a few kilometres across the Channel to them it was a land they knew little about except that they won the war seemingly single handed. They kindly took her to a Youth Hostel near Kingsbridge and there they said their good byes. They exchanged addresses and promised to write. She later sent them a postcard from Sunfield, but never had a reply.

The next day she found herself on a road where there was no traffic at all and she had to walk. All day she walked and finally came to a place called Torcross. She bought herself a bottle of orange juice and some fish and chips and then looked around for somewhere to sleep for the night. The best thing was to roll herself up in her tent plane and sleep on the gravel on the beach, tucked well under the rocks, high above the tide line.

She slept lightly, but enjoyed the stars above. It was quite peaceful, and the waves were gentle, but she heard the pebbles move beneath her.

At dawn she got up and since there was nothing where she could get herself something to eat, she went onto the road and started to walk. She walked all the way along Slapton Sands to Stoke Fleming, got herself some bread at the bakery and two bottles of milk and ate that, then walked on and somewhere got a lift into Dartmouth. She did some sightseeing and had a sausage roll and some tea. Late afternoon she took the ferry across to Kingswear and stepping off the ferry somebody called to her: "Where are you travelling to?" She looked around and saw a handsome young man. She had two more days before she had to be back at work and thought I can't dally I have to get going.

She said: "I have to be back near Birmingham in two days time". He said: "I am going that way, but I would like to see a little whilst I am travelling." They studied the map. It turned out that he was Canadian and had hired this car and was travelling around anywhere he liked just to see Britain, the home of his parents.

She was very hungry and had very little money left. She said:" I would like to buy some bread and milk and maybe some cheese for lunch. I haven't eaten anything other than blackberries. Do you want anything?" He grinned and said: "I can see that", but no thank you I had lunch." She wondered what he meant. They stopped outside a dairy and she went inside. There was a mirror on the opposite side on the wall, to make it look as if there was more bread on the shelf than there was and she spotted herself, blackberry moustache and all, and as she grinned, she discovered her teeth to be black as well. She got out her handkerchief and started wiping. Then it was her turn to be served and she got a small round loaf, two bottles of milk and a small lump of cheese.

Back in the car, she asked if he minded that she ate and he said:" go right ahead." She was starving, and the food tasted fresh and delicious. The milk had a thick layer of cream on the top. Satisfied, she got the map out. They were travelling along the seafront and headed towards Torquay. The sun was shining and the flowers were out and she thought she was somewhere in a southern country. Pines

175

and palm trees, blue sea, elegant houses. She was charmed and they got out and had a cup of tea in the pavilion.

They got back into the car and travelled along the coast to Exeter and north towards Taunton. They stopped at Glastonbury and Wells. Late in the afternoon they got to Bath. He said he was going to find a hotel, and Angela said to let her out near a campsite and they would meet in the morning to continue their journey. He offered to pay for her room but she declined.

She walked a little way out of town and then when there was no one in sight, she climbed over a gate and went into a field, and found a sheltered spot in the hedge. She ate the rest of her bread and cheese, washed it down with the rest of her milk, rolled herself into her tent plane, used the rucksack as a cushion and went to sleep.

In the morning her hair and the outside of the tent was covered in dew, but inside she was dry. She washed her face in the dew she gathered from the long grass and then went back on the road to see if her lift would turn up. She came past a dairy again. She could do with something other than milk and bread, but she was very short of money and had to get back. Tonight she should be back and there should be something to eat. So for now, bread and cheese and milk would do fine.

As she came out of the shop, she saw her lift about a hundred yards ahead of her. What a nice guy! She got into the car and they went to see the roman baths. He said that this was an important item his mother had written down for him to visit, should he be anywhere near Bath. Angela was impressed. She had not been aware that the Romans had come so far. She grew up with Roman history, because after all Regensburg, Castra Regina was a Roman city, and the medieval town had been built onto the roman ruins. Most of the foundations were Roman; even the cathedral had an old Roman temple incorporated within the church. But in Regensburg there was nothing like these baths. There were roman baths elsewhere in Germany; they always seemed to find the hot wells, but they were all still in use, now expensive spa's.

She told her companion about Regensburg and found he was interested. She had also learned his name. He was called Jean Paul.

By ten thirty, they were back in the car travelling towards Gloucester. They visited the cathedral and stopped at a fish and chip stand and had a greasy meal with lots of vinegar. He delivered her to her door by five thirty in the evening. They exchanged addresses, and would write to each other for four years, but never met again.

Barbara had changed. She did not talk to Angela any longer and did not want to share the same day off. Angela thought it strange and could not work out what had happened in the week she was away. What had she done? When she tried to find out, she got the cold shoulder from everyone. In the end she cornered Barbara and was told: "I don't know why I was ever friends with you. You are German. I don't have German friends", and she turned her back on Angela and left. Angela stood there not really understanding what she had heard. She felt like the tolerated enemy. But most of the young workers here were German. There was one girl from Madagascar and one from Kenya a few English people but most were from Germany.

She shrugged her shoulders and thought that there were too many women here. She had never been anywhere, where women ran the entire show.

There were some men, but they worked independently in the craft shops. Angela went to the various workshops in her lunch hour to see

what they were doing and got stuck in the wood working shop. Woodcarving! That was it! She learned to carve and Mr. Braithwaite was a good teacher and very happy to have her. She spent every spare moment, even some of her days off on the wood carver's bench. Her most ambitious project was the Sistine Madonna by Rafael. She was very proud with her achievement. She also learned how to sharpen her tools. Her woodcarving of the Madonna ended up in Regensburg. She gave it to her old teacher and she put it up in the "*Christengemeinschafts Raum*", the Anthroposophical Christian Community Chapel where it is on display to this day.

Bine had not yet come back to Sunfield. She wrote that she has lost her new work permit which had been sent to her from England. Now she had to wait for another one. Angela felt very unhappy and out of place. There were too many women here running everything and she found they were bitchy and frankly quite stupid with their petty attitude. She was used to working with men and they were straight and said what they meant and did not bitch behind her back. She kept to herself and stayed aloof of the gossiping which went on, and then one day a girl looked her up in her room whilst she was cleaning and listening to some music. She had found an old gramophone player and some records and had some Beethoven playing. Marie Louise knocked on the door.

"May I come in? You have such lovely music." Angela invited her in and they sat down and chatted. Angela had seen Marie Louise in the house and at mealtimes but never spoken to her. She seemed to avoid other women as well. And now she was here and wanting to talk with Angela. They spent the entire midday break together and then walked up to the house together and soon in the days to come they became great friends. They went to the woodworking shop together and travelled on their days off together and Angela found out that Marie Louise had been there two years already and had applied for a third year and would probably stay. Angela told her that she would not stay, that she was unhappy and would try to find another job somewhere. That she could not bear all this backbiting and bitchiness which was going on. Marie Louise agreed and said that the only way to survive these women was to keep to yourself and not mix with them. Do your job and that's it.

On the Sunfield Committee was a young man who had put a notice on the board and interested what it might say, Angela went and read it. It said: "There is a vacancy in Ireland for a young woman to help a family in the house and garden, and to help in the young business of organic flour milling etc. Telephone number..."

Angela went after him and asked for more details. It turned out that his sister had two small children and needed help and her husband who was starting a business needs help with milling organic grain into wholemeal flour which is being sent by post to customers all over Britain. Angela told him she was very interested and would he arrange it.

So six months after arriving in England, she left happily never to return. She got the train to Liverpool and the ferry to Ireland and the train from Dublin to Thomastown. On that train journey she got to know the Irish for the first time. The train stopped and nothing happened. People seemed to be quite alright and not worried; Angela felt that she wanted to find out. There was no station; it was the open countryside and only one track. What happens if another train comes along? She went through the train and found the conductor and the engine driver having tea. They told her that it was teatime and would she like a cup. She declined and laughed. She went back to her seat. The teacups were a bit black and greasy, and she did not believe that the train stopped just because they thought it was teatime.

Anthony, her boss, was waiting patiently at the station. He too was not worried. Trains are always late and this was Ireland. She met Eve and Anthony, their two children, Gabriel a little girl of two and Toby, a little boy of 8 months. She marvelled at their normality, and the things they were able to do. In Sunfield she had got so used to the fact that the children there were unable to do most things and certainly could hardly speak. She loved the family instantly and they loved her and she was really needed. They had not lived there for very long. They had moved there from Forest Row in England to start a new life. Eve's mother's sister had a large estate in Kilmurry and Eve and Anthony built their house in the grounds of the estate. There too was the mill to grind the flour. It was an ancient working mill still producing stone ground flour. She loved the old stone walls and the wooden gear-wheels. However the waterwheel did not work anymore and it was nowall driven by electricity. She met Eve's aunt, the lady of the manor whose love was horses. She had the most beautiful horses in her stables and Angela asked what she was doing with them. Was she breeding them? And the Lady said: "Some of these do not belong to me; they belong to the Queen of England." Angela was astonished. "The queen?" "Yes", she said," I only train them for the queen so she can ride them side saddle for the Trouping of the Colours. At the rehearsals I represent her in London". Angela looked at the horses and shyly asked if it was possible for her to ride one of the Kilmurry horses? Off course you can, I presume you can ride? Angela nodded her head. Yes, she said, I have ridden before. So she was introduced to the riding master and he promised that when she had a day off, just come along and I saddle up for you.

Angela felt happy, lucky and privileged. She wondered and marvelled at the ways of life and what it took to be able to get to this wonderful place and be able to work here.

About 6 weeks after she arrived at Kilmurry, Eve asked her whether she would be able to cope on her own with just Toby and Anthony to look after. Eve wanted to travel to Canada to visit old friends for a month. Angela assured her that all would be well. So Eve went to Canada and Angela had her little baby Toby all to herself. Anthony kept an eye on her and Eve's mother had come to visit her sister at the manor, and every now and then came to keep a discrete eye on Angela, asking her if all was ok and did she need any help.

One day, she had just finished to change Toby's nappies, when there was a knock on the door. She went to have a look and found a tinker at the door. He wanted to mend her pots, which didn't need mending, sharpen her knives and scissors which did not need sharpening and as she tried to get rid of him she saw in the reflection of her door window two boys chasing chickens in the back garden. She banged the door into the tinkers face, grabbed the broom at the back door and chased the boys as if they were stray dogs. Just then Eve's mother arrived from the manor house and helped Angela. She held out an imperial finger and pointing to the gate, she said: "Don't let me see you again on this estate. Next time it is the police". Angela was shaking. Mrs Broklebank, Eve's mother said, "get Toby and come to the house. Let's have lunch together and pick up Anthony on the way from his office." His office was just opposite from the mill on the estate.

When Eve came back, Angela noticed that she was pregnant. When Angela first arrived she thought that Eve liked her food a little too much, but now the reason was clear. Eve was having another baby. She noticed the look on Angela's face and said: "That is why I went to Canada now, I would not be able to go with three children and you won't be here all the time."

Angela congratulated her and said that she would stay until the baby was born and Eve was able to find somebody else to help her.

While Eve was away, Toby had learned to crawl, which he did flat on his tummy, just using his arms. He looked like a bay seal. Eve laughed and picked him up and hugged him tightly.

20

Rock of Cashel and the trip with Louise

On one of her days off, Anthony suggested that she should visit some ancient sites in Ireland. This was a country, where the Romans had not interfered and the Celts could develop and continue their culture undisturbed. He said that while she was here, she should learn as much as she could. He offered her the motorbike and she was off to the Rock of Cashel.

It took her quite a while to get there. The best way was to go to Kilkenny and then find her way through the lanes. It rained all the way. She was soaked on her arrival. She sat down in a sheltered spot and had her Marmite and lettuce sandwiches. As she was looking around, a man came up to her and said:

"Do you want a guide? " Angela had no money to spend and declined. He said:

" You don't have to pay, it will be a pleasure". Angela accepted his offer and put away the rest of her Marmite sandwich and followed the man. He took her around and explained some of the old carvings of beasts and human figures.

"Very old, one of the oldest sites in Eire!" he said. He pointed to the very top of the Rock:

"The ruined St. Patrick's Cathedral. He is the Saint of Ireland, St. Patrick is" Then he took her round and pointed to a big stone:

"Coronation Stone from the fourth Century and St. Patrick's Cross. Do you see on the one side is St. Patrick and on the other is Christ. This is the only Cross that shows the Christ." She had not heard of St. Patrick and why he should be a Saint, and the figures where so eroded, one could hardly tell what it was supposed to be.

"What did Patrick do to become a Saint?" she asked.

"He lived here in the fourth and fifths Century, came over from England when the Romans went back to Rome."

He looked at her intensely and said:

" Do you know why the Irish crosses have no Christ?" Angela examined the crosses and had not realized the absence of Christ as significant. One of the crosses in particular was so worn and eroded; it must be absolutely ancient, she thought. She just imagined it was the Irish way of looking at the cross, the symbol of the essence of life, the Celtic way of portraying this sacred symbol.

She said: "I haven't given it any thought really. Why don't they show the Christ?"

"Well now", he said: "Long before the story of the Christ and his crucifixion arrived in Ireland, the Druids saw the vision in the sky". He made a dramatic movement with his arm, taking in the entire space of sky his arm could reach. "What they saw was a huge cross and from the point where it crosses, came a bright light, as bright as the sun. Nobody knew what it meant, but it was there and the Druids saw it". He looked at her, waiting for her to say something.

"Did they then carve these crosses before the story of Christ reached Ireland?" Angela asked.

"Yes, this was a strong vision, and the people of Eire recognised it as a holy symbol. It took four hundred years before we knew exactly what happened on that day. It was then that St. Patrick came over and told it to us. The story had come with the Romans across the Alps and by sea to Britain, but in Britain they did not want to know about it, and so Patrick came over here, and we believed it because we had seen the sign. He told of the life and death of a man called Jesus, who became the Christ, and how he died such a terrible death. The Druids worked it out, that his Death occurred at the very same time as the Vision first appeared in Eire." Angela thought it a beautiful legend.

"Are there more legends like this one in Ireland?" she asked.

"Oh, 'tis no legend! This is the gospel truth, and he also drove all the snakes of Ireland into the sea. They were a terrible plague, and he freed us of it". Angela felt embarrassed; she did not want to offend.

"I suppose it must be true, since there are these crosses, and I have not seen any like them anywhere else." And then she remembered a story she had heard in Finland, and she said: "Just before a terrible battle the Finnish soldiers saw that the clouds in the sky parted, and very clearly the blue sky shone through the clouds making it look like a blue cross. They took this for a good omen and went confidently into war and won the battle. Since then the Finnish flag is a blue cross on white background. There must be some truth in legends? And what about Glastonbury! At Sunfield where I worked before I came here, they told me about Joseph of Arimathea, who was supposed to have come to Britain and visited the sight with Jesus when he was a teenager, and on a later visit he put his staff into the ground near the spot where he buried the holy grail, and it grew into a hawthorn tree, which still blooms today. Have you heard the story?"

The man said: "I have. My house is just over there at the bottom of the rock. Come and have a cup of tea before you go back". She was grateful, because the Marmite sandwich was still asking for a drink. They entered the little thatched cottage and Angela was amazed. There was only one room and no ceiling. She could see the thatch and the rafters. There was a fireplace at either end. Opposite the entrance door was another door, which led somewhere, Angela did not find out where, she imagined it lead into the garden. There was a fire in each fireplace and a black kettle made a quiet humming noise. It was very dark but clean and cosy. She had a very sweet cup of tea and the man asked her where she was from. She told her little story, which was ever ready and he grinned.

"We were not enemies did you know that?"

"No" she said surprised, "I didn't. Why not? I thought everybody in Europe was the enemy of Germany".

"No, not everybody, the enemy of Britain was on the German side". Angela did not know the in's and out's of British History, and thought it was probably too much to discuss right now.

"Were they still friends of Germany at the end of the war?" She wanted to know. After all, Finland started out to be friends, and then had to fight against Germany.

"Well, we were sort of neutral, we were not for nor against Germany, if you know what I mean". She didn't but wouldn't pursue the issue. She wanted to be on her way. It was just a little too much for the moment to take in. She got up and thanked the man and he opened the door. So far she found the Irish very talkative, and interested in everything, and something else, which surprised her, they liked classical music. Wherever she went, in public places, they played beautiful music, not popular hits.

"You have been very kind to me. I haven't been very long in Ireland, but I love it very much here." They walked over to the motorbike. The saddle was soaked and she wiped it as dry as she could and started it up. She shook hands.

"Just before you go" he said, "do you know a place called Regensburg in Germany?" She was amazed. "Yes, I grew up there why?"

"Well! he said, "one of our monks way back in the 12th Century went there to build an Abbey and church and it is called St. James. Two carpenters from St. James'workshop were sent back here in the 14th Century to help build this cathedral after it was destroyed."

Angela's brain raced, St James! And then it came to her. Die Schottenkirche St. Jakob am Jakobs Tor.

„I know it! We call it the Scottish church".

"That's right, Scoti, Celtic for Irish." She looked at this man. "Just imagine! and all that before trains, planes and motor cars!" He laughed..

"If you come this way again, drop in, please", he said. She shook his hand again and promised she would, and then she was on her way.

Halfway home, at a cross roads her motorbike suddenly stopped and she could not get it going again. "To much water" she thought, and started to push. There was no traffic on the road, so she could not flag anybody down. It rained heavily and the water stood in the road. In the distance she saw a lone farmhouse, so she decided to knock on the door and ask to use the phone. The woman who opened the door asked her to come in and invited her to take off her wet jacket and dry it in front of a huge fireplace. It was very cosy in the room and she was offered tea and sandwiches. The woman gave her the phone and Angela spoke to Anthony. After she told Anthony what had happened, he asked her to let him speak with the lady of the house, and she gave him directions as to how to get there.

While Angela waited for Anthony to arrive with the truck, the woman showed her all the photos on the mantelpiece.

'This is my oldest daughter, she is a nurse in New York, this is my second daughter, she is a nurse in Chicago, and she is married to an Irish American. They met over there and have four children. This is my third daughter, she lives in Melbourne and she is married to a doctor, whom she met in London where she was a nurse at the Royal Free. This is my eldest son, he is a priest in America, and this is my fourth daughter, she is a nun in London".

There were more sons and more daughters, but it was difficult to remember it all. None of the many children this woman had, lived and worked in Ireland. They had all left. How sad, how lonely, and they were all such a long way away. She had not visited any of them, had not seen any of them for many years. She would not have the money to travel, and anyway where would she start? All she had were dozens and dozens of photographs and letters to write, at least one a week to somewhere in the world.

Anthony arrived with the old truck from the estate and they loaded the bike onto it. Angela thanked the woman very much for her kindness and Anthony promised her a bag of stone ground organic flour.

They put the bike into the old barn to let it dry out, and after a little bit of fussing, it worked again perfectly.

"It is a great bike, it just mustn't get wet," Anthony said, "which is difficult in this country". Angela laughed. She had to admit, she had never been anywhere, where it rained quite so much. When she complained about the rain to a friend he protested!

"It doesn't rain in Ireland! This isn't rain! It is a fine fairy mist which kisses your cheeks". Angela laughed;

"It wasn't fairy mist when I went to Cashel. It was pelting down and hitting my cheeks". Anthony thought she ought to get herself an Irish driving license. She applied to the local Police station in Kilkenny, and got one send by post. No lessons, no tests. Good Lord! She has a driver's license. Anthony lets her drive the car wherever she wants to go.

One day she was introduced to a friend of Anthony's, a potter and stone carver who worked sometimes for the Kaye's. She said she would like to do some carving in her spare time since she had been doing it in Sunfield. His name was John and he invited her to come and see him at his cottage a few miles away. One evening she hopped onto the motorbike and drove over to see him and fell in love with the potter's wheel. John taught her to kneed the clay to get rid of all air bubbles, and then to centre the clay on the wheel and start making pots. She got so absorbed that she forgot all time. She spent one day a week and some evenings potting.

One day she asked Anthony: what do you do with the flour. Do you ever bake your own bread? He said no, he hadn't thought of it. So she used the flour and baked some bread for the family. They liked it so much and so she had to write out the recipe, which was then printed on the back of the bags they sold the flower in. Now only her bread was eaten by the family. Eve baked it herself.

On the whole Angela, although she was travelling and potting and riding, and even learning to do some stone carving, was bored. She had to do all these things on her own, there were no companions, no people her own age, nobody to go to the cinema with in Kilkenny, do things which young people do together. They had all left Ireland and only old people, some married with small children were left behind. It was a weird feeling, and she felt quite lonely. Also she felt, that she was a rarity, people looked at her and were friendly and helpful. A person her age stood out, people noticed her. It was embarrassing to be fussed over.

The lady of the manor invited her to go to the Grand National in Dublin. This took place at the same time as her 21st birthday. It is the first time she attended such an event, and there was so much happening, that she couldn't take it all in. Anthony had a stand where he showed his flour and some bread, which they had baked before, so that people could taste it and find out what could be done with the flour. Next to him was a stand, selling shirts and pyjamas. The man behind the counter pointed to a large jar of buttons on his display, and he invited Angela to guess how many buttons there were in the jar. She looked at the jar and counted the first layer of buttons, and then multiplied them more or less layer by layer down the jar. Light heartedly, she gave a number and laughed. The man took down her name and said: "If you win, what would you like? A shirt or a pair pyjamas?" She laughed again: "I'll have the pyjamas, medium size, and thank you".

The lady's horses were racing, and Angela, who had never watched a horse race, but was familiar with such events, because her grandfather was always talking to her about it and there were so many photographs in the old family album. Her grandfather had created the racecourse in Regensburg and bought horses, mainly from Britain to stock up the racing stable for the Prince of Thurn und Taxis. She decided she was born too late and into a warring time. Had she been born earlier, and if it had not been for the war, she could have been the owner of wonderful horses and take part in such events as these. She could have walked in her grandfather footsteps which had always been her wish. When she thought of her life so far, since she left school, this is what she was trying to do, but had failed miserably, because she had not been an apprentice on a stud farm. Nothing like this was available after the war. There were no luxury horses around, and she had made compromises.

Just as they were taking down Anthony's stand, a man arrived and handed her a light blue pair of pajamas and said: "You got the nearest to the number of the buttons in the jar. Here is your prize". Angela took the packet. "What do I do with that?" she grinned. She never thought she would win. She handed it over to Anthony: "There, a gift for you", she said. Anthony laughed and accepted the gift. They packed up everything and then the lady of the manor found out it was Angela's 21st birthday, and invited her to stop in a hotel with her and they did some sightseeing. They also climbed up Nelson's Column in Dublin, had a wonderful meal in the hotel and then came home, tired, happy and grateful.

She spent a lot of time as a miller, since Eve had come back from Canada. Toby had learned to crawl in her absence, and she was delighted with his progress. He also had grown   a lot of hair and two teeth.

Angela also offered to get some logic into Anthony's office, but gave up very shortly. It was a thankless job. Anthony wouldnever have a tidy office. Yet in all that chaos, he still seemed to find what he needed.

Angela enjoyed spending the time in this ancient mill. The noise of the stones as they were grinding the grain and the big water wheel, which had been reinstalled, making a rhythmic moving noise, the old wood creaking. There was an ancient smell of grain that had been made into flour for so many generations. The holes in the old stonewall indicated life behind it, mice maybe. She daren't think of rats. But high in the rafters under the roof there was a barn owl's nest. She had heard the noise one day, climbed the stairs and watched their silent flight from the top of the ladder.

Anthony said that she should have a few days off and take the little Fiat and discover Ireland. Eve's baby was expected in October and Angela had promised to stay until the end of November.

So she wrote to Marie Louise, her only friend from Sunfield, and asked if she would like to join her. Marie Louise arrived in the middle of August and they got ready for their trip. Angela pulled out the other two triangles of her tent from her luggage and buttoned them together and pitched it on the front lawn to see if it was fit to sleep in. They spent a night in it and decided it was ok.

They left happily singing and looking forward to a great adventure. Angela's first proper holiday, where she drove herself and did what she liked. She couldn't believe her luck.

First she took her friend to Cashel, she wanted to share this special place with Marie Louise. She said: "I came here and a man showed me around. But to be honest I have been here three times and every time discovered something else. Like these sun circles in the courtyard. Those circles are Celtic and pre Christian. And do you see the cross mounted on top of the stone with the circles? It portrays Christ on one side and St. Patrick on the other." They walked around and Angela pointed out things and then they found a notice, which was not easily readable because it was covered with moss and mildew. Type written it said: "The Rock rises 300 ft. from the plain of Tipperary. 370 AD the king of Munster used this ancient site to build the Abbey. Cashel remained the principal stronghold of the kings of Munster until the 12th Century. 450AD St. Patrick visited here and soon it acquired religious significance. What you see today included the Round Tower, Cormac's Chapel, the roofless cathedral, the archbishop's castle,   and the Cross of St. Patrick." There, it was readable after all. Marie Louise wrote it all down in her book, so she could write it up afterwards.

Just before they got to Cork they stopped off at Blarney Castle, home of the Blarney Stone. They had been told by Anthony and Eve, that they had to kiss the Blarney Stone. Anybody who did this can then speak on anything about everything with eloquence and aplomb, the gift of the gab, a load of blarney. So they kissed the stone and then looked around the castle. It was built in the 15th Century, a stronghold with a huge tower which withstood all of Cromwell's attacks.

From there they drove straight down to Cork. They learned that this was the place where they filmed Moby Dick. She had been to the local cinema, and had already seen Moby Dick twice. It always seems to be on as a first film before the film is shown which she went to see in the first place. She finds it very strange anyway, that there are always two films being shown. And everybody smokes. Sometimes the screen is almost invisible because of all the smoke in the cinema.

They walked through the narrow little streets in Cork, which all seemed to pour down to the harbor, and in the local pub they saw many photos of Gregory Peck on the wall. What a handsome man. Why are there only handsome men in films? Where do they find them? There are none around when we want to meet some.

They drove down a lane leading to the shore and started to look around for their first campsite. They will have to find a farmer who will allow them to park in one of his fields. She followed the narrow lane, and then she spotted the farmer. She called over to him and asked if they could pitch their tent in the field where there were some cows grazing. He looked a little bit suspicious, but then when he had a good look, probably thought there was no danger from two young girls and allowed them to spend the night.

They made themselves a cozy nest and then got the tiny stove out and cooked themselves a stew. It tasted wonderful and they drank some milk afterwards and Marie Louise broke up some chocolate for afters.

Later, at dusk they walked down to the beach with their toothbrush and towel and got ready for bed. A salty taste in their mouths and a bit sticky from the seawater, they crawled into their sleeping bags where it was cozy and warm and soon they were asleep.

Angela woke up in the morning to a strange sound. Listening she decided that it must be the cows gripping and munching the grass close to the tent, and then, most unpleasantly, a waterfall hit the side of the tent.

"Oi" She shouted again and again while she crawled out of the sleeping bag. By the time she was finally out in the open, the cows had moved away, leaving a circle of cowpats behind.

They carefully picked their way through the cow pats and went down to the beach to wash away the sleep from their eyes. The sky was black with thunderclouds, and the sea was an angry green and moving with a purpose onto the beach. It was not an atmosphere to linger. The wind got up and they thought they had better get back to the tent put it all away while it was still dry before it started pouring.

Then they saw it! A great round light appeared in the West and moved between the clouds and the sea to the East. It didn't move very fast, but nevertheless disappeared far too quickly. The two girls stood there, mouths open and pointing, but unable to say anything. It had completely disappeared over the eastern horizon. They were still staring and speechless, when it or another one like it, appeared again from the western horizon and moving to the East. Angela found her voice first:

"A round plane" she shouted over the noise of the waves.

"It doesn't make a noise, in fact it makes no noise at all" shouted Marie Louise. "And it hasn't got any wings" she added. Angela waded over to her friend and said:

"Do you think it could be a spaceship?" Marie Louise laughed.

"They said that they saw flying saucers in America last year. This could be a flying saucer". They waded out of the water and sat down at the beach and watched the sky.

"Maybe there will be another one, or the same one coming over again," Angela said hopefully. She was fascinated. Could, what she saw, be real? Nobody, absolutely nobody would believe them. They would find all sorts of explanations.

"If we told anybody, do you think they would believe us?" Marie Louise asked.

"I was thinking the same thing just now. But what would you say we saw? How would you describe it? It was fiery, round, yet flat and it moved not like lightning but slower". Marie Louise said:

"That is exactly what we saw, but I wouldn't tell it to anybody. They would think we are crazy". They waited another twenty minutes and then it started to drizzle and they ran back to the tent to take it down before it started to rain properly. They managed to get the tent down and put it away reasonably dry, and then had their breakfast in the car.

They headed out for Skibbereen, where they hoped to find some crystals, but didn't find any. Somebody had told Marie Louise to go there and find them but had not said where exactly they were to be found.

Then they were on their way to Bantry, Glengariff, Kenmare and Killarney. Their little Fiat had a tough job to clime the winding roads to cross the Caha Mountains. They are supposed to be the highest mountains in Ireland. They looked in awe to the gigantic and rugged mountain peaks, drove past mountain lakes, which were probably leftovers from the ice age, and negotiated many rugged tunnels. It all seemed like a wonderful wild fairy tale country. The weather had turned beautiful, with silver clouds and blue sky, but a storm raged as they got to the top and Marie Louise could not be persuaded to leave the car. She was convinced that if she got out of the little vehicle, it would blow away. Angela got out and braced herself. There were tall water falls and she thought one of the birds above could have been an eagle. But against the light and without binoculars she wasn't sure. She looked down into the glistening valley, which disappeared into a silver mist. She went to the boot and opened the box with the bread and butter, and prepared two sandwiches. She gave one to her friend and herself went over to the wall and sat down. She heard screeching tires on the winding road and thought what on earth...! Finally a car appeared, stopped abruptly, all four doors opened at once and five people poured out of it, braced themselves against the wind and took photographs in all direction, got back into the car and screeched off. Like a spook, it appeared and disappeared. The girls laughed: "Tourists!"

They drove on through this wild, wild country, on narrow roads hardly wide enough to pass the many donkey carts they met on the road. When they drove behind such a cart, Angela had to smile, because the wheels where so big, the platform where the driver sat hid the animal and all one could see were the thin little legs of the donkey in front of the cart it pulled. They marveled at the deep valleys, the big ancient trees, the rivers rushing over rocks into the valley, and way below in the silver distance the shining threads of the many rivers. They found a very small, green and mossy little spot in the middle of nowhere, sheltered and sweet near a little stream and decided to camp there for the night.

21

Getting to know Ireland

Angela had a terrible headache and only wanted to lie down and go to sleep. She pitched the tent and made the beds, sorted out the gear from the car and got the wash bags ready. It was already late evening and she could not see very well. She went over to the little waterfall, which was about three meters behind the tent and fed the little stream that ran past the front of the tent, and washed herself and cooled her aching head. Marie Louise sorted out the food supply from the tiny boot. Angela wearily slid into the sleeping bag and tried to forget about the awful headache, which plagued her. She was having far too many sick migraines. The song of rushing water soon put her to sleep.

Marie Louise got busy with cooking supper. Angela woke up to a delicious smell. In front of her was a steaming bowl of stew with all sorts of vegetables and bits of bacon floating in it. She still had a terrible headache but decided to eat, hoping that it might make her feel better afterwards. It tasted wonderful and she ate the lot.

"Just leave the dishes, we do them in the morning" Angela said, and Marie Louise put them outside the tent. It was just as well, because it started to rain heavily. They snuggled up in their sleeping bags and listened to the drumming rain on the tent.

They both slept deeply through the night and when Angela opened her eyes, she saw bright sunshine piercing through the weave of the tent. Her headache had gone and she crawled quietly out of the tent. She looked around the little campsite, which had been in almost total darkness when she pitched the tent. It was beautiful. The little waterfall ran into a basin, which was big enough to sit in, and that is what she did without hesitation. The smooth rocks fitted around her body and felt as soft as velvet. She marvelled at the wonderful water and drank it as she sat in it. She suddenly thought, if I had had enough money, would I have gone to stop in a hotel? No, she thought, I would not have gone into an hotel. I might have stopped in a youth hostel, like I did in Finland, but not in a hotel. I would miss all this. Marie Louise came up and laughed:

"Pity there is only room for one; I would have come and joined you". She was carrying the dishes from the day before and handed them to Angela. Laughingly she accepted them and washed them and handed the clean dishes back to her friend.

She stood up and reached for her towel.

"There you are, its all yours" she said and watched her friend undress and gingerly put her toes into the water. Then she stepped in, knelt down, jumped up and rushed out.

"This is freezing!" she accused Angela.

"Well yes, the servants forgot to heat the water" she laughed. "But I tell you something, it might have been cold to start with, but I am glowing now. It was wonderful". Marie Louise busied herself with breakfast and Angela dismantled the tent and put all the gear into the boot of the car. Then they sat down by the stream in brilliant sunshine and ate.

When they had done the dishes and put everything away and got ready to leave, they had one more lingering look. It was a fairy landscape, and the little people had probably been watching them and had made sure that they had a good night. Marie Louise went to the car and got out a roll of biscuits, took three digestives out of the packet and placed them on a little flat rock by the pool.

"There" she said, "That is for the little people, who did not mind us stopping the night". And Angela said with a bow in all directions:

"Thank you for everything". They got into the car, one more look at the lovely campsite and Angela put her foot on the accelerator.

At Muckross Abbey, the fairy landscape finished. At Castle Island they had a flat tyre, and as they looked around they found the countryside empty and boring. There were stones everywhere. So many stones! The local people used the stones to build walls, every little square had a wall around it, walls, walls up to the distant horizon, and still the stones lay around everywhere.

Angela changed the tyre. She found that her friend had absolutely no idea about anything practical or mechanical. The only thing she was good at was cooking. And she was a good and intelligent companion, but practical? No! And another thing she did, she moved the rear view mirror constantly to make up her face and forgot to put it back. When Angela was driving she had to readjust the mirror every time, and then Marie Louise got cross, because she had not finished using it. She simply had no idea what the mirror was for and thought Angela kept looking at herself all the time and laughingly accused her of vanity.

They continued to Listowel and Tarbert. Someone had told them there was a ferry, but when they got there, they found there wasn't one, so they continued on to Limerick. They parked the car and went walking around the town. In the little museum they found out a bit about the history.

Limerick was founded by the Vikings, and in the 12th Century fortified into a strong castle, King John's Castle. In a little booklet they read that Limerick is two towns; the old medieval English town on an island in the Shannon, and Irish town on the mainland, and then later in the 18th Century another development, Newton Pery.

There was a Crosier, made of gilded and enamelled silver; 6feet and 6inches tall, made in 1418 by the order of the Bishop of Limerick. It's quite unique and beautiful. Marie Louise said:

"It is amazing how the church always had the money for things like this, and the people were poor and starving."

They went to a bakery and bought some bread and butter, the dairy next door had milk and cheese. A little further down the street they found a greengrocer and got potatoes, carrots, leaks, beans and onions. Everywhere the sound of classical music filled the air.

Angela insisted on some fruit. Because Marie Louise did not like fruit, which Angela could not understand, she always had to insist that there were some apples or something.

They returned to the car and headed out to Ennis and the Cliffs of Moher. What a sight! There was nothing but sea, and the next bit of land would have been America. No wonder there were so many Irish people in America. And no wonder the first white settlers where the Irish. The empty horizon simply invited to go out there and find out what is beyond.

The Cliffs of Moher fall vertically 80 meters into the raging Atlantic, which breaks in massive rollers against these cliffs, sending the spray in slow motion back into the sea. They braced themselves against the wind, which blew unhindered from the Atlantic. The two young women lay down and looked over the edge. The dark green water rose slowly up, trying to reach up to them, and then fall back as white foam. The whole spectacle was unreal. Just a little frightened they rushed back to the car. Marie Louise said: "Lets get away from here, we might get blown away". Angela said nothing; she wasn't sure whether her friend might not be right. They drove away from the top of the cliffs. Between Lisdoonvarna and Ballyvaghan they pitched their tent for the night.

It was not a very comfortable night and the surrounding countryside was bare, but the sunset they watched was spectacular.

The thing they noticed were the numerous ruins. Abandoned cottages, four ghostly walls and the chimneystack, and no roof, probably because it was once a thatch, and decayed in the damp, Irish weather. Did the owners just leave their homes to rot and depart to America and a new and far more prosperous life?

There were also many round towers, some with conical roofs others with no roofs, as if something had chewed away the top. They were quite tall and getting narrower at the top, and Marie Louise thought they reminded her of fat pencils. Eventually they asked somebody what they were and were told that they were built for defence. There would have been dwellings near by and these towers would be manned and the enemy would be attacked from above, but if the ammunition ran out, they would dismantle the tower and throw the rocks at the enemy. There were no doors at the bottom and one could only get in via a ladder, which would then be hauled up and stowed inside the tower. There must have been numerous invaders judging by the many towers.

The next day was typical. Ten minutes sunshine and five minutes rain throughout. In Galway they sat on the beach and tried to get warm and even have a swim. When the sun shone it was warm and wonderful, but they had no chance to warm up sufficiently to get a swim before the rain came back and the drops where icy cold. They dashed back into the car to wait for the sun to return. Angela had a barometer at home, a little Black Forest farmhouse and in it was a man and a woman in traditional Black Forest dress. The man came out when it was raining and the woman came out in the sun. The two friends felt a little like that. They drove along the coast, past so many ruins. An abandoned land! How can any country be so deserted by its people. Something really terrible must have happened to make the people leave their home.

By the afternoon they reached the Slieve Aughty Mountains. They were back in fairy country, and were quite definitely aware of the little people about this place. The river and streams where crystal clear and sweet, numerous waterfalls rushed from the mountainside. There were so many different rock formations and crystals. Marie Louise got quite exited. She had spotted them first and Angela followed her, not quite sure what she was looking at. They were amazed! There were so many and they admired and touched and then found some loose ones and carefully removed them and placed them into the boot of the car. Irish Trophies! They were not quite crystal clear but the crystals themselves were beautifully formed.

Around five in the afternoon they looked about for a campsite and found another enchanted spot amid rapid streams and waterfalls and tall mountains. They met a camping companion in this lonely wilderness, a young English student. He had been camping there a whole month already. He was a geologist and had to chart and map the various kinds of rock formation.

There was also a farmhouse nearby and they bought fresh milk and brown coal, or turf. They lit a fire and invited the young English man to supper. He gratefully accepted. They were sitting around the fire and chatted. The farmer and his wife came over and sat with them. They drank a lot of tea, which the farmer's wife had brought along in a gigantic kettle. The old farmer liked the Germans and kept insisting that Hitler was a good man. There was no convincing him otherwise. He said that the English built up a pack of lies about Hitler. Angela thought, she would like to know what this man knows and would like to talk to him about it, but with the present company it was not possible. She gave up and just grinned. The old farmer was an intelligent and nice man. It started to rain heavily and the farmer insisted that they come to his house and continue the chat there.

It was an old Irish dwelling, a large room, which reached into the straw covered rafters, blackened by smoke, and a fireplace either end. Angela noticed that this cottage had no chimney either; the smoke found it's way through the thatch, hence the blackness of it all. There were hooks and stands to cook over the open fire, and the farmer's wife heated up some stew and offered it around. They weren't very hungry, having eaten earlier on, but the smell was so inviting, that they all had some delicious Irish stew. There were no doors leading away from this big room other than the entrance door and Angela thought that the large wooden wardrobe like boxes must have been hiding the beds just like in the north German Saxon farmhouses.

The young women stayed two nights; that gave them an entire day to walk and explore and follow the young man a little to learn something about this enchanting place. They bought two large river trout from the farmer, and cooked that over the campfire.

When they woke up in the morning, they found half a dozen eggs and a large bottle of milk and some fresh bread. Of the farmer no trace. They cooked breakfast, went over to the farmhouse to thank the farmer, but they could not locate them. They left a note thanking them. They shook hands with the English man and drove off. They left the mountains and continued into heathland, heading for Achill Island. This was brown coal mining country. If it hadn't been for the endless fuchsia hedges hiding this desolation, they would have been depressed. But they marvelled at these hedges. Curiously enough, these hedges had been stripped entirely of their leaves, only the fuchsia flowers bloomed in brilliant colours. The constant wind from the Atlantic had stripped the leaves. They marvelled at the strength nature provides to make sure the seeds are safe.

Angela took a photo and then made a quick sketch. She had to make a note of what she called a symphony of colour magic. The viridian green of the sea, the pink and grey-green-brown of the heather, the burnt sienna of the turf, the intense blue of the sky and the purple grey of the clouds, the deep red and blue of the fuchsias and the brilliant white of the cottages.

Their time was running out and they had to return to Thomastown. On the road between Castlebar and Claremorris they picked up two hitch hikers in Lederhosen. They had taken the coast road up to now and now they drove across Ireland to the other coast and Dublin. There were hills and mountains, rivers and lakes, bare mountains and areas with wonderful ancient trees, many castles and lots of ruins and always present those lone towers that reminded her of pencils, either with a led point or without, according to whether they had a roof or not. Another thing they encountered were stately homes, lots of them, all burnt out. They asked somebody nearby as they looked around and wondered, what had happened, but were told not to ask questions.

"Very sinister," Angela said to her friend. One of the German companions, who were still with them, said: "This is where they drove the English out of Ireland. Last Century I think it was". Not familiar with this part of the history of England and Ireland at this stage, she just said: "Oh yes?" and didn't feel very bright.

They all camped at Loch Ree in a lonely deserted and wild area, lit a big campfire and got everything out of the boot that could be cooked and eaten. They had onions, potatoes, fish, eggs, bacon and bread. They cooked the lot. The weather held until they had eaten, and then, naturally, it started to rain. They crawled into their tents and chatted through the rain and the thin tent walls until early morning. Close by were some donkeys in the field, and their plaintive eeaah's kept them awake anyway. They sounded so mournful and sad. Eventually they went to sleep and didn't wake until the sun heated up the tent and they felt too hot.

It was a great morning, and they all hopped into the Loch and splashed around happily. The young men busied themselves with the fire and the women got breakfast ready. They had gallons of coffee, toast, which they held over the fire on long sticks, butter and marmalade.

Then they had to say goodbye to their friends, who wanted to go to Northern Ireland. They waited until they had a lift and then the young women left for Dublin. Marie Louise said:

"Do we have to go into the city?" and Angela said:

"No, why, don't you want to see Dublin? And her friends answered:

"We had no towns and cities on this trip, only small dreamy places and wonderful country   side. Let's not spoil it. Let's just go back on the little lanes"

Angela agreed. Her friend was right. They headed for the Wicklow Mountains and arrived back in Thomastown the next evening. They had been exactly a week away. It seemed so much longer. What had they crammed into this week! Two days later, Marie Louise left for England. Angela missed her very much. She was a very good companion, and they were excellent friends.

She couldn't tell Anthony and Eve enough of the trip. It was so much better than the one she did in Finland. She had a companion, and in Finland she was alone. That was the difference. A good companion is worth everything, she decided.

*

Angela went back to do her pots, and found that John, the potter had biscuit fired her latest pots and of the first batch had sold quite a lot. Angela was disappointed, because there was one she had wanted to keep. It was her first real success and she wanted to remind herself of her achievement in the years to come. When she told John of her disappointment that he had sold some of her pots, he said that first of all he was in this as a business and he and his wife and children had to live, and secondly she was good enough to make more of that kind. Personally she felt she had lost one of her children. But she could also see that John and his family were living on the poverty line. She could not demand anything, because after all it was all John's equipment, his time and she was grateful that he was kind enough to teach her to pot.

She realized with a pang to her heart, that her time here would come to an end in a few weeks, and she doubted that she would ever pot again after that. Where could she pot, she wondered. Should she change her entire life and become a potter? She went home that day, unhappy with herself and unsure as to what the future held. She had been away three years; would they all count to her journeyman's years? She had collected all her references and all but Sunfield would count she thought. As she drove home on her motorbike, she decided to use the time to the full and make as many pots as she could, learn as much as she was able to, and not come too close to John. She admired him so much and thought his skills were not used to the full. He was an artist at heart and had to waste his time making pots, helping Anthony, in order to earn extra cash, mend bits of broken and eroded stone carvings on the various churches in the neighbourhood, instead of creating incredible sculptures and paint the most fantastic paintings.

Anthony had employed John to work in the mill, since there was no one when Angela left in November. So apart from seeing John at the pottery, she also worked with him in the mill now. She could tell that ever since they had been to Dublin in July for the Grand National, John had tried to be close. She had ignored it because after all she did not want an affair with a married man. Now, working in the mill, just John and Angela, he come over to her and cornered her. Without much preamble he kissed her. Angela felt very strange. She had never been kissed that way before, never been held that way, and what was going on in her body she could not tell. She felt quite helpless to stop it, and kissed him back. She was very shy at the same time. Good Lord! What was going on? She even felt her knees go soft. She got out of the embrace and looked at him. She became quite hot in the face and thought she must be beetroot red in the face. Her embarrassment was quite acute.

John too was embarrassed and said:

'I am so sorry, I don't know why I did that. Please forgive me?' But Angela, whose emotions went wild and was trying to work out what was happening to her said:

'Don't be sorry. I have to admit, I liked it. But we mustn't. You are married'. And John turned around and went back to work. Angela left the mill and could not take her mind of John. From now on, unless she was to avoid John altogether, she would have to control her feelings in front of everybody. Somehow she did not like it. She was not in control of it. It controlled her. And she did not know how to ban this feeling. Every second of the day she thought of John. She avoided the mill, telling Anthony, that John managed very well without her, and she concentrated to help Eve, who was heavily pregnant and had difficulty moving around. She could not avoid John all together and whenever they met when no one was around they kissed. Did she fall in love with John? How could she! He was far too old for her, he was married and had two children. She didn't even know how old he was. He must be at least fifteen or maybe even twenty years older than her. It had to stop. When she went over to the pottery, there at least Janet, his wife was ever present, and she liked Janet. She could not betray her behind her back. Had Janet noticed something? Angela was just throwing a large jug, when Janet came in and said:

'It is very hard to see you do all these lovely pots. I never have time to do anything but cook, wash, clean and look after the children. I would like to pot too. I used to before the children came.' She went away and came back with a beautiful green vase.

'I did this some years ago. It is a salt glaze. I can pot. But now I never get the time. Living here in this cottage, with no electricity, life is hard.'

When Angela drove home that evening, dodging the cats, rabbits and hedgehogs on the road, she decided not to return to the pottery.

Grossvater1957

Hitchiking in Europe 1957

1958 on the Rhein

Ross 1962

206

Richard , Angela Bangkok 1967

The Bluff NZ 1964

Cairo 1963

Addis Abbaba

Macchu Picchu

209

Station at Macchu Picchu 1968

22

Knights Hill House

The time for Eve's confinement came and she went to Kilkenny to deliver the baby. Her third child was also a little boy, Dennis. Angela stayed until Eve was able to resume her work, and had also found a young girl from the big house, which her aunt could spare, to help. Angela was now free to go back to Germany. She had a heavy heart and felt sad to leave all these wonderful people, which she came to love so much. Of all the people she had ever worked for and ever stayed with, Eve and Anthony, their children Gabriel and Toby and now tiny Dennis, their aunt at the big house and John, she loved them all, especially John and his pottery. Would she ever pot again. All she had were the photos of her pots. She had been in Ireland eleven months.

She had an invitation from one of Lady Archer Houblin's friends. Lady Gaylor had been to visit Lady Doreen Archer Houblin at Kilmurry, and Angela, just returning from a ride, had been called over and was introduced. They had a long chat, which resulted in Lady Gaylor asking Angela to visit her in London, and she prepared to go to Mill Hill, to visit Lady Gaylor's house, Knights Hill House.

Lady Gaylor's daughter, Hilary came to fetch her from the Mill Hill underground station in a little Morris Minor. They travelled for about fifteen minutes and then drove through huge wrought iron gates into a park and continued down what seemed a private road. They came to a large cottage with a big house behind it. There were also some stables joined in a square to the cottage, and the horse's heads looking out of the half opened stable doors. Hilary parked the car and a man came out of the cottage door and took her luggage. Angela had a duffle bag and a small suitcase. The rest of her luggage was at Victoria Station. She followed Hilary and the man into the cottage, passed a dingy corridor and came through a humble door into an enormous round hall, lit up by a huge glass dome high above in the roof. Red marble Doric pillars surrounded the hall supporting an upper landing to which led a wide winding staircase with ornamental iron banisters. Opposite the little door they had just come through, was an enormous double entrance door with window lights over the top. Very tall windows lit up the elegant staircase.

Angela wondered where she had got to. This was palatial and not what she at first thought was a cottage. Was this the famous back door front door phenomenon of the English people? Deliveries and services at the back, gentry through the front door!

The man went up the stairs and opened one of the many doors and showed her in. "This is your room while you are staying here". He bowed and walked away. She thanked him and looked around. A big four poster dominated the room; there was a washbasin and a makeup table, an easy chair and a rocking chair. At the door the man, Angela thought he must be the butler, said discreetly:

"They dress up for dinner, madam". Angela blushed and thanked him again. When she met Lady Gaylor in Ireland, she wasn't at all grand. Nor did Lady Doreen use a butler. So what is happening here? There was a knock on the door and Hilary came in.

"Mother wants to meet you. You don't have to change until later. If you like we have some tea downstairs". Angela was quite ready for some tea. She had travelled a long way by boat and train, and lastly by underground and now was tired, hungry and thirsty. But she would have to restrain herself until later.

She followed Hilary downstairs and was led into a spacious tall and long room with life sized portraits. Angela assumed they must be the ancestors. There was a roaring fire in the fireplace, two brocade covered settees, the glow of the fire reflecting on the gilt woodwork. Three crystal chandeliers suspended from the ceiling, and enormous brocade curtains hanging down beside the French windows of which there were four leading out into the park. Angela did not know much about this sort of furniture, which was displayed in this room, but if somebody had asked her, she would have said:

"It looks like Louis XIV" but whether this was true, she did not know and would not ask. Lady Gaylor looked quite forlorn in this big room, and Angela walked over to her and held out her hand,

German fashion. Reluctantly the lady took it and they shook hands. Angela was amazed. Here was this lady, in this palace of a house, gilt and gold, crystal and servants, surrounded by a beautiful park etc. and yet here she was in an old cardigan full of holes, a dirty old skirt and on her feet a pair of Wellingtons. Had she just come in from mucking out the stables? There was another woman sitting opposite and she was introduced as Lady Gaylor's sister, equally in Wellingtons and torn knitted cardigan, and she even wore fingerless mittens.

A maid, dressed immaculately in black and white, came in with a silver tea tray and served tea and biscuits. Gratefully Angela accepted her cup and now she had to negotiate the difficulty of the English way of drinking tea; elegantly balancing the tea cup plus saucer and the side plate plus piece of fruit cake, and no table to put anything down on. And as both her hands were busy holding the cup and saucer and side plate, the maid asked her if she wanted some sugar. Which hand should she have used to put sugar into her tea?

"No thank you, I don't take sugar," she said. Hilary came over and said:

"Here. Would you like to sit down?" This way Angela had a knee to balance the side plate and have a hand free to elegantly sip some of the much-needed tea. She drank greedily and looked around hopefully to be noticed and offered some more tea. The dutiful maid did notice and came over and filled her cup again. She was asked about the trip and were they alright over there in Ireland and how was the new baby. Angela answered all their questions.

She learned that Lady Doreen and her host had been to College in Tenterden together and whenever Lady Doreen comes over to represent the Queen at the rehearsals for the trouping the colour, she would stay at Knights Hill House. And any friend of Lady Doreen's was a friend of hers. She had learned that Angela had not been to London before and Hilary would be very happy to take her sightseeing. Angela was happy to accept.

The usual questions came. What did she remember of the war? Where was she at the time? Had she been bombed? Angela told her now familiar story. Then they wanted to know more about her grandfather and her connection with horses. How, because of the war, her family lost everything, and that her and her family's inheritance was not even in Germany anymore, but in Russia and Poland.

Angela felt, that had she been born fifty or sixty years earlier, she would have fitted into this environment very nicely. But now, it all seemed faded, used up and out of place. More members of the family arrived, and Angela saw that things were far from perfect. Hilary's sister had back trougle, her husband was a weak man with strange hair, and there were a lot of other people which had arrived but Angela was far too tired to take it all in. She was polite and took an interest, but it went into one ear and out the other. She could only concentrate to staying awake and to get through the evening intact.

There was a lot of talk of a safari and a cinecamera was put up and a screen erected and before Angela knew it, they were all seated, someone closed the curtains and she was watching a flickering film in black and white about Hilary and her recent trip to Kenya. Angela could not watch properly, because the images flickered about and nothing stayed on the screen long enough to be seen properly. Angela's eyes started to water and she developed a headache. There was a lot of commentary from Hilary, and a lot of knowing comments from the family. They apparently had all been on similar trips and were comparing their various adventures. Angela, who at this stage had never heard of Safaris and the sort of things that were available to people with money and connections to the colonies, was suitably impressed.

The film show ended and as if by a secret signal the butler came in and opened the curtains. It was now pitch dark outside, and the wooden shutters were closed. Hilary came over and said: "Do you have something to wear for dinner?"

Angela had no idea what one wears for dinner and said: What sort of dress should I wear?" and Hilary said:"don't worry, you can borrow one of mine," and left. She was back with a long deep green affair, which actually fitted Angela very well, except that she didn't like the style. She thought she looked ridiculous; however it was only for dinner. They all gathered in the red marbled hall until everybody was present, wearing dark suits and ties and the ladies in long dark dresses and some jewels. Very grand, Angela thought, over the top. Lady Gaylor led them all into the dining room, which surprisingly was a very small room with no special furniture, just one long table and chairs and only enough spare room to walk around the table to find your seat. Claustrophobic, Angela thought.

Lady Gaylor was seated at the top of the table and for the first time Angela realised there was no Lord Naylor. Angela found a seat between two of Hilary's brothers. The servants came and served the soup with white gloves. When everybody had finished and put their spoons down, the door opened mysteriously and the servants came and took everything away and brought in the next course. Angela wondered how they knew when to come in? When everybody was served they all began to eat, and again, when the last knife and fork was put down, the door opened and the servants came in, spotless white gloves and all, and cleared the table ready for the desert. Coffee was served in the lounge and the men went off into the smoking room. Weird! Angela said to Hilary:" Just tell me one thing, how did the servants know when to come in?" And Hilary said: "Simple, mum has a bell by her foot under the carpet, and when everybody is finished she steps on it."

Angela had to laugh. Of course, it is so simple.

The next day Hilary took her riding through the park and adjoining fields to a wide expanse of open land. It was a beautiful late Autumn day. What a life, Angela thought. She asked Hilary: "What do you do for a living?" And Hilary answered: "There is the estate to look after. I work very hard". Angela thought it was like farming; to see that everybody did their job, looking after the house and so on.

"Is there a farm attached to the estate?" Angela asked, and was told, that there were several and even one in Rhodesia and one in Kenya, and one in Ireland not far from lady Doreen's. Seven in all.

Angela was impressed. "Well, she said, I can see you have more than enough to do. Do the rest of the family help?" and she was told that they were all involved. "Tomorrow, you and I go into town and I show you our townhouse at Cavendish Square. It is empty now, and we are thinking of selling it. The Winter seasons aren't what they used to be, and with the public transport, one is in town so much quicker these days." Angela was curious, and amazed. The way these people still lived, even after the war! It just goes to show how little the war has affected them. And also, how protected they all were. How little they suffered, and yet they were convinced that they had suffered terribly. They had no idea, Angela decided. Absolutely no idea! But then how do you define suffering?

She had been told that sugar, butter meat and bread had been rationed during the war and for a long time afterwards. Even though the nation's rations were more than the average household needed, the mere fact that there was a restriction was to them suffering. To Angela suffering was not to be able to get any sugar, or butter or meat and only one slice of bread a day. That was suffering. To lose everything the family possessed, their land, their ground where for hundreds of years her family had lived and worked and grown food and had passed it all on to the next generation. To lose all that was suffering.

"A penny for your thoughts" Hilary said as they came trotting up to the top of the rise.

"Oh, I was just thinking, if it hadn't been for the war, I would be doing this sort of thing at home. But as it is, there is only wishful thinking. That will have to do. And I was wondering what I was going to do when I return home. Things will have to change, I suppose. I will have to move on. Actually, life is great. When you have nothing to restrict you, the world is your oyster. I can do anything I want to." After a while Hilary said:

"I have this job, but it is not paying. The estate is not making any money, and soon one bit after another has to be sold and the money put into the remaining estate to keep it going. It is not encouraging." Angela could see the difficulty. There was far too much to look after, too many managers and they would line their own pockets first. The family could not look after it all efficiently. They would have to travel constantly from place to place and even then they would not be able to see what was really going on. Angela did not envy them.

"The plantations in Africa are nothing but trouble, what with the blacks not pulling their weight. They want the white farmers off the land, and I tell you, when that happens, the blacks will all die of starvation. They don't know how to run anything. It will be the end of the colonies, I tell you", Hilary burst out angrily.

They were back in the park and Hilary said: "We are just right for lunch. Hungry?"

"Well yes, actually, very", and she was surprised, because breakfast was not so long ago, but when she looked at her wristwatch, she said:

"I didn't realize it was that late? How time goes by when things are wonderful. I love riding. I could do it all day long every day. I was born too late" she said again. Hilary laughed.

"I know what you mean; I go as often as I can, probably once a day. I can manage that most days. But we too are born too late. Times are changing fast and a lot of us are left behind. "

They had lunch in the little dining room. It was an ordinary event; soup and sandwiches, but enough to satisfy the hunger. Hilary said: "If it is alright, we go into town now and have a look at our house. Angela was eager for the trip and sightseeing. She had not been to London since Mike had taken her. It would be exciting to actually go into Westminster Cathedral and maybe the Tower? She mentioned it and Hilary was quite pleased to take her.

First they went to the house. It was a four-storey palace. Solid and square, and could easily be a department store. Hilary got the key out to open the front door. Angela followed her up the steps to the door. The entrance was covered by a flat roof held up by Grecian pillars. Angela could not believe that a family would have something like this as a second home for the winter season.

"Does anybody live here?" she asked.

"No, we have closed it down. We have not used it for the last five years. It is waiting to be sold."

The rooms were mostly empty, very stately and were called the red room, the blue room, the golden room and so on. The wallpaper was silk, but very old and worn out. So were the curtains. They went down into the basement and looked at the kitchen and other workrooms. The servant's quarters. It was a different world. An upstairs, downstairs world. Everything was covered in thick dust. There were some carpets, but they too were worn away. Angela became quite depressed. It was like looking at a dead person. Once there was life, hectic life, but now it was finished, only fit to be buried.

"Do you feel sorry it has to be sold?" Angela asked. And Hilary, sighing deeply, said: "No, not really, the times have changed so much, there are not the servants, the money from the colonies has dried up, and it has become a liability. It is cheaper to hire rooms at Claridges for our events, than to keep this house. Just to heat it costs a fortune. We have no central heating, only coal fires. Just to keep the fires going would need two staff". Angela nodded her head.

The rooms on the upper floors were mostly bedrooms with parlours attached, but strangely for all the rooms in the house and the people it must have housed at one time or other, the sanitary facilities were very poor. There was a very old fashioned bathroom at the very top under the roof, a lavatory on each floor, but not yet converted to WC. Even though it had not been used for several years, Angela did not like the smell when she looked into the closet. As for the servant's loo, it could have been in any peasants cowshed. Terrible!

They left the house and Angela had mixed feelings. She was relieved to get out, sad that it was not in use anymore, but then what would be the use? In the middle of London? Traffic roaring past, no horse drawn carriages, everybody busy to adjust to modern life, even though it still went slowly compared with the life at home in Germany. To think that offices and banks did not open until ten in the morning! In Germany business starts at seven thirty, banks at eight. This was England, Angela told herself. Life here is different. The houses were still very black and Hilary explained apologetically: "I am afraid it is because of all the coal fires in the houses. I know on the continent they already have central heating, but here we use coal. It is cheap fuel and keeps the people in the north and in Wales in work."

They went to Westminster Abbey and the Houses of Parliament and Westminster Hall and then to the Tower and then it was time to drive home and change for Dinner. Angela had two more days at Knights Hill House, riding over to a neighbouring estate and visiting friends of the Gaylor's.

Her last evening was spent at Covent Garden Opera House, to see and hear Tosca, with Maria Callas. It was a wonderful evening, Angela shining in one of Hilary's evening-or opera gowns, feeling like a princess. Everybody glittered and sparkled and was glad to see and be seen. Princess Margaret was there too and a lot of other sparkling royals, none of whom Angela recognised. Hilary wore a little tiara, and there were so many people Angela was introduced to, her head began to spin. People were pointed out to her discreetly: various politicians and public figures, all of them made no impact on Angela. She nodded and showed an interest, but none of it made any sense. She had the sensation of standing under a waterfall and not getting wet. She stood there, smiling politely, listening to all the chatter and laughter, watching the people walk this way and that, exclaiming delight when they saw somebody they knew. It all seemed so shallow and showy, unreal, strange. Is this what happens when high society meets? Angela thought. This was the time when her grandfather was young and they were at court in Berlin where he met his wife, her grandmother who was lady in waiting to Auguste Victoria, wife of Kaiser Wilhelm, grandson of Queen Victoria. Both wars had not really changed this country. But she felt that the British Empire seemed to be breaking up. At Hilary's home the signs were very visible.

When they finally came out, Hilary and some friends said they wanted to go to a café they knew at the market. They got their dresses hitched up and walked past endless vegetable and flower traders and came to a café which was open all night; a rarity in London, where everything closed more or less at eleven at night. Strange opening hours! The café was there for the market traders and the opera goers used it regularly to round off the evening. What a contrast after all the glitter. They had tea and toasted teacakes, and Angela thought it tasted wonderful.

Hilary's last words that evening before they said good night were: "Don't get up early. Have breakfast in bed and then I take you to Victoria Station. We do not have to leave until two pm. Angela slept well, and she had to admit it, she was looking forward to going home, to see Tissi after over three years away. She would have grown from a child to a young woman. And her Mum! Dear little Mum! Yes it was time she went home.

23

Going Home wherever that is

She arrived in Paris early in the morning and put her luggage into storage, and then went into the city. There was so much she wanted to see. She had only limited funds and had to be careful not to spend it all. She thought the first thing to do was to go up the Eiffel Tower to have a look around and see where everything was. She enjoyed the view, in fact it was three times higher than the cathedral in Regensburg. This was the highest point she had been to in her life so far, and she could not get enough. When she located Notre Dame, which she decided was a must, she thought one or two things to see in the Louvre, some lunch and then just a walk through Paris and see what there was to see. Just to get the feel of it, walk down the Champs Elisee, look at the Arc de Triumph and then collect the luggage and get to the other station. At four in the afternoon she had a cup of coffee and a croissant and afterwards went back to the station. She collected her luggage and then thought about getting to the other station. She had only a few coins and wondered if that was enough to pay the porter. Good Lord, she should not have had the coffee and croissant. She went over to a man who stood by a two-wheeled wooden cart and asked how much it would be for him to take her to the other station. It turned out that she had not enough money. Oh dear!

She had some German coins, about ten marks, her iron reserve, some English shillings; she counted about ten, and some francs. She laid it all out for him to see and hoped he would agree to take her. He shook his head. Well, she could not lug her suitcase over the cobbles to the other station that was certain. She grinned at him, lifted her suitcase onto the cart and started to push it down the street over the cobbles. She could hear the porter complaining behind her but she did not listen, she just pushed for all that she was worth. She guessed what it was he was shouting, but pushed the cart steadily on. Suddenly he became quiet and after a few moments took the handles from her and started to push the cart himself. She could not read his face, it was stony, but he continued to push it towards the other station, Gare del Est. He took her to the right platform, where the train to Basel SBB was expected. He stood there, stony faced and waited. Angela, embarrassed, offered all the coins she had, altogether with the shillings and the marks, it should have been a tidy sum. The marks alone was nearly a pound, the shillings half a pound and she wasn't quite sure about the francs. But he grinned now and closed her hand over the coins and said something like:"plesire". She smiled and rummaged in her bag and brought out two packets of Rothman's King size and held it out to him. His grin turned into a broad smile and he accepted the cigarettes. Just then the train pulled in and he helped her with her suitcase. When she was at her allocated seat, he held out his hand and said something and smiled, and then he gave her a peck on either cheek and left. Angela thought not for the first time, that she must learn to speak French. "Merci "she called after him, and he just lifted his hand and waved, took his cart and she watched him walk away.

She settled down into the facing seat by the window and thought it would be nice to have something to eat. She was starving. But she had no sandwiches and she doubted that she could buy anything with the remaining money on this train. It was getting dark and she would travel many hours through the night. It was quite warm in the compartment and she wondered who her travelling companions would be. She closed her eyes and did the trip through Paris again. It was a wonderful day and the episode with the porter was the cream on the pudding. She would never forget this day, even though it was spent in silence, apart from the few words uttered when she purchased tickets and bought the coffee and croissant. She spent several hours at the Louvre. She had to visit the Mona Lisa. Her mother had been given a live sized painted copy of the picture and it had pride of place at home during her childhood. She needed to see the original. She was sidetraked as she passed the ancient Egyptian artefacts but eventually came to the Leonardo da Vinci room. She stood a long time in front of the Mona Lisa, with memories flooding back to the time when this picture entered her life. Those were hungry times, when mother's American friend became a regular visitor to their room. It was a Christmas present from him to mother in 1946. He would always bring some food from the PX in return to speak German with the family and enjoy the company of them all. They were gentle times after the horror of war.

She moved over to the Virgin, the Child and Saint Anne. She marvelled at the movement and the gentle love, which came from the picture. Then she wondered why a grown woman would sit on another woman's lap, because quite clearly, the virgin sat on St. Anne's lap. Slowly she moved on to the Raphael's, the Sandro Botticelli's. Eventually she got to the Peter Paul Rubens's and felt quite strange, almost embarrassed at the white skinned, shapeless, fat cavorting women.

The sliding door of the train opened and a middle-aged man came in, wearing a Bavarian type Loden-coat. He settled down opposite her in the corner by the window. Then a woman came in and settled at the other end by the sliding door, leaving two empty seats between them, three empty seats on the other side. The man opened his bag and adjusted the little table under the window and put out a thermos flask and a box of sandwiches, a jar of little gherkins, a lump of cheese and an onion. He opened the box of sandwiches and offered it to Angela. They looked delicious and Angela said: "Sprechen sie Deutsch?" and he said: "Yes, I am from Switzerland". Angela smiled at him and said: "Thank you very much, I would love one", and he held out the box for her to help herself. He then offered the box to the woman at the other corner, but she lifted her hand and said: "Non, merci". The man then spoke to her in French and she smiled but did not take a sandwich. Angela enjoyed the bread, and when she took her second bite, the man opened the jar of gherkins and offered it to her. Gratefully she took two and munched away. Then he offered her a slice of onion and at the end another sandwich. She put embarrassment aside and helped herself gratefully. She had not eaten since she had her last meal at Knights Hill House, other than the croissant. She apologized to the man: "I am sorry I have nothing to offer you. I spent my last money sightseeing in Paris".

"Yes I know what it is with you youngsters. I have two daughters and a son, and they too travel by the seat of their pants". He smiled and then continued: "I get telephone calls asking to send money to all corners of Europe, because they have run out yet again. Do you call your father asking for money?" Angela shook her head: "I wish I could, I haven't got a father anymore. He didn't come home after the war. I work and save and then travel on". She smiled: "Where do your children travel?" He cleared his throat and said, offering her the gherkin jar again: "They went to Norway, Spain and Italy. At the moment my son is in Paris, which is where I have just visited. He wants to be an artist. He never has any money. And his paintings are rubbish. But as a father I have to encourage him, if that is what he wants to do with his life. I would have wanted him to study medicine. We need a lot of doctors in Switzerland." He cut a big chunk of cheese and offered it to Angela on his knife. She took it gratefully and the slice of onion which was the next thing he offered, and another gherkin. Something to drink would be nice, she thought.

"My father was a dentist and I always thought I would like to be a dentist too, but the war finished all that. I went into farming instead. But there is no money in that either. When I get back home, I don't know what I am going to do. Learn to type probably, which is a total change to my life, from driving tractors and horses, to sitting in an office typing. I don't know if I can cope with that. But then needs must I suppose".

Gosh, she thought, what do I sound like? What have I just said? She had actually never thought it through quite so thoroughly. Is that really what I am going to do? It must be, what else is there.

The man smiled and held out his hand: "I am Johann Pfitzner". Angela took his hand and said: "Angela Geppert". They shook hands and she liked the firm pressure of his hand. He held out his sandwich box again, but she thanked him and declined. She had eaten such a lot and felt happily satisfied. She could do with a drink. But he was already opening his flask and pouring some into the cup, which was also the outer lid, and offered it to her. She accepted it gratefully.

The world was a friendly place; the people in it to a great extent honest and good. She was full of confidence, feeling happy, and wanted to be in touch with all the nice people. She had been gathering addresses and hoped to write to all of them. And yet, at the back of her mind, she knew it was impossible. These were encounters which she would always remember, but that was all. Encounters in the night; shadows which were momentarily illuminated. Companions for the time their paths went the same way, but afterwards they would only be a memory.

They made themselves comfortable and went to sleep. Around 5am Angela woke up, stiff neck and aching back. She looked out and saw that they were in a mountainous area. She had never been in this part of the world and going 'home' was new too. It wasn't home, but it was where her mother now lived. It would be very strange. She felt excited and could not wait. She had to get from the SBB station in Basel to DBB station, one being the Swiss one and the other the German station. When they came near their destination, Johann Pfitzner got his thermos flask out again and the sandwich box and offered her breakfast. She had to laugh. "This is like the magic box of the Stuttgarter Hutzelmännchen, whenever you leave a little bit uneaten in the box, the next time you open it, it is full of food again".

"So it is" he said, "one of my favourite stories when I was a boy". She accepted the food and they ate together. The woman in the corner had left the compartment with her luggage. She stood in the corridor ready to leave the train. There were still 15 minutes before their arrival. They had time to eat, freshen up a little and say their farewells. They exchanged addresses, and Angela promised to visit, when her travels took her near where he lived. "You'll like my wife he said, and you might even meet one or two of my children".

She found a porter and a tram, which took her to the other station, and then she took the local train to Lörrach, which used up the last remaining ticket in her booklet. Her mother and Tissi were waiting at the little station. She recognized her Mum immediately, but Tissi was nowhere to be seen. She dropped her cases and rushed into her mother's arms. They spoke simultaneously and after a moment Angela said: "Where is Tissi?" and her mother pointed to a little miss, with a painted face and terribly high heals, in a trench coat with the belt so tightly drawn that it seemed to suffocate her, breasts bigger than those of her big sister, and she seemed to be in a huff.

Angela was taken aback and could not believe her eyes, but then rushed over to her and hugged her. "Tissi!" she called, "how you have grown! I just did not recognize you". She held her little sister at arms length, "Let me look at you", but Tissi pushed her away and said nothing. She glanced over to her mother and she only shrugged. So this is what her mother meant in her last letter, that she needed help with Tissi. Tissi, at sixteen was not listening to anyone anymore.

They did not have far to walk to the place her mother rented in the Baseler Strasse. In fact it was just across the road and fifty meters to walk. But it was up three storeys just under the roof of the house. As they lugged the suitcases and bags up the stairs, the curtains moved at every half glazed door to the various apartments in the house.

The first thing Angela did was to get in touch with the Ministry of Agriculture, Forest and Fisheries. She wanted to find out what her prospects were. The next thing she did was to get a temporary job, which would take her through Christmas and into the New Year. The business college she wanted to go to would start in April of 1958. She thought that modern farming would also have a business side to it and she wanted to be able to go back to farming with the knowledge of running a farm efficiently. There were five months of earning money left to her. At the labour exchange she was given work immediately at 'Suchard', the chocolate factory in Lörrach. Her workday started at 5 am until 1530 hours every day. She was offered nightshift as well, but her mother had asked her to be at home during the night, because of Tissi; her mother being on permanent night duty at the Hospital. There was no problem at the labour exchange, because the nightshift earned more money, and there were plenty of people who gladly accepted the night work. The money Angela was offered was four times the amount she had earned at the best of times. The amount made her feel dizzy.

When she arrived on her first day, she was ushered into a large hall and taken to a place along a very long and narrow table, and as she approached she saw many chairs and at least 10 women. The woman who guided her to her seat explained as two big wooden boxes of pralines were placed in front of her and a stack of little brown paper cups placed near her left hand. Just then the table started to move and frantic movements to her right took her attention. The woman said: "You see these boxes? " and already a chocolate box came rushing down the black table, which she now realized was a conveyor belt, and deftly the woman managed to separate two of the little brown paper cups, and put two chocolates, one each from the big boxes in front of her, and place them cleverly into the box which was rushing past her face, and already the next box appeared in the corner of her right eye and the woman had already got the next two chocolates in their little paper cups and placed them into the box rushing past and the next and the next, always in the same spot. After ten boxes or so she told Angela to carry on by herself now. Frantically and clumsily Angela tried to do the same, but she could not get the paper cups separated and the boxes rushed past without her two chocolates in them.

"You have to be quicker", the woman said, and Angela, sweating and concentrating managed every other box and slowly she managed two at a time, and a woman overseer came to the other side of the conveyor belt and filled the boxes she had missed. The woman leant over and said: "Don't worry; it happens to all of them on their first day. You'll do". Angela smiled relieved. By the time she went home, exhausted, there were no more boxed which she had missed and had to be filled afterwards. She had also been allowed to eat as many chocolates as she wanted, but did not find the time to pop one into her mouth. Every two hours there was a small break and everybody took a different seat and different flavours to stop the monotony. At the end of the day, she was given a small box of chocolates, because the box was damaged and could not be sold. She carried the box home like a trophy and shared it with her mother and Tissi. The next day she found that she had time to pop in the odd chocolate, and by the third day, swore at the end of it, never to eat another chocolate ever again.

She became nauseated by the chocolate smell as she approached the factory every morning, but she was going to work here until the time when she would be going to Regensburg and college. Strangely enough, she did eat more chocolates and before she knew it, her face was covered in pimples. Gradually it dawned on her, that it was the chocolates which caused the pimples, and that made her stop. It was coming close to December and all the Christmas chocolates had disappeared and the December weeks were filled with packing away Easter chocolates. It felt strange, filling chocolate Easter Eggs with chocolates, when it was dark outside going to work and coming home, trudging through deep snow. She worked every day except Sundays, and for working on a Saturday, she got treble pay. She could be a wealthy woman, if she continued to work in the chocolate factory, but then she thought, what work? She needed to be out, with animals under the free sky. Every Sunday she took the train and travelled into the Black Forest, which was on her doorstep, and walked up to the Feldberg.

Bine had returned from England while Angela was in Ireland and was now working as a receptionist in a doctor's surgery in Schönau in the Black Forest, which was very close and could also be reached via the little local train. However, Tissi remained a problem. She went out in the evenings, even though Angela thought it would be nice if they had time together, Tissi was not interested. One evening, Angela followed her secretly, because she always came home late. She watched her little sister as she stopped in front of a large shop window and looked at the unlit display. Then, to her surprise she started to whistle gently as a man approached, the man stopped and they started to talk, then they walked off together. Deeply shocked, Angela went home.

The next day, Angela questioned her. "Where did you go last night?"

"I met with some friends", Tissi replied.

"I haven't got any friends here," Angela said, "why don't we have a little get together on Sunday? It is the first of Advent, and Mutti will be home too, lets have a little celebration like we used to. Maybe Bine can come too? Anyway, we have not had a celebration since I got back. Ask your friends. What do you say?"

Tissi said: "I don't want to bring my friends here! This is a poky little hole. I would be ashamed to bring them here, and anyway, what friends, they are all in Regensburg". Angela's heart sank. "But this is your home now!"

"Exactly! Why should I live in such a poky hole, there is no room for anything. Small and poky, that's what it is,"

"What would you like to do then? Where would you like to live?" Angela asked.

"Oh, I don't know." She shrugged her shoulders. Angela urged: "Don't tell Mutti how you feel. All she wanted was to give you a home as well as she could provide under the circumstances. Life is not always as we want it". Angela felt sorry for her sister. She had to leave her friends in Regensburg, had to change school three times since her mother had to go back to work, and now she was a young adult in a strange town with no friends and no sisters and only a worried mother.

"When will you finish school?" Angela asked.

"I finished this July, and I have been put down to start at the hospital as a student nurse soon, but I don't like to do that, I would like to do something different." Angela thought, what about getting her to go to Sunfield and learn English to start with and work with the children.

"What about Sunfield", Angela asked. Tissi looked at her and Angela feared to have her head bitten off by her little sister, but Tissi grinned. "If Mutti lets me, I'd go tomorrow."

"Why shouldn't she let you?"

"Because she can't keep an eye on me when I am not here anymore. She does not trust me," Tissi said.

"Well, is she right, can she not trust you? What do you do when you go out at night?" Angela looked her in the eye and Tissi avoided her.

"I meet with friends, I said so before, didn't I?"

"Yes you did, but you also said you had no friends here. So what is going on?" Tissi did not look at her when she said: "I shall bring my friend here. His name is Peter, you'll see he is nice."

*

Angela laid the table for the afternoon coffee and cake, a traditional German afternoon occupation, when visitors come. It was

228

the second Sunday before Christmas and her mother had a night off. There was a happy atmosphere, just like it was years ago, when the entire family, mother and the three girls and Günter were still together in Regensburg. Cosy, for the moment free of worry, Bine had come too, and there was chatter and expectation as they all expected Peter, Tissi's friend.

He arrived with an enormous bouquet of flowers, several little parcels and a wide grin on his face. He had greeny blue eyes, and raven black hair and a very fair skin, and looked quite handsome in a strange sort of way. Angela could not put her finger on it. He was very pleasant, talked a lot and helped with the washing up. It turned out, that his father had died long ago and his mother brought up the children, two girls and one boy, Peter, all on a own. Peter being the oldest took on responsibilities, which usually fell on the parent. He had a sweet sense of humour, but was a little put off, when he learned that Tissi was only just sixteen. He thought her to be nineteen, and told her off for not telling the truth. Tissi was furious, because somehow, innocently, Bine let it slip, not knowing that Peter did not know. With them all there, it was only natural, that by getting to know all about everybody, it would have come out anyway, Tissi being the youngest.

They had one of their impromptu evening meals, a large plate of smorges brod, which Bine and Angela prepared, black tea with sugar and lemon, and Christmas Stollen to finish. Afterwards they sat around the table and played cards. By eleven Peter got up and said he had to go home now. It was a truly pleasant afternoon and evening. As Angela found herself alone with Peter in the little hallway, she whispered: "Why do you dye your hair?"

"I didn't think it shows?" he whispered back. Angela said: "Don't be embarrassed, it doesn't show really, I just guessed, because your eyes go with red blond hair, not with black." And he grinned broadly: "I have coppery red hair and at school they called me carrots". Just then Tissi came into the hall and said: "What are you whispering about?" Angela said: Oh, nothing", and said her good byes and went back into the living room.

Peter came back the next weekend, already a part of the family, but he had un-dyed his hair and it was now coppery red and purple, where the black had not been properly removed, and his hair was cut very neatly around the sides and top. He looked very handsome, because his face had a much more chiselled appearance. Tissi was devastated. Peter did not come up to her expectations anymore. She sulked most of the evening, but Peter managed, with his good nature to bring her round.

Angela had got in touch with Sunfield and Tissi could go there in the New Year, the date to be confirmed. With Peter, now a regular and pleasant visitor in the little flat, Tissi became less sulky was even happy to talk to Angela. They became friends, having bridged the gap of growing from a child of twelve to a young woman of sixteen; a very difficult time to overcome.

Shortly before Christmas, Angela was called into the office at the chocolate factory. She was called away from the conveyor belt and another woman took her place immediately, so that there was no interruption in placing the chocolates into the box.

When she got to the office, she found two very stern policemen, the lady foreman and the factory manager staring at her. Angela's felt her knees going soft, and a strange feeling spreading in the stomach area.

One of the policemen showed her his identification, and as she looked intensely at the identity card, she read: 'Sittenpolizei'. (Police for immoral behaviour). She looked up, puzzled:

"What does that mean?"

"It has been reported, anonymously, that you have a man in your mother's flat, and he leaves every morning at four thirty. Now your mother is working all night, and probably does not know about the immoral goings on in her flat." Angela asked: "What man, I don't know of any man, who would stay in our flat all night." She felt herself blushing and also became deeply embarrassed. The manager asked:

"Where do you live?" and Angela said: "In the Baseler Strasse, just opposite the station". The manager turned to the policemen and asked:

"How many people are reported to come down the stairs at four thirty every morning?" And the policeman said:

"Only one is reported".

"Well, then I suggest this is an evil hoax. Because it is this young lady who comes down the stairs every morning to come to work." Angela felt a great relief and said:

"Who would report such a thing anyway? How mean people are." She could guess, it was one of the busybodies living downstairs behind those curtains she saw moving every now and then. The policemen were also embarrassed and apologized and said they would tell the persons involved to mind their own business. The trouble was, they had already been to the hospital to find out what shifts her mother did and troubled her during the time she should have slept. And now she was worried and did not know what to think, Angela feared. The manager allowed her to go home, since there was only another hour and a half left to work on her shift.

Angela was taken home in the police car and found her mother up and in tears. One of the policemen had come up with Angela and explained to her mother the dreadful mistake. But at the same time explained that they had to follow up complaints like this, because they could not allow immoral behaviour in the town. Her mother put her arms around Angela and said:

"I did not doubt for a moment that my daughter would be involved in such a thing. I am just so sad, that my neighbours are capable to do this. Since you can't tell me who it was, I have to suspect all of them and that makes life in this house pretty awful."

The policemen said: "Leave it to us this person will not trouble you again". They left and Angela and her mother sat down to talk.

"You will have to explain in the hospital why the police wanted to see you. They were everywhere. As if we are criminals. I didn't know, things like this happen in Germany." And her mother said:

"In a way, I have to admit, that it is good that they keep the morals up. It protects young girls." Angela thought this is directed at Tissi and mother's worry at not being able to keep an eye on her youngest daughter.

*

Christmas came and went, Bine and Peter were there too and it was a happy and peaceful time. By February, she was laid off in the chocolate factory, because the Easter rush was over and a lot of extra staff, who were only taken on to cope with the rush, were paid off. She earned a fantastic bonus, and immediately found herself a new job, helping out in a children's home in the Bavarian Forest.

It was a job for 7 weeks only, just long enough to see her to the start of college. Tissi had departed to England in the first week in February and Angela two days later, leaving her mum totally by herself for the first time since she had given birth to her first child. It would be a very hard time, Angela could feel the pain her mother felt, but could do nothing to help. Everybody had to leave the nest one day, and mother would have to remember when she herself left the nest. How she felt then. Angela reminded her and her mother smiled through the tears.

"I will be back in the autumn", Angela promised, and stepped into the train to Regensburg, where she would change to travel on to Cham, near the Czechoslovakian border.

She had to supervise the boy's homework. It was, as she found out later, a boarding school for young offenders and children with learning difficulty. Right little hooligans they were and she had quite a job to work out how to handle them. They watched her suspiciously, tricked her and took no notice of what she tried to do with them.

There was deep snow outside, and one day, she shouted furiously into the noise:

"Right you lot, anybody who is not pulling their weight and does not do their homework in an hour and a half, stays behind and does not join me when I go out skiing." There was instant silence and the boys looked at her in disbelief.

"Are you allowed to do this miss?" one of them asked.

"I can't see why not? If I take some responsible, young men skiing with me, what should go wrong? Of course if there is trouble it will not be repeated and all the fun is over, that is certain." Angela paused and looked around. She focussed on a handsome angelic looking boy, who looked a little forlorn.

"What is your name?" and she pointed to him. The boy blushed and said:

"I am Ingo and I come from Cologne".

"How old are you?" she asked and he said:

"I am twelve."

"How long have you been here? She asked.

"I think I came here when I was six, I can't remember".

"What do you think of skiing when you have done your homework?" He smiled shyly:

"I think it's great">

"Ok, I am going now to ask permission and to see if there are enough skis to go round, and you sit here and work hard and I don't want to hear one word when I am gone, not one sound, except pencils scraping on paper, right?" They all just looked at her quietly. She left the room and stood outside for a little while. All was quiet. She waited a little longer and still all was quiet. So she went to find the matron. There was doubt in the woman's face as Angela put her plan before her, and together they went to the manager.

"We have not done this before, but if you do not go too far, I have no objections if the boys behave". Angela said:

"They are sitting through their first test at this minute. If they fail, we are not going anyway. I just wanted to know if there were enough skis to go round and if you approve. The director, the matron and Angela went back to the classroom and stood outside the door. All was quiet. All three of them grinned.

"There are enough skis to go round. See me when you are ready".

Their skiing trip became a regular occurrence and she taught a lot of those youngsters to ski. One of the teachers said:

"We did not know you could ski. You did not mention it in you application. Finally the skis are being used. They have been standing around for years. Where did you learn to ski?" And Angela explained:

"I was taught by boys a lot younger than the lads here. The Finnish children learn to ski when they learn to walk."

They had snowball fights and built snowmen, and the children from other classes and their tutors came and joined them. Angela built a snow castle, igloo style, and one afternoon in her third week

233

there, she decided to build a very small ski jump. Just by making some big rolls of snow, like they do to make a snowman and then to built it up, so that they would fly into the air a little and land about a meter further down a small hill and continue to the end. The queue for the jump was never ending, and even the tutors stood in the queue, slid down the hill and walked up again to the end of the human snake. There was laughter and tumbles and happy faces and red cheeks. Angela enjoyed herself so much, that she thought she might change her career. However, when the director asked her if she would like to have a permanent job with them, she realized that it would not suit her. She needed to be out in the world. This would be a job in the sticks and she said that she could not take up his offer, and anyway she was down for the business college in a couple of weeks. She promised to give it some thought after she finished college.

The boys were sad to see her go and thought that all the fun would now stop. But Angela pointed out that if they behaved and did their work, there was no reason why the tutors would not continue to do things with them. She told them that only hard work and discipline would get them anywhere in the world.

They wanted to know what she did in Finland and she told them that she had been an agricultural apprentice and had passed all exams and did her practical years in Finland and England and Ireland. That she had had a most wonderful, adventurous time and met great people as well. But it takes hard work and application to achieve all that. The boys listened and thought that they would also want to be apprentices.

Just work out what you would like to do most in life and then go for it. But first of all you have to pass your exams here and get your leaving reports with A's and B's and not too many Cs. They grinned. Many years later, via her mother's address, she had a letter from Ingo. He had become a pilot for Lufthansa. Her heart made a little jump.

24

Saying farewell to Grandfather

When she arrived at her old home, where she had lived with her mother and sisters from 1948 to 1951, a great sadness overcame her. So much happened in those three years before she had to leave for her first year as an apprentice. She looked at the empty rooms, where they had existed and survived great hardships. Her grandfather lived in the same apartment, but self-contained with several rooms to himself. He lived in the grand style he was accustomed to, and even then he felt he was reduced to poverty. Angela could never quite remember the elegance of his former homes. The house where he had lived when they came to Regensburg after his arrest in November 1944 was beautiful, elegant and had many rooms, which he had to share when he returned from Berlin. He grumbled and complained and blamed everybody for his 'hardships'. His daughter and grandchildren got two rooms, grandfather's housekeeper had one room, and he complained that his living space was reduced to only four rooms. Even worse, he had to share the bathroom. In February 1945 they were bombed and Angela, her mother and sisters had to move to Eichofen. In the autumn of 1945, they moved back, after the house was temporarily repaired and were given only one room and their other room was rented out to a young woman who had an American fiancé. Her rent money was food from the PX, the American supermarket.

Then, after the Währungsreform, (change from old Reichsmark to the new Deutsche Mark) they had moved to this place and some happy, although still cramped years followed. Even though they still had only the one room, it was a lot bigger and it had a balcony and they were given a kitchen, which was wonderful. There was also a larder attached, and since the money changeover there were things to buy in the shops and therefore food in the larder.

She looked into the rooms, and nothing seemed to have changed since they had moved out. The same wallpaper, her corner, empty now since her mother moved south to the Swiss Border only 2 years ago. She was aware of ghosts or were they just vivid memories? She was overcome with sadness.

She was shown into the box room, a tiny room which in the past housed the cleaning stuff. They had put a bed into it and there she would live whilst going to college. She was a bit put off, their old empty room would have been nice, but grandfather's fourth wife, just a year older than Angela's mother, ruled here. She was nice enough and also inviting. Angela could live there rent free, and was invited to share their meals and could work in the big living room, even use grandfather's desk and typewriter to practice on. She was content. The only thing she did not like was the window in her little box room, which was a very narrow affair high up above the bed, so that she could not look out. The only thing visible was the sky. She imagined a prison cell. But she would not grumble. Without this room she could not afford to go to college. She had paid back the money her grandfather had lent her for the trip to Finland and when it was done he invited her to keep paying because he had put all the money she had sent him into an account for her and if she wanted to she could send money every month to make her account grow. This money plus what she earned in the chocolate factory now paid for college.

Grandfather was so pleased to see her, and invited her to a game of cards. He had become frail and Angela could tell that he would not live many more months. She loved his smile, and he had become very kind and even loving. Angela spent a lot of her free time with him and they talked and played cards and checkers.

For Angela this was the first time she did not do physical work, her hands recovered and she found herself looking at them more often and came to the conclusion, that she had beautiful hands. Beautiful hands need looking after, and grandfather offered to teach her how to do just that. He manicured his own fingernails and even used clear varnish on his nails. Angela looked often at her nails and one day decided to buy coloured nail varnish, something, which had never before entered her head. In fact she had never looked after her nails at all, she just cut the excess off and that was that. She had never owned a nail file, lipstick, or any other make up stuff. She decided it was time to change that. She went to the shops and looked for ages at make up. She had no idea of what she was looking at and didn't dare ask in case they thought she was ignorant, which of course she was. She didn't know what Cold Cream was or where or how to use it. Whilst farming she had never used any face cream except maybe Nivea. She bought a lipstick, which turned out to be too red, and it frightened her when she saw herself in the mirror. She didn't use it.

Grandfather had also given her a signet ring so that she could go and have it copied. She had found a little job cleaning her old teacher's house once a week to earn some pocket money. Her teacher's brother in law was a goldsmith and she took the ring to him and asked him what it would cost to have a ring made like it. He gave her a special price; all she had to pay for was the gold and the stone. She chose Lapis Lazuli, beautiful blue. 3 weeks later it was done and she put it on her finger and she wore it all the time. It was too big for her ring finger so she wore it on her right forefinger.

Then, one day, she entered her grandfather's room as she did every afternoon, but she had painted her nails red. Her grandfather took one look and pointed to the door and cried: "OUT"

Confused, she left immediately and went to her aunt and said:

"What happened? He shouted and told me to get out!" Her aunt looked at her fingers and said: "Take this off, and then try again"

Sure enough, he was all smiles when she returned. The wicked old thing had a good giggle to himself: his old regal nature raising its head once again, even if just for a minute. She grinned at him and said: "What's the difference between clear and coloured varnish?" And he answered: "One is for tarts and the other is discreet elegance". From that day on, Angela would never use any other varnish than the most natural clear pink

She met an old flame from the Christian Community, who was confirmed with her in Munich in 1950, and they spent a lot of time together. They went on cycling tours and long walks. Then came grandfathers invitation and Johannes came to visit. Grandfather thought there was more to it than friendship, and Angela felt embarrassed, until they both explained that theirs was just a friendship. Grandfather was happy about that, as he explained later when they were alone together: "He is a bit puny, isn't he?" Angela agreed, he was but he was an intelligent young man, good companion and a friend.

She shared a desk in college with a young woman and they became friends. She felt, that after having spent most of her youth with men in a farming environment that it was time to have a girlfriend and they talked mostly about men and make up. Angela learned from her most of what she wanted to know about buying the right makeup and deodorant and the right soap for her face. And then half way through the course they had lessons in how a secretary should do her face up to look discreetly elegant without attracting too much attention. After her fourth lesson, Angela went shopping and then experimented in her little box room. She did not dare wear make up in front of her grandfather, but she started to wear it to college. She kept looking at herself. A beautiful stranger looked back at her from the mirror. That's me! She said to herself, pleased.

Angela had taken her bicycle to Regensburg, and so she cycled to college every day. She had to get her head around these dreadful shorthand symbols, which she hated. She felt like being back in Berlin in her first ever class when she was seven, and first learnt to write. When she had finally written her text, she was not able to read it back. Terrible! Typing was different. She borrowed her grandfather's typewriter and practised every day at home. She quite enjoyed learning to type 'blind' and proudly hammered away. The other thing which was difficult for her to grasp was book keeping. She would never be any good at that she thought. There were all these strange names and banking jargon and all she could do was dream of driving a tractor or plough a field or drive the horses into the field.

At the end of her time in college, she passed well enough though. This time her departure would be final. She would leave Regensburg and never return to live there. She was quite aware of this, and felt sad. But there was nothing here for her now. Thinking about it she realized that she had never felt at home. Home was a long way away. Home was where you could not go anymore, where they did not even speak German anymore. She had become rootless. It made her feel vulnerable. Once Grandfather died, there would be nothing at all. Her aunt would still be there and she would visit her because she felt duty bound. In the meantime she would visit her grandfather as often as she could, and hoped it would be for many more years, although deep inside she knew it would not be. He knew it too. On the day she left, he gave her a silver St. George. It was a beautiful little silver knight in armour on horseback, fighting the dragon. The statue was standing on a large crystal which itself sat in a silver garden with a fence and flowers surrounding it and all of it was mounted on a silver plinth studded with semi pressures stones. It was an exquisite thing and Angela looked at it and was speechless. Since she had first seen it when they moved in with her grandfather, she loved it and often polished it.

"Take it," her grandfather said. "When I am dead, the vultures will come and take it all. I had to make my will so that whoever wants something they will have to buy it, because Tata (his fourth wife) has no pension and my pension dies with me. And you and your mother have no money, so you will not get anything. Your mother's half sister inherited all the lands in her family's duchy and lost nothing in the war. She can afford to buy anything Tata is willing to sell. I want you to have this. That is my wish." Angela's eyes filled with tears. She suddenly realized that when she leaves now, she will not see her grandfather ever again. She could not bear it, but had to be strong, the last thing he would want, was to see her in tears. Not the done thing.

"No tears, go on and be quick. It makes me happy to know you will look after it. I got it as a prize from the old prince of Thurn und Taxis for driving the coach and six. Go and live your life. I trust you are the best of the bunch". Angela bent down and put her arms around him and hugged him gently, shocked at the frailty of him. Then she left the room, unable to say a word without bursting into tears. She did that on Tata's shoulders. Tata too cried and said:

"I am not looking forward to his passing. I was happy here with him, and when he is gone, this will all go. It is very sad and so unpredictable. I will have to go back to work, and have not worked for 14 years. But a friend has already got me a job, whenever I need it with an American General as his private secretary. He has been here and met Rudolf and it is all very safe."

Angela kept hugging her. Tata married her grandfather in 1947, a lady from Magdeburg, and she had been there when the Napalm bombs fell and lived and survived the terror and lost everything and ended up in Regensburg, where she met Angela's grandfather. They fell in love, and although she was so much younger, just a year older than Angela's mother, she had looked after him well and had made an excellent wife. It was not easy when they were first married, because she resented Angela's mother and the children. But bit-by-bit they grew to respect and even to love each other.

"I will come and visit, that is a promise" Angela said.

"And I am looking forward to see you often."

*

Whilst still at college, she had arranged with Marie Louise to meet up in Lörrach, and hitch hike to Italy. Marie Louise now lived and worked in Stuttgart. So when she got back to her mother's flat, she only had about a week to get ready, pack her rucksack, and be off. She took on three days at the chocolate factory, with overtime and made enough money, she thought, to go to Italy with. She counted what was in her account in the bank and what she had earned was 300 Marks. She would not need all of that, and took out DM200. She felt rich and free and prepared for her holiday of a lifetime. She had not hitch hiked in

Germany before, only in England, and not gone from one country into the next not knowing where to sleep at night. She would take the same tent they had in Ireland, and Marie Louise and she would carry it together. They would miss the tiny Fiat, but it would be such an adventure.

Her mother was full of misgivings. They both reassured her that all would be well. They took the tram outside the house into Basel and stayed on it until they got to the last station where they got off. The first lift took them the short distance to Olten and there they put themselves onto the road to Italy. The first car stopped and said he could take them as far as Lucerne. Great! Thank you very much and they climbed in. He was a businessman, travelling a lot. When he found out they were off to Italy, he enthused about all the places they had to see. They told him about the trip they had done in Ireland just the year before and the things they had encountered and their time in England together.

When they got to Lucerne, instead of letting them go, he asked them to wait in the car. He just had to make a telephone call and then he would be back. He was back in ten minutes and said he had changed his schedule, and was now going to Bellinzona, on Lago Maggiore. He had business there and would have had to go next week anyway, and so he is doing it now. He was grinning all over, took his jacket off and said:

"First we are going to eat." Angela looked at Marie Louise and said:

"Sorry, we have not got the money to eat out. We prepare our own, it is so much cheaper".

"I should have said I wanted you to be my guests. I am having so much fun, not to have to sit in this car on my own, but to have company. You are so entertaining, and I am grateful. So please, let me invite you". Marie Louise thanked him and said:

"This is really very kind of you. We did not expect anything like this. We just want to visit Italy the best way we can afford to. We have been students and not earned much. We have worked out what we can spend each day, and we have to stick to that." The man now introduced himself as Herr Schmidthuber who was a leather bag salesman, bags of any sort, from little elegant evening bags to anything as big as leather suitcases.

"I have been a student once, but my father paid for my travels. We did not "tramp" like you do. But this is now the thing and everybody does it and I must say, it is much more fun and entertaining all round. What do your father's do?" Marie Louise answered this:

"We don't have any fathers. They went off to war and didn't come back. They have been gone for so many years, I suppose I don't miss mine. Do you miss yours, Angela?"

"I can't say that I do, but every now and then I dream that it would be nice to have a father, only because there might be a little bit more money to go around, and I might have had an easier childhood, at least after the war finished. I have no idea what it would be like to have a father of my own."

Herr Schmidthuber stopped in front of a huge Swiss farmhouse.

"Here we get fabulous food. It is a farm, and they have a restaurant where they cook their own produce. I always stop here when I pass." They entered a big room, all in wood with beautifully carved furniture, typically home made in the long winter months, when there is nothing to be done outside and everybody carves in wood, to make their own furniture or carve for visitors" he continued. "All along the road from Pforzheim in Germany through the Black Forest into Switzerland and Austria and Bavaria, the most skilled Woodcarvers show their art. It is passed on from father to son since they settled in these parts. Woodcarving and painting, in fact anything that is possible to be made from wood, is being created in these parts. Every bit of wood is being used, be it ever so gnarled. People come from far and wide to purchase one or two pieces, or buy the nativity sets. And here in this beautiful room are things discreetly exhibited, which had been made by the family."

She saw musical instruments placed in a corner and they were told that all the family play the harp or violin, wind instruments and the accordion and all of them sing. This is the same in Austria, Bavaria the Tyrol, Switzerland and the Black Forest. It is a tradition which has never died. When the snow is thick outside and the animals have been dealt with, it is by the fire they gather and carve, spin, knit, sing, and make music. And it all happens under one great roof.

They ordered roast pork, red cabbage and dumplings, and apple juice to drink.

*

It was the first time for Angela and Marie Louise to see the European Alps. They had been together in the mountains of Ireland

and that was grand and exciting, and Angela had been to Norway, but what they experienced now was breathtaking. Herr Schmidthuber took them over all the passes, missing the tunnels, as he explained, you miss it all when you go through the Gotthard "Loch" (hole). They passed Interlaken and the Lakes and went up Wassen to the Susten Pass. Up and up into the clouds the road seemed never to stop climbing, past the massive Stein Glacier, and looking back into the valleys, it seemed as if they were flying, looking back to earth. They saw the Stein Gletscher Inn, and it was a tiny spot in a vast, wild landscape, and they could not believe, that they had passed it half an hour earlier. Herr Schmidthuber could not stop talking enthusiastically about all they saw, and in the end they could not take it all in. They arrived at the Gotthard Pass and got out. It was freezing and in spite of it being Summer, there was a huge amount of snow and brilliant sunshine. There were tiny areas where the snow had melted and deep blue giant gentian and purple tussle flowers grew. They thought they should also see some Edelweiss but Herr Schmidthuber explained, that Edelweiss only grew in inaccessible places and could only be found by daring climbers on dangerous ledges who pick one or two for their sweethearts as a token of their sincerity. They went into the *Gasthaus* and had some coffee and buttered *Brezeln*.

From the Balcony where they were sitting they could see the great divide, looking north, although the weather was beautiful, it seemed to be a dark light, and looking down into Italy it shone golden. They could not wait to get down into that light. It seemed to glisten. Herr Schmidthuber explained:

"What you see is the light reflecting off Lago Maggiore, even though you cannot see the lake." The girls looked on in wonderment. What a sight!

"We will soon be in Bellinzona, and there I will have to leave you, reluctantly, because I would just as soon go all the way to Rome with you" He laughed. Angela thought, if all our lifts are as good, we have nothing to worry about. What luck they had this morning, when they got on the road at Olten.

"We can't thank you enough, you have been wonderful. We will never get such a great lift again. This is a one off" Angela said. They got back into the car and now it was serpentines all the way down to Bellinzona, where it was so hot, they could hardly breathe at first, but soon got accustomed. They found a place where they could put up their tiny tent and shook hands with Herr Schmidthuber. They did not exchange addresses.

The next day they had a lift with a huge juggernaught which took them all the way to Milano where they were let off in an area where there were no houses, no trees, an enormous open space of grassed land and in a little distance ran a sparkling stream with crystal clear water. They decided to pitch their tent just there.

"What luck", Marie Louise said, "to find such a place. There are no people around, a few cars in the distance and one deserted house over there. What a strange place". Angela started to pitch the tent with the opening towards the stream. It was so clean, they could surely use the water for cooking. Marie Louise began to prepare the vegetables for the evening stew and decided that they would have to do a little shopping soon. They never carried a lot, only enough for about two meals. They needed milk. Angela had spotted a mobile shop a little further on from where they were let off and said:

"As soon as I have finished putting up the tent, I shall go over there and get some milk and whatever else we need if they have it." She took the purse which contained their joint food money and went off. It occurred to her that she knew no Italian and had no idea how to ask for what she wanted. The mobile shop turned out to be a roadside café as well as a shop. She asked first of all if somebody could speak English, but no one did. Then she said: "Spricht hier jemand Deutsch?" As an answer somebody said:" Ich liebe Dich". She grinned and asked if he knew the Italian word for milk. He didn't. They were all grinning and talking in Italian and she laughed and asked for a piece of paper. She indicated that she wanted to write something. She got a paper bag and a pencil. Quickly she started to draw a cow with an adder and a bucket underneath and a line into the bucket and a line from that line to a bottle which she drew. The all laughed and shouted:"Latte!"

The woman behind the counter asked her something, but Angela shrugged her shoulders, and grinned. She did a lot of grinning, it seemed to help. The woman put her hands together and placed them like a pillow to one side of her face. Angela understood and pointed to the little tent in the distance and nodded. The woman made noises of astonishment and acknowledged she understood as well. She got out a loaf of bread and a small packet of butter, a soft plastic litre bag of milk and she charged Angela only for the milk. She refused to take more money and from the waterfall of words and smiles from the woman, Angela understood that she was happy to give it with compliments. The coffee drinking customers around her also spoke all together and smiled. Angela thought it a good idea to take her piece of paper with her drawings and her shopping and thanking them in English and German, left to walk back across the wide grassland to the tent. Would they leave them in peace in the night? She wondered and had mixed feelings.

They settled down to their evening meal when in the distance they saw two men walking towards them. They were wearing some sort of grey uniform. The two girls looked at each other and said as one: "Police!"

Then Angela said: "Just act normally, keep on eating". One of the men was quite tall and the other only half the size. However, their uniform looked very formal. When they reached the tent, they sat down opposite them and started talking. Angela said: "Do you speak German?" the little one said: "si" but no more. Angela tried again and said:" Do you speak English?" They did. It turned out that they were employees of the Milano Airport, Linate, on which ground their tent stood. They camped on the perimeter of Linate Airport. They pretended to be worried and made as if to move their camp, but the two men said: "No no, it is a ok." They pointed to the deserted house and said: "We a live there, we a watch a nothing happen to you."

25

To Italy with Marie Louise

Very early the next morning the two men arrived again in swimming trunks. Angela and Marie Louise had also put on their swimsuits because they were going to have a dip in the stream to wash away the sleep. Apparently the two men who now introduced themselves as Theo the tall one and Pierro the short one also came here every morning to dip into the cool water of the stream. Angela was a head taller than Pierro, but Pierro took a shine to Angela. They splashed around happily with not a care in the world. Afterwards the girls made coffee for all 4 of them and shared the bread and butter between them. At midday they had to go to work. They had two Vespas and explained that the girls could borrow one and they would go to work on the other.

"You go a visit a Milano. We are home to night a". And they left. About 15 Minutes later, they drove over from the house, Theo got off his Vespa, parked it and hopped onto Pierro's Vespa and laughing and shouting they drove off. Angela got onto the scooter to try to get the feel of it and drove around until she was happy that she felt safe. She got off and they secured the tent and took the valuables with them in the small rucksack that held all their papers and Angela asked her friend to get on. She wanted to ride Italian style, sidesaddle, but Angela told her no, it would be unbalanced, and anyway knowing her friend, she would probably loose her on the first bend they came to. Grumbling Marie Louise straddled the scooter and after a few rounds in front of the tent, they dared to join the traffic. They took with them a map and headed to the center of town.

They could make out the cathedral and headed straight for it. Somebody once told Angela to go and play with the traffic. She never really knew what that person meant by it. Today, she found out. She 'played' with the traffic with the crazy Italian road users and risked her neck on several occasions. She parked in front of the Cathedral and the two girls walked around the outside and then went inside. Eventually they climbed up the inner tower and got onto the roof of the building where they found endless rows of souvenir stands selling the tackiest religious bits and pieces they had ever seen. The girls walked from stand to stand, looking in disbelief at the rubbish for sale. How could this happen on this roof of a wonderful beautiful cathedral! They left slightly bewildered. Next they wanted to find Leonardo da Vinci's Last Supper. They asked and were directed. Here they found a building which was bombed in the Second World War, three walls dreadfully damaged, two almost totally and the third which was opposite the Last Supper badly cracked, but the one wall with the Last Supper was not damaged at all, apparently not even a crack. Was that a miracle? The building had been restored, and the girls stood in wonderment before the mural. A museum's official came over and explained that over the centuries this place was amongst other uses also a stable for guard horses, and the walls were regularly hosed down. That could explain the faintness of the colours. What a terrible thing to do. People were so dreadfully ignorant. But then hosing it down repeatedly is not as bad as throwing bombs.

The girls examined and discussed the painting from a little distance. The colours were still quite strong and the perspective incredible, the movement of the men at the table was such, one could almost hear their heated conversation, and the depressed silence of Judas. And then there was the calmness of Christ. It was a unique place and a unique portrayal of the Last Supper.

The girls finally left and rode back to their campsite. They did not want to see any more today to spoil what they had just seen. They both talked about the mural, something they were quite familiar with however had never seen it in its natural setting, and that was overwhelming, especially that it survived the bombing.

The next day their two friends, who, by hook or by crook, both had a day off, took them to see Milano properly. The two Vespas coursed through Milano all day and at the end of it they could not quite remember exactly what they had seen. There were lots of stops for cappuccino's and gelato's and spaghetti Milanese. There was a lot about the Sforzas, a prominent ruling family in Milan, and their forts, castles and palaces. They saw a picture of Ludovico Sforza and found him looking very formidable with a prominent nose and a big double chin; it seemed he would not tolerate any argument.

They went to the cathedral again and noticed things they had missed the day before, and once more the Last Supper. It was a fantastic and very happy day.

They spent two more days in this peaceful place, and even learnt a little Italian. On the day of their departure, the two friends took them to the outskirts of Milano and deposited them on the road to Piacenza.

They exchanged addresses and Pierro gave them both a little present of a Chinese porcelain spoon wrapped in a white gauze netting filled with white sugared almonds. The girls looked at him a little perplexed and he explained:

" I a getting married next a week in a Napoli. My fiancé is a called Angelina and you come to the wedding?" Angela and Marie Louise laughed out loud. Marie Louise said:" That is sweet of you, but we are not able to come to Napoli. It is too far, and in German she said to Angela:" The little deceiving rat". Angela grinned. She wasn't interested anyway and aloud she said in German: "He is far too short for me". The girls thanked them for the use of the Vespa and for the time they spent with them. Then they watched them as they drove of in typical Italian macho style. What a pair!

That evening they managed to get as far as La Specia. They found the campsite at La Specia so full of people, they did not want to join the masses and found a quiet spot outside the fence in a sandy bit of forest quite close to the sea. They pitched the tent and found the sand a soft place to sleep on. They went shopping for some supper. They found onions, tomatoes, some cheese and spaghetti. On their little burner they first fried the tomatoes and onions in a little oil and set it aside. Then they boiled the spaghetti and when they were soft drained the water and added the vegetables and later the cheese. They stirred it all up and ate from the pot. Total luxury! They shared half a bottle of wine and felt like kings on a royal holiday.

It was a hot day and still light, and they went for a swim. Marie Louise didn't want to go in with a full stomach, but Angela went and enjoyed wave hopping. After a few minutes her friend joined her. They slept well that night and before going to sleep they decided to stay here for as long as they didn't feel bored.

A week later they thought it was time to move on. The local youths, who would not be in the campsite visited and lounged outside their tent and tried to speak to them in German. They were all dreaming to become guest workers in Germany. The girls learnt some more Italian, and taught German to the lads. In turn they brought food, some ready cooked and some raw, bread and milk. It was quite incredible. However, they wanted to be by themselves again and get on with looking at Italy.

They hitch hiked down to Viareggio and Pisa and their lift to Pisa took them as far as the campsite there. They walked through the town and took some straight photos of the Leaning Tower of Pisa and climbed up to the top of the tower. An experience of wonder. Why did it not topple? Angela supposed that every tourist must have asked this question.

They stayed one whole day and moved onto the road to Firenze. Their lift took them to the campsite on the side of the hill called the Piazzale Michelangelo. It was a small site for tents and the view was marvelous. All of Firenze was at their feet. Loads of steps led down to the Arno and the bridges across into the old city, with the cathedral of Santa Maria del Fiore squatting in the foreground, dominating the scene. That evening they just sat on the steps outside their tent and marveled at the excellence of the campsite and the view in front of them. They decided to cross the river on the Ponte Vecchio and that would undoubtedly take them to the first tall tower they had seen, and from there it could only be minutes to the cathedral. What a beautiful wonderful city. They got out their Baedeker guidebook to mark out all the things they wanted to see. They also bought some postcards and guiltily wrote to their mothers. They hadn't written since Milano.

They were still sitting on the steps when it got dark and gazed over the city as it gradually lit up. Both the girls had never seen such wonders before. Marie Louise put an arm around Angela and said: "I am grateful to have you as a friend. I would not have been able to do this on my own". Angela said simply:" Same here!"

*

For seven days they walked through Florence and each day discovered more treasures. There were so many galleries and museums, churches which were full of art treasures, piazzas and cafes, Botticellies and da Vincies, Giotto's Bell Tower and frescos in the Basilica of S. Croce. They discovered the golden Doors of the Baptistery by Ghiberti. They visited the Uffizi Palace and the Ponte Vecchio and Brunelleschi's Dome and more endless wonders. They felt like the first ever tourists and there were no crowds and the place was virtually theirs to explore.

On the morning of the seventh day they counted their money and decided that if they wanted to see Venice, they would have to leave that day. With a heavy heart they rolled up their tent, packed their Rucksacks and shouldered their load and looked for the road to Venice. They were picked up quite early and got to Ferrara by two in the afternoon, and sat by the road in searing heat with not a single car passing. A farmer passed with a cart full of watermelons and they bought two. They got out a knife and ate the lot there and then. Then they decided to walk. By four in the afternoon they had another lift which took them to Mestre. Another lift took them into Venice across the causeway, and there they caught a waterbus which took them via the Canale Grande to the Lido, a long stretched out island facing Venice and San Marco. They found a deserted little spot close to the water and pitched their tent. They spent three wonderful days crossing over in the waterbus in the morning and coming back exhausted but happy in the evening.

By day three, the money situation got serious. They had to get back to the mainland and have enough for food to get them back home. At Mestre they put themselves onto the road to Verona and then headed for Trento and the Brenner Pass. As luck would have it, an enormous light blue, brand new juggernaught picked them up on their way to Germany. Ha! They climbed into the big cab and put their rucksacks behind on the driver's bunk and looked at the world from a great height. They saw the signs to Lake Garda and promised themselves another trip with more money and a swim in the lake. They climbed higher and higher as they came up into the mountains and tried to have a conversation with their driver, but he was not interested to talk. At the border their driver got out and told them to get out too but not take their rucksacks. Then he said he was not going any further that day he was going to sleep in the cab and one of them could sleep with him in the bunk bed. The girls looked at each other and said no thanks, could they please have their luggage. But he would not hand over the luggage. He locked the cab and went into the restaurant for a meal. The girls looked around, very embarrassed. Angela spotted the little side window open. She climbed onto the wheel of the cab and then squeezed her arm through the little window and reached out to open the door, grabbed the rucksacks and the tent, threw it all down to Marie Louise, closed the door, jumped down and ran into the nearest bit of forest, where they hid for ages. When the driver got back, they saw him look around and then open the cab, jump down again and ran around, looking, no doubt searching for the girls. Then shouting he jumped up into the cab, started the motor and drove off.

Slowly the girls came out of the woods and walked through customs and on and on until they found a spot to sit down. Marie Louise was crying quietly. Angela looked around and found a field of white grapes, which were big and juicy. She decided to walk into it a bit and then pitch the little tent. They had no food and so they went to bed immediately. They were well hidden from the road and before they settled down, Angela had earmarked a few bunches of grapes. When it was dark she slipped out and cut the grapes down and came back into the tent. They ate so many grapes, that they were near to bursting. Deliciously juicy and sweet! Then they slept deeply.

The next morning early and bright they got a lift through Austria and just across the Border into Germany. They were deposited outside a baker shop. The girls looked at each other, starving. They had not had a meal since Venice. They counted their money and found they could buy 6 bread rolls, which they did. Then they sat down and started to eat the dry rolls, when suddenly a man appeared with a liter glass of fresh milk in each hand and gave it to the girls.

They were quite speechless, but found words to thank him. He said: There is more if you want some, don't hesitate. What a wonderful man.

Milk and bread rolls never tasted better.

They got a lift that lunchtime to take them all the way home to Loerrach, and they were even invited to a meal by the kind man. What a wonderful, marvelous, exciting and adventurous trip. They slept for almost two days.

*

26

Working for the German Railways

Angela had to find a job away from farming or maybe with farming? She went to the jobcentre and was shown various jobs, which might interest her. There was one, which attracted her, working for the German Railways. A Pfennig per kilometer on any trip anywhere in Germany and some trips abroad. Her workplace would be in Basel and she would have to cross the boarder every day and there were more perks. She would get a Grenzkarte (Border pass) and with that she could bring back chocolate, coffee, cigarettes and lots more duty free every week. She took the job.

Now she had to learn to use a Telex machine. That was not a problem. She was good at typing. The difficulty was to learn the telex language, the symbols and how to use all the abbreviations, and to read the tickertape. After 6 weeks of instruction by her new colleagues, she was sent to Karlsruhe to sit a test, which would decide if she was suitable for the job. She passed well and signed her contract. She had already made friends with all the girls who apparently had done this job since the year dot. Her salary was so high she could not believe that all that money was hers. It was more than she had earned in the chocolate factory and for the first time in her life she decided that money mattered. She had to work shifts, seven days in the week, which meant that in one week she would cover 24 hour duties, different hours every day and in one week she would work from 7am to 12noon and from 8pm to 7am and then sleep that day and night and the day after that she would work from 8am to 6pm with two hours for lunch, the day after from 12noon to 8 pm with one hour break and then again from 7am and so on. She had not done the shift work up to her exam but now she was fully employed, and during the nightshift, she was entirely on her own with a great deal of responsibility. The 'Badische Bahnhof' Building had the police station directly below her offices and in the night she often heard the prisoners shout in their cells, who were picked up because they were drunk and disorderly. 'Let me out' they would howl in Swiss German most of the night.

Doing this job made her grow up and look at herself. She was 22 years old and had not given her life much thought. She had enjoyed her life, worked very hard for little money and had taken bad times as part of it. Now she had grown up and had to give her life direction. Was it because she suddenly was earning real money, and was doing a real job? The years, which led up to this moment were learning years and she always believed them necessary. She was sad that she could not go back to farming, but then all that had changed anyway and she did not like the modern way of factory farming. The horses were replaced with sophisticated machinery, mono-farming was introduced, farmers concentrated on just one or two crops. Farming, although it was hard work, used to be fun work, they were fun years, they carried responsibility, but that did not rest on her shoulders entirely. And her earnings were poor. She had grown out of this sort of life. Her childhood behind her, her farming years done, they had been invaluable and she had learned a lot, but now she was starting a third phase in her life? Freedom! Wonderful!

Now everything seemed to be perfect. The women in the office were great mates. It was exciting work. It was mostly negotiating between Swiss, French and German Railways. Cargo and Passengers, trains coming and going! A freedom she did not know before, since she had to live, eat and work at the place of her employment whilst farming.

At home she was living with her mother, who was happy to have her home after all those years apart. They shared the rent and food, which meant her mother had a little bit more money to herself. Her mother still worked for the hospital in Loerrach and was working nights.

Then her mother was offered the job as Matron at the Old Peoples Home in Rheinfelden, which was a town half German and the other half, across the Bridge over the Rhein, was Swiss. The old people's home had only just been built and was a huge complex. There was one building three stories high with a basement and on each floor were ten apartments where single people or couples could live in self contained sheltered accommodation with a small section in the cellar. The middle Building, also three stories high and was a nursing home, housing approximately 80 patients. The third building was a two story one and housed the caretaker with his family, all the nurses and other staff. All three buildings were connected by a glass corridor. Mother had a flat in the first building and Angela shared it with her. It was very small, but very cosy. They moved there in the spring of 1959.

Angela joined the Rheinfelden Rowing Club. Since she was a newcomer, everybody thought she might have to learn first, and they were astonished when she showed them her skill at rowing. Soon she was in the top team and there were friendly races up to Basel and back. It was easy and fast to get to Basel, it was not so easy against the current to get back to Rheinfelden. The long summer evenings were mostly spent on the Rhein whenever her shift allowed it. A young man, who also was a member at the club, showed a special interest in her and it turned out that he too worked for the Railways, but not in Basel. He was the stationmaster's assistant at a small station three stops outside Basel towards Freiburg im Breisgau. That meant he had to travel via Basel and often the two would travel together to work. Angela thought him to be very handsome, tall, blond curly hair and very blue eyes. He did not speak the local dialect and seemed well educated. His name

was Dieter Matties. However, she was still thinking of Mike, even though he had not written for nearly a year. He had not answered her last letter and she felt she did not want to press for mail lest it should look as if she was 'running after him'.

Angela and Dieter and a lot of friends often went skiing on the Feldberg in the Black Forest. Angela had to get different skis because the Finnish ones were cross country skis and no good for down hill runs on the Feldberg. She amazed her friends with her ski jumping skills and felt proud, but tried not to show it. Always remembering her grandfather's words: 'Pride comes before the fall'. Inwardly she grinned a lot.

She joined the Carnival festivities in February. There were lots of costume balls. Every weekend somewhere else and Dieter took her to the ball whenever they were off together. Since Dieter was also on shift work it needed careful planning. Dieter was a flirt, and the girls were swarming around him like wasps on a piece of cake. Angela watched from a distance and was glad that she was emotionally free. He was a good friend and she was attracted but nothing more. That would have to do and she was quite content. There were quite a lot of young men who danced with her; in fact she did not sit out one single dance. What a lot of fun it was to be free and not have to ask your boss if it was alright to go out. She was her own life's manager.

On the first of May Angela and Dieter had the day off together and it was decided that all the members of the rowing club should go for a long walk in the Black Forest. They packed their Rucksacks and started off at dawn. They took the train to Wehr and walked up the Wehra Valley to Todtmoos. It was a beautiful day. All the trees had fresh spring leaves which shone golden in the May morning, the meadows were strewn with millions of different wild flowers showing off their bright colours, glistening diamond dewdrops, piercing blues and greens, red and purple, as the sun broke through the dew. The bark of the birch trees snowy white with deep black crusts and the Black Forest trees showing in darkest green, which probably gave the forest its name. The birds were singing and they counted the cry of the cuckoo. The number would indicate how many years you had left to live. They all laughed, because there were twelve cries and the entire group would die in twelve years? Ha!

As they walked they sang 'Wanderlieder' and Dieter turned out to have a wonderful voice and his friends Uwe and Max could sing Russian songs and started to teach Angela, and although she did not know the words, she learned to say them parrot fashion. She remembered the time before she left to go to Finland. She was singing Russian songs then. Such a long time ago!

They found a forest 'Wirtshaus' and had a delicious and extended lunch and a few glasses of wine. Then they began their return walk. It was 14 kilometers to get back to the station, which they would have to reach before 11.30 pm.

By the time they came home, late and tired but very happy, Angela had fallen in love with Dieter, could sing like the Don Cosacks and they decided that they would give a Russian concert at one of the clubs functions.

One of her colleagues, Hildegard, was a refugee from East Berlin and had managed to flee into the West. After the 17th June 1953 floods of refugees fled the GDR into the West, which eventually lead to the building of The Wall 10 years later.

Hildegard, her husband and daughter had over many weeks deposited their valuables in luggage deposit boxes at different railway stations in West Berlin. They carried their possessions in small plastic bags, everyone taking a separate trip and different underground stations to avoid suspicion. Then came the day when one of them was questioned on the way over to West Berlin. That evening they decided to leave the next morning, regardless. They would not take anything with them on this, their last crossing, except a shopping bag each with nothing suspicious in it, and find their separate way across into West Berlin, buy a suitcase each, put their stuff into it and meet at Tegel Airport and fly the hell out of Berlin to relatives in Stuttgart.

Before she fled East Berlin, Hildegard had been a secretary to a Russian General and could speak fluent Russian and even type in that language. Angela asked her if she knew those songs, and could she write them down the way they are spoken, so that Angela could read them and learn them and could she put the translation down as well so that one knew what the story in the song was. That would help when she sang the song and she would then be able to give meaning to the words she sang. She knew some of the songs, and Angela had to dictate a couple. They had lots of laughs, because Angela did not really know what she was saying and Hildegard had to guess. But in the end they had a nice repertoire and even some songs, which Hildegard knew and taught Angela.

Hildegard was quite a remarkable woman. As a girl and teenager she was a ballet dancer and even danced in Moscow and was quite famous. A very handsome, Russian Officer from Siberia made her pregnant, not entirely with her consent. She always maintained that it was a semi rape. She would have liked to be married to have

257

children, and the officer later promised marriage when he found out she was expecting a child. However, he disappeared in the vastness of Russia, and she never saw him again. She never forgot his wonderful blue eyes though. She called her daughter Gina and that was her only child. The husband she had when she fled East Berlin never managed to make her pregnant. They divorced a few years later and Hildegard was heartbroken at first, but her Berlin humor soon helped her to get over that. She was a true and honest and very funny Berliner and Angela and she became lifelong friends.

Not far outside of Basel was a place called Arlesheim and there beat the heart of Anthroposophy. An incredible Building called the Goetheanum dominated the hillside. It was designed by Rudolf Steiner, the founder of Anthroposophy. Angela and her family belonged to the Christian Community since 1945 and that too was part of Anthroposophy. She went often on her free afternoons, before the night duty, to Arlesheim. It was easily reached by tram which came past the station. There were lectures and art galleries and then she saw a poster advertising Goethe's Faust Week. There were performances morning and afternoons with lectures of explanation in between. She went and bought a ticket and managed to wangle changes in her shift which made it possible to see most performances, but she had to skip some lectures. It was an experience which would live with her all her life. She thought she would easily see it again. It would be performed every 4 years.

Entering the Goetheanum was a unique experience in itself. There is no building anywhere in the world that would equal this one or compare in any way. As one walked up the road from the tram station, the tall building situated on the brow of the hill, seemed like a temple from another world. On entering one got the feeling of grandeur of an extra terrestrial kind. The concrete wall made it very physical and yet strongly spiritual in the wonderful form it was fashioned! The tall windows alone were breathtakingly spiritual. The staircase leading up was inspiring. The stage at the time was the largest in the world with scenery that could not be seen anywhere else in the world. It all was simply unique, which it should be, since all Anthroposophists the world over come here for inspiration. And anyway it was also the University for Spiritual Science. Where else in the world would there be such a place.

Dieter showed disapproval and argued in ignorance. She felt somehow, that it was pointless to explain. He was prejudiced and closed his ears to any explanation. Her leaning towards Anthroposophy would become a stumbling block to most of her relationships in her life.

Towards the end of 1959 she was called to the head of the department, her boss, and he said: "You speak English pretty fluently, do you have papers to show me?" She didn't, since she had learned it by picking it up and not at college. He suggested she should take a break, go to England and take an Exam and then he could promote her to his office. More money! So Angela made arrangements to go to England as an Au pair to the same family she had stayed with in Ireland, who had by then moved to Forest Row so that the children could go to a Steiner School. They were pleased to have her and so she went early in 1960.

Once a week she hitch hiked to Tunbridge Wells where she prepared herself for the Exam with other foreign students. She took her exam in London and passed. Tissi meanwhile had found a job with a family and their handicapped daughter in Bayswater Road in London, and Angela stayed with her for the last days before returning to Germany. She was walking down Piccadilly with Tissi and some friends and as they passed Lufthansa German Airlines, Angela said: "Wait here a minute, I'll just have to ask something".

She went inside the Ticket Office and said to the girl behind the counter: "Can I speak to the manager please?" and the girl said: "Have you got an appointment?" And Angela said:"No", and the girl said: "What is it all about?" Angela answered: "It is about the job" (She had absolutely no idea what job or if indeed there was a job).

The girl went up the stairs and soon came down again and told Angela to go on up. There was an elderly woman up there and she asked her a few questions like: "Where do you live, where have you worked before, why do you want to work here" and Angela answered all her questions and the woman went through a door into another room. Soon a tall handsome grey haired man came out with her and said:" Dubral!" and shook hands. When can you start?

Angela replied: "Any time". So Herr Dubral gave her a date which was 3 weeks away, to arrange the working permit.

When she joined Tissi and her friends she grinned: "I have got a job with Lufthansa.

*

27

Working for Lufthansa in London

It was not easy for Angela to tell her mother that she was not coming home again but would go back to London. She had enjoyed living with her mother and they had become good friends, but life there was crammed and she was not used to living with her mother. She had lived away from home for nearly 10 years and needed to be free. Her mother was upset to lose her daughter again, but also realized that she had to live her own life. And the chance she got was wonderful. Something her mother never dreamt would happen. The world would now open to her and the war forgotten. Maybe? Her mother still dreamt that one day they could all go home. Angela did not think so. The attitude to Germany and the Germans outside of Germany was so different. People blamed Germany for both wars, and who could say differently after what happened to the Jews. Nobody seemed to think that Austria and Sarajevo had anything to do with it, or that the Kaiser, a grandson of Queen Victoria, could also have a little bit of Africa, but not as long as Britain thought it was all theirs. There were truths which were hidden, truths which one day would come to light and Angela believed fervently that this day would come. She also knew that while Germany was nailed to the Swastika, it would be a long time to wait. She kept her thoughts to herself. She learned not to talk about things to anyone but she studied and learned about what led to the First and consequently to the Second World War. She sifted through the history books. She remembered what her grandfather had told her. The English had little idea of what had happened to Germany or weren't interested because it didn't suit. She found that the English population judged the war and the Germans by the propaganda films made in the London film studios during the war years. She also learned that the English Nation is a warring nation. They think war as they see it is an honorable thing, and you have to win. How did they think the world became a British Colony? By the people around the globe peacefully surrendering their nations to Britain to be ruled by them? But stoically they defended their right to rule the waves, rule Britannia and rule the world. But for now, Lufthansa in London would be a great place to be.

Angela had to face Dieter next. He accused her of being unfaithful and flighty. Angela thought what right had he to call her unfaithful? They were good friends and she liked him but he was vain. She told him that she intended to stay in London for a year, to find out what it would be like and then she would transfer to a Lufthansa base in Germany, Stuttgart maybe or Frankfurt. Dieter did not agree, he wanted her to be near him and to get engaged. Dieter's attempt to dominate her and pressure her into staying made her even more determined to go to London. No one would dominate her. She was a free person, and even if she would marry, she would try to be an equal to her husband. Or she would not marry. She would be her own boss in life. Would she find a man who would let her? She wondered. Dieter accused her again of being unfaithful. She turned round to him and said: "What sort of basis is that for an engagement? You haven't even told me that you loved me. Do you think I take it for granted that you do just by saying you want to get engaged? She walked away, with a thought at the back of her mind that she had escaped imprisonment.

It was a dismal Christmas. Her mother was depressed and cried a lot. Angela could understand. She was so completely alone in a part of Germany, which was absolutely not her home. Her mother still grieved for her own homeland and that grievance she bravely kept to herself. But her roots were in what is now Poland, all her relatives and cousins lived behind the iron curtain, in the Russian Zone or so called GDR, German Democratic Republic. She had made only few friends in Loerrach, because when she had worked in the district hospital, she was always on night duty on a ward where patients were terminally ill. Still, she understood her daughter and would not stand in her way. It was a repeat of years earlier when she left to go

262

to Finland, only then she had her youngest daughter to spoil at home, now there was no one left. Angela tried to imagine what it would be like when the time came and her children would leave home. She would have children and they would leave home and she would be alone, only she would have a husband, she hoped, and there would not be a war which would tear her family apart, like it did her mother's. Spontaneously she hugged her mother and promised many visits, and that her mother could travel anywhere in the world with Lufthansa and only pay half fare, wouldn't that be wonderful? Fly to London and visit your two daughters. She hugged her mother. It was so difficult to leave her Mum, who was never happy unless all her children were around her or at least near. Bine was working for a Doctor in the Black Forest not far from Rheinfelden. She hugged her Mum again and said: "Bine will be home often I am sure. "

Angela had explained to her Boss in Basel, that she would not return and explained why, and he had written her a fatherly letter, saying that he understood and that it was a vast improvement to working for the railways. The world is yours he said. What a nice boss he would have been.

Angela took the train from Basel to London. Tissi was at Victoria Station and together they went room hunting and found a tiny room in Earls Court, near the Underground station. It was on the 4th floor and had a wardrobe, a bed and a cupboard with a tiny stove, a basin, pots and pans and some shelves for food. No fridge, a small table and one chair completed the outfit of her room. The window looked down onto a green square with a little church in the middle. It looked almost rural. She liked it.

She tried to make her money last the first month, because she would be paid monthly. For the first time in her life she had rented her own accommodation. Her funds ran out a fortnight later and she had to go to her boss and ask for an advance in her wages. Very carefully she put the money she needed for each week into envelopes, because at the end of the month, she would only get the other half of her wages and that would have to last until the end of the next month. There was the rent and the fare, and if she was strict with her smoking allowance: 2 Cigarettes a day, for meals just bread and jam or marmite and lots of milk, baked beans, and for Sundays an egg. She had the money worked out to the penny, and would not spend a penny more, no matter what. She would survive, she must survive! To her joy she found that she would receive 'luncheon vouchers'. What lifesavers!

She always went straight home after work and did some painting and went to bed early. It was lonely and she missed her friends from the rowing club and she missed not being able to row any more. She missed a lot. What was she thinking off, leaving a good job, friends, a beautiful area, with Switzerland just across the river, Italy a half day's drive away, skiing in the Black Forest to this black, noisy and dirty city.

She had not yet made any friends at work because she had not the money to socialize yet, go to the cinema or eat out. It was the winter and there was no snow. She missed the snow. It rained a lot and there was painful yellow fog, which the English called Smog. It came from the millions of coal fires, because even now in 1961 the English households appeared not to have central heating. She loved her work with Lufthansa, but she was wondering for the umpteenth time if she had not acted hastily, leaving her job in Basel and moving back to Britain which she did not really like at all. She consoled herself though that she would stick it for a year and then go home.

Her room had no heating other than an electric fire which she had to feed with shillings, lots of them and she could not afford to run it. Her cooker and kettle and her light had to be fed with half crowns as well, and so she kept it all to a minimum. The first two months would be hard, but after that, if she was careful now and not borrow any more money, she would be fine.

Then she was invited to Bill's home in Kew, a colleague from Lufthansa and they still had an outside loo and no bathroom. To her amusement she discovered a tin bathtub hanging on the door of the outside loo. She could not believe it. It was very cosy though in Billy's house, and it was lovely to sit by the fire. Only she found, that whilst it was warm and cosy in front from the fire, it was freezing on her back and the back of her legs were ice cold. William turned out to be a very nice friend and she saw a lot of him. He was going through a sad stage in his life, because his childhood sweetheart from next door had dropped him for a famous pop star,

(Manfred) Freddy Mann, and there was no chance that Will could compete with that.

Angela liked the work with Lufthansa; it was exciting and instead of just handling passengers and trains in a small section of Europe, she spread her wings worldwide. To make bookings to destinations, which she only knew from her Geography lessons with a prospect to someday go there herself, was fantastic. She was on the telex machines and sent messages about bookings to Frankfurt, where the great Lufthansa Computer was housed which handled all bookings worldwide. She was so fast that she could manage 2 Telexes a minute, which no one else managed. She had incredible stamina, which even surprised her, but she was determined to make this a success. She would not be forever in the telex room; she would advance and do different things. She would be with Lufthansa until she had seen the world.

Gradually she made friends with her colleagues. They had three tiny rooms on the 5th floor in a building in Regent Street on the corner of Vigo Street and opposite Brewer Street. It was an exciting part of London, down to Oxford Street up to Piccadilly Circus, the cinemas at Leicester Square and down Piccadilly past Swan and Edgar's to the Town Office of Lufthansa where her boss had given her the job. That was where she was determined to work in the end. The Ticket Office! Would she stay in London that long or would she transfer to Frankfurt, or Johannesburg, Sidney or Hongkong?

Her colleagues often walked down to Lyons Corner House between Piccadilly Circus and Leicester Square and afterwards talked about the wonderfully cheap food they got in the Salad Bowl. "Such a big plate full for only 2and 6pence!" they told her. "You can fill your plate as full as you like". The next day Billy said he would take her and show her where it was. Together they walked down Piccadilly, crossed the Circus and Angela could already see the big Eating House. There were so many restaurants in there, something for everyone. Billy and Angela went up to the first floor and entered a large, rather dark room, got a tray and a big bowl and started to fill it, handed over their two and sixpence luncheon voucher, found a place to sit and started eating. Angela had not had a proper meal for three weeks and found this was the most delicious food she had ever tasted. She went there every day for lunch, until she was clear with her money. She owed nothing, she had not borrowed a penny, and she was all right with her rent. Life was beginning to be more wonderful than ever before. She was appreciated in her job, she had not yet made any mistakes, her colleagues liked her and she liked them. They joked and got on so well. Dieter was soon forgotten. She felt, that if she could forget him so easily, it could not have been serious anyway. If she had been in love, she would have stayed with him and not come to England. So she was entirely free, happy and content.

As she sorted out her third month's wage, she realized she had quite a lot of spending money left over. She divided that into four packets and marked it spending money. Some of if would be for food, and maybe a cinema. Smart clothes was a must and she put some aside for that. She learned quickly to dress up London Style. She had plenty of friends now and since she still worked shifts, covering from seven in the morning to 10oclock at night, often the late shift would go and have a drink before heading for the underground.

Life was suddenly so very different from anything she had ever done before. She was always dressed smartly, wore great make up and Vidal Sassoon had just opened a salon down the street in Bond Street and cut and ironed the hair for airline staff with a sizable discount. She noticed that people looked at her, and she felt not embarrassed but reassured.

One of her colleagues, Klaus Tobias, was an opera enthusiast and soon she found herself among some of the staff from other departments queuing for tickets to go to Covent Garden. They took turns to queue all night and other colleagues brought them tea and sandwiches.

Angela felt that she had suddenly been propelled to the center of the world where everything was happening, where the stars met and politicians walked. And the world opened a door and Angela walked right through it; from the outer sticks of farming right into the epi-center of world affairs.

A year later the entire offices moved from Regent Street to number 10 Old Bond Street. It was a very large and beautiful office with new equipment and new ways, and Angela was asked to instruct two new people into the telex room and as soon as they had been trained, Angela was promoted into Reservations. She was now talking to travel agents and customer and made the actual bookings. She was still standing by to relieve in the telex room at lunchtime and when somebody was too ill to come to work. But on the whole she was making bookings. She was good in Geography and soon her English colleagues put difficult long haul bookings her way, because she did not have to take out the Atlas first to find out where the destination was. It surprised her that they were so vague about geography, even within Europe. They all knew where America and India was, but the rest of the world was a haze. Incredible! Being able to speak two languages also gave her an advantage over her English colleagues, because only few of them spoke German. They were told that they had to learn it within 12 months, but when the time was over they stayed on and on and on. Fifty percent of her workmates were German, and they created a 'Denglish' language, where the sentences were put together the German way and the words half English half German. Her English colleagues were baffled and could not understand the German humor or what they were saying.

Lufthansa was expanding fast. More and more destinations were added to the timetable. After the war Lufthansa was closed down to die. It was re awakened to life in 1955 and then five years later the offices in London were opened. Angela joined at the very beginning of it all and the excitement of new destinations into the wide world was wonderful. In her first year she had to book with other World Airlines, mainly BOAC and Pan American. Every destination inside Germany was also shared with BEA and Lufthansa was not allowed to fly to Berlin, its erstwhile home. These Airlines dominated the sky, with PAN AM being the only Airline to fly right around the world. Pan Am 1 going one way and Pan Am 2 going the other. To start with Lufthansa was only permitted to operate within Europe sharing with BEA. Outside Europe any other Airline would take the booking, mainly the ones that belonged to the country of the passenger's destination. Of course BOAC and PAN AM dominated the world's destinations.

Lufthansa added New York, then South America but only to Rio and Buenos Aires, Johannesburg via Lagos, Honkong via Bangkok, Karachi and Calcutta. Cairo and Beirut to their timetable. But to fly to places, which were not handled by Lufthansa, Angela soon found out that she could fly with other Airlines who were in 'pool' with Lufthansa. The world had become her oyster!

This was also the time when she decided to find better accommodation. Tissi had left her employment in Bayswater Road and found a job in a restaurant in Chelsea. She found a room in Beaufort Street in Chelsea. 3 weeks after she moved there, another room became free and Angela moved to Chelsea as well. She now had a room next to Tissi's. They went out together and had a lot of fun with other tenants who shared the flat. It was a lovely area, very near the river and within walking distance of Battersea Fun Fair.

Angela had to find a Dentist. Her wisdom tooth began to ache again and she decided something had to be done. One of her colleagues, Don, gave her a telephone number and a name in Number 1 Church Street in Kensington and the dentists name was Peter Maloney. She rang and got an appointment. Her wisdom tooth was growing sideways into the molar next to it and her gum was swollen and painful. It was decided by the dentist to eventually pull the molar to let the wisdom tooth grow in its place. But before that there were some cavities to fill. So she made appointments, which would not interfere with her work. She managed to be the last patient of the day which was convenient when she worked the early shift. A month later it was decided to pull the tooth. She had an early appointment on her day off. She wanted to recover in peace at home before she went back to work. She had been told that she might require one or two stitches because it would leave a large cavity where the tooth had been..

This dentist made strange jokes and she laughed politely although she was not really sure what was going on. He seemed to have a sense of humor, but not being British she did not understand.

She was sitting in the chair not at all feeling happy. He gave her an injection which she didn't feel at all. He was gentle and careful. Half her face felt numb as if it did not exist. She could not control her lips. He stuffed some cotton wool into her mouth and then he proceeded to pull her tooth. He began to yank at her tooth and after some dreadful minutes he said: "There are complications. I shall have to take you to the Eastman Dental Hospital, where I shall be this afternoon. I can take you because you might feel some pain in a little while". Angela had not a lot of choice. She agreed and they walked across Kensington High Street to a small mews behind Barkers Department Store, where her dentist had a small flat. He opened the door and made himself a sandwich, then they walked across to Barker's Car Park where he parked his little Morris Minor. Angela felt very uncomfortable, because she could not close her mouth. The tooth must have been half pulled out; it became very painful. However, she could not stop a grin, when she saw her dentist walk in front of her to the car park, with his 22 inch trouser cuffs flapping around his ankles. How very old fashioned she thought, and he was getting bald on top, he must be at least 40 years old!

They arrived at the Eastman Dental Hospital in Grays Inn Road, and Angela was deposited at the tooth-pulling department. Several hours later, her dentist showed up, and when he saw her sitting there, he said: "Good heavens are you still here?" Angela got up and said she had most terrible pain. "Come with me we'll have a cup of tea in the canteen and I shall give you an aspirin. Then I shall see to it that you are the next patient."

She was the next patient. She got another injection and then a very short dentist got his pulling equipment ready and got a grip on her tooth. Then he called out to his nurse: "Nurse, I need a stool" and while the nurse got a stool he kept a tight grip on her tooth, and while still holding on, climbed onto the stool and finally got the tooth out.

"You have to see your dentist for after treatment. You need a plug into the socket where your tooth came out. It is quite a large hole". Angela nodded; she could not talk very well. She went out to the waiting area and hoped to see her dentist. A nurse came by whom she recognized. She had seen her as she entered the Hospital with her dentist at midday. "Can you tell me where I can find the dentist with whom I in came in with at lunchtime?" Angela asked. "What's his name?" Angela realized that she did not really know if it was Peter Maloney or whether his name was Western. She plumped for

Western. "There is no dentist with such a name here" she was told. "Mr. Maloney then?" "Ah, said the nurse, you mean Ross Valentine!" "I don't know his name really. It is just that I am supposed to see him to change the plug in my socket, and I wanted to ask when it would be convenient." "Hold on, I get him for you". Angela sat down. She felt quite weak and shaky, didn't know if she was able to get home, or even exactly where she was in London. Where was Grays Inn Road? Which way to the underground. All she wanted was to be at home and in bed. She would have to ring in the morning to tell them at work, that she could not come in, because she felt so lousy. This must have been the worst dentist she had ever been to, she decided.

"Let me take you home, you look awful" she heard a voice. It was her dentist. She was really quite unable to protest. "Thank you" and like a sheep she followed him. She wasn't even able to be cross with the treatment. It had been sheer torture, and why wasn't he able to pull her tooth, like the little chap did in the hospital? He used no special equipment, there was no special operation, just a tooth being pulled. She was too tired to think, too sore to speak. She told him where to go, and then closed her eyes. When they arrived at her home, she departed through the door without saying good bye. She did not have to see him again for 5 days. She went straight to bed. When she was in bed, she realized that she had not even thanked him. "What the hell, thanking him for what!" she thought, "he put me through agony. When that treatment is finished I shall look for a different dentist. I shall never go back to him!"

She was in considerable pain and had to ring him before the five days were over. The plug had come loose and the nerves were exposed and she was in terrible pain. He planted a new plug and prescribed antibiotics. She went there every other day to change plugs. Slowly, 4 weeks later, the hole had sufficiently closed up; she only had two more appointments left. She had always been the last patient, going without a lunch hour to leave early so that she did not miss any work, and could go straight home. As she left the surgery, she realized that her dentist wanted something of her. She could imagine what it was and was not interested. She dashed down the stairs, and as she got to the corner of Kensington Church Street and the High Street, an 88 Bus slowed down at the corner and she jumped on, looking back she saw him running after her and seeing her safely on the bus, stopped running. "Aha! So he was after her. What everfor?" She thought on her way home, that he was old enough to be married and have children, even though he lived on his own. There must be a wife somewhere. What did he want with her?

There would be two more appointments. She would be watchful. She was not interested in him, especially since he made such a botch of whatever it was he could not do.

When she saw him again, he said he wanted her to take these vitamin pills. She looked peaky after the antibiotics and needed building up again.

"Ok she thought, maybe he is right. I hope he feels really guilty".

When she came for her last appointment, before he even started the treatment he asked her for a drink in the pub opposite. She looked at him properly for the first time. Before he had just been a dentist; what she mostly saw of him, where the deep, dark and hairy cavities of his nostrils. And she had noticed that he limped. He had huge, clumsy looking hands and a much wrinkled neck and his suit was at least 40 years out of fashion. "He is harmless" she thought and said: "Ok, just a little drink".

He had two pints of beer to her half. He asked her where she was from, since he detected an accent and she let him guess. South Africa he thought. No, much closer to England she offered. He could not guess and finally she said: "I am from Berlin". She felt pride in saying that. Yes, she was happy to be German and proud to be a Berliner.

"I am from New Zealand. My wife left me three years ago. She went back to New Zealand and took our children with her. I miss them terribly", he said.

"I am sorry to hear that" she murmured. What else could she say, and thought, I was right. He is married and he has children.

Angela was getting desperate to go to the loo, but felt too embarrassed to say so. So in the end, she pretended that it was high time for her to go and without much ado, got up and said goodbye. He still had some beer in his glass and so stayed behind. She rushed, more to get home than to go to the loo, and to escape from him. But just as well, she had made no arrangements to see him again, and would not see him again. She was still determined to find herself another dentist anyway.

28

Getting to know Ross

It was several weeks later, when she came home late from the theatre, that she found a note on her bed.

"Give me a ring when you get in, it is urgent. Ross Valentine" and added was the telephone number.

What does that mean? She went out to the pay phone in the hall and rang the number. "What is so urgent, that you need to speak to me so late at night?" she asked and he said:

"I want to see you. Could we not meet again?" She did not have a moment free at that particular time in her life; what with late shifts and doing extra shifts so that she could fly to Cairo as a guest with UAA, along with a lot of other staff from different Airlines on what they called "familiarization trips". She was going to learn all about Cairo so that she could tell customers where to stay and what to do. She had no time for an elderly dentist, who felt a little lonely.

"I am afraid, I have no time for at least 4 weeks"..

"I shall ring you in a months time" he said. "Good night, and sleep well." "Good night" she said and hung up. That will be the end of him.

Her trip to Cairo was fantastic. Apart from staff from other airlines, Billy and several Lufthansa colleagues came too. They stayed in the El Borg hotel, had dinner in the Sheiks tent in the Hilton across the Nile, went to the incredible Egyptian Museum, to the Bazaar, the ancient Mosque, which is supposed to be the oldest of all mosques in Egypt, the Pyramids, had a camel ride into the desert, a boat trip up the Nile through Cairo. One of the Qantas staff slipped in the shower and cut his bottom into shreds on the glass partition and knocked himself out. The next day he was ok but could not come for the camel ride. The last evening there was spent at the Pyramids watching and listening to the 'Son et Lumiere', which was overwhelmingly beautiful. There were great photos and slides as a reminder. It was her first of so many more wonderful flights and experiences to familiarize herself with the world..

She flew back via Zurich and took the train home to visit her mother. Two days only and then she had to fly back to London. It was lovely to see her mother. Her mother was still unable to take it all in; that Angela, little farm girl, was now flying around in the wide world. She wanted to know everything that happened. They talked long into the night.

She was back in the office and her opera-loving colleague, Klaus Tobias, had, without asking her, got tickets for Tosca at Covent Garden. He had looked at her rosta and found that she had the evening off. Gratefully she thanked him for thinking of her. Four of them went, dressed in long gowns and looking like royalty. It was a great performance and afterwards they waited at the back door for the stars, and Angela got autographs from Maria Callas and Titto Gobbi. Whatever would she do with them? At least she was in the crowd and took part of an excting event. They went to a late night restaurant at Covent Garden and had some Goulash soup and then took a taxi home. When she got home and got the key to open the front door, a figure came out of the shadow and stood in her way.

"Mr. Valentine, what are you doing here?"

"I've been here for two hours. Your landlady said you were at the opera and so I thought I wait until you come home. I wanted to see you again, and here I am. I told you I will get in touch with you in a month".

Angela's heart sank. "Well you can't come in", she said. "The landlady is strict that way".

"I don't want to come in", he said. "I just want to ask you out to dinner next time you are free". She was embarrassed. She did not want to go out with him. However he looked at her in such a way; it touched her just a little bit.

"I finish work on Thursday at 5.30 pm", she said "is that ok?"

"I will pick you up at seven then" he said and went. As he walked away, she thought: "He has a definite limp!"

She walked down the short distance to the river and stood by Battersea Bridge, watching the murky water. It is strange how she ended up to live near water most of her life, but this was the murkiest, muddiest, dirtiest water ever.

She felt strangely troubled by the interest her dentist showed her. She would ring him up and tell him that she has to cancel the Thursday date. She would tell him a white lie. She felt relieved and free again and walked back to number 99. She got out the key and opened the door and Tissi, on her way from the kitchen to her room, stopped and said:

"Who was that bloke out there? We told him you would be late. He waited all that time. Who is he?!" Angela ginned.

"He is my dentist and he wants to take me out. We made a date for Thursday, but I shall cancel it. I shall tell him that something has come up". Tissi said:

"We could go to the cinema when you get home, and then if he comes here again, you won't be here. How did he get your address in the first place?"

"He took me home after they pulled out the tooth at the Eastman Dental Hospital. I felt really lousy and could not face the Underground. I suppose he felt guilty because he really botched the extraction. He just could not do it, and yet the little chap at the EDH did it just like that, after they brought him a stool to stand on." Tissi laughed. June, another flat mate came out and said:

"I saw him too. He is an old geezer. He could be your dad". Angela laughed:

"Not quite, I think he is 15 years older than I am. He has two children in New Zealand; seven and eleven I think he said. His wife left him three years ago"

"Keep away!" June said. "My wife does not understand me anymore!" she mimicked. "Have I heard that before? Anyway, if he were such a nice guy, why would she leave him? Ask yourself that!"

"Well, I shall cancel our date anyway, I don't feel happy about the whole thing." He will eventually get the message, I hope". They decided to call it a day and go to bed.

"Good night everybody" Angela said and closed the door behind her. On her bed she found yet another note from her dentist.

"Sorry you are not in. I really want to see you again. I just can't get you out of my mind. Please get in touch? Ross" and he signed it with two crosses, whatever that meant. She had not seen that before. She went over to her sister's room and showed her the note.

"Did you put that note on my bed?"

"Oh, sorry, I forgot to tell you. Yes, he gave me that note, and then he went away, but he was back by ten, and then just stood out there. Really stubborn! He must like you a lot." Angela pointed to the two crosses and asked:

"What does that mean?" Tissi laughed.

"Don't you know? They are kisses!" Angela felt embarrassed and trapped.

"Oh dear! I must finish this before it becomes serious" She hugged her sister and went back to her room.

The next day she rang her dentist from work and told him something had come up and she could not make it. As she left work on Thursday evening, he was waiting for her outside the exit of 10 Old Bond Street.

"I just want to see you again. Can we not make it another day? Anyway what is so important that you can't make it today?" Embarrassed Angela said:

"I had forgotten that I had a date with my flat mates and my sister to go to the cinema. Afterwards there is going to be a party at one of our friends, who is from Rheinfelden, where our mother lives. She wanted to come to England and we arranged for her to come over and be with a family to learn English. That's all".

"Can I not come too?" he said?

"Well I suppose you can, but I am sure you will find it very boring. There are mostly Germans there and then you won't understand a word."

"That does not matter." They were now walking towards Piccadilly Circus Underground and mingling with the rush hour crowd. As they were queuing for the tickets he said:

"In the month that I waited to see you again, I have been to the University Hospital in West Berlin for 10 days to see what is happening in the Dental Department over there". Angela was amazed.

"Was it a study trip, where you invited or what?" she asked.

"No, I wanted to see your home town. You told me your father was a dentist in Berlin. I wanted to have a reason to visit, I put it to the EDH, that someone should go and see how things are done elsewhere." He looked at her in that strange way, which always touched her somewhere. She looked away. How could she get rid of this man? They got onto the Piccadilly Line and got off at Knightsbridge and took the Bus to Chelsea. They got off in the Kings Road at the bottom of Beaufort Street and walked down to number 99. Angela asked him to wait outside. As she entered, Tissi saw him out there:

"What is he doing here?" she asked.

"He was waiting outside work, would you believe!" Angela shrugged her shoulders. "He wants to come too."

"Oh well, it can't be helped then". When Angela and Tissi came out of the house he asked: "Where do your friends live? Do we take the underground, bus, taxi or walk."

Tissi laughed: "Kensington Gore, a little cottage. It is not so very far by bus. We have to change though in Knightsbridge."

"Have you had a meal yet?" He asked the sisters.

"We'll get some snacks at the party, and we have a bottle of wine here", Tissi said. Ross smiled this special crooked smile and said:

"I would like to invite you two out to a meal. I know just the place." Tissi looked at Angela and Angela at Tissi. They both did not know what to say. Angela was just about to say no, when Tissi happily said:

"That would be very nice, thank you."

That's Tissi, Angela thought crossly. She looked at her sister and hoped she would read the anger in Angela's eyes. However, Tissi took Angela's arm and to Ross she said: "Where are you taking us then Mr. Valentine?"

"A surprise" he said and hailed a taxi. To the taxi driver he said: "The Mandarin in Exhibition Road."

Angela thought, the cinema is forgotten, the friends would see the film without them and they would all meet later at the party.

Angela had never in her life had a Chinese meal. They entered a very oriental establishment, very private on the first floor. They were given a round table and Ross ordered, since both the sisters did not know what was what. He has been here many times, Angela thought, the proprietor knows him well. I wonder if he brings all his girlfriends here. Her mind was full of suspicion

They had a most delicious meal and by now it was 9.30 pm and high time they made it to the party. Ross tried to hail another taxi but Tissi stopped him.

"We are almost there. We can walk the rest". They got to the party and there everybody spoke German. Then somebody said:

"We will have to speak English, because there are quite a few non German speaking guests here. Everybody laughed. It turned out to be a very pleasant evening and Ross fitted in well and was very gallant. He managed to be liked by everyone.

"He is charming!" they told her later, "a very nice man!" Angela was still uneasy. She did not know him and was unable to make him out. What does he really feel about me? She thought. Her heart did not soar, she felt depressed. It was all very strange.

Angela and Ross met once a week and went for little drives and walks outside of London, when they had a weekend together, which was a nice change from rushing to work every day. Angela had to work at least one weekend in the month but because they were collecting days to go away, it could be that there was only one free weekend in the month. They would then meet in the evenings and maybe go to the cinema after Ross had taken her to a restaurant for a meal. There was a lot of insisting on both sides. Angela wanted to pay for her supper and Ross insisting that he wanted to pay.

"I earn a lot more money than you do, believe me!" he said.

"That is beside the point" Angela argued, "I don't want to feel obliged. I have always paid my way."

"I don't doubt that for a minute, however it would be my great pleasure to invite you with no obligations", and he would give her that crooked smile which captivated her against her will. She tried to ignore it and because she felt confused, she smiled weakly and said:

"All right then but I have to return the favor". Ross smiled and agreed.

"I am sure that I would like and appreciate that." She began to enjoy his company. He was charming and witty and always there. She began to rely on his company too. She even looked forward to his telephone calls, which was every evening when they did not meet. At the back of her mind she felt that it was wrong, because he was still married. Then she laid her conscience to rest; 'he hasn't seen his wife in three years, so maybe their relationship is truly finished'.

She began to make sandwiches to take to work, and save her luncheon vouchers. When she had enough for two to go to the 'Shanghai' in Shaftsbury Avenue, knowing that they accept her vouchers even in the evening. She invited Ross for a meal and he accepted gracefully.

Then in May he invited her for a trip to the New Forest. Somehow Angela knew what that meant, and she declined. They had not yet kissed properly. It had never been more than a peck on the cheek and Angela had to sort out her feelings. She enjoyed his company, she was not a child anymore, she was 24 years old. Ross had not said a word when she said no, she wouldn't come. He just looked at her, as if he could guess the turmoil in her mind, and she was embarrassed. Many of her friends had sex just for fun. She had never done that, because emotionally she knew she would have to love this person. Just for fun with just anybody; she could not do it.

She looked at Ross and he still had not said anything to persuade her to come, to talk her into it. Suddenly he took her hand.

"You can trust me", he said and Angela looked down at her feet and said:

"I would love to come" and she felt herself blush. Out of the blue he put his arms around her and kissed her like she had never been kissed before.

She felt like a stupid little girl, not like a grown woman. There was no fight in her, no contradiction in her mind. She freed herself however and stepped back.

"Good night" she said, "see you next week." He gave her the customary peck on the cheek and left, murmuring a "Good night Little One."

Little One! Is that because of the age difference? Oh my God, what am I doing? Yet, she missed him every time they parted. Do I really fall in love? Is that what it feels like? Wanting to be together all the time? She didn't feel like that with Mike or Dieter. Even her fist love, Heiner so many years ago! A teen crush, nothing more.

She was getting seriously involved and it seemed there was no turning back. And yet, there was a wife and she had no right to interfere in that marriage. There were children. She really had no right to him. What was she thinking! She didn't even know him properly. What she has seen so far was a very charming man, well mannered and courteous. He is a lousy dentist who cannot even pull teeth out.

Why did his wife leave him? What reason did she have to take their children back to New Zealand, and deprive the father of his son and daughter?

Why did his wife leave him? What reason did she have to take their children back to New Zealand, and deprive the father of his son and daughter? He keeps telling her he misses them. Then why does he stay in Britain and does not go back to New Zealand and be with them? These were questions, which crowded her brain. Until she was convinced about his sincerity, she would have to be on her guard.

29

7 Neville Street South Kensington

They met early in the morning. Ross came in his Morris and picked her up at 99 Beauford Street and they travelled south towards Portsmouth on the A3. At Guildford they turned off to Gomshall and on to Abinger Hammer where they stopped at the Old Mill and had cinnamon toast and coffee.

They continued to Portsmouth and visited HMS Victory. These were all things Angela had never heard of and knew nothing about. Ross told her about the role it played in British History. She would have to learn a lot about that, as she knew very little about the English side of European History. She knew about Henry the Eighth and Charles the first, also about the Conqueror, but not in depth.

They had a late lunch in a doorway, sheltering from the rain each holding newspaper wrapped fish and chips. This she learned was the most eaten food in British held territories.

Getting back to the car they were drenched and travelled on to Fareham, Southampton and then dropped into the New Forest to Lyndhurst. There, Angela discovered he had booked a double room and they were Mr and Mrs Brown. She felt herself blush but at the same time she would not make a scene. In a disappointed way she realized that she had given him the ok by accepting to come with him. 'It is time to grow up and do the modern thing', she thought. At the back of her mind she remembered his words, 'you can trust me', and in her naïve way she believed they would have separate bedrooms.

It was a charming bed and breakfast cottage, with flowery wallpaper and matching curtains, frills everywhere, a fire in the open fireplace and comfortable chairs near by. It was beautiful. They booked in and then looked for a restaurant to have supper. Angela prepared herself mentally for what was bound to happen. She had ladled out her soup, and now she would have to empty the bowl. It was time she lost her virginity, and even if this was not the man she would marry, she would find out today what sex was all about.

He was charming, gentle and funny. When her English wasn't enough to understand what he was saying, he patiently explained. She watched him and kept thinking about what was bound to happen when they went to their room. Did she really want this so much older man to be her first? How many women had he slept with so far apart from his wife? She disliked her train of thought and missed something he said.

"Sorry, I don't quite understand" she pretended her English wasn't adequate.

"I said a penny for your thoughts, you were miles away", and she said:

"A penny for my thoughts? They are not for sale", and she laughed. There was that crooked smile again. How does he do it? It sends darts straight into my heart. Suddenly she wanted to be loved by this man. Would he be able to love her? Sentimental twit she thought in German and then made up her mind that it was going to be an initiation, an experience and she would move on afterwards.

They didn't sleep a lot that night, and he kept telling her how much he loved her and she assured him that she loved him too. They were lovebirds when they came down to breakfast the lady serving them had a knowing and understanding look on her face.

"Could it be that they were listening, that they could hear us through the walls?" Angela was embarrassed. There was this grin again.

"They are quite used to this. Honeymooners come here on their first night before they rush off to the Ferry to go to Paris for the real honeymoon."

Had he been here before and how many times? He deliberately took her to a honeymoon hotel! He planned it all very carefully and Angela in her stupid and naive way fell for it. What a country bumpkin she still was. But from now on she would be aware, grown up, sophisticated and experienced. And yet! She had this strange feeling, that she would never want to be parted from him again. In a way she could not quite understand it. Her head told her one thing and her heart something else. Somebody once told her that hormones confuse the brain. One thinks its love, but it is only a hormone driven sexual feeling.

In the office she told no one about her weekend away. If Ross was going to be a regular feature in her life, he would be a secret. And until he sorted out the business with his wife, she would just enjoy his company and no matter how much she wanted to be with him, she would restrict herself to once a week.

They often met on Wimbledon Common and walked and lay on a blanket under a tree and cuddled and talked. She was sure with herself that it would not be a permanent relationship. Before he took her home in his old Morris, they would have supper somewhere and visit a pub afterwards. Angela became quite fond of the English Pub. They were lovely old places, usually two or three hundred years old and if they weren't then they were made to look medieval. Strangely though, there were some benches on the edge of the room mostly, but no tables and everyone stood crowding the bar. It always seemed a struggle to get a beer, and people standing around and talking, one had to use ones elbows to get to the barman. In pubs outside London she found that there would be a blazing fire and some armchairs around an enormous fireplace and if they were still free she would dash straight for that and sit with her feet stretched out towards the fire. She would want to live in a place like this; ancient dwelling, roaring fire, dark beams and cosy windows with window seats in the thick walls, instead of the bar a dining table and behind a way into a cosy kitchen with a big stove and a hood over. Dream on!

"What would you like to drink" Ross asked and she said her usual:

"a small sherry please". She did not like the English beer, to her it was an insult to drink this foamless, warm and stale liquid, and actually call it beer. There was no bite to it. The English would have to learn a lot about decent beer, decent bread and decent coffee. The only edible English food she found was Sunday Roast and Yorkshire pudding, and the way they drank their tea was acceptable. They could keep the rest.

Then came the day when Ross asked her if she could get four or five days off. He wanted to take her to Jersey for a few days. Yes, she thought, I would like to do that, but she said:

"I don't know I have to see if I can change my roster. It is always done for the month ahead and I have to find someone who would swap with me" She wanted to go and at the same time she felt uneasy. Her conscience would not leave her alone. She turned to him and said:

"Ross, I think I am falling in love with you, and somehow deep inside I know it is wrong. You are still married and I don't know if I should be the one you get divorced for."

"You are not. I am going to get divorced for myself and for Alison. She does not want to be with me. She does not want to live in Europe, and my job is here, at the Eastman Dental Hospital. That is where I need to be at this stage of my life. And Alison has never had a job, she is not working, she is a housewife and needs to be where her husband earns the money. She chose to leave me." Angela nodded. It sounded like the truth. And then Ross continued.

"When we lived in Opotiki, on the East Coast of New Zealand's North Island, she rang her mother every day, and cried a lot because she could not see her parents when she wanted to. So I had to sell up and move back to New Plymouth. Then we took a year off and left the children with her parents and travelled around the world. It was a slow and wonderful cruise. When we got to London, I wanted to work for a while with English dentists to exchange ideas and to further my knowledge. I went to the Eastman Dental Hospital and got a temporary job. I believe that Alison got bored, but there was so much to see and do in London. However, she just moped around in the flat and when I got home she cried. I found that the Eastman was exactly where I should be and work. I got myself a job for a year and we had the children come over to be with us. Then, when my time was nearly over, I was approached by the head of the department and invited to work there permanently for four sessions in the week, which meant that I would have to find at least 5 sessions in a dental surgery somewhere. A friend of mine, Pete Maloney, who has the practice where you came to, offered these to me and I was set. When I told Alison about this, she went mad and cried and wanted to go home the next day. I persuaded her to stay and we moved into a beautiful flat in Notting Hill, not far from the Church Street surgery. She managed to stay a year and then she left taking the children with her. We had too many rows. Nothing could persuade her to stay. I was glad in a way when she left. At the same time I grieved because I missed the children. I felt guilty about Alison too. I did a terrible thing when we were in Otago University together. She was a prize. Everybody courted her and I won her. And then I had to marry her because I believed that I loved her. She was a beautiful woman, but she changed after we got married."

"How did she change? Angela asked.

"She only wanted to live in New Plymouth were her parents lived. It had never occurred to me to live in New Plymouth. Christchurch, Wellington or Auckland even, but not cliquey New Plymouth. Everybody knows everybody, no privacy, and a very small town, albeit a beautiful town. But to be a successful dentist and to make any money one has to have a well-populated town. However that is by the by. I have moved on and Alison has moved back. It is best really except for the children."

Angela nodded; she was not convinced and said nothing. She thought about her own father, who left to go to war and then was listed as missing. When he finally made it back, he did not try to find his family, who had gone through absolute hell since he left and several times nearly lost their lives, whilst he very likely was in his own hell. However she watched as the fathers of her classmates, who survived the war, came home and no matter how difficult it had been, they left no stone unturned to find their loved ones. So many times she wished with all her heart that her dad would come back. She wished that no matter what, he would love his children enough to risk hell and high water to find them. But he did not. She looked at Ross and said:

"Don't children come first even above your feelings for one another?" And he answered:

"It is not good if the children see unhappy parents. Alison was never happy unless she was living right next door to her mum and dad. I could never make her happy. And when we rowed the children were upset. So it is better she is with her parents."

Angela nodded. She supposed this was the case with her own parents. She did not know. Her mother kept this all to herself. Was she suffering? She never ever talked about it. And she rarely looked at another man. Angela never gave it much thought. It had become the most natural thing to just see "the four of us". But now her mother was all alone. Her three children were out in the world and had left the nest. She felt a knot forming in her throat, and quickly changed the subject.

"I was in Jersey only last year as a mother's help. The people I stayed with in Forest Row, where I prepared myself for the Cambridge Certificate in English, went there for a holiday. Their parents lived there and we went with three and a half children. I think it was St. Brelades Bay where we stayed. It was very beautiful and the weather was great."

"Good. Then I wait for the dates," Ross said. Angela nodded. They were almost in Beauford Street. It was late and they kissed good night.

A month later they flew to Jersey for a week and those were beautiful days. The Queen Mother had arrived on the Britannia. They were standing looking out to sea at a big ship anchored in the bay. They had no idea that this would happen, and suddenly people surrounded them waving flags and cheering as a small launch detached itself from the big ship. Angela watched as a tiny lady in a ridiculous hat with lots of feathers and flimsy clothes which fluttered in the wind alighted, and came up the steps, where the Islanders had placed a red carped. A set sweet smile and a hand raised, graciously waving at the cheering people, she walked briskly up the steps and into a black limousine and was whisked away before anybody had a chance to say anything. When everybody had gone, Angela graciously went down the steps and waved at Ross, who took a photograph. Ross had hired a Morris Minor with an open roof and they travelled round the Island. There was nothing they missed and by the time they left, they had "done" the Island and Ross had become part of Angela's life.

He had persuaded her to come and stay over in his new flat in Peel Street, right next door to the Windsor Castle Pub. So it became a habit, that when they were to spend the weekend together, Angela packed an overnight bag and stayed on every free weekend with him.

In July Angela had to go to Germany to attend a training course. She had persuaded Ross to go back to New Zealand and sort out his family. So he agreed and just in case he was going to stay in New Zealand for good, he ordered a Mercedes to take with him. It coincided that he had to pick it up from Sindelfingen around the same time that Angela was there too.

"Why don't you come back with me? I can arrange it so that I don't have to pick the car up until you finish with your course." He looked at her and put his arm around her.

"That would be wonderful," she said.

They met again at Stuttgart airport where she had flown from Hamburg where the course had taken place. She had passed the course and now she would get her first pay rise. She was happy and proud. What a change to her farming days.

Ross had booked them into a small hotel near the airport and they would start back next day.

"How many days have you got left before you have to be back at work?" he asked

"Only four days. How long would it take back to London in the car?" Angela asked and he said:

"We make it in a day easily. So where do you want to take me then? I want to go somewhere romantic and beautiful where I have not yet been. I took Alison on a trip through Europe, hoping she would like to stay, and we saw some beautiful spots." He took out a brand new road map and opened it. It showed Stuttgart in the bottom left hand corner. Her finger went north, searching and ended up at the top middle of the map.

"Here!" and he read 'Rothenburg ob der Tauber'. She laughed at his pronunciation.

"Have you been there on your travels?" and he shook his head. "Then that is where we are going. I used to work near there and my most favourite place to cycle to was Rothenburg. It is romantic, beautiful and unique. You'll see. We drive over to here that is where we join the 'Romantische Strasse, which leads directly to where we want to go. I starts at Füssen, where the chocolate box castle is, 'Neuschwanstein'".

"Oh, we went to Neuschwanstein, and that is the only place Alison liked. It was a difficult trip."

They travelled over to Dinkelsbuehl and then up to Feuchtwangen and arrived late at Rothenburg. They found a Wirtshaus and had supper and drank a bottle of delicious local red wine. Afterwards they asked where there would be a hotel where they could stay for two nights. They were directed to the Gasthaus zur Sonne, where they found a lovely four-poster bed and Bavarian painted furniture, beams and cosy chairs. They settled in and then went downstairs into the attached Wirtstube and drank some more wine and chatted with the locals. Angela felt a little unsteady on her feet and kept apologizing and giggled a lot.

Next day they roamed through the medieval town, which in itself is a lived in open-air museum. They went into the gothic St Jakobs Church with the twin towers, each of a different design. They went upstairs to the gallery and admired the Heilig Blut Altar (Sacred Blood Altar) by Tilman Riemenschneider, carved in Linden-wood. They visited many little museums and walked around the city wall, looking into the town and through the arrow slits out into the beautiful countryside, climbed some tall towers, of which there are dozens and dozens. They climbed up to the top of the Klingen Tor and Ross pointed to a deep valley, and Angela explained that this was the Tauber Tal. She pointed to a little church in Detwang and said: "There is another Riemenschneider Altar."

The next day they went out through the Klingen Tor and down the steep path to Detwang, then along the Tauber to the Toppler Schlößchen and the Fuchsmühle (Fox Mill) and along to the Hans Röder Mühle (Hans Röder Mill) and over the wonderful bridge which would later be a location for the Chitty Chitty Bang Bang Film. They continued up the steep hill to the Koboldzeller Tor (one of the many guarded gateways into the town, which could still be locked up at night if the citizens wished) and back into the little town. Ross could not get enough of it all and Angela happily took him around, glad that he appreciated something she held so dear.

They arrived back in grey, drab London and Angela felt a pang of homesickness. She got to her room and busied herself with her dirty washing. June, another flatmate, came and joined her and said:

"How would you like to move with me into a flat? We share all expenses and then we are just the two of us. Our own flat! What about it!" Angela thought it was a great idea and said:

"Have you already found a flat?" And June answered:

"In the house where my boyfriend lives. He said the basement flat has become vacant, it just has to be cleaned a little. The man who moved out was a bachelor and did not do a lot of housekeeping." I thought it would be a good idea to have a look.

They found a filthy place with mouldy food still in pots and pans and on plates. Not a single thing had been washed up and the flat itself was in a terrible state.

"We have to do a lot of cleaning and decorating and getting rid of all the rubbish in the garden. I can see great potential here". Angela said.

With the backdoor from the kitchen leading into a little garden, full of rubbish at the moment, she could see herself getting the garden into shape. They had a word with the landlord and he agreed to let them have the flat rent-free for two weeks while they got it into shape and cleaned it. They gave in their notice to their landlady. Tissi was surprised but said:

"I have a boyfriend. I met him in the 'Hide-away' and I am in love. You'll see Ange, I want you to meet him soon". Now it was Angela's turn to be surprised. Tissi said she would let her know when they could meet.

June and Angela went every evening and Sundays when they did not work to get the flat ready to move in. There would have to be a lot of work still to be done once they had moved, but in the meantime, they cleared the rubbish from the garden and the flat and scrubbed and cleaned until it glistened. They had a living room or lounge, a bedroom, which they decided to share, and a kitchen with an adjoining bathroom. The kitchen had a back door, which led into the garden, where some roses tried to recover.

On their first day of clearing the house Ross arrived with a thermos and some sandwiches. Angela thought at first he would be joining them and help, but he took one look at the filth and put down the thermos and sandwiches and excused himself and left. Angela laughed:

"Men!" and June said:

"Tell me about it!" They continued to scrub and polish, tear off mouldy wallpaper and wash the walls. They would paint them later. They scraped the loo until it shone and glistened white, sanded off the wooden seat and varnished it, and moved in towards the end of the second week. It was all very cosy. However they agreed that the walls had to be painted white, and very soon to get the light. The front door and the sitting room window looked out to the street and all one could see of people passing by were their legs up to the knee. There was a little courtyard leading to steps up to the pavement. Angela put flowerpots down and immediately it looked homely.

Angela didn't stay at Ross's house in Peel Street, even though he asked her often. She excused herself, saying she had a lot to do getting the flat ship shape. June however went upstairs to visit Stanley, her boyfriend often for the night. He was a mystery; Angela never got to meet him.

The nights that June and Angela shared the bedroom, June told her all about her childhood in Birmingham and her discarded old boyfriends. It sounded strange. She lived in an area where all the houses were built in rows. As far as the eye could see the same houses, row after row, small and snaking up the hill, millions of chimneys smoking into the air, making it difficult to breathe, every house had a front with one window and a door, fifty in a row, parlour and kitchen downstairs with an outside loo in a tiny garden just big enough to dry the washing. The three girls and the parents shared the two bedrooms upstairs. They had no central heating but a coal fire in every room. In the tiny garden they kept the coal in the old air raid shelter, which every one had to have during the war. The houses were built in such a way, that the gardens of the opposite row met with a small lane just wide enough to let a fire engine in, separating them. She told Angela that it was lovely on washday, when all the mums where out in the garden at the same time hanging the washing and chatting away. The children would play in the lane, or in the street. Angela got the feeling that too many people lived in a small place cramped together. June confirmed this one day when she said:

"Since I moved in here with you sharing this flat, I never really knew how tightly we were squeezed into our house. It wasn't even our house; we had to pay rent. It was still only two and six pence a week when I left to come to London. Just imagine, for the room in Beauford Street I paid three pounds!" Angela said:

"How come you paid only two and six pence rent when so many people lived there? That was so cheap! What sort of houses where they?" June laughed:

Queen Victoria had them built for the workers and the rent then was six pence. They are council houses, which is good, because if there are repairs to be paid for, the council pays for it. Not like this flat, where we have to pay for the decorating. Mr. Swift, the landlord told my boyfriend that he would not pay for it. As far as he is concerned, it only needed cleaning. The rest is up to us. However, you and I don't qualify for a council flat. Anyway I would not ever want to live in a council estate again. It is taken over by hooligans."

"Hooligans? What are hooligans," Angela asked.

"They are street gangs, roughs, mostly teenage boys who have left school and have no work. But they make life in those places unbearable." Usually around this time Angela would drift off to sleep. June never asked about Angela's life and Angela never ventured to tell her. Angela's childhood was looked up tight. The English don't want to know or would ever believe her or understand. Later, much later she would write about it.

*

A few months later Angela came back late one evening and found June in the kitchen preparing supper:

"Oh, you are back. Shall I put some extra potatoes into the pot?" she asked.

"Yes please, what else have you got? I have some vegetables and some ham" and Angela said, "and I have some eggs, looks like we are going to have a feast tonight".

They both laughed. When they sat down by the kitchen window, looking out into the little bit of garden, Angela told June that she was worried about Tissi.

"She is vague and doesn't tell me anything. I somehow feel she is in trouble."

June had been listening and now nodded her head. "Men, she said, I bet there is a man. The thing with men is that you have to know them for a long time before you actually know what they are like and even then you still don't know until after you are married. Take my husband for instance…"

"You are married?" Angela was surprised, "you never told me".

"I was married. I am divorced now. He lived two doors down from our house and I had known him a long time. The marriage didn't last. He was a drunk, and he beat me. He was sweet when sober, but that didn't happen very often. I tell you he was a nightmare. He usually came home after I had gone to bed. He would be drunk and I knew he would come into the front door, groan, kick off his shoes, drop his jacket and head for the bog. I always had to remind him to take out his teeth, because when he vomited and didn't miss, they would go down the bog with the vomit. He lost that bloody set of teeth so many times. I tell you. I am well rid of him. I don't even know if he is still alive. Sad really, because when you get married, you think this is the best thing ever and you think you would die if you ever get parted from that man. What a laugh! I am never going to get married again, I tell you. I will have boyfriends and have fun, but I shall have my own flat and live my own life without having to cow tow to anyone".

Angela looked at her friend. She was shocked. So young and so disillusioned. She felt so sorry. She asked:

"Where there any children?"

"I wouldn't have children with that drunk, no way. Most of the time he was too drunk anyway to get his pecker up. I was grateful for that". They both laughed until the tears came. Angela had never heard the work "pecker" but she knew instantly what it meant.

*

When Ross rang her at work the next day, she agreed to spend the weekend with him at Peel Street. She was going to look at him with different eyes she promised herself. She reminded herself that he was a married man. She had great difficulty with that. He promised her to trust him but deep inside she didn't trust him.

She arrived on a Friday evening after work, and Ross asked if she had ever been to Hampton Court or Windsor Castle. And she said no she hadn't and so it was agreed that they would go and visit those palaces that weekend. Ross went into the kitchen and opened the fridge, got out four lamb-chops, frozen peas and potatoes and started on their evening meal. It was always the same meal he prepared.

"That is the only thing I can cook", he explained.

"Then I have to teach you some more recipes" Angela offered. She never had lamb before in her life. In Germany they didn't eat sheep because of the high fat content. But Ross explained that only old sheep had this sort of fat. Lambs didn't.

But they are baby lambs, how can you slaughter them when they are so small?"

"No they are at least a year old, they are still lambs then. They become sheep when they become pregnant".

Well, Angela thought that was what animals were for after all, to be eaten. She had learned that much when she was still farming.

They had two wonderful days, the weather was beautiful and Angela was made to feel as if she was the most precious person in Ross's life. He would not let her pay for anything, he read most of her wishes before she asked, and they went to magical restaurants.

"I have missed you so very much since you moved into that flat. I thought I would never see you again. Let me spoil you just a little. I gives me so much pleasure". He looked at her with that crooked grin of his and she felt her heart melt. His hand moved over and covered hers. He made her feel so wanted, so important. The touch of his hand made her senses explode. She wondered at herself, how very attracted she was to him. She felt she could not even wait to get home to his house to make love. And yet she felt annoyed that he could make her feel that way. This is not what she wanted; this is what he made her feel like. But she could not resist his charm. Yes, he was gallant, charming, and sweet and she let herself fall for it. She realized she was manipulated, but she pushed this realization right back in her mind. Her conscience however told her that this was to be enjoyed only briefly, that he would be going back to New Zealand and she would very likely never see him after that. So enjoy him while you can, but prepare yourself for the parting. She pushed back the tears at the thought and swallowed the lump that appeared in her throat. I shall not break my heart over it, she promised herself.

*

Some months later Tissi arrived at the flat, expecting a baby. It was difficult and there wasn't room in the flat for Tissi to permantly live with Angela and June. Angela, with the help of a colleague secured the travel money from the baby's father's partner and Tissi could go home to Germany to stay with their mother, who had already found her a job in the maternity hospital in the town where they lived.

Ross came on the last evening to invite them to the Chinese restaurant for dinner and they had a lovely time. The next day Ross came with the Mercedes and picked up Tissi's luggage and took the sisters to Victoria Station. There was a tearful good bye and Angela said: "I shall come over for a quickie trip and visit" and then Tissi was gone.

Immediately Angela said, "I have to go and find a room". June had moved out two days previously. It had become very difficult. "Now I have only a few days left before I need to pay my next rent. So this weekend I have to move out. June found the flat too small for the three of us, and Tissi hadn't got any money to help with the rent and I could not afford the entire rent on my own."

Ross said: "I know and I shall help, but first we go to a pub for a drink" "first we go and have something to eat, I am starving." Angela was exhausted and depressed. The joy of being in London and working for Lufthansa had somehow vanished. She wanted to leave it all behind and go. But she did not know where to go. She just had to pull herself together. In a way she was jealous of Tissi that she had reason to go home back to Germany. That is where I would like to be right now.

That afternoon they found a room just off the Gloucester Road. It was on the first floor and was very small and narrow but long and ended up on a balcony. The balcony sold her the room.

"I shall have flowerpots here and have the door open most of the time when I am home", she thought. It had also a cupboard, when opened it turned into a little kitchen with a cooker, basin and small cupboards. That will do nicely for me. I will have to be happy here. She looked out from the balcony and saw a huge building site. Later she found out that it was going to be the West London Air Terminal and that the building of it went on day and night. That must be an omen working for an airline and living right next to the place where all the coaches leave for the various flights. Yes, and it was not far to the underground. She moved in that Sunday and was back at work on Monday. She had managed it all on her days off. How quickly things change, she thought sadly. She had not seen June at all when she moved out. She left a note, but had no answer. She never saw or heard of June again.

It was going to be the last thing that Ross would do for her. His departure was getting ever closer. Angela did not want to think about it. Every time she imagined his trip back to New Zealand, her heart seemed to stop beating and all her nerves seemed to knot in her stomach area. She always had to take a deep breath to steady herself. "I shall be alright" she promised herself.

Ross had bought two big red trunks and filled them with his things. He left one in her room under her bed.

"These are things I don't really need in New Zealand, but I want them when I get back, which I might. If I don't come back you can keep what you like and get rid of the rest. Here is the key to the trunk."

Angela took the key. He told her that he had booked a passage on HMS Conrinthic, which would leave Southampton in three weeks. Three weeks! Angela moved into his open arms. They held each other, but already they took their leave. They had not made love for many weeks for one reason or another, and they would not make love ever again. Angela did not want to reawaken those feelings.

What they had now was love without sex, and she would want to cherish that forever. She didn't not go to Peel Street again, but they met almost daily in either her place or in town. They went to the cinema and theatre, and into lovely restaurants. Ross said:

"I have to take all this with me, because in New Plymouth there is nothing, except boring people". Angela offered:

"When you are back and made it up with your wife, would she not now move to Christchurch, Wellington or Auckland with you?" Ross said nothing, and Angela kept quiet.

Ross gave her all the addresses where the Corinthic would stop and said:

"You can write to these addresses and I can post all my mail to you from there. The trip will take all together six weeks and I can only post my mail from these stops." Angela said:

"I think we should not write to each other anymore. It would interfere with you making your peace with your wife. Once you left, we have to assume that that is forever. You owe it to your children". Ross did not reply.

They stood in front of the lift door at Earls Court Underground station. Ross had come to her room to say good-bye and she had come with him to the station. What she had not told him was that she would go immediately to the Airport and take a flight to Frankfurt to see her sister. She could not go home. She had taken a week's holiday to take her mind off it all.

The Lift door opened and Ross stepped inside. He looked at her with that crooked smile that always got to her. She wanted to rush to him and stop him from going, but she made no move. She smiled and as the door closed, she gave him a small wave. Her heart seemed to have sunk right down into her shoes. Mechanically she walked to the left luggage locker where she had deposited an overnight bag the day before and caught the coach to the airport.

'Look at it this way' she told herself, 'this is a new phase in your life. You will find the man who is meant to be with you, and he will be about your age, and you will live happily ever after',

At Frankfurt Bine came to the airport to pick her up and they went to her room. She was training to be a physiotherapist. They went to the swimming baths and up to the Hennninger Turm, which

296

had a revolving restaurant with views all over Frankfurt. They met some nice men when they went to the swimming baths the next day. The one that was interested in Angela was a count form Hungary who had fled in 1956 to escape the horrors of Communism. He was very gallant and kept kissing Angela's hand, which was an old imperial custom, she remembered from her childhood, when she was still living with her grandfather.

Bine's admirer was a friend of his and they wanted to take them out in the evening. Bine had a boyfriend and did not want to cheat and Angela was not ready for a new relationship. They exchanged addresses and Angela decided to fly home on the Monday. Somehow she thought Ross might have written before he left on the Conrinthic. She did and did not want a letter. Bine understood. She was going down to Rheinfelden the next weekend to see Mutti and Tissi.

"I haven't seen Tissi for such a long time. Just imagine, the youngest and the first to have a baby. I let you know how things are" They kissed and Angela went to board the LH222 back to London. When they were over London, they circled for a while and Angela thought they were in a 'stack' waiting to land. But then the voice of the captain came over the loudspeaker:

"Ladies and gentlemen, please fasten your seatbelts. There is nothing to worry about but we have difficulty landing, because the nose wheel is jammed. I shall have to jettison fuel and the airport will prepare the landing strip and we shall land in about one hour".

The people looked at one another but said very little. There was no panic. The stewardesses came round with extra cushions, smiling reassuringly, making sure everyone was belted in and answered charmingly all the questions that were thrown at them.

Angela, sitting by the window had a prime view of London and identified various sites. Then the plane veered off over the countryside. Angela thought that this would mean that it would be safer to crash where there are no houses. How quickly one's life can end! And then she thought how ridiculous" I am not going to die today. If God has kept me alive throughout the horrors of the war, he would not let me die in such an absurd way.

The voice of the captain came over again:

"We are going to land ladies and gentlemen. Please put your seats into an upright position, put the pillows on your knee and bend down. We will be all right. It might just be a little bumpy when I have to slow down"

The captain's voice was soft and calm. It was very quiet on the plane. Angela would have liked to see outside, but all the shutters were down. She felt the plane land softly and the engines reverse and thought: 'what was all the fuss about, then there was a bump, a tremendous shudder and screeching noise, which carried on until the plane stopped. Immediately, the stewards and stewardesses were everywhere and opening the escape hatches. The inflatable shoots rolled out and people were told to take off their shoes and hop onto it and slide down into waiting arms. The landing strip was lined with fire engines and men and there was foam everywhere. The first woman to jump was so eager to get off the plane she jumped with her high-heeled shoes on before anybody could stop her and punctured the shoot at the end, which is the bolster to catch the sliding passengers. An employee from Lufthansa Cargo had to be the catcher. He was in the end the only person seriously injured. He was taken to hospital with kidney damage and spent a long time off work. Captain Dofel did a most incredible job putting down the aircraft without the nose wheel. The aircraft itself suffered no permanent damage. Four hours later he took off that afternoon and flew the empty aircraft back to Frankfurt. The English Newspapers were full of his praise and showed his photo on all the front pages. Hero they called him. Lufthansa give him the sack. Everyone was in shock. The papers were full of it and Lufthansa was forced to apologize and reinstate captain Dofel. What must he have felt? That his company had so little faith in him? Angela wrote a little comment in the 'Lufthanseat'

*

She had to wait some time before she could collect her luggage and identify her handbag from the cabin, then she went home and thought: 'what an absurd life I lead. There is never anything, which is ordinary about my life.' What an experience! Was I scared? She wondered. She had felt no panic, no fear, more an interest at what was happening. Was it her complete trust in the captain, or her

298

knowledge about what she had been through and survived, and therefore felt that she would live until old age?

She rang the office and asked if it was alright to save the rest of her days off for another time, she wanted to go back to work and not be at home. It turned out that one of her colleagues was not well and they were glad for her to come in. Great!

There had been a letter from Ross, but she had not opened it. She kept looking at it. But he was now on the Corinthic and she would not answer this letter anyway and so she just propped it upright on the shelf above the table. She so wanted to read what he said, but this was over. She would keep this letter unopened among her things. She would never read it. Strangely she felt painfully relieved.

Wedding 1966

Mallorca 1969

19 A Forde Park

Angela's and David's wedding day 1996

Camping France 1983

Elizabethan Tuesday in the dress that Angela made.

Louise and Angela 1975

Nile Cruise David and Angela 2007

305

My favorite box. made like all the others of scrap wood.

One of my Boxes

the wendy house that mum built

30

A cold and dismal Winter

Angela enjoyed her little room. For the first time since she worked for Lufthansa she was entirely on her own. She never heard from June again. June seemed to have vanished, probably she and her boyfriend moved into a flat together. Angela never found out. She was sad. They had got on so well together.

Angela spent a lot of time visiting the National Art Gallery and the Tate; she went to the National Museum. She visited the Greek and Egyptian sections over and over. She had discovered Leonard Cotteral and was reading his Archeological books about the Mountains of Pharaoh, Lost Kingdoms, Tombs and Temples. The Bull of Minos and the big digs by Sir Arthur Evans at Knossos, and Heinrich Schliemann in Mycenae! Lost Cities, Lost Kings and Queens of Egypt. These are the places I am going to visit. She planned her trips. She had not time for anything else. Work and my trips! She felt happy and relieved and ready to get on with her life. She even thought that she might spend one or two holidays working on a Dig herself.

Coming home from work two weeks after Ross had left, she found 14 blue airmail letters bundled up with an elastic band in her letterbox. Her heart sank. Immediately her feelings were aroused. She had tried so hard to get on without Ross. Ross must be banished from her life. She wanted to put this bundle on the shelf with the other unopened letter when her eye caught something on the first cover. It said:

"You must read me!" She opened it and it read: "I miss you so much, Little One. I don't think I can live without you". She closed the letter she did not want to read any more of it. She opened the last one in the pile, and it read: "When we docked today, I was hoping to get a letter or two or three from you, but there was nothing. I miss you so terribly much. How are you my Little One? I know we said not to write, but I need to know that you still love me." She put the letters aside. "He must be crossed out of my life." She wrote to him and he would get this letter in Bangkok. She told him that they must stop writing and finish this affair. He must make an effort for his children's sake, and that she herself had to get on with her life. In Time they would forget each other. She posted the letter. Angela was overcome by a feeling of grief. A terrible longing! She must rid herself of it all. She needed to be free to lead the life she planned. There should be no room for anyone, and she certainly did not want to be hampered by these all-consuming feelings. But would she forget? She would never forget! The feelings would fade and hopefully a nice memory would remain.

Then a thought struck her like an arrow. It had been lurking at the back of her mind and she had ignored it. Ross has not been faithful to his wife. Would he be faithful to her, should he come back and they were together again? She would never be sure. All that he had said about Alison and her homesickness and she being a prize! He had not made her happy and that was why she was homesick. She could see it as clearly as anything. Was he the conquering hero? Would he pursue her until he was sure she was his and then drop her? What morbid thoughts! He was gone and by the time he got to New Zealand and saw his children, his wife, his mum and dad and all his friends, he would surely never come back to England.

Then came the colourful letter from Pitcairn where the Corinthic docked out at sea and the islanders came to collect the mail and goods in their little boats. They also took the ships mail to be sent off with the next ship that would pass to go the other way. Pitcairn's stamps are very rare and very beautiful. He put just about every stamp available on the envelope. She put it with the others on the shelf.

A week later came the telephone call:

"Little One, I am coming home. I can't stand it. Alison came on board and told me not even to get off the ship but to go right back again. She wouldn't let me see the children and I took a flight to Christchurch to see my mum and dad at Ashburton. Then I flew back to Wellington. It just about broke my heart to see the children at

Norma's. They had come to stay with my sister. They have grown so much. Richard was crying. Jo was hiding behind her mother who had come too. My sisters were very understanding. But Alison and I had a terrible row. She accused me of having affairs, but I swear I did not until I met you, and you happened a long time after Alison went back to New Zealand. I am coming home. Will you be at the Airport? I am leaving here on Friday. I arrive on Monday." Angela was speechless. This would turn her life upside down. It did not fit into her plans anymore.

"Please say something. Don't you love me anymore?" came his voice over the phone. She still did love him; she could not deny it. But she was not happy with the relationship. It was too involved. She could not stop him from coming back.

"Yes, I love you. But it seems to me that you did not say the right words. You are letting your children down. To build our relationship on their grief would not be a happy one. They would always miss you and resent you and me." Again she thought back to her own childhood and how she so often wished with all her heart that her father had cared enough if only to see them now and then.

"I will be at the airport. I will have to take the day off. Take care"

"I love you, Little One. I can't be without you" and they rang off. She should have been happy to have him back. Seven weeks ago she was devastated that he left and now she was unhappy. What is this! What is going on with my emotions! Is this the end of the life I know? Am I going to have to change everything to be with this man? I have to be loyal, since I love him. He is coming back here because he loves me and I seem to be more important than his own family. It made her sad and it upset her terribly. She did not want him. To make matters worse, it made her feel guilty.

She was at the airport and was shocked when she saw him. He looked tired and so small. He only had a little overnight bag. He dropped it to hug her.

"Oh my darling, it is so good to hold you", he said. They kissed. Slowly they walked to the coach station and caught the coach back to London.

"I am utterly broke, Little One," he said. I owe my sister Elaine £80 pounds for the flight. (Angela earned forty-two pounds and ten shillings a month) I have nowhere to live. I have no job. Pete Maloney said I could sleep in the waiting room at number one Church Street until I find a place to live. Alison's dad is a lawyer and he made sure everything goes to his daughter and our children. That is ok. But I am skint! I have not a penny." Angela was stunned. Well she could not now tell him how she felt. She thought that she would have to give up her room, which would never be big enough for them both and find somewhere else to live. It would have to be cheap, since he had no money and she would have to find the rent herself.

"We will have to find a cheap flat somewhere," she said with a heavy heart. She thought it is all happening too fast. I have only known this man for a year! What of my plans, what of my life!

They went to the surgery, and found Pete Maloney still there. He was also a New Zealander and had known Ross since they were in Otago together, Pete being a little older, had graduated before Ross did. Pete said:

"How are ye, ye stupid bastard! How can you get yourself into such bloody shit?" Then he turned to Angela and said:

"I don't mean you, I mean him and his in laws. He should have had a lawyer before he went back to New Zealand and arranged it before hand." Angela said:

"That would have defeated the purpose. He went back not to divorce but to mend his marriage. That was the idea." Pete laughed.

"There was nothing to mend. They should never have married in the first place". Ross pulled a face. He had been standing there, probably too tired to argue. He just said:

"I am grateful that you offer me this place to kip. I shall tidy up and before the cleaners and the patients come, I shall be out of here. Can I have my old job back?"

"I am sorry mate, but I have somebody who took your place. Couldn't manage all my patients on my own." Ross nodded:

"I thought so." They took their leave and Angela and Ross went across the road to have a bite to eat. Then they went to Angela's room and talked. Angela had to go to work next day and had to make up for the day she borrowed to pick up Ross. She did not see him for three days. She had given him ten pounds and he went back to the Eastman and was reinstated. Then he found a dentist in the Edgware

Road who would employ him for four sessions and give him five pounds per session plus if he had a patient he would get his percentage less the five pounds. But as yet he had no patients and had to wait for an overflow, which would be passed on to him. Then on the fourth day he rang her and said:

"I have found a flat!"

"Where? How much is the rent? When can we have a look?"

"I have already seen it. It is behind the Olympia in a little street. It is a basement flat. It is ok. It hasn't got a garden like your other one had, but it will do until I have found my feet. You will have to trust me, Little One".

"Can we have a look tonight?" She did not want to end up in a dark underground flat. The one in Neville Street had been light and warm and had a garden, and really was only a semi-basement. Well she would have a look, and as Ross said, it would only be for a short while.

It turned out to be dark and cold. It had no passage or hall to lead to the rooms. One entered directly into the sitting room from the street, and the front room window looked out into a black hole, which was the coal cellar under the pavement. There was a rail, which stopped pedestrians from falling into the well. The front door did not fit very well and a terrible draught came in from the street. The door opposite from the entrance lead into the kitchen and then there was a narrow passage to the bathroom and further to the bedroom. The kitchen, bathroom and bedroom had windows under the ceiling, which looked up to a grid covered in dead leaves. There is no daylight into this place. It smelt of musty damp. Angela felt deep depression ooze all over her. "I can't live here?" She thought. Ross said:

"It is not much, but we can make it cosy, and we have each other. By the spring I will have enough money together to be able to afford a better place." Angela realized, perhaps for the first time, that she was going to be with this man for the rest of her life. She was caught! She went over to him and he put an arm around her and together they went round to have another look. There were things on the kitchen table; three mugs, plates and two pots, some dreadful cutlery and a bent and battered frying pan. The double bed had blankets and two changes of sheets, the bathroom was damp and cold and the hot water came from a little gas boiler in the kitchen. The rent was three pounds and ten shillings a week. She stopped herself from crying. "I have to be brave. It will sort itself out. You have to stick it for now" she told herself. "This man has come round the world to be with you, he loves you, you love him, and things will work out. You are not yet committed" She reassured herself. But deep inside she did not want this.

Angela gave notice to her landlord and he offered to let her go before the two weeks were over because he had a waiting list for the room. So they moved that weekend into the dark, miserably cold flat behind Olympia, and Winter was just beginning. They found some shops at the bottom of their street and Angela saw some orange boxes. They would make furniture and shelves, which we haven't got, she thought. She asked the greengrocer whether she could have some boxes and he said:

"Take em lovey, I won't have to get rid of them then". Angela laughed and said:

"I shall have some more next week, will you keep them for me?"

"Sure ducks", he said. Ross asked what on earth she wanted with those boxes and she grinned and told him to wait and see. They put the groceries in and carried them home. There she put them against the wall and put her books into it. Ross had nothing so far, except what was in his trunk, which he had left with Angela before he travelled to New Zealand. This trunk doubled up as their only table. His other trunk was still on the high seas, being shipped back to England. It would take at least three months before it arrived. In time they had kitchen cupboards, shelves for her clothing and shoes, since there was no wardrobe. They found a very cheap cupboard in a second hand shop. It only cost six shillings and they carried it home between them. A young lad, who saw them struggling, gave a hand at Angela's end and they got it down the stairs and into the bedroom. The place was beginning to look like a home. Angela bought some cheap material and made curtain to hide the contents of the orange boxes. She had stacked them three by three and they hid an entire wall in the sitting room. The curtain made it look very respectable.

The 'kitchen cabinets' had cheerful bright colours, and they even had two bathroom cabinets, all orange boxes. Ross said:

"What a clever little child bride I have". Angela did not like the phrase 'child bride'. She was never that, she was not even a bride. She did not have to stay with him, in time when he found his feet, she would find a way out. And yet, she still thought she loved him. Her heart jumped every time he touched her.

"What happened to the Mercedes? Where did you leave it? Did Alison get it?"

"No it is with my parents and they are going to build a garage for it and house it for when we go to New Zealand. You must get to know my parents, little one. Anyway it must be in the country for at least a year before I can sell it legally for a good price."

As Winter approached they realized that this would be a very cold place to survive in and Angela decided to fly over to Frankfurt and shop for German duvets. Bine collected her from the airport in her little Carman Ghia and took her straight to the department store because she had to catch the afternoon flight back to Heathrow. She bought two Rheuma Decken, which were filled with pure sheep fleece and had cotton covers. Delicious warm comfort! She also bought covers and sheets, German sized pillows and covers. Back home Ross said:

"They are singles! Why didn't you get a double one?" "No way" Angela thought. I need my own cover. To Ross she said:

"I don't want to have to fight in the night for my bit of blanket. This way we can snuggle up tight and if we want to be together, one duvet is big enough for both of us." Ross grinned.

"They are lovely. They are so soft and light! I will have to get used to this sort of cover. We only ever had blankets." Angela laughed:

"Those awful English blankets! They let the draught in both sides and if you want to be warm you have to pull them out from under the mattress and then they are a terrible mess. I never got used to them. They are incredibly awkward, messy and typically British. I think they are the reason why English people rarely make their bed in the morning. They make no sense. If you get into Winter, you have to pile up the blankets until you suffocate under the weight. You'll see!

You will wonder how you could ever have been comfortable without duvets".

*

Angela got her first proper holiday in December, and she had decided long ago to go to South Africa. Ross took her to the newly completed West London Air Terminal. He wanted to know if she flew by herself or if she was meeting up with someone.

She shrugged her shoulders: "How am I to know who I am going to meet in Johannesburg? I might make friends with somebody, surely you don't mind that? I have always made friends with people". He grinned and kissed her goodbye.

The flight went via Nairobi and on to Johannesburg. It was hot summer and since the Gold Town lay on a high plateau, she had been warned to be careful not to get sunburned in this high altitude. She arrived, wearing winter clothes. Feeling hot and uncomfortable she headed for the ladies room to change. She just put her hand on the door to open it, when a heavy hand landed on her shoulder. She looked round and into a stern police officer's face. He wore a brown and sand coloured uniform and to her he looked like someone who had come to life from the Nazi time in Germany when she was little.

"That toilet is for blacks only. For whites it is over there" and he pointed into the opposite direction. As she walked over she passed a sad scene. A tall white man held a ten Rand note high up above half a dozen black porters with outstretched hands, and then he dropped it and so did the men, trying to get the note. She reminded herself, that black people here were the lowest of the low. Forgetting this could get you into trouble. She remembered the American soldiers after the war who treated their black comrades similarly.

She had booked herself into the Hotel Quirinale and her first walk into town was to the Lufthansa Office. She wanted to find out what she could do whilst here. She wanted to see something of South Africa, but had no idea how to go about it cheaply.

Mr. Staudte, the Manager was friendly and helpful and said:

315

"Tomorrow we have sales managers from Belgium, Sweden and Holland arriving. I am going to take them to Krueger Park and then over to Mozambique you could be one of the party. The trip will take about a week." Angela asked how much it would cost and was told, that she could count it as a business trip, familiarization, after all she would have to tell her customers what the country and the hospitality would be like. It would cost her nothing. All she needed was her own pocket money, passport and some clothes and a bathing suit. She went back to the hotel and went swimming in the pool on the Quirinale roof. She felt happy and excited. She put the thoughts of London or the dark hole, which was her home at the moment to the back of her mind. In fact she would find out whether she could work somewhere else in the world for Lufthansa. Maybe even work for Lufthansa back in Germany. Happily and light hearted she plunged into the water.

Afterwards she went out into the street and wandered around looking at shops. She bought a big bag of Mangoes and wondered how to eat them. She had never even seen one and now she was going to eat one. She went back to her room and attacked the fruit. She found it peeled easily, was very slippery and juicy and she had to rush over to the basin and to bite into it. It was delicious, soft and hairy. She slurped, sucked and chewed with relish and decided to have a second one. Just for this lovely fruit she would live here, she thought.

31

South African Safari

The next afternoon she was introduced to the sales managers. There was De Chief from Belgium, De Kruyff from Holland and Kuoni from Sweden. Afterwards they went window-shopping and sightseeing in Johannesburg. The sun was beating down and some of the men got their noses burnt. Communication was difficult; their English was limited. But they managed as they slowly remembered their school English. They decided to have a beer in a pub. When Angela entered she saw a lovely garden at the back with tables laid out with gingham tablecloths. They all agreed it would be lovely to sit in the cool, mottled shade under the trees. As they all headed out towards the beer garden an 'Nazi type' policeman stopped them.

"Where are you going? You know that the back is only for blacks!" Since Angela was the only one who could speak and understand English fluently, she became the spokeswoman, even though the policeman totally ignored her and turned to the men, who looked to her.

"We are sorry, we did not know," Angela said to the back of the policeman. "We only arrived in Johannesburg yesterday and have not got used to the rules". The policeman did not look at her. Ignoring his rudeness, she then introduced the men and told him where they were from. He became reasonably friendly and told them to enjoy themselves here not out there. They didn't like the dingy dark pub and left. They went back to the Quirinale and sat in the air-conditioned foyer in deep leather seats and soon a black man came and asked what their wishes were. When he came back with their drinks the Swede tried some conversation and the black boy got nervous. While the Swede searched for words and Angela tried to help, a fat woman behind them clapped her hands and shouted "Boy!" Immediately he bowed politely and left to go to the woman.

He then hurried away and the woman, without looking in their direction said:

"We don't engage the blacks in conversation. They are scum". The men all turned to Angela and asked what she had said, and when she explained, they were all stunned. She didn't know the word 'scum' and had to fish out her little pocket dictionary. She read it out and had to translate it: Scum: 'Impurities that rise to the surface of liquid especially in boiling or fermentation.' To the men she explained: When you make jam, the white foam, which collects on top, you fish it out, and throw it away. That's what it means. The Dutchman said in halting but good English:

"One does not really understand what it means when you hear that they separate the blacks from the whites. Not until you see it with your own eyes." Angela said:

"You speak Dutch, that is the same as Africans, isn't it? "And he answered:

"It is the same, yes, but they have a most peculiar dialect. I have difficulty working it out. It is very old fashioned Dutch". Angela imagined that it would be equivalent to German and Swiss German.

"There are difficult days ahead" De Kruyff said and the Swede explained that the blacks were all Communists and that there will be an uprising, so he had heard in Sweden before he left. The papers were full of this terrorist called Nelson Mandela. Apparently they caught him in 1956 but was released with a lot of others. He is still fighting Apartheid he is accused of rousing the blacks. De Kruyff said that Mandela's days were counted, and he will end up in prison probably for life or even get the death sentence.

Angela was still pretty ignorant about the politics in South Africa to know what the rules were. She too had been warned by her colleagues about this discrimination, but to see it was a different thing altogether. It was not in her make up to separate human beings into upper and lower categories. On her first day into town she had taken a bus. It all looked so familiar, red double-decker, just like London. Except that the queue parted at the bus stop, whites this end and blacks that end. When the bus arrived, the whites were entering first and she tried to head upstairs because in London smokers went upstairs. She was yanked rudely down again and told:

318

"Upstairs is only for blacks." The whole thing was against the grain. She could never live here, not with this sort of thing going on.

*

The next day they set off early in two Beetle Volkwagen cars out of Jo-burg and into the wilderness. Herr Staudte wanted to get to the Krueger Park in one day, 259 miles.

"We should do this in a day easily", De Kruyff said. Angela sitting in the back of the first car with Staudte felt hot already. But she enjoyed every minute. She had no sunglasses; they would have been an expensive luxury. She was wearing shorts and a sleeveless blouse. Looking out of the car window, she missed nothing of the countryside and the places they passed. All was wonderful, strange, exotic and African. There were all sorts of monkeys on the road, mountains in the distance and they were still above deep valleys. They drove through Bapsfontain and headed for Bronkhorstpruit and saw the big dam. They stopped at a village and took photographs of the villagers, bedraggled poor Blacks, whose husbands travelled to the town every day to work for the Whites. They saw very few men, only women who changed the further they got away from Jo-burg. It was too far to travel to work and poverty was seen everywhere. So sad and so shocking. They watched disinterested as her little safari drove through their village.

At Middleburg they had lunch at Lufthansa's expense. Angela could not believe her luck, to have chosen this time for a holiday, and to be included in this incredible trip. They stopped when they saw a black man with a bicycle on his shoulder teetering over a ropy suspension bridge, which dangled across a white water river. There were slats missing and the entire thing looked as if it was just about dropping into the depths. Staudte's secretary and Angela got out of the car and asked the men to take a photo. Angela had first photographed the man with his bike as he struggled across the missing slats, and then bravely the women went to the middle of the bridge and had their photo taken.

This was Angela's first big adventure outside Europe and she could not yet grasp the fact that she was at the bottom end of the globe. Unbelievable! Even three years ago she would never have dreamt that she would ever have enough money to travel outside Europe.

They were more or less the only two cars on the road and when they came through the villages, the road was lined with women and children dressed in rags who stared.

They got into forested country and had to slow down considerably, because the road was populated with baboons carrying their babies and climbing all over the beetle car. At three thirty in the afternoon they arrived at the Bushman Rock Hotel. Soon they all gathered at the swimming pool to cool down. Afterwards Angela went to look at the flowers and shrubs surrounding the pool and found a snail bigger than her fist. They had a wonderful evening meal with wine and went back to the pool afterwards and swam in the moonlight searching for the Southern Cross. They all went to bed early because as Staudte said:

"We are off early in the morning. People who oversleep stay behind", and he grinned.

They travelled slowly through the park. A white warden, driving a land rover, accompanied them part of the way, so that they would find the animals. They passed several hippo pools, crossed the Sabie River and stopped at native villages. Angela suspected that the villagers had been warned that visitors were coming and so they dressed themselves up in colourful blankets and lined the track, which led through the village. They stood there like wooden statues. They had nothing to sell and were not begging. Angela wondered what they were thinking. She felt embarrassed. The roads were surfaced, except in the villages. There was poverty and hardship everywhere. The natives seemed to have no hope or pride, and as it seemed to Angela, no future.

They visited the Tschokwane Tea Room and continued towards the Olifants River and spent the night in Shingwidzi. They slept in comfortable straw huts under mosquito nets, listening to the noisy birds and other animals and the constant crescendo of the crickets. It was all incredibly noisy, however Angela fell asleep and did not wake until the call came from outside that it was morning and that breakfast was in ten minutes. They travelled back on a different route and crossed the Crocodile River, but there were no crocodiles. At Komat Poort they got onto the road to Lorenco Marques. Angela saw a boy selling mangoes by the roadside and asked Staudte to stop. She wanted to buy some mangoes. She asked the boy how much they cost and he said 'six pence'.

"Can I have three please?" and the boy said

"For the box" and Angela purchased the entire box of mangoes but gave the boy a shilling, which was a rand. They put the box into the nose of the car and continued. She was being teased for having bought the fruit; no one else liked mangoes. Angela wondered why, when they were so delicious. They got to the boarder and were stopped for hours. No one had a visa to allow them to enter. Staudte disappeared into the office with the black official, who was wearing an immaculate uniform. He insisted that he had it all cleared up before leaving Johannesburg. Apparently these border guards had not been informed. Angela noted that there were no European officers working here.

After two hours of waiting in the heat, feeling tired, thirsty and hungry, Angela got her box of mangoes out of the nose of the beetle and sat on the ground in the shade and started to eat. The juice was running down her arms and dripping off her elbows. She enjoyed herself so much, and invited the others to join her.

"Help yourself, they are sweet and juicy and delicious". Gradually they took her up on the offer and had a fruit each and began to peel them. An hour later the box was empty and they were looking around for a water tap. One of the Border Police came out and Angela asked where they could wash their hands. His stern face cracked when he saw the box full of mango stones. He herded them to the lavatories. The loos were terrible, but welcome. There was a tap. Everybody was relieved, satisfied and clean, and almost immediately their passports came back and they were off into Mozambique. It was getting very hot and more and more humid, as they descended down from the mountains into the valleys and towards the Indian Ocean. They arrived at the Polana Hotel and as soon as they had a shower they went out into the town and on to the beach. The sand was soft and white, and so fine that they could not hold a handful. There were extraordinary shells on the beach, huge and beautiful, as if fashioned from bone china. They found sea creatures in the wet sand, left behind after the receding tide. They came to tumbledown shacks and were amazed that people lived there. They must be swept away at high tide, Angela thought, and all that sand! The floor in the hut was sand. They must be fishermen's huts she realized by all the netting hanging out to dry. She followed the stench and found fish hanging up to dry behind the hut.

They did not have a swim in the sea because the hot wind was strong and the waves too high. Mozambique was a Portuguese Colony and she realized for the first time that the world had been carved up and slices of it given to the seafaring countries. Britain got most of it, Spain a fair slice and Portugal close behind. What right had any of them to any of it!

They visited some night clubs and in one of them the "Los Paraguios Band" played and they all enjoyed the South American music and danced half the night. Angela bought a record and had them sign it.

After two days they were on the road again, back to Jo-burg. They watched queues of children in cobalt blue uniforms going to school, all very neat and tidy. They looked clean and organized, and the black people were not downtrodden as in South Africa. Mozambique was different. Black people had dignity and order and seemed to be in charge. She thought that if she were a Black in South Africa she would flee to Mozambique. But maybe that was not so easy. She decided she did not like South Africa, even though she had a wonderful time, and it was an incredibly beautiful place. Sadly she realized that it could all be so beautiful everywhere, if people or politicians, to be precise, did not mess things up all the time and made life so difficult for ordinary people. She was still young and felt uninformed, naïve even, but the thought struck her that maybe it had all to do with insatiable greed and money? There were always people who had loads and people who had nothing or too little to get anywhere.

The road back to Jo-burg was beautiful, climbing up into the mountains again from sea level to 7000ft or 8000t.

When they finally got back to Jo-burg, Angela had four more days left of her time. The sales managers took extra time out and stayed too and together they roamed around the city and outskirts.

Johannesburg was a fairly new destination for Lufthansa, who had been given the permission by the Allies to reopen as an airline in 1955 but was not flying until 1959 / 60. Then it was just within Europe, and gradually more and more destinations were added. So in these early years, staff had more or less Carte blanches to explore and come back with travel news, which was always good for sales. Every customer who came into a Lufthansa Office could get first hand information as to where to stay and what do to. Air Travel was still new to most people and everyone who travelled by Lufthansa was made to feel like royalty.

Angela and the sales managers did not enjoy what they found in South Africa as far as separation of races was concerned, and this they could not pass on to customers who came into the Lufthansa Ticket Office. Travellers had to be herded on to the tourist trails by guides who made sure there was no contact between the black population and the European whites to see the beauty of the land and it was beautiful. That the black people were nothing more than slaves for the whites, and that they seemed to own nothing, the tourists had to find out for themselves and make up their own minds about it.

The black people lived in awful poverty outside of Jo-burg and Angela and her friends were not allowed to walk the streets of Johannesburg after dark. The hotel staff were there to serve, but every one else had disappeared. They found that the villages were fenced off and gates locked.

De Kruyff tried to strike a friendly conversation with the man at the hotel reception desk in Dutch and the Afrikaner pretended he did not understand. He spoke in English, and De Kruyff said in Dutch, that his English was not so good, but that Afrikaans was the same as Dutch. The receptionist got cross and insisted that Afrikaans was a language in its own right and had nothing to do with the Netherlands, Dutch or Holland. De Kruyff walked away, shaking his head. Then he said in halting German and English:

"I have heard back home from a man who was born here, but returned home to Holland, because the Afrikaner will insist that when the Voortrekkers came here there was nobody living here and they made it their own country, and that they have not taken anything away from anyone. The black people came later to find work. Anybody who argued differently was locked up. So this man came back home to Holland seeking asylum".

Angela too knew some people from South Africa, working for various airlines in London, even one of her colleagues Anna came from Capetown, but none of them worked for South African Airlines. Maybe she knew the answer now. Her colleague was half Indian and half South African, but since this South African, her father, had married her mother he was forced to leave and live in Kashmir where Anna's mother originated from, or face prison.

The sales managers all had first class seats on the Lufthansa flight home. Angela had tourist class ticket. It did not occur to her to spend a few pounds more to sit in first class. But she learned fast. De Kruyff spoke to the check-in person and Angela was upgraded and sat with them all in first class. What wonderful luxury. On entering the flight, she was given a bunch of dried South African flowers. She had also brought a brown paper carrier bag full of mangoes and had placed them on the floor by her feet. A woman who sat next to her, getting the strong scent of the mangoes into her nose, importantly explained to Angela that they carried monkeys in the hold. With tongue in cheek Angela said:

"Ah, that would explain the smell."

In Nairobi they had a refuelling stop and a small delay gave them extra time to go to all the incredible shops to see the goods made by the Kenyans. She bought a lovely little carving in black wood. She ignored the smelly leather goods.

*

Ross was there to pick her up at the West London Air Terminal in Gloucester Road. He wanted to know what she had been doing. Apparently the postcards she had sent had not yet arrived. Poor Ross! She was so brown and in the cold December evening she looked even darker than she was. Happily she started to tell him about her adventure but he kept interrupting her all the time, asking questions. Suddenly she realized that Ross did not really want to know about her trip, he wanted to know if she had been faithful. Is that what he wants to know? He hadn't actually asked the question, but that was what he was after.

"What are you asking me? Do you want to know if I slept with some stranger in South Africa? Is that what you want to know?" Angela was cross, disappointed and embarrassed. She heard Ross say things but she did not want to listen. She looked out of the bus window into the yellow foggy gloom. Bloody Hell! How could he even think that she would do such a thing? Did he think she would sleep around? Had she not still been a virgin when he first made love to her? She felt deeply insulted, and trapped, and suddenly she wanted to be a million miles away from here, without any body holding her strings. She was not a puppet on a string and nobody should even attempt to put strings on her. Slowly his apologies came through the fog of her anger. She turned to look at him and there was this crooked smile and he promised never to be jealous again, that he trusted her and he was so sorry.

They got back to the dark, cold and miserable dimly lit flat. A miserable coal fire burned in the dreadful fireplace, not giving any heat. She found a vase and placed the flowers on the makeshift table. They looked very much out of place. She put some mangoes in a bowl and put those on the table as well. Ross had been cooking and the smell from the kitchen was promising. He had kept the place very tidy. She turned round to him and said:

"The place looks lovely and it feels really cosy." And he said:

"I know what the place looks like, it's not lovely and it's not cosy and it is freezing cold and miserable. But wait until the spring. We are going to move. I promise." They hugged.

At Christmas she had to work on the 25ths and 26ths with Denis, Billy and Brigitte. They would have a cosy time in the office, and Ross had to stay on his own in the miserable flat. He said he would stay in bed all day and sleep. She had gone to Schmidt's in Soho and bought a lot of German Christmas goodies, which were not available anywhere else in the country. That would make it all feel a lot more like home. She had even been able to get some Knoedel powder and the delicious red cabbage, which was also not available in the green grocer's shops. She often thought how uneducated and ignorant the English were when it came to cooking and food. English food was poor. They didn't even know how to make decent gravy. They used Bistow! She soon taught Ross how to make the gravy and he liked to cook when Angela had to work late. She taught him how to make bread, and they never bought another loaf.

"It makes a change from chops and peas", he said.

In the middle of January the snow came and they had to shovel themselves free every morning before they could go to work. Money was very short, Ross still had no patients of his own and the money he earned at the Eastman went all to New Zealand. Angela was still the main earner. They decided to give up smoking because they could not afford it any longer, but in the end, they had to give up not smoking, because life was so bad, that not smoking made it worse. They decided to only smoke when they got home in the evening and at weekends. The cold continued and the coal fire did not give any warmth. They sat on the floor in front of it and got roasted facing the fire and froze on the back. They decided to have a hot bath and go to bed and be warm there. The water coming from the miserable little boiler was cold by the time it travelled through the endless freezing pipes to the bathroom. Eventually in March the snow melted and the water ran into their little flat. And then Ross came home and said he had a lot of patients and soon he would earn enough to get a better flat further outside of London, maybe Richmond or thereabouts. The days got longer and warmer. In April they took a free day and looked around the estate agents to see what was available. They found a place in Upper Richmond Road, and went to see the Landlady. It was a grand Edwardian house with a huge garden and a half moon drive, in at one side and out at the other and steps leading up to the front door. A half round rose bed and a hedge separated the drive from the busy road. The lady was friendly and immediately took to them and after some questions said:

"Come and have a look at the flat, and if you like it you can move in right away" They went upstairs and she opened a door into a little hall. To the right it led into the kitchen with a view of the beautiful garden. A serving hutch gave Angela a glimpse into the sitting room which they entered again from the little hall and that too had a big window into the garden. An ancient birch tree partially blocked the view of the entire garden from there. They got out of the room and back into the little hall and into the bedroom, which had a window showing the drive and next to that, also reached from the little hall, was the bathroom. Angela was delighted. The lady was sweet and so friendly. Angela looked at Ross. Did he earn enough to pay for the rent, which was not a lot more than she paid at Neville Street. He gave her a reassuring nod. They arranged to move in a week later. The lady smiled happily and made them feel very welcome. 397 Upper Richmond Road was theirs. They had to catch a bus from Barnes Station to Hammersmith and from there the Underground. It worked out fine. Barnes Common was a lovely green area where they could walk in the evenings, and Angela even found a riding stable in Roehampton, and booked herself in. Riding was not expensive, because some of the horses belonged to private people who did not have the time to ride them regularly and they were happy to let some experienced person exercise them. Angela happily obliged. On her own she would not have moved out of London, she would have stayed in town, got herself a bigger room, but ultimately she would have left England and moved to another Lufthansa office anywhere in the world where her fancy might have taken her. Did she regret getting settled? Ross was very good to her and they were very much in love. Granted they were still very poor and often Ross asked her for money, but things improved all the time. The fare into town was a lot more now, but they would survive. They lived in Paradise and they could use the garden, and although the landlady had an old and trustworthy gardener, Angela was allowed to potter. They would lie in the garden looking up into the sky and watch the planes come in to Heathrow, so low that they could read the logos on the planes. They were directly under the flight path into the airport, but since she worked for them, they did not mind. The noise was deafening but the planes were exciting to watch. People still went to the perimeter of the airport to watch the planes at weekends, Angela and Ross only had to lie in their garden to watch. The noise of the planes was one reason why the flat was so very reasonable.

A month after they moved in, on the first of June 1962, Tissi gave birth to a lovely little boy. She named him Steve. Apparently Steve had got in touch again and phoned Tissi sometimes, but he turned out to be a lame duck. It fizzled out and nobody ever heard of him again.

A year later Ross bought a brand new car, a white Rover 2000 with red leather seats! Their lot had changed dramatically. Ross was well established as a Dentist, and had even left the practice in Edgeware Road and moved to Cavendish Square with the prospect to becoming a partner there. There were so many private patients which were his own patients that he could well afford to pay the rent. He also contributed to the housekeeping a bigger share than Angela. It was now Ross who was the main earner. Angela could now afford to spend money on clothes, which she could not do since Ross had returned. She also decided that Ross had to look more like a European and not like a Kiwi in his old fashioned, terrible suits. They had gone window- shopping and Angela had seen some clothes that would look really good on Ross. So they went and spent a small fortune on two pairs of trousers, shirts, two jackets and a hat. His coat would still do, but he needed some ties and some weekend casuals. He was also in need of some decent shoes. His old wardrobe was chucked, he did not even want to have a second look at it. It went straight into the bin. After that spending spree, they had to count their finances and had to tighten their belts again for a while. But Ross was earning well and he liked to show off his money. That was something Angela did not like. However she thought maybe it was just a passing phase after the long suffering poverty period.

32

The Pyramids of Egypt

In the spring of 1963 Angela flew to Egypt with quite a few of her colleagues and other airline staff; guests of Egypt Airlines. They had rooms at the Elborg Hotel and were taken around the city and the bazaars, ancient mosques and the Egyptian Museum and finally out to the Pyramids. Angela had always been interested in Egyptology ever since her mother gave her 'Gods, Tombs and Scientists' to read. She was astounded by the beautiful things which were found in Tutankamun's tomb, could not get over the fact that these things existed when in Europe people lived in simple round huts and made basic but beautiful jewellery and pots. Such an exquisite civilisation, such incredible temples and when she came out to Gizah and saw the Pyramids with the Sphinx gazing out over the desert and seeing a thousand lifetimes past and future, she was overwhelmed. For thousands of years the tallest buildings on earth! She had seen plenty of pictures of these extraordinary tombs but to see them in reality was amazing. They went into the great Pyramid of 'Kinga Chops' (King Cheops) as their guide called the Pharaoh, and Billy and George, two of her colleagues took her into their middle to protect her from pick pockets, goose marching first bent double because the corridor up was very low, steep and narrow and then it became as lofty as a cathedral until they reached the burial chamber at the top of the passage. The entrance was low. Strangely, even though they were so deep inside the Pyramid, it was not airless or stifling, as she had feared before entering. It all seemed too amazing to fathom and to take it all in.

Angela was told that it was the equivalent of Easter in this Muslim country and everybody was out by the Pyramids celebrating and having a picnic.

"But they don't believe in Christ" Angela said. She did not understand the explanation and their guide was vague, so she left it at that. There were about a dozen people in her group and after they had walked around and taken photos of everything several times over, they were taken to the camel enclosure and were invited to hop on for a ride out into the desert to see the pyramids from a distance. There were mishaps and giggles and stifled screams from people who had never ridden anything. All the camels were on the ground with their long legs tucked neatly underneath. They all got on and then the camels lifted their behind up first and then the front. They all made it ok. Angela was thrilled. She watched the guide on his camel and also crossed her legs Arab fashion and not use the stirrups. She found it a lot more comfortable. They all had a handler to hold on to the camel, just in case it would suddenly take off and gallop away. The guide soon sorted the experienced riders from the novices and promised a ride once they were away out in the desert. Angela watched carefully what their guide did to learn to speak to the camel and found the camel responded. After an hours ride the Pyramids became smaller and smaller on the horizon and there they stopped and had a pic-nic. The camels sat down and everybody got off. One of the camels got up again immediately and started to pee, and Angela, after some time, which she thought was a long time, timed this camel. It took another 7 minutes before it finished peeing. It peed with great dignity, even though everybody looked on in wonderment, it then walked away from the wet area and sedately sat down again.

The guide then took the experienced riders for a gallop as he promised he would. They rode away and soon lost sight of everybody, because now nothing was flat in this desert; there were huge dunes everywhere and if it had not been for the guide they would have been lost in no time at all and not have found the rest of the party again. However, if one climbed to the top of a dune one could make out the Pyramids on the horizon sometimes not distinguishable between the dunes if they were hidden in the shade of a cloud. Angela felt the galloping rhythm of the camel thrilling and would have wanted to carry on. It was a wild ride and the camel's lips were flopping and spit was flying. She found it a much more exciting ride than on horseback probably because the camel's legs were so much longer.

They returned to the Pyramids the next evening after dark and watched the 'Son et Lumiere', the nocturnal magic of the Pyramids. The lights were incredible and Angela listened to the words:

"You have come tonight to the most fabulous and celebrated place in the world. Here, on the plateau of Gizah, stands for ever the mightiest of human achievement. No traveller- emperor, merchant or poet- has trodden on these sands and not gasped in awe.

The curtain of night is about to rise and disclose the stage on which the drama of civilization took place.

Those involved have been present since the dawn of history, pitched stubbornly against sand and wind. And the voice of the Desert has crossed the centuries ".

Then the face of the Sphinx was born out of the dark night as if coloured by the light of dawn:

"With each new dawn I see the Sun-god rise on the far bank of the Nile. His first ray is for my face, which is turned towards him. And for five thousand years I have seen all the suns men can remember come up in the sky.

I saw the history of Egypt in its first glow, as tomorrow I shall see the East burning with a new flame. I am the faithful warden at the foot of his Lord – so faithful, so vigilant, so near him that he gave me his face for my own. I am a Pharaoh's companion, and I am he, the Pharaoh. Through the ages I received many names from the people who came to me in adoration. "

Angela had to take this home with her and bought the booklet and the record to be able to listen to it again and again at home and have Ross share it with her. (Which he never did)

Thinking again of the difference of civilization between Europe and Egypt she came to the conclusion that in the sun things ripen better. So did the Egyptian civilization advance in the sunny warm and golden climate. In the cold and dark north with the short

Summers and the long cold nights and Winters it took thousands of years to catch up with the Middle East. There was a blip when the Romans came, but when they left; it all sank back into darkness. Even they could not exist in the cold and dark North. The Mediterranean sun would also account for the wonderful bright colours the Egyptian people used to tell their story in the tombs of the Dead which were discovered thousands of years later.

She did not fly back with the group; instead she took a flight to Zurich and the train to visit her mother and Tissi in Rheinfelden. There she wrote a letter to Ross.

My dearest Darling

At last I am in Rheinfelden. I am so tired. We had so much on our agenda for Cairo, that I only had about ten hours sleep while I was there. On Friday we arrived at 10oclock Cairo time 8oclock London time. We had to wait quite a long time, while they got all the papers ready. We finally arrived at the El Bourg Hotel, went to our rooms and got ready for dinner. First we had a little stroll through Cairo and on the way back we had dinner at the Nile Hilton, which was on the other side of the Nile right opposite our Hotel. We went to bed at 4am. We got up the next day and after a dreadful breakfast we started the day at the Museum. It was great. After that we got back into our minibus (All vehicles in Cairo are Mercedes, Taxis, big and small busses trolley busses etc.) and drove out to Gizah. Oh Darling, I really wished you could have been there with me. It was wonderful. One really felt awed in front of those terrific monuments, especially when I went inside the Pyramid. It was unbelievable. From the village to the Pyramids we went on Camelback. After that we saw a few mosques, all very interesting. And then we were taken to the bazaars. What a stink! It was so filthy, everything turned upside down inside me. They just put their turds wherever they please and pee in the middle of the street. Apart from that (you don't know where to put your foot) all the waste goes on the street to rot as well. Very unpleasant! Our guide took us to the upper class bazaar after that and this was very pleasant. We made real good business. We didn't buy anything unless we got it half price or less.

. It was great fun. Back to the Hotel, change and bath, (actually shower as the bath was filthy) and then we went to the Nile Hilton

for dinner in the sheiks tent with belly dancers and all. Back to bed at 4am. Sunday morning assembly at nine o'clock for a ride in an old sailing vessel down the Nile, lunch at hotel and then back to Gizah, camel ride into the Sahara and back to the Pyramids, drinks at the Pyramid Hotel and at 7.30 pm back to the Pyramids for the Son et Lumiere. It was great. I'll show you some pictures and one day I'll take you there. Oh I wish it were soon. The last day we could spend as we liked.

Darling, I'll see you soon. I'll arrive on Sunday afternoon at 1.50 at London Airport.

Darling I am a little homesick, I love you and I hate leaving you, I really do. All my love, your Kleines.XXX

Little Stevie was a sweet baby of ten months, very cuddly and huggable. Angel's mother and Tissi were happy. Angela stayed for three days, enjoyed the baby and then flew back to London. At Stuttgart Airport, where she had to change flights, she had a coffee in the departure lounge and read an English magazine and next to her cup lay several brochures, which she had picked up in Switzerland regarding precision attachments for people who did not want bridges and dentures in their mouths, but fixed firmly onto remaining teeth or just roots. She thought it would be interesting if she translated it for Ross. She had an hour to wait for the LH Flight to Heathrow and would translate them presently. A very young and handsome man asked awkwardly whether he could share her table. "Sure" she said and continued to read. They both drank their coffee slowly. The young man grinned at her every now and then, and grinned to some people at a neighbouring table. Angela grinned back and thought somehow he looked a little like somebody she had seen somewhere before. Shyly she asked:

"Do I know you?" and he said "I don't know, do you?" and she added: "I am sorry, I must be mistaken." And she went back to translating the brochure. However, this man distracted her again.

"Do you listen to Rock Music?" and Angela shook her head. "I am more for classical music and German folk songs."

"Do you speak German then?" He asked, and she said: "Well yes, I am German, but I work in London". He turned to the neighbouring table: "She is German and works in London". Angela grinned and said:" Ok and what do you do and where do you live?"

He grew in stature and replied: "We are the Rolling Stones, I am Mick Jagger". Angela felt embarrassed. She had no idea who the Rolling Stones were. She realized she was blushing and she felt more and more awkward. His mouth was enormous and became even larger when he laughed.

"Ok, ok don't worry. There are people like you, but it won't be long before you hear from us." It was only then she discovered their luggage. They were musical instrument cases. It must be a group like the Beatles, she thought. And then she remembered a television program, and how quickly she turned it off. A group of noisemakers she called them, and had asked Ross if he was interested to listen to them. They were wildly hopping around the stage and made a most dreadful noise. Ross had said no turn it off.

"I must seem like a boring old woman in your eyes, not having heard of you before. I think, now that I remember it, I have seen you on television once. But I couldn't make out the words, or lyrics you call them? And if I don't know what the music is all about, I don't understand it." She hoped that would satisfy him. He said:

"But there are no words in classic music. They have a title, but no words."

"You are right, there are no words, but the music speaks, you listen to the music and you see the sea, the forest and the birds singing in it, you see the sunrise and sunset and you see the northern lights as in Sibelius Finlandia, you hear the ice crack in terrific thundering music which gives you goose bumps." She smiled at him, hoping he would understand. But just at that moment the announcement was made that their flight was ready for boarding. The group picked up their instruments and they all walked towards the exit. Just before their ways parted, he said:

"You work for Lufthansa in Bond Street? What is your name" and she called back "My reference is GE, George Edward" and they lost sight of each other, he travelled first class and she tourist, but since she was a standby, she had to wait until everybody had boarded to see if there was room on the flight for her. There was. She never saw the group at Heathrow after they landed, and never heard from him again, not that she expected it. But the rest of her life she would remember their conversation through all the things that she read in the papers and seen on TV. All his marriages, all his conquests, his women and his children, all his excesses and successes and all the questionable fame that went with his name, the change in his face due to drugs and the change from the beautiful fresh young man into the thin and haggard character he had become.

She had translated the pamphlets for Ross. It was all about precision attachments all brand new in Britain's Post Graduate Dental Hospital. Ross booked himself immediately into a two-week course in Switzerland and learned all about it and introduced it into Britain and was the only person to be able to perform the work on patients. A big boost to speed him up the ladder past the other lecturers at the Eastman! Suddenly he was very much in demand thanks to Angela's quick thinking and ability to speak two languages.

Angela went to Nice on a daytrip with Air France and came home late. However they saw so much of Nice, so many hotels and cafés she did not remember the names of them, only the luxury, the extraordinary food they had to sample and the elegant people going in and out and lounging around and shopping in shops, which to the group of Airline Staff who were supposed to familiarize themselves with the essence of the Riviera, could only gawp at in awe. Boarding the plane, in which, by the way, they flew first class each way, they were presented with a huge bouquet of Riviera flowers and an elegant brief case with a golden Air France emblem on the front filled with pamphlets, brochures and advertisements, which they were 'allowed' to take back home.

*

Later that Year, Angela and Ross got ready to fly out to New Zealand to meet Ross's parents. She had heard so much about the land, and the black Mercedes was at his parent's house, so that they had transport to 'do' both Islands and meet all the family. It would be 6 weeks of intense travelling and meeting people. Ross had to buy his full ticket, but Angela only paid ten percent of the fare, but had to be standby and didn't get onto the flight. So Ross went on ahead and

Angela flew to Frankfurt first, to catch the LH flight to Sydney. She had a Teal Ticket with NZ Airlines, which was free. Such generosity she thought. It was all standby off course, but to hitch hike by air half way around the globe, who minded! Alas the flight from Frankfurt was full and she had to fly to Rome to catch an Alitalia Flight to Sydney, and all that would delay her by at least two days. She sent telegrams to Ross's parents. Ross would arrive in New Zealand when she left Rome, if she got on.

She did make the Alitalia Flight. It was so full with human cargo, that she thought the flight would never take off. She was sitting in the tail end of the 707 looking out of the window and wishing the flight to lift off. At the very end of the runway, the plane laboured into the air and Angela sighed with relief. As soon as the seat belt sign was switched off, the Italians started to get off their seats and walk around the plane. It seemed to Angela that the entire plane load was related, because everyone seemed to know everyone else. It turned out, that they all immigrated to Australia, entire sets of families from babies to grandparents and later she found out they were all from the same village. Children started to play in the gangway and stewardesses had a hard time to come through with the food trays. Then the men ordered drinks. Apparently they were under the impression that drinks were free, which they were not. When it came to paying for the drinks, a row started which needed the captain to come into the cabin to sort out, and then the food they had consumed came up again and ended mostly on the floor and not in the bags provided, and when all that was sorted, they came down for refuelling in Karachi. Back up in the air the load of immigrants went peacefully to sleep and a stewardess came up to Angela and said:

"I see that you are staff. I wonder if you would be so kind and help me with these?" and she showed Angela a stack of papers and passports and explained:

"These people have to fill these in before they get to Sydney, and they don't speak English and don't know how to do it. We have well over a hundred of these to do, and all these forms are in triplicate".

"Sure, Angela said, it will give me something to do". Gratefully the stewardess handed her the stuff and said: "On this flight there is no first class. They are all emigrants. Anything you want, just ring.

Would you like a coffee now?" Angela accepted the offer and got stuck into the work. What a job! When you got into it, it wasn't so bad. All she had to do, was to sort out the families, enter all the details from the passport into the immigration papers which were in every passport provided by the Immigration Authorities in Australia in triplicate, put an elastic around each family pile and go to the next one. She could see every stewardess and steward sitting somewhere and doing the same job. Afterwards they all sat together for a midnight snack and a chat. It was all very pleasant, except for the penetrating smell of vomit, which would not go away.

Because she had to fly from Rome, her TEAL flight from Sydney had gone and she had to wait 8 hours for her next flight. Forlornly she sat under a very strange Christmas tree, very tired and trying to sleep. Someone had offered her a shower after she had secured another flight to Christchurch, and she had changed into summer clothes, but it was still very hot and she could not leave the building because she had no visa to enter Australia. She listened to the announcements and grinned at their strange accent. She went and had some food, and then went back to her seat under the Christmas tree. Staff from TEAL telling her that her flight was ready for departure woke her up. She would have missed it had the lady not woken her up.

Ross and his parents were at Christchurch to pick her up. She was so very tired that she could hardly cope with meeting his parents. She excused herself and said that she had not slept for three days, or was it four. She turned to Ross and said:

"Since you left on BOAC I have not slept, however long ago that was."

"My poor Kleines" he said, "you can go to bed as soon as we get home and sleep as long as you like", but she went to sleep in the car on the long trip from Christchurch to Ashburton and Ross put her to bed without supper. It was a lovely morning when she woke up and she heard voices somewhere in the house. She got up, put on her dressing gown and washed her face in the little basin in her room and walked barefoot into the kitchen, where for the first time, consciously she met his mum and dad, Val and Chas.

33

1964 First Trip to New Zealand

Angela learned that Chas had built the house all by himself. It was entirely made of wood except for the tiles on the roof. It was a small cosy bungalow. The front door was reached via a long path from the road, flanked either side by flower beds and rosebushes and continued past the house to the back of the house and the garden, where she found a bench under a rose arch close to the back door. From there she could see the garden and the vegetable beds, the fruit trees and right at the bottom of the garden, a wooden shed. This, she learnt later, was Chas's world and workshop. A large area on the front lawn was now used up for the garage to house the black Mercedes. There were apples and plums on the trees and runner beans grew up poles. There was also a veranda with an overhanging roof. Angela fell in love with the little house. She also fell in love with Chas and Val. They were uncomplicated warm people and Val was easy to understand and comfortable to be with. Her main topic were the women in Ashburton of her own age mostly, and how high their Pavlov's had risen in comparison to hers and her Pavlov had risen to the highest, although Mrs. Heffers from the store, hers came close. There were loads of cream puffs at the Christmas party, mostly hers. Christmas had just passed and there were still lots of puffs at the house for them to have with afternoon tea. As she chatted away telling them things, Angela had to smile at the way she confused some words, but nobody corrected her. From the 'optessen' she got her spectacles and from the 'delicatician' she bought the Bluff oysters and the special cheese in honour of their visit. She worried about the use of the telephone in case the electric bill went up. But it was no use explaining the difference, she knew how it was and that was that. They spent a week in the little house and explored the area around Ashburton and then made ready to drive south to Dunedin and the Bluff, where the Valentines apparently originated from. They visited the old University where Ross studied and because it was the Summer-cum Christmas holidays, only the Caretaker and his wife were there to show them around. The wife was borne and grew up in Alaska and Angela asked:

"How do you cope with Christmas being in the middle of summer?" She herself found it strange, her first Christmas in shorts. The woman said:

"I love it here in New Zealand. There is just one time in the year when I am homesick, and that is Christmas. I really miss the snow and the darkness and the cosy togetherness we have at home in Alaska." Angela agreed. Val sniffed loudly but said nothing. When they were back in the car on their way to the Bluff, Val said:

"Really, what a thing to say! Why doesn't she go back where she came from"? Angela looked at Ross who was driving, and Ross said:

"Mother, she meant nothing of the sort. All she said was that at Christmas she misses home. It is totally different from New Zealand. It is dark most of the day and deep, deep snow and very cold, colder than your deep freeze and people have fires going and huddle cosily inside."

His mother said nothing but started to sniff and Chas kept stroking her hand. Angela kept passing paper tissues to them in the back. It took his mother a long time to stop sniffing. Angela tried to tell her from her own experience in Finland and how she coped with the constant darkness albeit lit up by the Northern Lights and the bright Moon when it was full, how the snow would fall until it was up to two meters high. His mother still said nothing, only sniffed and Angela gave up consoling her. She was wondering what went on in her head. She had never been out of New Zealand in all of her life, the furthest she had travelled was New Plymouth in the North Island, and she talked about that trip as if it had be a round the world once. Angela realized that she had no idea how far England was away. The New Zealanders asked visitors from England: "Are you just over from home?" which could not be that far away.

By the time they got to Invercargill, Chas was coughing a lot and Val, having finally recovered, thought it would be a good idea to stop at a chemist and get some Hacks. She headed for the chemist and we all entered. She found some scales in the corner of the shop and thought it would be a good idea to weigh herself. Carefully she took off her shoes, coat and cardigan and before she stepped onto the scales she picked up her handbag, shoes, coat and cardigan and proceeded to weigh herself. Ross laughed and took it all off her again. Chas called her silly billy and Val couldn't stop laughing.

They continued to travel down to the Bluff where they were supposed to stay with cousins who had a kind of a pub and rooms above. When they arrived, after 10 pm, all was dark. They heard muffled voices and knocked on the door. Immediately all was deadly quiet. Ross knocked again and nothing happened. Then he knocked again loud and louder and then they could hear footsteps and the door was opened a tiny crack. Ross said:

"Raymond?" and Raymond opening the door further said:

"What the f... do you want? Didn't I tell you how to f...ing knock? You could have been the f...ing police. And you are f...ing late." Angela did not quite believe what she heard. She stood a little behind the Valentines by the suitcases. Ross said: "Do you mind, there are ladies present". Raymond opened the door and Val and Chas entered and Ross wanted to go in too when Raymond turned on him and said:

"Are you going to let the f...ing lady carry the f...ing bags all by her f...ing self?"

Angela burst out laughing and walked up to Raymond and said:

"Hello Raymond, I am Angela, and if you think I have a funny accent, I am German". She didn't quite know why she said it, but she thought it would be good to get it out of the way.

"A f...ing Hun! Do you remember the bloody war?" But Ross stepped in and said, we can talk about that in the morning, we have had a long day and I am sure mum and dad want to go to bed. Raymond slapped Angela on the shoulder and said:

"Pleased to meet you." I am not always so rude, but I had to get my f...ing guests out of the back door first before I let you in". Angela reassured him, that she was not offended. She had already found out that that word was used a lot down under. It emphasised a lot of things and expressed situations where a Kiwi would just not find the right words.

They left at lunchtime the next day with keys to the summer house in Te A Na U . It was a long and dusty drive up and up into the mountains. Breathtakingly beautiful! The hut was by Lake Te A Na U and Angela thought it would be a good idea to have a swim since it was so hot. But she got no further that her ankles when she leapt out of the water thinking she had lost her feet. It was so icy cold, and her feet were instantly hurting. There would be no swimming here in that glacier lake. The Valentines had a good laugh. Later Chas came down with sunstroke.

They spent some very relaxing days and then Ross decided that he had to show Mitre Peak to Angela who had no idea what that was. He said it was going to be a long and dusty drive but it was going to be worth it. Mum and Dad came too, sitting as always in the back of the black Mercedes.

It was a blue sky day and the snow topped mountains glistened in the sunshine and the waterfalls fell crashing and foaming down the mountain side. The roads were unsurfaced and full of holes, and looking back Angela saw a huge yellow dust cloud. As they got over the pass they all got out and had a play in the snow. Eventually they came to the Homer Tunnel, a rough hewn hole through the mountain with water rushing into it through cracks and a stop sign saying: "Drive through every hour to quarter past and oncoming every half hour to quarter to the hour". It was now quarter to the hour and they had to wait 15 minutes for the cars to come through the tunnel. Ross explained that this is the only land route to the other side of the mountain. The easiest way is still by boat up the fjord. There is so much to be explored still and forest to be cut down to making room for settlements. One car came through and they waited a few more minutes for the full hour and then entered the unlit tunnel. It was pitch black with deep potholes and the rocks so dark from the water rushing down that the lights did not reflect and Ross had to find his way in gloomy darkness. She suddenly thought aloud; what if a driver thought there is hardly ever a car coming this way and enters and they meet in this gloom and can't pass each other. Ross said:

"Don't even think about it."

They got to the other side and drove on to Milford Sound and parked by the fjord in front of the hotel. It was unbelievably beautiful and peaceful. Angela sat for ages on her own in front of the hotel and looked out towards the peak.

The Peak rose steeply out of the water into the blue sky, first wooded green and then snow capped. It caused a perfect mirror image in the still water. Ross and his mum and dad were having tea and cream puffs indoors and Angela wished Ross would come out and share the moment. It was too beautiful to enjoy it by herself. But he did not come. So after a while Angela went in and sat down and poured a cup of tea and reached for a cream puff. Later Tthey had dinner later and stayed the night. Angela rose early and walked back to the fjord. The peak was shrouded in deep mist with just the very top showing. If the mist sinks down it will be a lovely day she remembered from her farming days. She watched some Albatross gliding past. Just amazing.

They left early in the morning to head back to Te A Na U. They stayed another day and then hid the key and drove on to Queenstown and eventually back to Ashburton. They had to say their fare wells to Val and Chas and drove on to Christchurch and Littleton where they boarded the ship to take them to Wellington.

After staying with Norma, Ross's sister and Bruce and Susan, their grown children they continued to New Plymouth to pick up Ross's children Richard and Joe. Angela was just a little nervous to meet them. How they will take to her, she wondered. She was right they were totally hostile. It was not until Ross explained that they had not met until three years after their mother had taken them back to New Zealand, and she had nothing to do with breaking up the family. Angela was taken aback because she had no idea that there had been something going on between their father and someone else. She was under the impression that Alison, their mother left because she was homesick and missed New Zealand. However, Angela left the three of them to sort things out. She was quite prepared to step back should Ross want to go back to his family. She would never take the father away from his children if they wanted to be together. It turned out however, that neither Alison nor Ross wanted to be together, and Richard and Joe had to make the best of it. They continued together to Whitianga, to visit Chum, an old friend whom Angela had already met in London when he came over with the All

Black Rugby Team. After a little while Angela got on really well with Richard and Joe, who seemed to have come to terms with their father having a new woman in his life. Angela made it quite clear, that she did not want to be a step mother. Joe especially became quite attached to Angela and as a token of friendship, Angela gave her a ring from her finger. Joe blushed with pleasure. Angela felt that there should be some happiness in their sadness. They promised to come and visit them in London.

*

34

Riding Trip to Ethiopia

Here Angela describes a riding trip to Ethiopia with the Interline Horse Riding Club for the Lufthanseat, a staff magazine

Friday the 14ᵗʰ of January 1966 seven people met at the West London Air terminal in Gloucester Road. They were members of the Interline Riding Club in London and staff from various Airlines: Ian from Olympia, Greek Airlines, Mike from MEA, Brenda from Qantas, Glenda und Julie from BUA, Ralf from Bea and myself from Lufthansa.

We were all quite excited because we intended to pack a lot into this amazing trip. We took the coach to Heathrow and flew with Olympic to Athens. The weather was clear and we had a wonderful view over the Alps and then Athens where the pilot circled to have a good view of the Acropolis. The service on board was great. In Athens we were the guests of Olympic Airlines and Ian showed us around since it was the airline he worked for and we were well looked after by his Greek colleagues. We were guests in a Greek restaurant and then went to visit the guards at the Palace. At 2300 hours we continued our trip on Ethiopian Airlines. Since it was late and we had already eaten, we lay down on the empty benches in first class. Even before the aircraft took off we were fast asleep. I woke up above Khartoum where I watched a wonder sunrise. We enjoyed a great breakfast and shortly after that landed in Addis Ababa.

The Public Relations Officer of Ethiopian Airline was there to pick us up. He was extremely helpful to get us through passport control and luggage inspection quickly and then took us to a wonderful hotel. We were full of expectations. The weather was hot, in fact too hot since we were all still in our winter clothes. We all had a room to ourselves and went straight into the shower. Opposite the Hotel was the Ethiopia National Bank and we went immediately to change some money. It was a round ball-shaped building with a glass roof and hollow in the middle, three storeys high. Huge arrow shaped pillars rose up and met in the middle above the building. It was brand new and quite beautiful.

We all met outside on the steps after we had changed our pounds and traveller cheques and counted out Ethiopian Dollars. We hadn't planned anything in particular and therefore decided to roam around in the town. We stopped a small taxi and learned that it only goes in one direction and then we would have to get out and find another Taxi. Every trip in all directions in these Fiat Mini busses cost 24 cents. Our map showed "The Old Market". Haggling is necessary and we bought a few little souvenirs. Life at the market is primitive, however interesting and original. We took a few photographs and suddenly we were inundated with children who followed us everywhere. They never left us even when we walked all the way back to the Hotel. We gave them all some cents and they skipped happily back to their place at the market. I went to bed early because the next day was fully planned.I was deeply shocked because a heavily veiled woman wanted to sell me her baby, a tiny bundle in her arms. I refused but my heart was close to breaking.

We met early dressed for riding. A chauffeur from the Imperial Bodyguard Headquarters took us to the stables. The beautiful white Arab stallions waited readily saddled for us. They made a lovely sight. We climbed on and immediately had our hands full to quieten the fiery horses. We found quite a difference between the docile horses we ride at the odd weekends in England and the stallions of the Imperial bodyguard. We started off down Russia Street and past the embassies of Haiti, Britain, Belgium, Russia, Germany and Italy and out of town into the hills.

The Banks, the Embassies and the official buildings, Government house and Africa Hall and hotels are modern and beautiful building set along wide new roads. In-between stand the poor native houses, no more than biggish sheds. Animals graze alongside. rode into the hilly outskirts and had a great view of Addis Ababa. We passed a long line of donkeys with heavy loads leaving town on their way back to their villages.

We returned to the stables in the late afternoon and passed the French Embassy. We were invited to a pic nic and a local beer at the officer's mess.

Back at the hotel we went for a swim. We enjoyed an excellent evening meal and then we went with our Ethiopian Friends to several night clubs. There were no floor shows as you would find in Soho, but you could dance your heart out. We all had a great time and everybody wanted to dance with us. Such fun. There were brand new clubs with colourful lighting and the music was partly modern but also plenty of Amharic Music. This too is very good dancing music. We also visited true Ethiopian clubs, mostly for natives only and the walls were covered with monkey skins and the room was lit with candles. The visitors there were more the well to do natives. The way they danced was fascinating and we just watched. We left there as well because we wanted to see as much as possible in the short time we had. We stopped outside the city in the purely native quarter. There was a dance hall, not a night club and the guests were all teenagers. The girls sat all in one corner and the boys in the opposite corner, and every time the music started the boys walked over to the girls, bowed politely and the girls got up, curtsied and off they went to dance. Afterwards the boys took the girls back to their seats and bowed again and returned to their corner. There was lot of discreet giggling.

At four in the morning we returned to the hotel and came across some hyenas who roamed the city by night. It was eerie and the sound of their laughter was mocking.

The next morning early we went for another ride and then we watched the Emperor how he fed the horses. It is a ceremony. Officers of the stable carry a silver tray with hey and the emperor walks behind, (he is a short gentleman) and tosses a few bits of hey into the horses crib. Fascinating! Afterwards we went sightseeing and visited Africa Hall, Haile Selassie Jubilee palace and the private gardens with wild animals like lions, panthers and tigers etc. Later we returned to the stables because a local paper wanted to have some photographs of the European riders who actually rode on the imperial horses.

Our last evening was celebrated quietly. We counted our finances because we still planned a day in Athens. The farewell was so nice, everybody turned up to say good bye and we shook hands endlessly and thanked all these lovely people and then we left for Bole International Airport. First class on Ethiopian Airlines. It was great. We felt like royalty. The view from the Aircraft was clear and we stopped in Asmara and Beirut and got to Athens at midday. It was cold and unpleasant after the wonderful weather we had. We visited the sites as one does and left the next day with Air France to Paris and on to London with Olympic Airways. It was freeeezzzzzing in London.

35

Macchu Picchu Peru 1968

Over the next two years Angela was taken on various trips all over the world to get to know the product she was selling to customers. She learned about hotels and bars and clubs, exotic resorts, white sands and emerald seas, exotic flowers and remote places of interest, archeological sites in Greece and the Middle East, Egypt further down the Nile, Africa and the Caribbean, Ethiopia and South America.

Ross was a jealous mate und watched her every move. Whenever she came back from her business trips he wanted to know exactly who she had been with and had she been unfaithful. She felt insulted und could not really believe that he was serious. But he was. Relentlessly he questioned her. She became unsure of herself, felt humiliated and enslaved. Did he love her or did he just want to possess her. She decided to leave him. She packed a small suitcase and walked to Barnes Railway station and waited for the bus. She intended to go to work and ask her colleagues if anybody could put her up for a few days until she found herself a bed sit in Kensington or somewhere. She did not care where, so long as she was free again and not possessed by a jealous man. She felt that he wanted her to be his adoring slave, but that she could not be.

She had been standing there devastated and furious for 20 minutes and no bloody bus came. Then she noticed Ross limping fast across Barnes Common and he reached her just as 3 red busses turned by the Red Rover Pub into the road which lead up to Barnes Railway Bridge Bus stop. He just took her suitcase, put an arm around her and kissed her.

"Come home Little One" he said. "We will sort it out. I am so very sorry. Will you forgive me?"

As she walked back with him she knew it was a mistake and that she should have been firm. She felt increasingly that she could not breathe and felt trapped and not herself. He wanted to make her his, and although she wanted to be with him, she wanted to be Angela, the woman who came through the war, who got a degree in Agriculture, who worked in various parts of Europe, who had had a life before Ross and who wanted to share her life with the man she loved, not be dominated by him. She wanted to be loved for who she was and not what he wanted her to be. But she found he was not interested in who she was. He tried to control her and he made her feel that she owed him something. He made her feel ungrateful and he made her feel guilty.

When they got home they had a long talk. Angela told him exactly what was on her mind and Ross promised he would trust her and believe in her. Angela said:

"What point is there in living together and making a life together if there is no trust? We have to be able to trust each other and I don't want to lose my identity. Do you think that I would be unfaithful because you have been in the past?"

"I have had one relationship with a woman after Alison left that is all. You can trust me a hundred percent, Little One" he said. "I have never loved anyone the way I love you," and he took her into his arms and made love to her and she let him. Angela believed that you could only make love to someone if you truly loved and trusted the person. She loved him, but did he love her? Was her love for him enough for both of them? She wasn't sure. She wasn't even sure of his love. Was he in love or in sex with her?

On her weekends off they did things together, usually to play Golf somewhere around London with his dentist friends. He became a regular member at the Farnham Golf Club, and that was where they mostly went. He and his friends said she was his good luck charm. It was always pleasant and the Golf course beautiful, and Angela just walked along, she never played. At the end of the game they would usually have a pint or two and play the one armed bandits. There would be a syndicate, everybody put in two and six pence, half a crown, and so everyone had five goes. Any winnings would be shared and the game could go on for a long time. They never played for more than 2and 6pence each. When that finished the game finished. He never went anywhere without her. He made her feel desired and wanted. She seemed happy.

Then came the day when Alison's father, Mr. Sheet, let Ross know that he had been given a decree nisi, in other words he was divorced and only had to wait for the decree absolute.

"Now we can make plans to get married," he said and Angela felt sudden panic. On the one hand where her private life was concerned she was already Mrs. Valentine, but at work and in London she was still Miss Geppert. That untruthfulness at least will be over. But it would have to be a quiet wedding, because they still did not have their own home. They still lived in Upper Richmond Road, where they rented a beautiful flat, but it was not their home and not a place where you could have a wedding.

Ross came home one day and said:

"Fred and Elaine Harty have offered to have the reception at their place in Ealing, what do you say to that?" and then a letter came from New Zealand announcing that Normas's son Bruce was coming over to England and he would bring the wedding cake, baked by Norma. Tissi, who had come back to England with little Stevie the year before to work in Gloucestershire with friends, would come. Somehow it was all arranged by Ross with the help of his secretary. Angela hoped that Bine and Mutti would come from Germany, but they had other plans. Angela was hurt. When her eldest daughter or older sister gets married, you drop everything and come, unless it is the other end of the world and you can't arrange it that quickly or whatever! There were still six weeks to go, plenty of time to make different arrangements. Angela suspected that her mother did not like Ross and disapproved of the marriage. It made her sad. So Tissi would be the only member of her family to be at the wedding? Did she want to get married at all? The pressure was on and she could not wriggle out. Angela felt she was being managed, it just did not happen with her own free will. She was again at war with her upbringing. Would she ever shake this "You do as you are told" bit of her childhood? All her life since she had left home, she had to make up her mind as to what SHE wanted, not what other people wanted her to do. She loved Ross so much. Should she not start to trust him? Since that long talk they had had no fights. Getting married meant a lifetime together. Would he stay with her? Did she want to spend a life alone? Did she want to be with anyone? No! That was not it. She loved Ross, he had become her life, but there was something! Was it that she had been her own boss for the last fourteen years, and no one told her what to do with her life? But if you meet someone you share your life, and it seems that someone has to be the head in a relationship. But she did not want that, she wanted equal rights. She would never be the underdog or door mat.

She talked to Ross about it and he gave her that crooked smile and hugged her. "Little one, Kleines, what are your worries? We have managed so well since I got back and we are going to pull this wagon together. You are my life and I love you so much. Trust me and don't worry". They made love.

When the day came Tissi was there to help her and it was so good to have somebody there who represented her own family. Angela promptly got her period that morning a week early and suffered abdominal pains, and was nervous because the suit she wore was white! Then she mistook the air freshner as hairspray and ruined Tissi's hair. But in the end they arrived in Wandsworth Registry Office and the deed was done. No Church wedding. Angela had always hoped to have a traditional white church wedding, but because of Ross's divorce that was not possible. Then they went to Henley on Thames for a drink and snacks and it was a beautiful day and later to Fred and Elaine's for a big wonderful meal. The guests were Dermott and Ann Strahan, Bruce Truscott, Tissi, John Kinghorn, the head of the department at the Eastman Dental Hospital, and his wife Margaret, Maurice and Desiree Berman, all of them Dentists or dental nurses except Bruce and Tissi and Angela. A remote connection was there after all because Tissi's and Angela's father had also been a dentist. As she was thinking that she felt a stab into her heart. Mike came to mind. But Mike had long ago lost interest and she had quite forgotten him. And then she smiled to herself. His father too was a dentist, that's why she remembered.

351

They went to Greece on their honeymoon for ten days and enjoyed every minute. They stayed in a hotel in Athens and took prearranged trips to many sites. There were some sites she enjoyed most, Epidauros and Corinth, Mycenae and Delphi, Sounion and the Acropolis. There were other sites, but she only found out exactly where they were and what they were, after they returned home and she studied the books and sorted out her photographs. She enjoyed the Agora below the Acropolis, mainly because it was reconstructed, and one could see what the ruins once were.

She had been to Athens before, but it was to see the beaches, the Hotels and some sites in Athens itself. The rest she only learned from slideshows in the various hotels where the tourist offices showed them the trips that they would offer to tourists.

While visiting the ruins she had this feeling of having been here before. Ross said it was because she had been there in the slide- and film shows. But she felt that it was all strangely familiar, she had the feeling of having come home after a long absence and even though the buildings were now ruins it did not upset her.

*

Since her wedding she found a change in Ross. Whereas she was included in everything he did before with the "Boys", like meeting after work in a pub in London or go to the Golf Course on a Sunday, she was now EXCLUDED.

Nobody takes their wives" she was told. There was to be no argument. He took the car and she stayed at home. She was deeply hurt and very angry.

Well she didn't stay at home. She took the bus and the Underground and went into London. There were the Galleries and the Museums and she had a good time, albeit a lonely time. She was back at home to cook the supper for when Ross came home, usually very late and worse for the many pints they had had after the game, and so long as she did not tell him what she did all day on her day off, there was no strife.

"Did you have a good rest?" he would ask and she would say she did. She was sad. Was this now the pattern of their life? Were they to spend separate lives? Why did he want to marry her if now he did not want her company? She did not tell him where she was all day and it was not a lie, because she did have a rest, a rest from having to go to work and battle with the rush hour, to see beautiful things and not to sit at home like a good wife. What was there to do anyway? And Ross did not seem to show any interest how or what she did on her day off. What made him change? She wondered and could not find anything that she might have done. Was it really only because she was the wife now?

Then one day he rang her at work and asked to meet him after work. He took her to a pub on Cavendish Square, just opposite from his surgery and when he had bought the beer he said:

"I have good news. We can go and look for a house. I have got a mortgage agreement. Where do you want to live?" He never discussed money matters now that he was earning properly. He did not discuss getting a mortgage, he hadn't even talked to her about buying a house. And now he asked her where she wanted to live? She did not know England very well. The few places where she had been and where Ross had taken her were all in the South. She loved Forest and thought maybe Epping Forest?

She simply had no idea at all. She liked to be somewhere in the countryside, but close enough to the Underground and the busses because there was the daily trip into work and the late working hours. There were so many thoughts crowding her mind. Could he not have told her that he intended to get a mortgage?

She said: "what about Epping Forest, I have never been there but forest sounds nice."

They took the Underground and found no forest. Forest in England does not necessary mean trees. Very disappointed they went home. They spent many weekends looking and became very close. He was loving and thoughtful and she felt that he would like to live somewhere where she was happy. Eventually they found a sweet little bungalow in Ewell with a beautifully laid out garden and a greenhouse as well. She saw herself sitting in that when it rained with a good book and watching her lovely garden. They bought it and moved in very soon in the lovely month of May. The Azaleas where in full bloom and the roses looked promising. She worried a little about that. She was good at farming but with a flower garden she had little experience. I'll manage she promised herself. They could park the car outside the station at Tolworth all day and if she was on early shift, Ross would take her, and if she came home late, Ross would fetch her and she would come home to a cooked meal. Often they came home together when her shift allowed it. It seemed to be wonderful. At weekends he slept until lunchtime, which was not so nice, because she could not stay in bed that long. She never learned to sleep in. It gave her headaches and made her restless. So she would get up and tiptoe around the place, and often volunteered to work weekends. That gave her extra days off and she would fly off somewhere with the Interline Riding Club or even just fly home for a weekend to see her sister Bine and Mutti. Ross was loving and Angela was happy.

*

Angela was planning their next trip. She had planned a trip for a customer to South America and this is what she decided would be their next journey of discovery. The only difficulty would be to find out which airlines Lufthansa was in pool with so that she could ask for 10% tickets. Staff would never pay more than ten percent of the fare, or chose not to go at all. She found the airlines and all her applications were accepted except the one between Lima and Cuzco. She wrote again and as a reply got the tickets sent through the post free. Complimentary tickets. So they would go to New York, Quito, Lima, Cuzco, Lima, Santiago de Chile, Rio de Janeiro, and Home. Five weeks in all. She found out that if they wanted to go and stay the night in Macchu Picchu they would have to take bedding and food because there was no accommodation. So Angela made a travel bag which she could sling round her shoulder, where they could put all the necessary items for the trip to Cuzco and Macchu Picchu.

When she discussed it with Ross he was full of misgivings. "That means we have to rough it" he said and his face fell. On top of it all there was a currency restriction. One could only take 40 pounds sterling out of the country. "You can never do all that on 40 pounds"

354

he said, "it is out of the question. Angela looked at him. "I have worked it all out. We can pay for the tickets here, the tickets between Lima and Cusco cost nothing, they are a gift from Peru Airlines, I have a book which says you can do South America on 5 dollars a day. And we have £80 and live frugally".

A few days later Ross came home and said:" A client of mine lives in Rio de Janeiro and he owes me £100 and I told him to pay me in Rio. He then asked when we wanted to travel and when I told him the date he said we could have his apartment on the Copa Cabana with his chauffeur and his maids, because he wouldn't be there for a month. What do you say to that!" Angela jumped for joy. "Aren't we lucky, we shall have a wonderful adventure."

They arrived in Lima and found a hotel which they had chosen from their book "South America on 5 dollars a day", which she had bought at Foyles. "Casa Alemana", old colonial wooden hotel, run down and miserable, was recommended in the book. The Hotel owner was in bed, apparently sick, it was difficult to tell. She directed them from her bed to their room. They had to climb narrow wooden steps to the second floor and go through a door on the left which led out onto a balcony. They looked down into the inner courtyard, as the house surrounded this courtyard on all four sides. The rooms were numbered and theirs was number 227. A big rusty key with an even bigger tag opened the door and they found one wooden bed and a table in this room. There were sheets and blankets on the table and one pillow.

"This bed isn't even big enough for me on my own let alone for two of us or to make love in" Ross complained. Angela got the giggles.

"What a place, nobody will believe this when we get back". Angela enjoyed the adventure. They would stay here for two days and two more on their way back. Angela would have to ask the landlady to look after their suitcase until they get back, because they did not want to carry everything with them to Cuzco. They tried to sleep that night. It was a narrow bed and the mattress had a hole in the middle and Ross and Angela were squeezed together, which was something they didn't mind, but it was too hot to be comfortable. They turned in unison and threw off the covers and pulled them back on again because the flies were a pest. They woke up early and left the hotel to find somewhere to have breakfast. There was no food in the "hotel". They also found the airline office and got their tickets confirmed for Cuzco. They amused themselves in front of the palace watching the fancy dressed soldiers and guards goose stepping up and down. They enjoyed freshly squeezed fruit juices on the big square and visited some churches and the museum. There they discovered a little Inca girl which was obviously sacrificed to the gods and miraculously preserved in the glacier, still holding her little bag of marbles. There were hundreds of sculls which had belonged to warriors who had been injured in battle; the enormous holes in their sculls were caused by clubs and then were operated on afterwards and the pieces of bone removed and then left to close up by themselves. One could tell, that they had lived afterwards for quite some time, because the bone had grown, stretching out like crystalline fingers to finally grow together in the middle. Some made it and others did not.

They got the flight to Cuzco. A small 24 seater which seemed to hop over the peaks of the Andes, or squeezed through them and its shadow went down the valley and raced up towards them again. Angela watched with fascination. Then they circled and came down on the little runway in Cuzco. As they came out of the plane she could not get enough air to fill her lungs. She had been told about this phenomenon but to feel it, was different. She remembered to stay calm and told herself that all the others had the same problem, except that the locals were used to it. Their chests were huge like the wardrobe size bundles they carried on their backs. Everything was carried on their backs held there with a broad band tied around their foreheads. Bundles of wood larger than their bodies. Their necks must be as strong as an oxen's. They walked in quick short steps. Their clothing was very colourful and the women wore many skirts one over the other. Angela was so fascinated with everything she observed, that she forgot about her breathing and soon found it did not trouble her anymore.

There were so many taxi drivers who wanted to take them and offered them hotels. But because of their precious little book they knew where they wanted to go. They mentioned the name of the hotel and one taxi driver came forward and said that the hotel belonged to his brother. He spoke a mixture of English and Spanish and said he was very pleased to take them. It was a cheap and clean hotel, but did not cater for meals. Their taxi driver told them that they had built the dining room and put down the parquet floor before they put on the roof. They decided that it would not rain but it had and the floor was ruined.

Angela and Ross discovered a cosy little restaurant with lots of atmosphere on the Plaza des Armas, the Roma. Among other thing it offered "Rose Biff" on its menu.

They also planned to visit a dentist in Cuzco, somebody who had had some correspondence with the Eastman Dental Hospital and Ross had dealt with that. He had invited them to visit any time they were in Cuzco. Ross rang him up and invited him and his wife to the Roma restaurant for a meal. This Dentist was so pleased and delighted to see them, he would not accept the invitation but instead insisted for them to come to his house and stay with him. Angela and Ross wanted to keep their independence and stayed in the hotel, but were his guests for everything else. Louis and Martha Davila took them everywhere in Cuzco even to places which were not open to ordinary tourists. He also said that they should take the local train to Machu Picchu and avoid the tourist train. It would be a wonderful adventure.

In his mixture of language he told them about Cuzco. Here Angela re-tells the story as Louis told it to her and then carries on to tell the rest of the journey of South America.

"When the Inca culture was at its height, Cuzco was its capital and cultural centre. Peru's gold, which only the Inca was permitted to own, was kept here. In the Beginning Cuzco was a small house of stone with a roof of straw, which Manco Capac and his wives built. They called it Curi Cancha, the golden wrapping.

Manco Capac, the offspring of the sun, and the first Inca, came forth from the depths of Lake Titicaca, accompanied by his spouse, Mama Ocllo. He is said to have followed the path of the sun to find the most appropriate spot to found his kingdom. He carried a magic wand and when he came to where Cuzco is today; his wand fell to

357

earth and was swallowed up. Cuzco is supposedly the centre of the world: Qosqo.

From here grew and was ruled the empire of the Four Geographical Points, "Tawantinsuyo" the powerful civilization of the Incas, and ranging among one of the greatest in the world, covering the southern portion of Columbia, almost all of Ecuador, the Upper Amazon, the greater part of what today is Peru, all of Bolivia and the northern part of Chile and northwest Argentina, a total area of nearly two million square miles.

By the time the Spaniards discovered Cuzco they found a golden city. They saw fields of maize, potatoes and grain, herds of llama and other domestic animals, made of pure gold. The straw covered houses had so many stalks of gold amongst the straw that the roofs shone like pure gold as well. The Spaniards were confounded and had great difficulty to hide their greed.

In the end they took all the gold in Peru they could lay their hands on and shipped it to Spain and had the Inca, his wives and all this children murdered, his subjects were forced to become Christians. A minor relative of the murdered Inca was made king. He gathered his people and tried to fight off the Spaniards, but he could not save his kingdom. He fled across the mountains to the royal city of Vilcapampa, 112 Kilometres to the north. There were no roads as we know it. These were lanes and endless steps which wound around the mountain tops. The Incas never discovered the wheel. There was no need, nowhere long, straight or wide enough to build a road and use a vehicle. There were rope suspension bridges across the deep ravines. Vilcapampa was impossible to detect on the high ridge, now we know it as Machu Picchu, and it was the refuge of the last Inca. So it was known in the 1960's but since then more archaeological digs have discovered more about this history.

In 1911 Hiram Bingham discovered Machu Picchu and found that this mountain range was never mapped.

Here Angela continues the story herself;

We took the local train from Cuzco to Santa Ana. The tickets only cost a few Sol and some centavos, a tenth of what it would have cost on the tourist train. Three quarters of the journey to Santa Ana we got off the train. Louis had told us that there was a hotel up there but

358

we would have to take our own bedding and we would find no food. We had been prepared about the bedding and we had bought some rolls, wine and cheese for three days. This would be our breakfast, lunch and supper. We also had found some terrible biscuits and chocolate, but that was all there was which would keep for three days without a fridge. The train left at six in the morning and we got to Macchu Picchu at midday. (Much later it had become one of the incredible train journeys of the world on a BBC Program)

Our fellow passengers were local farmers with their livestock and produce. Although we were early, all seats were already taken, and the rest of the space was occupied with chickens, geese, ducks, goats, rabbits, pigs, and some strange animals which I have never seen before or since, even in zoos. It looked like a giant overgrown rat without a tail.

The train was packed and there were more people standing, but we were the only Europeans there. We were stared at. We found the local people fascinating and admired quietly the beautiful clothes they wore. So colourful and generous. Every one wore a poncho. The women's hats had stories to tell, I am sure, there was such a variety. I found out one thing, women, no matter what age, who wore hats which looked like upturned bowls with flowers in them, meant they were not married. All very beautiful. We returned their stares and there was a lot of grinning all round. A friendly people.

There were many stops. They all looked like the inside of a quarry. Although there were no stations as such, but where the train stopped were huge crowds with loads of bundles. Amid loud chatter and laughter there was a great exchange of bundles of all sorts of vegetables and animals through the open windows. This happened at each station and I wondered if not the bundles exchanged at one stop were swopped at the next one for something else. There was very little money changing hands.

A board had been laid across the train lavatory and a gas fired hot water boiler was placed on it and so the convenience was turned into the cafe. The washroom was stacked from floor to ceiling with Fanta, 7Up and Inca Cola and dozens of crates of bottled beer. The 'restaurateur' brewed coffee and then with a large enamel jug and a basket full of tin mugs, came around and sold coffee, black and sweet. We bought a cup each and it was delicious. Somebody near us offered us a sticky something to go with it. It was all very happy, friendly and helpful. However no one offered us a seat. We stood for 6 hours. Getting off the train at the various stations was not easy because there was no platform, so I did not bother.

The train moved along the Urubamba River and it was a very narrow canyon with the mountains rising high on each side. The train never emptied, everybody seemed to go to the very end. After the fifth stop the coffee came round again, but the mugs were not washed in between. What the heck, it was hot and we were thirsty. At Ollantaytambo was a lunch stop. Again there was no station or houses to be seen, but the entire village was gathered there with large cooking pots on open fires or makeshift stoves, they stirred the food which looked quite terrible, but smelled delicious. Our passengers had their own bowl and cups in their bundles which they handed out through the windows with much laughter and chatter had them filled. We had to go without, because we had nothing to put the food in, so we had one of our rolls each and drank wine from the bottle and a bite of cheese. Very nice and appreciated by the local people. They nodded approval. There were other tiny passengers on this train and they did not leave us in peace! Fleas!

As we arrived at Machu Picchu, the tourist train was ready to go back. It had to wait for us, because there was only a single track. This train had left two hours after us and had overtaken us at one of the stops while all the trading took place, took the tourists up to Machu Picchu, herded them through the city and down again ready to go as we arrived.

At the station we found a short row of stalls, just packing up because the tourists were departing. They did not count on two more getting off the local train. They did not know whether to unpack again or what. We just had a quick look around but made it clear that we did not want to buy anything. We had nowhere to put it anyway. A rickety bus, having just made the journey down with the tourists offered to take us up. He tried to tell us that there was no one up there and we indicated that we knew and wanted to go anyway. There were at least 12 hairpin bends zigzagging up this steep mountain side's un-surfaced road to dizzy heights.

We arrived at the hotel and found a sleepy man in there. He was surprised to see us, and we learned that two relief workers were also staying there. He showed us to our room and to our surprise we found a bed with clean sheets. We dumped our rucksack and went to find Machu Picchu. We had to skirt a mountainside of terraces, which once grew produce to feed the town, but we found terraces way up the mountain and wondered how anybody could get there in the first place. Coming round the mountain terraces we saw the city. Three thousand feet below we heard the rushing Urubamba. It was so quiet here that we could hear the river clearly. Then we came to the gatehouse which had been thatched and beyond we found the city. We caught our breath at the astonishing beauty of it.

High up in the wildest and most rugged Andes, on a topographical saddle between two mountains, the Machu Picchu (old mountain) and the Huyana Picchu, lies the mighty city of the last Inca, Vilcapampa. Later, when Hiram Bingham rediscovered the city, he named it after the mountain, Machu Picchu, not then knowing the real name of the city.

Hiram Bingham wrote, when he first set eyes on the site;

"Formidable, green precipices dropped deeply to the white rapids of the Urubamba; immediately in front of us, on the north side of the valley, rises a gigantic granite block to 2000 feet, and beyond that, snow covered mountains reach thousands of feet into the clouds above us.

To his dying day Hiram Bingham believed he had not found Vilcapampa, not realizing that he actually had found it.

To tell all about this city would take an entire book and there is no place here. I have written about it in my travel album.

We went back to Cuzco after 24 hours all to ourselves on this amazing mountaintop discovering for ourselves this marvellous place. Our friend Louis Davila and his wife took us to Pisac, a few mountaintops further into the Andes. There is a famous Sunday market where the Indians come from all around on foot to trade. It is a most colourful happy event. People chat and laugh and most of all trade by exchanging bundles or even money. Louis Davila took the chance to investigate the local people's teeth, which were brown *from chewing the beetle nut leaf like the Westerners chew gum. Louis found that there was no decay in their teeth.*

I bought a few things, mainly a poncho and a fur mat, soft and of all the Llama, Alpaca and Vicuna furs sewn into a wonderful pattern. Sadly our week ran out and we had to return to Lima, onto Santiago de Chile where we stayed some days.

We visited the zoo which somebody said was the most southern in the world and we found it really beautiful. It was situated on a hill and you went up on a cable car and then walked down. Having seen everything and done everything we decided on the day of our departure to go to the airport early and have lunch there. In the taxi to the airport we saw a plane take off and I jokingly said: there goes our plane. We were standby passengers on this airline, but Ross thought it could not be that a plane takes off 4 hours before time. However when we got to the airport we found that it had been our plane and since we were standby we were not on the list. All passengers had checked in and they took off. We were assured that on the next plane there would be room and we were actually checked in right away. The departure lounge was totally crowded out with the Brazilian Football team, amongst them Pele who at the time was THE football hero in the world. A little wiry man who recognized the only non football players in the lounge and came to make us welcome. So since we had missed our plane, we were taken on the next plane full of footballers. What fun it turned out to be. They all got off in Buenos Aires to play Argentina and we flew on to Rio de Janeiro. We came in to land in the night and looking out of the window into the black void I saw the Christ on Corcovado, huge and shining white and seemingly floating in the blackness of the night. I thought it was very beautiful.

The apartment which we could use was wonderful. The chauffeur had collected us from the airport and took us up in a lift which took us directly into the apartment. An African cook and chambermaid waited for us, dressed in a blue uniform with a white frilly apron, and we were guests as far as food was concerned as well. On their first morning an English man arrived with a brown paper carrier bag stuffed full of money. The hundred Pounds! After the cup of tea the English man left and Ross sat in the middle of the floor of the sitting room, emptied the bag and found that we were millionaires. He threw the notes into the air and let them rain on top of him, saying I am a millionaire! We went to the beach with was just across the 12 lane Avenida Atlantica, beautifully paved and we felt like millionaires as well. The sand was very hot underfoot and I ran very quickly into the water which was icy cold. I lost my Bikini top in the rough surf and we had to go and buy another one. We also bought some wonderful crystals and some jewellery.

All together we had an amazing time, surfing on Copacabana Beach, going up to the Corcovado Christ and looking down, across the city onto the Sugar Loaf, and going up to the Sugar Loaf and looking across to the Christ. What a place! The apartment on Copacabana Beach overlooking the bay!"

Here ends Angela's story of her fantastic trip of a lifetime.

When they got back Angela discovered that she was pregnant. She was over the moon about it. She already thought that she would never get pregnant, because she was now over thirty years old. She watched herself for symptoms of the new life inside her. It would be at least 6 months before she would feel anything. The doctor confirmed that she was expecting, and Ross seemed quite happy too. Angela had the feeling, that to him it was a routine thing, nothing special. To her it was a miracle.

They wallpapered Ross's den with the remainder of the Brazilian money, about £5 worth and it papered the entire wall above his desk. The rest was papered with the remaining maps of South America, so that they could do the trip several times over. A large photograph of Macchu Picchu was hanging on the all as well.

There came a trip to Greece to explore a new resort and she was allowed to take her husband. She asked Ross and he told Barbara, his secretary not to book any patients and to cancel the ones already booked. They got to Patras and from there a bus-ride to a remote spot, which they found was infested with mosquitoes. They were supposed to stay there for a week and give a report afterwards. The accommodation was primitive, the food very good, the mosquitoes a plague. Angela had brought some repellent which helped wonderfully, but there were colleagues from Austrian airlines and Swissair who became terribly ill with the bites and they had to be taken back and the whole trip was cut short. Angela wrote a damming report on the resort. There was nothing to recommend the place and the good food they had did mot make up for the primitive state of the place and the terrible mosquito plague.

On a day off, working in the garden she suddenly without warning lost the baby. She was devastated and when she told Ross he seemed not to mind at all. There was no loving cuddle and reassurance. She went into depression but could not allow herself to wallow in self pity. She had to go to work and being with her colleagues was a great help. They had more understanding than Ross had shown. She was glad to have so many good friends at work. They were like an extended family especially since they had been together for so many years. Nobody wanted to leave Lufthansa, there was nowhere a better job to be had, and there were no rivalries amongst the staff, every one got on so well with every body else.

Then came the day when Richard announced that he would come to Britain and stay with his dad. Angela looked forward to this because Ross had often mentioned that he missed his children very much. They expected Richard in early spring and waited for the telegram that would announce the time of arrival at Heathrow. But nothing came. He had left New Zealand but did not arrive. It turned out that he took the chance to visit India like so many young people did in the 60s and apparently he was with a group of young hippies doing the hippy tour. Ross was very angry and tried to get in touch with his son, but there was no way of trekking him down. There were postcards, but they had been a long time coming and by the time they reached Ewell, Richard was not at that place anymore. Angela said, when he has run out of money, he will come, you'll see.

He did come and within a day of his arrival, Angela was disappointed and unhappy. His cigarettes smelled terrible. He was lazy and began to mess up the place. He arrived at her office and she had to ask him to wait until it was her lunchtime. She realized that he was lonely, because both she and Ross were working and he had nothing to do. She suggested he should find a job to earn some money and to have somewhere to go during the day.

"I have just been freed from school, why should I imprison myself with a bloody job so soon?" Richard said.

"Well you had some months in India, why don't you earn some money for your next trip?" Angela offered

"No need, dad will pay my return trip if I want to go back to New Zealand, which I don't think I will. I like it here"

But his Mother had other Ideas. He was to go back to University in New Zealand and Ross was in full agreement. He could fly with a 50% reduction on flight tickets because of Angela's job and they all decided to fly back to the Antipodes together via Hong Kong, Bangkok and Sydney which was a fantastic journey. They took in all the sights. In Hong Kong they visited Tony Jackson who was a dentist friend of Ross's. They stayed a week in Hong Kong. Coming in to land was just a little hairy. A thick cloud was hiding the city.

Angela said: "Suddenly it seemed we were landing on water and I thought Oh God, here we go!" Just a split second before touchdown the runway came rushing in and the pilot put the plane down." Phew!!

The airport and the hotel where they stayed was in Kowloon on the mainland. To get to Hong Kong they had to take the ferry. Tony told them to go in first class because there it was forbidden to spit. They went to the market, they looked up a tailor which was the father in law of one of her colleagues and ordered a suit for him. They visited Aberdeen, the boat city and found only charcoal sticks. It had completely burnt down a week before. They found Hong Kong very hilly, the streets go up and down and the backdrop to the city when you could see it is surrounded by mountains. The skyscraper apartment houses stand shoulder to shoulder with tiny windows, just small cells where people go to sleep, because during the day it seems that everybody is on the street, selling things and cooking and eating in the markets everywhere. They visited silk spinners and pearl fishers and admired the beautiful things. Angela bought a lovely silk wall hanging for Bine who was getting married at the end of Angela's and Ross's trip. For herself she bought a silk cushion with exquisite embroidery and four hand painted silk paintings; summer autumn winter and spring.

They took their seats in first class on the way back to Bangkok and waited and waited for one more passenger. As they looked out of the little window they saw a woman and a few men rushing through the drizzle to the aircraft. They could not see her face because she had her mackintosh over her head. After they were all in and settled behind them the plane took off without delay. After the seatbelts were off it was announced that it was Jane Mansfield and once she got the makeup on and was presentable, she would give an audience to all the men. Ross and Richard could hardly wait and when it was their turn, Angela knelt on the seat in front of Jane Mansfield and listened. She asked a few daft questions and one was where Ross from was and he said New Zealand and she said: Oh, wonderful, I did not know they spoke English there! She was wearing a wig and her false eyelashes were slightly loose, and Angela felt sorry for her. She looked terribly tired.

In Bangkok they were the guests of the Tavarankhol's, a Thai dentist Ross had met at the Eastman. The time in Bangkok was silk and gold, wonderful temples and a trip to the water market, exotic fruits in barges and beautiful materials.

They were invited to a restaurant on a hill, where they sat on cushions on the floor, admiring beautifully laid out tables and even more beautiful people sliding on their knees to serve the many dishes and using what looked like golden cutlery. It was entirely beautiful and if you want to read more about it read it in Angela's travels.

They delivered Richard to his mother safely.

Ross told his son to study hard and train for anything academic, anything he liked and Ross would be happy and then he could come back to Britain and Ross would help him find a job. Richard promised.

When they returned to Britain they stopped off in Karlsruhe because Bine was getting married to Joachim Liehmann, a tall and handsome man. He was an electronics engineer and had already invented some clever gadgets for his firm. It was a beautiful wedding and all the entire family was there, little Stevie the only grandchild was loved and spoiled. They went to a medieval coaching inn which had not been modernised and still had the stables where the horses went and the carriages stood. It was just so special. Bine was expecting her first child. Then it was time to return to work.

Richard dropped out of Uni and was back in Britain via India a year later. His mother sent frantic letters, but he could not be traced in India. When he finally turned up in Ewell he brought with him a kilo of cannabis resin, which he hid under his mattress and which Angela found the next time she changed the sheets on his bed. He had repeatedly denied smoking drugs, even though Angela had asked about the strange cigarettes he smoked. She did not know enough about cannabis and those smoking habits nor did Ross. When Ross asked him out right he denied everything and when Angela produced the huge lump of resin, he lied about what it was. Ross turned to Angela with an icy stare and said: "Don't drive a wedge between me and my son."

From that day on, Richard was allowed to do anything he wanted to do and nothing that would have been in any way useful. He did not work, he asked for money all the time, he messed up the house and never helped anywhere, and when Angela once asked him to help her in the garden he said:

"Why should I, it is not my garden" and Angela said:

"Well you live and eat here, you have your clothes washed and ironed, the place is cleaned and all without your help. Don't you get bored not doing anything? Just lying around sunning yourself watching others working and just smoking that stuff all the time? Even though your father is in denial about you smoking pot, I know, and I tell you it will lead to harder stuff and before you know it you are a junky. You will turn to the harder stuff when you don't get a kick out of Cannabis anymore and then you are lost. You are an addict."

"What do you know about it? Cannabis is not addictive."

"So you now admit you smoke cannabis?" Angela said.

"Well you have known it all along anyway, but don't tell dad. I shall just deny it and then it is my word against yours and guess whom he will believe?" Angela turned her back on him and ignored him. He was out to annoy her and he was right. Ross did not want to know. He gave Richard money to go into town and often he came back dirty and drunk. Then one day he came into the office, sweet and friendly, asking her out to lunch. Angela was amazed. This young man was two faced. What brought on this change? In the morning he had just got up, unwashed, heavy with sleep he sat at the table, spoiling her breakfast with the terrible breath which he yawned deliberately into her face. Angela had left without finishing her breakfast and had gone to work and had breakfast in the little Buttery around the corner from the office. And now this! He wants something, I wonder what it is, she thought. They went to a little bistro and had a lasagne. He wanted a ticket to go back to India.

"Shouldn't you find a job or train for something? What money do you use in India? You haven't earned anything! What do you want to do with your life, Richard? You can't rely on dad for the rest of your life. You have to learn to stand on your own two feet. "Angela said.

"Dad owes me! He left us and now he can pay".

"Do you want to say that it was my fault that dad left you?" Angela looked at him.

"No it all happened before you. You are just another victim," he said, grinning.

"What do you mean, another victim", but Richard just shrugged his shoulders. Angela thought it was just something he said to annoy her.

"Anyway, we have to talk to dad about that. He has got to agree to your trip to India.

"I am 18 I don't need his permission.

"Ah, but you need his money! You won't get it from me!" Angela was angry. This young man had an attitude, which she had not encountered before. He was greedy, impolite, lazy and provocative. Totally without ambition!

"You still have to talk to your father. I shall not get you a ticket without his permission. And anyway, since I am not paying for the ticket, you will have to ask Ross."

"Fuck you then, you silly bitch" and he left without paying. Angela paid for the lunch totally disgusted. Poor Ross! She went back to work, and relieved the person in the telex room. There she could get down and concentrate and type away without having to think. Let's see how many I can do until it is time to go home. Two

368

a minute, that will be about 480 telexes unless there are long itineraries.

By the time she got home, at seven, both Richard and Ross were sitting at the kitchen table, drinking a beer. Ross had cooked the supper and they were laughing. Angela smiled and said hello. Ross said that as soon as she is ready, they can eat. She was hungry and looked forward to a nice meal. As she sat down, Richard looked at her and said:

"Had a good day? I meant to see you today at work, but I didn't make it." They looked at each other hard. Angela wanted to say something, but Richards stare stopped her. Alright she thought. I will have nothing to do with him. It is entirely between him and his father. There was something else she wanted to say, but that can wait until they go to bed. She was pregnant again and this time she was not going to lose the baby. She would concentrate on this child inside her and accept it right from the start. No matter what was happening around her. It would now be only mother and the child. Richard's mother, Alison, demanded that he come home and finish Uni. So Angela and Ross decided to take him back via Honkong and Bangkok and visit her mother in law and show off the bump.

On the 27th of October 1968 she wrote a letter to her mother:

My dear little Mother

News! Imagine, but first sit down, I am pregnant. What do you say to that? I can't believe it myself, but I have missed my second period, so it must be true. I am so excited I can hardly write. So you can start knitting! Ross is convinced it is going to be a boy, Can you think of a nice name?

In January we are flying once more to New Zealand, which is probably going to be the last time, because when I stop working for Lufthansa we won't be able to fly anymore so cheaply. I shall miss that awfully but you have to be there for twenty years to be able to fly after you stopped working for them. Don't tell Tissi yet, I shall tell her when I see her on the 13th November. I would like to surprise her.

I won't need the ox for the crib this Christmas because we won't be here. I shall have to work on the 24, 25 and 26th of December and on the 27th we fly to New Zealand. I shan't bother to put up a Christmas tree this year, but next year with Baby!

I wrote to you to ask you if the parcel has arrived. If not then it must have got delayed in the post. They are striking again. There is a post dispute going on at the moment. They argue over the 4 penny and 5 penny stamp. They don't ask us, the people. We have no rights, as always.

When I came home from work today I had to pass a huge student demonstration. 30000 students were on the march and our poor policemen had no Sunday off. It was supposed to be an anti Vietnam demonstration but the freedom fighters from Wales and Scotland joined and also Africa for the Blacks etc. Everybody who had an axe to grind was there and the whole thing was a fiasco.

I am happy that you like the work in Todmoos, and that you have a hobby. Bine has not written at all. I had no idea that they are going to move after they did so much building at the place where they live. I have to stop now, I have 5 more letters to write. I will have more time when I stop working, behind me is a big basket with clothes and Ross's shirts, a new one every day, white! There is little time when I am working.

I love you very much, always your Ange and Ross

36

Life in Epsom

The Christmas 1968/69 was Angela's last trip to New Zealand to see her mother in law. Chas had died the year before and it was all very sad. They travelled to see all the family in the South and North Island and in New Plymouth they took an Ex Ray photo of the baby in Angela's belly but in those days one could not tell if it was a boy or a girl. She didn't want to know anyway. She was so very happy.

Happily she continued to go to work and fight her daily trip through the rush hour. Nothing mattered, she was expecting a baby. Such wonderful happiness.

In May 1969 Angela gave in her notice to Lufthansa with a very heavy heart. She could not believe that she was now going to be at home all the time. She started to sew clothes and curtains and baby things and she worked hard in the Garden. The little house became so very cosy. The baby room was complete, with a baby basket with a lace canapé over the top. Small cut out fairy figures on the wall which were amazingly saved from before the war and had been hanging in her own baby room in Berlin. Funny, the things that were saved!

A big chest of drawers, which she bought for £5 from a neighbour was restored by her and looked great in the little room. It had been standing in the Garage covered in paint blobs, where her neighbour's husband had stored the paint and stirred it and splashed it all over. Angela could see the potential through the mess and asked to buy it and the neighbour was glad to get rid of it.

On the 5th of June the baby was supposed to be born but there was no sign. The queen came to Epsom and she would pass on the main road near the bungalow at the Grange and Angela went to stand by the road and watch with her neighbours. On the 8th of June Angela started and went to hospital, but the baby did not come for another two days and eventually had to be induced. It was a forceps birth and Angela was badly damaged during the birth. She had to be sown up with 32 stitches and was very sore for weeks. It took a long time healing and Ross got very impatient, because he thought that she should be able to do her duty as a wife in the marital bed. Angela was unable to even think about sex, let alone have sex. She was trying to feed the baby and

unable to sit comfortably. She had to acquire new skills, and having to get used to looking after her child, doing a new job and having to learn fast. Ross was totally uninterested and she found, that having had two children

already was bored with the fact to having to start all over again.

However he adored this little baby which they called Sarah Jane. She was a golden baby with tight corkscrews curls and the biggest blue eyes. She laughed a lot and made her mum very happy. Angela adjusted to be at home, shop and cook, sew and garden, clean and iron, and be a good mum and wife. But Ross did not come home for supper any more. He arrived later and later. She had to put baby to bed and eat by herself and try to keep his food from drying out in the oven. When asked if he was going to be home for supper he always said off course he would but never did. When he came home at nine or ten, he would go straight into the baby room, wake up Sarah and play with her, reeking of beer and whisky and being silly. For peace and harmony's sake Angela kept quiet. Ross overlooked her, she might have been invisible as far as he was concerned.

She said jokingly one day:

"I feel like the wrapping paper the goods came in, and now that you have your present the paper is thrown out" He ignored this and Angela might as well have spoken to the wall. He was a stranger.

When Sarah was a year old, Ross and Angela took Sarah in the white Rover 2000 to Germany to take part in the Tiedemann Gathering in Hersfeld. On this occasion she met for the first time Hasso Weichbrodt, whose mother was Dorothea Weichbrodt von Tiedemann, whose father was a brother of Angela's great - grandfather. Then they travelled on to Berlin in the company of Angela's mother.

They visited Hermann von Stuckrad, whose father was the gynaecologist who had delivered Angela and her sisters in Berlin, her mother's cousin. Hermann was the sole survivor of the family in 1945. They had all died together in a suicide pact as the Russians entered their street in Berlin.

Angela, Ross and Angela's mother with the baby Sarah were going to cross into East Germany to visit her mother's aunt, Ta Echen. She was the sister of Angela's grandmother. As they wanted to cross over at Checkpoint Charlie, her mother was refused entry, as "the relationship was not close enough" Angela lived in England and married to a British Citizen, and therefore, with great difficulty got a visa. Her mother stayed with Hermann until it was time to take the sealed bus to Hof, through the GDR where Angela and Ross picked her up.

Meanwhile Angela and Ross finally got to Halle on the old motorway, which seemed deserted except for their car. Weird and eerie! Angela spotted a sign pointing to the Wartburg and thought she could go and visit, like any other tourist. But just 10 meters off the motorway they were stopped by armed soldiers and told to turn back onto the motorway. In Halle it turned out that Ta Echen was finally given two weeks in a holiday home for the elderly, which she had asked for two years earlier. So when Angela and Ross got there, she was not there. Deliberate chicaneries! Angela could not believe that authorities could be so wicked and devious. She had spent months of negotiations to be able to visit and finally got permission only to find Ta Echen gone. However her neighbour was willing and happy for some police deception. At midnight Ross and the neighbour went off to find and bring back the aunt. Happy to do something illegal and with a mischievous smile she arrived at two in the morning. They all went back to bed, Sarah slept through it all. In the morning they found that absolutely everything had been stolen out of the car. Ross forgot to lock up after they got back and everything, except what was in Angela's handbag was stolen. All Sarah's clothes and nappies, the potty, Angela's spare clothes and her Peruvian Poncho, Sarah's little poncho which Angela had knitted, taking the pattern from her own poncho, the Pentax camera which they had purchased in Hongkong, a rare piece of equipment at the time, especially in Russian Occupied Germany. The thieves didn't get the money, and they didn't get the passports.

Ross and Angela had brought a lot of food for TaEchen which was already in the flat so the thieves didn't get that either. The neighbour offered to go into town to buy some bread rolls to go with the butter, honey and real coffee, which was not available in the GDR. The hours went by and the neighbour did not get back. Eventually she arrived with a bunch of radishes. That was all she could get that morning. No bread, no rolls, nothing. Luckily Angela and Ross had bread and crisp bread.

They reported the theft to the police station and were told that they would not get anything back except the camera. They would get that back because in the entire GDR or Poland or Russia there would not be a camera like it and when the thief put it up for sale, they would have him. And sure enough, later that year in October, TaEchen came to West Germany to visit Angela's sister Sabine and their mother and brought the camera with her.

Every day they had to go to the East German police station and exchange west mark into east mark. They tried to buy things with that money, but could find no shops of any kind. So they decided to change it back when they left, but could not. So they thought they could buy petrol with it, but petrol could only be bought with west mark. When they got to the border they were asked if they had any east mark and they thought now we can change it back into west mark, but that was an entirely innocent thought. The deviousness, chicanery and criminality of the GDR was beyond anybodies imagination. With stony faces they declared that it was illegal to export GDR money into the West. They made Angela and Ross feel entirely guilty. Angela suddenly felt that it was all too much. She shouted in German that it was entirely illegal to steal money from people, and that was exactly what they were doing. A soldier appeared with a gun and just stood there not moving a muscle in his face. Stony faced the lot of them and the woman said:

"You have stayed here a week, 6days at 30 marks that is 180 marks. Have you bought anything, can you show the receipts of the goods you have bought?" Not taking any notice of the armed soldier Angela shouted:

"Ha! Where are your shops? Where are the goods you produce in the Zone? What could we have bought in the Zone?" That stopped the stony stare of the woman and she shouted back:

"This is not the Zone, this is the GDR", and Angela shouted back that they should be ashamed to call this Germany and to do this to fellow Germans.

Ross got frightened and nervous and said:

"Give them the fucking money and let's get the fuck out of this fucking place. I have had enough of this, they can keep their shit money". Angela grinned. Here spoke the true New Zealander, not the elegant dentist who so carefully tried to get rid of the New Zealand accent. She put the money on the counter and they left. No doubt they would never ever get permission to visit the GDR again, nor would they want to. They got into the car and crossed the border. A very lonely figure waited for them on this large, empty, windy place. The bus had come and gone and Angela's mum stood there forlornly. She got into the car and got a blow by blow account of what had just happened. Afterwards they laughed. Ross said that he would never do this again, but would not have missed it for the world. What an experience!

They travelled on to Bine in Karlsruhe who had finished her training as a physiotherapist and was busy starting her surgery. Tissi had returned to Germany because things had not worked out in England for her. She was working for Brecht's Spices, a good job. Little Stevie was going to a German school. Bine was thinking of building a house outside Karlsruhe. Her mother in law was putting up the money for the deposit.

Angela's mother had also retired and now lived near Sabine in Karlsruhe and would also put some money towards the building of the house which entitled her to the granny annexe. So now that Sabine had her first child, called Yvonne and a business, granny would look after the child whilst Bine worked. Achim had to travel to Bretten to work. It was hard for Bine but their mother was there and Tissi and Angela felt a little out of it all. She suddenly felt that she would love to come home and live in Germany. But her home was now in England and with Ross her husband and she loved him even though she felt more and more that he did not love her. Angela was troubled and worried and tried to work out what it was that she did wrong. But her thoughts turned around about in circles and always arrived back at the point where she knew she had not changed. The one that had changed was Ross, and she suspected that he had become unfaithful.

Back in England, it wasn't long before Richard was back. He was on hard drugs, Angela knew it, Ross was in denial. Richard was totally useless to himself and to the family. He was a total nightmare and Angela lost another baby. She was depressed and Ross impatient.

"Pull yourself together; there will be other babies, no doubt". And Angela busied herself quietly and left Richard and Ross to themselves. She was now a fulltime housewife, and felt like a domestic employed by two uncaring blokes, but had to endure it because she had a baby. She also felt that both Richard and Ross ganged up against her. She had never expected this from Ross, such blatant disloyalty. Quietly she did her job and hoped that there would be some escape from it all eventually.

Ross still used her regularly in bed but there was no love on his part. She was very unhappy and tried hard to make him feel that she loved him. But Ross was not interested. He just relieved himself and then turned his back on her. She felt totally humiliated.

Richard had met Ross's young dental nurse and started to take her out. Soon Angela found that there was a strange rivalry between Ross and his son.

It wasn't long before Ross gave him the money to travel again and Richard was off to Bali. No one heard any more from him. His mother kept writing trying to find out where he was but neither Angela nor Ross could give her any news. Richard had become a Druggy. Heroin was now controlling him. Angela kept quiet. Ross had to work this out for himself. He had not listened to her. There was nothing she could do. Ross never talked about it, except that he had made up his mind that Richard deserved to be where he was. It never occurred to him that giving him the money to go back to Bali would mean the loss of his son to drugs.

Then Joana announced that she would come and work in Britain for a while. Ross was happy and looked forward to her arrival. He came home one day and said that they were "financially under-housed" whatever that meant. So they went looking for a bigger house.

Angela was pregnant again and felt unwell most of the time. She could not bear to go into a butchers shop, with all that sawdust covered in blood on the floor reeking of stale blood. She retched uncontrollably and felt embarrassed, and every morning she felt sick. "You are expecting a boy" they said to her and she looked forward to this little baby.

However, Ross was hardly ever at home. He had lots of excuses. He gave lectures in Birmingham, he was playing Golf in Scotland, he had to go to Yugoslavia to give lectures to dentists there. In the evenings he was always late. Angela had to have her evening meals on her own and wondered if she should even cook for Ross. She suspected that instead of Yugoslavia he was quite close in some flat making love to someone else. It turned her stomach upside down.

"Are you going to be home for Supper?" she would ask and he would angrily answer: "Off course I'll be home." What time can I expect you then?" "The usual time after work. Don't ask silly questions".

Angela saw him leave for work and thought that if he had behaved like that to Alison, then no wonder she had wanted to go home to New Zealand. No one wants to be with him, I don't want to be with him anymore. He is a nightmare of a husband. There was a solicitor in the little shopping precinct in Ewell and often she stood outside his door with Sarah in the pushchair and herself very pregnant and then she thought she could not do it. She loved Ross and he loved Sarah and what would his mother say. She was fond of Ross's mother and all the other relatives. Leaving your husband because of adultery and mental cruelty did not just mean you leave him; you leave all of the family as well. She could not do it.

One day he surprised her in the bathroom. It was late and she prepared to go to bed. She heard the key turn in the front door, her stomach turned and she felt sick fear. What awful thing is he going to tell her this time? He opened the bathroom door without knocking and came in, took one look at her naked body and said:

"Oh my God you are fat! Disgusting!" and left. She did not even have the time to remind him that she was six months pregnant with his child.

She was devastated, sad and depressed. She could not go on like that. This was not the man she fell in love with or was it? He hated her and she could not tell why. She felt so guilty. What was it she had done? Quietly she gave way to tears and felt the baby turn. She must not be depressed; she must be happy and cheerful. The baby must feel that she is happy. She tried to think of things that would make her happy. She did not need Ross to be happy she decided. She would carry on, loving her children and she would make a life with her children and she looked forward for this one to be born. But, she could not get rid of her heavy heart. What about the father of these children. He did love Sarah but what about the family. She concluded that he was not a family man. He was a man to be happy with "The Boys" as he called his dental colleagues with whom he still spent a lot of time. To meet the "boys" after work, even though two of the "boys" had also got married and stayed at home now because they had started a family. But new "boys" had joined and Ross still belonged to the bachelors. He would probably always be a bachelor and Angela had to accept this. She had to accept that he was not a family man.

One day in late autumn he wanted her New Zealand Greenstone Tiki. She asked him what for and he said it was to be a surprise. Sometime later he gave her back the Tiki.

Angela spent a very lonely Christmas in Ewell. Ross had to go on business somewhere he did not tell her where. January was spent on her own. Ross told her that he was overworked and it had made him impotent. On a trip to London she ran into a mutual friend, Tom Hill, another dentist, who asked her how she liked the golden Tiki which Ross had made for her for Christmas. Instantly she knew. He had made it for *her*. She just smiled at Tom and they parted.

February came and Valentine's Day and Ross wanted to know if the baby was due on the 14th. Angela said she could not make the baby come; it would come when it was ready to come.

"Oh have it your own way then" he said and left. He did not come home until 3 or 4 in the morning and even though Angela knew he had a new love, she tried to put it out of her mind. But she asked anyway and his answer was:

"Off course not, what do you take me for? I have not got a mistress, trust me"

On the 21st of February he rang her at 4 in the morning: "Sorry, Kleines, now don't get worried or upset, I had an accident with the car. I am fine, however the car is a write off" I will be home as soon as I cleared everything with the police. How close are you? I won't be long".

Angela sat up in bed and was very angry. He was drunk, and probably had his mistress in the car. Trust him to write off the car and not get injured. He has the luck of the devil. And I bet he is telling the police a bunch of lies and leaning heavily on his pregnant wife at home who is having a baby any moment. The bastard!

He was home by six in the morning and rang his secretary to tell her that he could not come in today because Angela was about having his baby. Would she cancel all the patients please? He went to bed after that and straight to sleep.

Angela rang the Epsom District Hospital and asked for an ambulance. "But you are listed here that you are coming into hospital in your own car." the man on the phone said.

"I know", she answered, "but unfortunately my husband had an accident and the car is not useable".

"Well, Mrs Valentine, how often do the pains come?"

"About every ten minutes"

"Ok, I shall try to book an ambulance right now, and you give me another call in about an hour?"

"Thank you" Angela said and rang off. She had her suitcase packed and the baby clothes ready and the little cot was beautifully renewed after Sarah had been in it. Angela's mother had come over from Germany a few days earlier and stayed in the room upstairs. She was there, but very depressed to be in this loveless and unhappy home. Everything was strange and foreign to her. She would be there for Sarah while the baby was being born. Angela and her mother hugged and her mother said:

"It will be alright once the baby is born, you'll see". But Angela now knew her husband. Nothing would be alright. He just could not help himself. He needed young and beautiful women and that would never change. A victim, Richard had said and that's what she was. And he was a liar and didn't even know it himself.

Then it was time to ring the ambulance and it came within a very short time. The driver came in to escort her to the vehicle and went for the little suitcase when Ross came out of the bedroom to see what was going on. The man asked:

"And who are you?" and Ross answered:

"I am the husband" and grinned stupidly. The man turned to him and said:

"Well come on man, get dressed you are coming aren't you?" and Ross went and put his trousers on over the pyjamas and the jacket over his pyjama top and rushed out into the ambulance and off they went. Through the window she saw her mother stand alone and forlornly in the doorway. Poor mum, Angela thought. "How am I going to get home?" Ross complained.

Angela was busy with the pain and the baby struggling to get out. She also had to smile because Ross's pyjama trousers bottoms showed under his elegant trousers and he had no socks and only wore his slippers.

She could not care less how her "beloved" husband was going to get home. "Get a taxi" she squeezed out whilst coping with the pain. Ross sat opposite her looking totally miserable. It must be the shock of having had this accident just a few hours earlier. "You shouldn't have come, after the accident" she said but he did not hear her and she could not care less. She was very busy right now. They arrived and she was whisked away and the baby was trying to be born almost immediately. But there were complications and Angela was put on the operating table and given an anaesthetic injection which lasted just a few moments and she was still able to hear what was going on. It all sounded far away. When she was fully conscious again, she held a tiny boy in her arms. He too had to be fetched with forceps and one of his tiny ears was folded up like a letter. Angela gently touched it and tried to unfold it and the nurse reassured her that it will be ok in a day or two. Ross came in and took one look and said: "Oh well done, see you later" and left. He did not give her a kiss. Was he embarrassed in front of the nurse? The nurse said: "In a hurry was he to get to work? Why did he still have his pyjamas on?" Angela hugged the baby and said: "It's a long story, don't ask"

The next day, Angela had an embolism and was rushed to intensive care. She had very little milk for the baby either and he had to be supplemented with bottled milk.

The doctor visited her and said:

"Whatever happened to you? You are in a terrible state. By the way I have fixed your 'undercarriage', the damage caused by your last birth. You should have no more problems now. We have also cleaned out your womb. But you have to be on blood thinning pills, you must not drive a car, peel potatoes or anything that might injure you and make you bleed for the next 6 weeks. You must not injure yourself".

And I must not cry, I must not feel depressed. She was back in the ward and the baby was in a cot by her side. She held him tight whilst feeding him of her own milk and then pretending for his sake that he was breast fed whilst suckling on the bottle. He could feel her skin and hopefully hear her heartbeat. She looked at his little fingers and his little toes. He cried a lot. She was hoping that Ross would bring her mother and Sarah. She wanted to see her other child and show Peter to Sarah and she wanted to see her mum. But Ross did not come. His secretary sent a bunch of flowers and wished her well. Nothing from Ross. Angela suddenly had a dreadful thought. He is afraid to tell his mistress about the baby. Why should Angela have a baby when he was with her? Oh my God! Put it out of your head. Here is this lovely boy, who needs Ross! Both children would need their father but she now realized quite clearly that Ross was not a father. He had conquered her the same way he had won Alison, and now that he possessed her, he was out for new conquests, what did Richard call her?: A victim! Would she have to accept his mistresses? Is that what was expected? First she has to beat this embolism. The doctor said she was lucky to be alive. The blood clot had travelled through her heart.

A week after the birth her mother came to visit. Poor mum, left in a household where she was not familiar, in a town which was totally strange to her and with a bus service she did not know and how to find the hospital she had no idea where it was. But here was her mother and Sarah came running up to the bed and tried to climb up. Angela kept back the tears:

"Oh Mutti, how did you get here? Did Ross bring you? Where is he?" Her mother gave her a hug and a kiss and said:

"Where is the baby? I came to hold him and to show Sarah her little brother. She has been asking for you and her dad." Angela looked at her:

"Isn't he at home?" Her mother avoided her and held Peter and talked to him in German and Sarah snuggled up to Angela and needed to be hugged very much. Angela hugged and kissed and caressed her daughter. Such a lovely child and so loving and in need to be loved back. Her mother handed the baby over for Sarah to hold. All three of them on the bed, Angela holding Sarah and Sarah holding Peter, and granny taking a photo! Almost as an aside her mother said:

" Ross hasn't been home since the birth". Angela's heart nearly stood still. And then her mother asked:

"When are you coming home? I must be back in Germany, Bine needs me".

This time she thought her heart would truly stop. But she became furious. She looked at her mother and suddenly realized that her mother had been suffering at home with Sarah, no Ross, no help, worried about the situation and she also realized that her mother had known Ross's character and tried to warn her about him. What had made Angela so blind and so stupid? Here she was with two children and no husband and no job, because after three years she could not return to Lufthansa unless she started as a newcomer, and anyway who would look after the children? The children! She would not be without them.

"I have had an embolism and I have to be careful with knives etc. Her mother being a nurse knew exactly what an embolism was. She hugged her daughter again. Angela also knew that Bine relied on her mother because of the business. She was a working mother and Mutti looked after her household and the children. Angela rang the bell for the nurse. When the nurse came into the ward Angela said: "I need to get home as soon as possible, can you arrange it? I make it my responsibility not to cut myself or be involved in an accident." The nurse said I see what can be done." Without saying much, they all knew that Angela's husband had not been to visit and that things were not right. She was an abandoned mother. They were so sweet to Sarah, remembering her from when she had been born three years earlier.

Ross was in the house when Angela came home with the baby. A hospital car took her home and her mother had rung him at work in Cavendish Square and he had promised to be home that weekend. To Angela he said that he kept away to make it easier for her mum not to have to worry about him cooking and all that. He said he stayed in a hotel near work and it was less stressful than to travel every day. Angela said nothing, because she knew it was a lie. She didn't know how to react and so she busied herself with the children, mother had cooked a wonderful evening meal and they all sat down together. Ross was very uncomfortable and Angela guessed he felt guilty or couldn't wait to be away again? Two days later, her mother left for Germany and Ross returned to London and Angela had no idea where he spent his nights. He always came home for the weekend, but stayed in bed most of the time.

*

They found a beautiful house in Epsom, in Woodcote Green Road, a house called Tyrrelcote and she loved it. She was hoping that this house would be their home and that the children would love the garden. She was happy. They would be able to move in around August. It was in a terrible state of repair and every room needed decorating. The bathroom had been used as a coal cellar, because the central heating had only just been put in to make the house more attractive for the potential buyer. But the bath tub was black and scratched and filthy. So the first thing would be to install a new bathroom. Then the kitchen! The kitchen sink was rotten und the wooden draining board was so soft and black with rot that she could put a knife right through it as if it were a ripe tomato. Disgusting!

However she saw the potential of the place and the big windows and the lovely staircase and all the beautiful rooms. This had once been a beautiful, almost stately home. It had a coach house with a room upstairs and an enormous garden, and a huge chestnut tree stood over the coach house and in the garden was an orchard, a tennis lawn, a fruit garden and vegetable garden and loads of exotic trees and flowers and a jungle for the children. She would have to find out what was in the jungle, it looked as if there was a plum tree but she couldn't tell for sure. At the bottom of the garden were two tall poplar trees and later she found out that they were a landmark in Epsom. The RAC country club was not far.The Racecourse was just up the road. Ross was satisfied; the place suited his status, so he said. What kind of a man had Ross become? She hardly recognised him. He was a complete stranger. It frightened her. How could anybody change so much?

Peter was six months old when they moved to Tyrrelcote. Angela insisted on separate bedrooms. She did not want to be disturbed anymore when he came home in the early hours and told lies as to where he had been. She was tired of listening to his lies and wanted her peace.

She busied herself in getting the house clean and nice. They had the bathroom installed. The colour was blue and Angela bought matching toilet paper which Sarah called blue paper. "Mum, there is no blue paper in the loo." "There is more blue paper in the cupboard, darling" her mother would say and Sarah would go and fetch a roll and busily try to hang it up.

Angela ripped the old linoleum out of the kitchen, in readiness for the new one to be installed. The underlay was newspapers from 1930's! A Maharajas wedding in Lahore and about King Edwards VIII abdication. She tried to read the article but the small writing had been eaten away by tiny creatures. She put it all into the garden incinerator and hoped to have got rid of whatever it was that was eating the paper.

They had chosen red brick coloured vinyl tiles and deep blue kitchen cabinets. Angela had chosen an oranges and lemon roller blind for the wide kitchen window. There was a room which led in the garden and must have been used like a garden shed by the previous owner. She made this room into her work shop. She housed all her tools there and she invested into a Black and Decker Jigsaw with many different blades and went out to buy a whole load of tongue and grove panel boards, nails and batons and went to work on the cloak room and downstairs lavatory and panelled it all over with wood.

She soaked and stripped all the various layers of old wallpaper from the walls in all the rooms and repaired the walls with plaster and that covered the awful state of the walls which she then re-wallpapered. It looked beautiful. She also made a lovely wooden toilet seat. She took the pattern from the old cracked seat. She had become a wood worker. How easy it all was. And she did not miss Ross. She had so much to do, but at the back of her mind was: Would Ross like it. Would he appreciate it?

When he did come home he would inspect all her work very carefully and then start criticising what she had done. But to Angela it looked good and since he did not do anything, was hardly ever at home, what was she waiting for? And she found that she did not care for his opinion any more. She carried on.

She also went up to the little shop and advertised for a gardener. Somebody rang and as they discussed terms over the phone, she decided she liked his manner of speaking and employed him there and then. Would he come round for a cup of tea to get to know one another? His name was John Stuart Black. He turned out to be a handsome white haired gentleman, retired tea broker from Ceylon, wanting to do some gardening to keep him busy. They became great friends and much later, he confessed to her that had he known in the first place that she was German, he would not have taken the job, and what a loss that would have been for him, not knowing her. She answered him that that was the nicest thing any English man had ever told her. He also did some babysitting for her when Ross demanded that she had to attend at official functions as his wife.

This husband of hers was truly amazing! What a liar, what sham, what did he tell his colleagues? She would show herself off, put on her grandmother's jewels and trail her white mohair cardigan like a mink. She was not a grey mouse, she was Angela, who had an aristocratic background and no carpenter's son, be he ever so grand could put this Angela into the shade. She was the dutiful wife, spoke to all their friends who frequently in the past came to dinner at her house, she knew that all of them knew of her husband's affairs even before she did but nobody showed it. Did they think she still didn't know? What two faced people they all were. Insincere! She smiled and kept her feelings hidden. She felt, she knew that soon she would never ever see any of them again. What friends! After the grand dental gathering was over, she would grandly descent the stairs of the Cafe Royal on her own, head held high get a taxi and go to the station and to hell with Ross, wherever he wanted to spend the bloody night.

When he did come home for clean shirts and to have a good bath every now and then, she tried to have a talk and sort things out. His complaint was that she was not always able to come to town when he needed her to come: "You should have a permanent babysitter".

Then Joana arrived and moved into one of the spare rooms. She found herself a job in London almost immediately and for a while Ross would be home every day and to Jo it looked as if all was well. They went to work together and came home together and Angela always had a good meal ready. They ate together and Angela thought that maybe all will be well after all. He was even nice to her and praised the children. He agreed with Jo when she commented on Angela's work, that it was well done. He praised Angela!

Jo decided on a job change and Ross suggested a tour around Europe and maybe a drive to Greece where Angela's Berlin cousin had a house he had offered it to her anytime she wanted to holiday there. Jo thought it was a wonderful idea and Ross suggested that Angela should take Jo and the children and do a tour through Germany first and then Ross would join them in Munich and they could all be off to Greece together.

Angela had employed a cleaner to come once a week and do a thorough clean up throughout the house. This was a young girl from the Philippines, Flora Bao In, a nice religious girl and a good worker. Charlotte Montgomery, her immediate neighbour and friend asked if she could employ her too and soon Flora had a job for every day of the week. Angela instructed her to come even though she was away because she wanted to keep the house clean for Ross whilst she was away. Charlotte also had a key to the house. Ross would be at work and Flora would have the house to herself.

Angela packed their Crown Custom Toyota Car and what did not fit in went on to the roof. Peter got the playpen in the back to sleep and play in and Sarah had a little bed made up next to that and Angela and Jo sat in the front and they went on a grand tour, visiting Angela's friends and relatives and 3 weeks later, as arranged with Ross they camped at Munich's campsite and waited for Ross to tell them with which plane he would arrive at the airport. Angela rang the house many times and at work and heard from Barbara, his secretary that he hadn't been at work for two weeks. At home he finally answered the phone and told her that he was standing by to fly to New Zealand because his mother was very ill and probably dying.

Angela's reaction was that they would all come home immediately, but Ross said no, no, they should enjoy themselves and visit more people in Germany, and the trip to Greece would have to be shelved, such a pity, he would have been happy to take them, but now it was more important to stand by for his mother.

Angela talked it over with Jo, it was after all her dear granny which was so ill. Jo wanted to go home immediately and be with her dad. So Angela suggested ringing him again which Jo did. She was persuaded to stay in the Munich campsite and wait for further news. Angela began to smell a rat. This is not normal. She decided to ring her neighbour, Charlotte Montgomery.

"Oh Angela, am I glad you rang. I don't know how to tell you this, but Flora discovered Ross and a woman in your bedroom, and she has not been back to the house since. She was so upset and worried that she had done something wrong. But she did not suspect anybody at home and barged into the bedroom to clean it. She is still upset and I must admit so am I. I am so sorry".

Angela felt strangely calm. She had known it all along, but could not really believe it. Now was the time to face it. Her marriage to Ross was over, that much was clear to her. She took Jo aside and told her what Charlotte had just told her.

Jo's reaction was: "That fucking bastard", she shouted, and Angela looked around to see if anyone had heard it. "He is at it again", she said and then gushed like a waterfall; Angela heard for the first time what sort of a man she had married. She heard how he had had affairs with all his dental nurses one after the other. How her mother had been humiliated and how one of the affairs had rocked

387

New Plymouth and turned so nasty, that her parents had to go for a trip around the world, so that things would settle down again. But then her dad had found work in London and did not want to go back to stuffy small town New Plymouth and demanded that the children joined them in London. They got a lovely flat and Richard and Jo went to school in Kensington and very soon Ross had a new affair. Then he had two on the go all at the same time and one of them rang her mum and told her about the other one and her mum had had enough and left and went home taking Richard and Jo along with her. Now you know the whole story. I don't know what he told you, but you certainly were his next victim. Angela had to grin even though she was devastated. "Richard called me that too. "His next victim."

Angela rang Charlotte again and told her that she was going back to her sister and think things over, give Ross a week to sort himself out and then come home and sort things at home. She also rang Ross and told him that he need not lie anymore, he can make his mind up: his new woman or the children. Angela would be at Bine's, her sister. And Angela demanded that whoever it was he slept with to leave the family home immediately because she wanted no trace of her in her home.

*

Jo was very kind and helpful. Angela asked her if she wanted to have a glimpse at the Alps before they go to Bine's and she said that would be lovely if it was alright with Angela. "Well there is not much we can do at this stage. Your Dad has got to sort himself out. If he has any feelings for his family he will." So they headed for Mittenwald and after 3 days headed back to Stein and Bines home. Angela had a terrible headache. It had finally hit her hard that all these years she had been deceived and her marriage was at an end. Her dream of a happy home with children and a loving husband were shattered. She remembered all the things Ross had ever told her, ever promised, the hard times they managed together. Why did he come back to her? For what reason? Why did he want to marry her? Was she just a pretty conquest, a trophy wife, he could have let her go when she wanted to go. He insisted he could not live without her and now all he wanted was to get away from her. It was all such a terrible puzzle and her head was about to burst. They got to Stein at midnight. They had left little Peter with her mother and she went in to hug him but not to wake him. Suddenly she started to cry. She hadn't cried since Munich and now she let her tears flow. She cried herself to sleep. Her heart felt heavy, as if she carried a ton of stones.

Angela did not want to go home and delayed the journey day after day. She waited for Ross to ring but he didn't. In the end Sabine and Jo persuaded her to leave the children and the car in Germany and for just the two of them to travel back to Epsom.

37

Can this be the End?

Jo and Angela arrived at Epsom Railway station and took a taxi to Tyrrelcote. Ross was in shorts and no shirt very busy cooking a delicious meal. The smell was wonderful and Angela was immediately suspicious. He was very surprised to see them and the first thing he did was excuse himself and disappear through the hole in the fence to see Charlotte next door. Later Charlotte told her that he rang the woman to tell her that they had returned unexpectedly and she could not come to supper. He returned through the hole and Angela and Jo were still in the kitchen, Jo making a cup of tea. Angela watched Ross crawl back through the hole. She grinned grimly inwardly: Her beloved husband crawling through a small hole, feeling as guilty as hell. What was he going to tell her this time?

"Who is this lovely meal for?" she asked and he said," just for me, I am expecting no one. You should have told me you were coming back. Where are the children?"

"They are still in Germany and there they will be until I know what is happening here. You have told me so many lies, I wonder if I could believe anything at all from now on. I am devastated and totally exhausted"

"Cup of tea anyone?" Jo had prepared three cups of tea. Angela thanked her and said she would be back shortly and went upstairs. She heard Ross and his daughter arguing and shouting. In front of the door to her room she collapsed and went unconscious. She never knew how long she had been lying there but she came to when she heard Jo shout from far away, calling her dad to come quickly. Together they lifted her and put her to bed. All she wanted was to be left alone. She didn't want to see or hear anyone. Just to be alone. But then she felt such a strong longing for her children and she started to cry quietly. She didn't sob, she just let the tears flow. Was this the end to everything? Had Ross so completely and callously abandoned her? Was this what Alison had been through? Never trust a man who is divorced. Never trust what he tells you. Who had told her that? June, her flatmate of long ago. Dear June, she wondered where she was now.

She was still unable to get up after two days. She just did not have energy or strength or the will to get up. In the end Jo insisted that they rang the doctor. Angela had also developed a terrible migraine and was unable move the pain was so terrible. When the doctor came he pulled back her eyelids and then gave her an injection. Angela felt the pain swim away and herself sink into beautiful oblivion.

The doctor came back the next day and asked her how she felt. She said the headache had almost gone, but she was totally exhausted and needed a lot of rest. He asked her where the children were and she said that she had left them with her mother in Germany because there were "things" to be sorted here first. He looked at her hard and then said: "I understand, I will be back tomorrow to see how you are. You must rest. You will need a lot of strength to get through this". She looked at him gratefully. He had been her doctor for many years and he knew her well.

Jo looked after her while she was in bed. She stayed in bed for a week. Ross had left the day after they returned and had not been back at all. Jo was embarrassed and hurt and mad with her father. Angela found that she had to console Jo and tell her not to worry. They both cried together and then Angela said: "He isn't worth shedding any tears over" and Jo added that her mother called him "an idol with clay feet". Angela wasn't quite sure exactly what that meant, but it seemed appropriate. A charming bastard! A vain idiot! A lying bastard! They were both finding words to describe Ross, to make their hurt easier. Jo used the F-word a lot, but then she was a Kiwi and they both laughed through the tears.

Angela realized that blood was thicker than water and knew that Jo would naturally forgive her father because he was her dad no matter what. Angela resolved that she had to do something. She was longing to be with her children and she got up and started to clean the house. She rang Flora and asked her to come back and help with the cleaning. John, her gardener also came back and Jo found herself a job in London. She did not ring Ross, just got on with getting the house cleaned. She wanted nothing remaining of the woman who had slept in this house while she was away with the children from his first and second marriage, probably trying to make more children with a third woman. She tried not to be bitter or heartbroken. Just keep working, things will sort themselves out.

Two weeks after her return Ross came back. He said he was sorry that everything had turned out the way it had, but the woman he was with, threatened suicide if he left her and so he could not leave her. (Sorry excuse, Angela thought. What about the children?) From Jo she found out who this woman was. It was his 17 year old assistant dental nurse in the Eastman, the very one Richard had taken out. Apparently she had come up to Ross and said that she preferred the father to the son.

Now it made sense to her why Richard wanted to go back to India or Bali or whatever and why Ross was so willing to give his son the money to leave. The Bastard! And Richard had called her his father's next victim.

Slowly she came out of her thoughts and still heard Ross talk. She hadn't heard anything he was saying and now heard him say: "Can't you be more sophisticated and accept that I want to live in town, I shall come home every weekend and spend it with you and the children. The daily travelling into town is too much for me."

"Are you sharing a flat with this nurse of yours?" and he answered: "Does it matter? I still love you and the children and I don't want to lose you, Kleines".

"I am not your Kleines anymore. And I shall not share you with anyone. You have to make up your mind, who you really love. I think you love only yourself and can only think of what is good for Ross Valentine. Well I will not play your game. You want this girl, who has barely left school and is younger than Jo, for goodness sake! "Angela turned and left him standing. She heard him say: "Darling, don't throw everything away that we have together. I want the children home and I want you as my wife at home. Let's have a week away in Spain and find ourselves again. I do love you, you know!"

Throw away everything we have together, she thought bitterly. She wasn't doing the throwing! He was! That was typical. Making her feel guilty! Making her feel miserable! She wasn't being unfaithful. She was at home with the children, waiting, waiting and waiting for him to come home and be the man she married. But whom did she actually marry? Who was this man? God knows!

And Angela agreed to the trip and they flew off to Spain. He told her that the girl had gone to Israel to work on a kibbutz and she was out of his life now.

Angela tried hard to forgive him all his meanness and lies, but found it difficult. She simply did not trust him, she tried not to show it. He was sweet and Angela was lulled almost into believing that it would turn out alright. She did feel spoilt but could not help thinking how he can turn it on when he wants something. Such a charmer! She wanted to believe that he was serious and agreed to go back to Germany and fetch the children home. She also said she would come home with an Au Pair girl from Germany, so that she was able to come to London whenever he needed her to be there.

She took the train a week after they returned from Spain.

When she got to Stein, Peter who had done his first steps in Cloppenburg in Northern Germany, was toddling along the corridor to find his granny in the kitchen and cling to her legs, his baby grow unbuttoned and wearing no nappies. She saw Sarah and Nicole, her cousin, playing and went over to her thinking that Sarah would remember her and said: "Hello Darling Dudi, come and give your mum a hug" and Sarah burst into tears. Bine said to her sister: "Try speaking in German to her, she might have forgotten how to speak in English." Angela grabbed her daughter and hugged her and she hugged her back and then she felt a little hand and turned to see Peter standing there and she opened one arm and grabbed him too and there they sat on the steps to the loft and kissed and hugged and spoke German and laughed and cried and Angela was so happy to hug her children that all the other worries fell away.

She had to listen to all the things her children had been up to while she was away in England sorting out her life and their future. She had missed so much in the life of her children, but she vowed she would never ever leave them anywhere again. She looked at photos of her two living with their cousins like sisters and brothers. She was so grateful to her mother to be there and she was so moved to see how her children loved her mother. They were so intimate and so trusting, and she hugged her mother gratefully. Here in this house was true love. Honest love. Love which could never be destroyed. If only she could have that in Tyrrelcote. But this love comes freely and if Ross does not love her, her love for him would finally wither and die. She knew that. You needed to love each other deeply and honestly, not just be sexually attracted. She had suspected a while ago, that Ross never loved her, probably never loved anybody, was only sexually attracted and believed that that was love.

It was a shocking revelation, but very likely to be true. So be it!

"I have to advertise for an Au Pair to take with me to England" she said to her mother and sister. "Which would be the best paper to do it in?"

They advised her to use the Pforzheimer Allgemeine and Karlsruher Newspapers. She had several answers to her advertisement and arranged interviews. She chose a young hairdresser called Connie. She was accepted by the children right away while Angela was interviewing her and they came to an agreement; Angela would ring her that evening. She was seeing two more girls that day and would let her know.

Bine and her mother had been there as Angela interviewed all the contenders and they all decided that Connie was the right one. She also had a number of smaller brothers and sisters and it seemed she would be good in the house as well, and was keen to learn English.

Angela rang her that evening and also explained the situation at home and said she could change her mind if she thought it would be stressful and embarrassing. Connie reassured Angela that she would keep out of any confrontations that might occur and that she would try to help Angela as much as she was able. She did not mind the possible stress. And she was looking forward to be part of the family for a year or so. Angela informed Ross of everything that was happening almost daily; when he was not available she left a message with Barbara, his secretary.

Connie had to give two weeks' notice and Angela enjoyed two weeks of rest with her beloved children, mother, sister and nieces.

She helped her brother in law, Achim laying the foundation of a terrace at the back of the newly built house. There was as yet no Garden and the front had to be made into a car park for the patients, who had to park opposite in a little layby. Angela and Achim worked hard laying gravel to make the car park. Although she worked hard, she felt at peace. They sat down together and had a beer every now and then. It was a very hot August into September and the children all helped with their toy wheel barrows to get the gravel shifted. It was so harmonious and joyful, granny-mum was cooking and baking and at mealtimes the beloved voice called everybody together: "Essen" and tools were put down and everybody went to wash their hands, big hands and tiny hands and happy laughter and "denglish" spoken. Angela's heart soared. Everything would now be alright. It had to be.

Angela fetched Connie from the Koenigsbach Railway Station and together they loaded the car. The children did not want to leave and Sarah kept asking why they had to go. This was home, wasn't it? And Angela explained that home was in England where Vicky, Alastair and Adam lived next door. Could she not remember her friend Vicky? Sarah could not remember and after all, she had been away from home for just over two months. There were hot tears everywhere and her sister said: "If it gets unbearable, come back. Live in Germany. Don't be lonely over there. Angela thanked her for all the help with the children. "Don't thank me, thank Mutti" she said and Angela hugged her mother. They got into the Toyota Crown Custom and drove off with a very heavy heart.

Angela drove through without stopping, the children mostly asleep in the back and so they arrived the next day, Saturday at lunchtime in Epsom. Ross was there to welcome them and they had a very happy weekend together. Connie was happy with her room and could not enthuse enough about the house and the garden. Everything was so beautiful she said.

Ross went to work on Monday and did not come home until late. Angela said nothing. It had to run its course. Maybe Brenda (Angela had learned her name from Jo), did not leave him alone. Or maybe they had not finished at all and she had not gone to Israel. Angela kept her peace and carried on with her life and the children and the garden and decorating the rooms bit by bit. Painting the window frames was a lot of work. The French windows in the dining room and the garden room took a lot of time and she was cursing a bit with all those little squares. John, the Gardener was a good friend and sometimes she confided in him. He advised patience. The days came when Ross did not come home until 3 in the morning. He would open her door to her bedroom and brag about the wonderful time he had had. Why did he do that?

Working in London Jo moved into a flat sharing it with other Australians and New Zealanders.

One day in November the ultimate happened. Angela could not sleep and went downstairs to make herself a cup of tea and read the paper in the kitchen. Connie, who had become a good friend and a great helper with everything in the house, saw the light as she went to the loo and came down too and joined Angela for a cup of tea. They sat and chatted. It was three in the morning when she heard the key in the front door and Ross came home. He saw Angela and Connie having tea in their dressing gowns and stopped at the door, leaning against the door post and said: "The lovers having tea! What is she like in bed, eh?" Angela was dumbfounded. She had heard what he said, but said nothing in return. She was totally embarrassed and hoped with all her heart that Connie could not speak English well enough to understand what her husband had just accused them of. She forced herself to sound calm and quietly said:

"If you have an ounce of decency you would pack your bags and leave". He said he was sorry and didn't mean to say what he said. Angela took no notice and looked at Connie and casually said: "I am tired, I am off to bed, "andConnie got up too and said:" Yes so am I "and they both went upstairs into their bedrooms.

Angela did not speak to Ross again. He came home to change clothes and have a bath every now and then and then go again, leaving his dirty washing. As Angela picked it up to put it into the washing machine with their clothes as usual, Connie said she shouldn't do that, he can take it to the woman where he spends most of his time. Angela grinned and put the washing back into the basket.

Next time Ross came for his clean laundry and ironed shirts he found none. He had taken a bath and found no clean towels and no clean shirts and came dripping and naked onto the landing and shouted for clean things.

Angela was in the sitting room with the children and said quietly that it was time Brenda did these domestic chores. "She has everything else of yours she might have your dirty washing too, don't you think?" She had no answer to this, but a little while later Ross left by the front door and she did not see him again for weeks, nor did he ring or enquire about the children. Christmas came and she decided to take up the invitation from Tissi to visit her and her husband in Totnes. Her mother had come over as well and it would be nice to spend Christmas with the family. So Connie and Angela got all the presents for everybody and packed the car and drove down to Devon. Sarah was missing her dad and asked Angela:

"Is daddy spending Christmas with his sweetheart, mummy?" Angela thought her heart would break. Did he introduce his daughter to Brenda and if so when? She could not believe what she had just heard. That man was impossible. Calmly she said:

"Yes Darling, I believe he is".

"Why can't we be all together at Christmas, I like daddy's sweetheart" she said.

Sarah had no idea about parents, she suddenly realized. She thinks it is quite alright for her father to have a sweetheart. She said:

"You know darling, I was once daddy's sweetheart, but now he has a new one, and she does not like me, so we can't go. We go to auntie Tissi and your granny and we shall have a wonderful Christmas. I think the *"Christkind"* is going to bring you and Peter and everybody some lovely presents."

*

They had a very harmonious Christmas Eve, quietly celebrating the birth of Christ and singing some carols, and then looking at their presents. The fire was crackling and the food was delicious and everybody seemed happily content and watching the children play. Tissi was pregnant. There was snow on Christmas day and they all went for a wonderful walk in a fairytale landscape and came back to a glowing fire and Jim put more logs on and in no time it was roaring in the fireplace. There were Christmas cookies and chocolate and mince pies, the tree glowed and gleamed and glistened and the children kept looking at the nativity figures which had been carved by a black forest artist. It was just lovely. Angela wished to have a loving husband and father for her children by her side and it hurt her terribly that he was spending it with a stranger and that he had not even given her any presents for their children.

On Boxing Day, Tissi told Angela that Connie would from now on stay with her and Jim at Maryland House because Tissi would pay her more.

Angela was shocked and sad. She thought that Connie had become her friend and was quite content with her pay which was more than the average Au Pair got. She looked at her mother but found her face blank. Quietly she got up and went upstairs to pack her bags. She could not stay here another minute. She put everything into the car and then dressed the children and got all their toys and made a cosy nest for them. Nobody spoke a word. They all avoided her. She had no idea what had been going on behind her back. Her mother came to the car as she got ready to go and said:

"Must you go now? Can't we talk?" Angela looked at her mother.

"What has been going on? All behind my back? What has been said?" But her mother had no idea. She started to cry and hugged her daughter.

"Let's not cry, I don't want the children upset". She got into the car and told her mother that she loved her and drove off. She thought her heart would break. Was it something she did or had said, was it her character that made people leave her? She looked at herself and could not see what it was. She kept the children fit and healthy and clean and made a lovely home for them, she tackled all sorts of things because there was not a man to do it for her, and she tried to be brave. The children behind her played happily and her heart went out to them. She loved them beyond anything. She didn't need anybody, she decided. She was sorry for her mother who seemed to be the 'pig in the middle'. Poor Mum, I wonder what was going on in her mind this Christmas. It began to snow as they drove past Exeter and headed for the A303. By the time she left the A5 and turned into the A303 the children were both asleep. It was 4 in the afternoon and dark when she got to Tyrrelcote. The house was empty and cold. She turned the heating on and quickly made a fire in the living room, and then had a look at the children. Peter was just stirring and she opened the door and got him out. And then Sarah woke and scrambled on her own out of the car. With a happy squeal she ran upstairs into her room and found her favourite toys. We are home, she cried and Angela put Peter down and he crawled upstairs too and said: "Peter home". Those children will save my life she thought. Then the telephone rang. It was Jim.

"Angie, I am so sorry about what happened. I had nothing to do with it". Angela did not want any confrontations. She said:

"What about Connie's things, is somebody going to pick them up?"

"Well that is what I wanted to talk to you about. I have to come to London to pick up some things and Mutti thought if it was alright with you she would like to come down with me and stay with you for a couple of weeks before she is going back to Germany, and I shall pick up Connie's things then." Angela thought that was a great Idea and on the second of January Jim came and brought her mother and took Connie's things. Angela spent two happy weeks with her mother in Tyrrelcote. They did not discuss the matter "Connie or Tissi". Angela did not want to talk about it, the subject was closed and she was much more concerned as to how she was going to face her sister again. At the moment she felt she did not want to see her ever again. She was an arrogant, selfish, greedy, spoilt, ignorant egotistical little bitch. Tissi cost her her friendship with June, her lovely little flat in Kensington, strife with Ross when the garage at 7The Grange was full up with her things for more than a year and Ross's lovely new Rover had to be parked in front of the garage. The job as nanny and house keeper Angela had found for her with Angela's boss from Lufthansa, a wonderful job with cheap travel etc., she abused and had to leave in disgrace to Angela's embarrassment. Nothing but trouble! Then she finds this man and marries him within six weeks just because he has a big house and seemingly a lot of money. Angela did not want to think about it and did not want to have any more to do with that sister of hers. I shall not forgive her ever, she thought and then she thought about the

399

Lord's Prayer, and "forgive them their trespasses." Well, eventually but not now.

There were tears at Vitoria Station when her mother stepped onto the train. The children were confused:

"Why can't granny stay?"

"Well because she is needed in Stein with Bine. That's where granny lives, she only visits us, Angela explained.

"But granny will come and visit often." They waved until the train went out of sight. They drove home and Angela blessed the fact that she had two such wonderful children. Peter was actually a problem, he was a furious little man. He could so easily get into a rage and often Angela wondered why. There could be so many reasons. Angela decided to just try and give them a secure home, happy and cosy and lots of playmates and friends. She was new in Epsom and had no proper friends only acquaintances. She would have to change this.

*

Connie only stayed for one month at Tissi's and then found herself a job in a hotel near Chagford. Sadly, not used to the narrow lanes, she had a dreadful car crash and somebody died. Angela felt very sorry for her, but could do nothing. Tissi never ever mentioned her again.

*

Angela started to rip off all the old wall paper right down to the plaster. There where at least 4 layers of wall paper, one on top of the other. She soaked the walls well and then scraped it all off. She was amazed how easy it all was and how great the walls looked with nothing on. The house looked so much bigger and lighter. She continued until the rooms were quite "naked" and let it all dry out and then she went to look for wall paper.

There was a telephone call from the Airport. It was Richard.

"Angela may I come home, please?" Angela was surprised. Did he not know that Ross and she had parted? She said:

"Richard, Ross does not live here anymore. He moved out to be with his new woman. You will have to ring him and find out if you can stay with him. Good luck." Half an hour later Richard was on the phone again.

"Angela please, may I stay with you, I have nowhere to go. Dad doesn't want me and he said I can't stay with you. What shall I do? "Angela asked:

"Why come here, why didn't you go to New Zealand?"

"My best friend died of an overdose in Bali and I am scared, Angela. Let me come home?"

"Are you on Heroin, I want the truth>"

"Yes"

"Now listen carefully. You can come here if you have nowhere else to go, but only if you bring nothing home. I want none of that stuff in this house. I shall help you do cold turkey, but the moment I see you doing drugs, you are out and I shall inform the Police"

"Anything you say. You have my word I shall bring nothing, I will do cold turkey. And you were right. I see that now. Dad said I should not go and stay with you because you would only say I told you so. But you haven't said it."

Angela told Richard to grab a Taxi and come on home.

He arrived looking grey and sick. The next thing Angela did was to ring the doctor because Richard had yellow eyes and was in pain. Then followed pleading with the doctor not to inform the police because there was no "stuff" in the house, and he put the house on quarantine for at least 6 weeks because Richard had infectious hepatitis.

Angela rang Ross and asked for his assistance since she could not go out or receive visitors, to do the shopping for them.

"I told Richard not to bother you. Why did you let him in?"

"He is your son, he is in trouble, and he needs help. Where should he have gone other than to come home? And this is still your children's home. And by all accounts he could not possibly go to tight, pretentious, stuck up and prejudiced New Plymouth. I shall write to Allison though. Tell her not to worry too much".

"What do you need in the way of shopping?" Angela told him to buy loads of vegetables, onions, carrots, leeks, tomatoes and cucumbers, rice, eggs cabbage and beans. Whatever they have to make a healthy stew.

" Get some lamb as well, Richard would want to have some good meat, but maybe not lamb, that is too fat. I leave it to you. You can make some enquiries what people with hepatitis are allowed to eat." Somehow she would get through this and get Richard well.

What she had not foreseen was his behaviour whilst doing "cold turkey". He was hunting through all the drawers and cupboards hoping to find something. At first Angela watched him opening and closing the furniture drawers and doors hunting for something. She asked him:

"What are you looking for".

"Stuff", he said. But Angela assured him that there was nothing of the sort in this house. So he started to hold onto her skirt and followed her where ever she went. When she went to the loo, she had to tell him to wait outside and he would stand right outside the door until she came out again. When he went to the loo, he left the door open and kept talking to her all the time to make sure she would not go away.

Richard's nose started to run constantly with a clear slime, he did not close his mouth and dribbled everywhere. So Angela gave him a tea towel to hold and when it was soaked she put it straight into the washing machine, which was going every day on the highest setting. In the night Angela had to go to his room often because he was sitting up and screaming in terror. She was afraid the children would wake and be scared. She would sit with him and rock him back to sleep. She had to be meticulously clean to stop infection. It was all a nightmare.

Ross brought the shopping and left it on the doorstep never ringing the bell to say he had been. Angela was sad. He never inquired about the children or Richard.

The weeks went by and Richard was feeling a lot better. A big bag of shopping with a load of tins lay on the doorstep and a note: Away for a few days, hence the tins. Then a postcard arrived from Disneyland Florida where he had taken the girl he was living with: To my Darling Sarah, having a wonderful time, love Dad. What about Peter?

The Bastard! Angela was speechless. Sarah saw the gaudy card and wanted to know what it was. Angela told her it was a picture of

Disney Land. She didn't tell Sarah her father sent it. Sarah studied the card and then asked: "Is it near here?" Angela lied and said, it was in Chessington Zoo and they would go there with Richard just as soon as he was better and we an go out again.

Richard saw the card and only shook his head, he stroked Sarah's head and said: "We shall have such fun, you and I".

The quarantine was lifted but Richard was still craving and Angela was feeling more and more unwell and had quite severe stomach ache. After X-Rays and a barium meal she was told she had stomach ulcers. She was prescribed some dreadful medicines which she was told she had to take forever 4 times a day, and the doctor told her not to get stressed. Ha!

Friends told her of a doctor in London, Japanese, and he would prescribe diets which would also help Richard. So the four of them went to see doctor Kawahara! Without touching Angela, by just looking into her eyes and later at her hands he told her that she had stomach ulcers. Amazing! Richard was next and without even looking at him he said he was on Heroin and now suffered withdrawal symptoms. Angela agreed to all of it and asked if he could give them a diet which would include the children and help Richard with his craving.

He dictated a list of things they could eat and Richard wrote it all down, then he added specific items for Richard and separate ones for Angela. He recommended for them to get a book with Macrobiotic Recipes and to go to a shop called Ceres in Baker Street. Laden with food and the cookbook, they returned home and Richard offered to do the cooking for all of them, prepare the teas which they had to drink several times a day and Angela had no pain in her stomach even after the first meal Richard had prepared, even though the rice was not cooked through. He asked Angela what he had done wrong and she told him that he forgot to add the water. They all had a good laugh and Richard became an excellent cook after that. Angela continued with the decorating and Richard looked after the children and did the cooking. Richard was still under house arrest which he had to agree to as one of the conditions to be able to live with her and the children. She did not want him to secretly meet up with dealers and get stuck into the drug scene again. He stuck to the agreement and only came out when Angela had to go out. They went everywhere together.

A year after he had come to stay with Angela and the children, he found a job at Chessington Zoo to look after the monkeys. He loved the job and Angela and the children often went and visited the Zoo.

Eighteen months after he came to stay to do "cold turkey", Chums daughter Louise came to stay from New Zealand. She had had a terrible car accident in which her twin brother had died and she had barely survived. She was paid a large Insurance sum and came to travel in Europe. Richard had not seen her for several years and now he seemed to see his chance for a new life. He had been great friends with Louise when they were children together and now he offered to show her the world, although he had no money, but Louise offered to pay for everything. Angela had dark forebodings. As they prepared to leave, Angela took him aside and said:

"Just remember, if you go back to Bali, as planned, and you get into drugs again, you don't even have to think you can come and stay here. I shall not go through all this again, ever. Do you understand! Never! I am glad and grateful that we have come through this together and that we are still friends. You have been through hell and back again and I with you. We have had a good time together and the children love you. It is up to you. You are fine now. Stay this way. Good luck and God bless." He kissed Angela good bye and thanked her and told her he would never forget what she had done for him. He said his own mother would not have done as much. Angela said, that his mother was far too close to him to see her own flesh and blood do this to himself. I could not bear it if one of my children did this to themselves.

Happily Richard and Louise left Tyrrelcote. She was sad to see him go. He had become part of the family and he had fitted in well.

38

Life goes on

Three Years later they returned, both heroin addicts although they denied it. Angela could see it in their eyes. They were changed people and lied as soon as they opened their mouths. They found somewhere to live and Angela saw them occasionally when they thought they could get some money from her. Soon they were living on the streets and sleeping at Piccadilly underground station. Then Louise was caught stealing. She had bought hundreds of pounds worth of goods from Marks and Spencer in Marble Arch and paid by cheque and then took them to the Oxford Street Circus branch and exchanged them for money. When she was finally caught she owed M&S £800 and in order not to have to be jailed, Chum, her father, paid Marks and Spencer. Then they moved in with Ross, pretending they had stopped using drugs. However, they had not and then, thinking it was all Louise's fault, Ross told her to leave. So she went to live on the street, stealing and only having a plastic bag with a jar of Malt a teaspoon and her "gear". Her sister Jenny came from New Zealand to look for her at Piccadilly Circus and was run over by a red Double Decker Bus and ended up in intensive care. Louise, when she was told of the accident did not even blink and never visited. Her mind only revolved on where to get her next fix.

In Autumn of 1976 the police called one Saturday night on Angela's door. Could she go and pick up a young woman in Banstead and he described the exact address of Ross.

But that is where my ex-husband lives she told the policemen. They told her they knew nothing of that, the woman lies semiconscious in a bus shelter and only asks for you, Mrs Valentine.

She argued with the police that she couldn't pick up Louise because she has two small children sleeping upstairs and she would not want to leave them alone in this house, could they not pick her up and bring her here?

No, they said, we can't touch her. She has no stuff in her bag and if we touch her and take her here we could be accused of manhandling her. Angela rang her Swedish friend a few houses up in Sunny Bank, and asked her to come and help and bring her daughter Christel to babysit with her she would explain later. Luckily Eva was still up and came immediately. Eva and Angela went over to Banstead and found Louise apparently asleep in the bus shelter. When Angela shook her she barely reacted, but with the help from Eva and Angela, she got up and got into the car. They took her home and Angela put her straight to bed where she went to sleep immediately.

The next morning, Sunday, Angela was in the middle of preparing breakfast when the doorbell rang. She went to open the door and a man and a woman stood there:

"Sorry to trouble you, but we are friends of Chum Allan and came to see if you knew anything at all about Louise. I am a doctor." Angela was very happy to see them and invited them in and said:

" She is here, I picked her up at one o clock this morning. She is asleep upstairs, come and see her"

His name was Peter van Praag. He followed Angela upstairs and immediately went over to see Louise, lifted up her eyelids and then turned to Angela and said: ⸱

"She is dying, you know. She needs an injection of heroin or she will die." Angela panicked:

"I thought she was sleeping, I was just about to bring her some breakfast. Am I glad you came! What a fantastic coincidence".

He told her that he couldn't practise in this country, since he is not registered with the BMA and so she would have to involve her own doctor. She rang her own doctor who came to the house immediately. The two doctors introduced themselves and discussed the situation and it was decided that Louise would have to go to hospital but he could not ask for an ambulance since she was an addict. So Angela decided to take her to Epsom District Hospital just down the road in her car herself and Peter van Praag came too and his wife offered to stay with the children. She had already taken over from Angela and continued to give them breakfast.

"Don't worry, I shall be alright' she told Angela.

The first thing they did after yanking her onto a hospital trolley, was to give her an injection and it was amazing how this girl came back to life and then started to insult everybody around her. Her language was filthy and Angela, embarrassed, looked around to see the reaction, but these people obviously had heard it all before. They took no notice and a doctor came and took Angela and Peter van Praag aside and said: "We can't keep her here, she is now free to go".

Angela was astonished. She turned to Peter and said:

"She has to be locked up. She has to be weaned off the stuff. If she goes out now, she will be dead in a week, and I can't have her as an addict living with me, and she cannot go to New Zealand, she will be arrested there." Peter agreed and turned to the Doctor:

"Is it possible that she can be locked up? "And before the doctor said anything Angela said:

"In a mental home, locked up, and it all has to be in secret so that her boyfriend does not know where she is. He sends her out to get the stuff for him, and then he takes more than his share and leaves her to suffer. She has to be rescued and saved from him".

The doctor looked at her and said: "We can't do that against her will?" Angela turned to Peter:

"If we don't get her locked up, she will die."

"If it is possible to find a place, somebody would have to take the responsibility," the doctor said. Angela turned to Peter and said:

"We both take the responsibility and we shall get in touch with her father, who is a doctor in New Zealand and he will certainly agree with our decision." Peter agreed with that and with the verification of Angela's doctor she was transferred to a mental home just outside Epsom. The staff at the home were told not to reveal her name to anyone on the phone. Angela told them that her boyfriend, Richard Valentine, would certainly ring and demand for her to be released. But she was to stay there, incognito until her father arrived from New Zealand.

Louise was given a nice room and she certainly behaved like a lunatic and seemed to fit in well in with the rest of the mental patients. She was given methadone. Angela visited every day. She was civil and polite, but everybody else got frightful abuse. The nurses just shrugged their shoulders.

"She gets the same treatment as the rest of the patients".

Richard pestered Angela to reveal where Louise was. Angela told him that he should know, she was living with him. So how could he have lost her?

Richard told her that dad hat thrown her out.

"Oh, and what did you do to prevent her from ending up on the street?" He told her that he argued with his father and by the time he was allowed to bring her back, she had gone and he did not know where, but the police told him that she was in Epsom. Angela told him that she had been briefly in the house but friends of Chums had come and taken her away. Now she does not know where she is. Is she in Hospital, he wanted to know. Angela said she did not know, and frankly she didn't care, because this time she was going to tell him:

"I told you so".

Richard rang every hospital in London and Epsom including the one Louise was in. But he did not find out where she was. Angela knew that the only interest Richard had in Louise was that she provided him with stuff and now this source had disappeared.

One early afternoon Angela had a phone call from Richard when he said he wanted to say good bye.

"Why, where are you going?" She wanted to know. He sounded very drunk and she hardly understood what he was saying.

"What is the matter, are you drunk?" She wanted to know but he just mumbled and then she heard him say that he had taken an overdose." She put the phone down and rang her good friend Eva. Eva came with Christel in tow, who looked after the children. Angela and Eva drove over to Banstead. There they found Ross's flat open and a trail of blood from the bathroom, which looked terrible into the sitting room and a seemingly unconscious Richard. Without any hesitation they grabbed him and dragged him downstairs and into the car and drove over to Epsom District Hospital. The emergency doctor took one look and told her that he would not treat this man. Angela explained that he tried to commit suicide and cut his wrists, (very badly because he missed the main artery completely) and took an overdose of some sort. The doctor still didn't want to know and Angela shouted at him to do *something!* Eventually they pumped out his stomach and then sent him packing, threatening to call the police if he did not disappear immediately. He came home with Angela. It was now 5.30 in the evening and Eva and Christel went home. On the way out, Eva said:

"He is such a fraud. Attention seeking! He would never have died! Anyway send him packing. He is not worth your attention." Angela cooked supper and gave him a good feed. He kept looking at his bandaged wrists, and Angela said:

"If you had been serious, you would have cut your pulse. Surely you know where that is?" and then she thought to have a good talk and find out what was on his mind. But all he could do was blame his father for what he had become. Angela said that he was a grown man and could work out for himself what he wanted of life instead of looking to his father for everything and added:

"I never had any support from home at all. I had to stand on my own two feet when I was only 15 years old. I had to make my own decisions and believe me, I never chose to ruin myself. My father never showed any interest in his children and I did not sit down and feel sorry for myself. No time for that. It is time you took responsibility for your own life instead of relying on others to live it for you."

At eleven o clock that evening the police arrived at Angela's door. Was she Mrs. Valentine? Did she know somebody called Richard Valentine? Yes to all those questions and please come in and talk to Richard directly. They came into the kitchen, saw that he was ok and left. They returned with Ross who opened his arms and crying said:

"My son! I am so glad I found you!" Angela watched with disbelief and Richard said:

"O fuck off dad!" the policemen rolled their eyes and made ready to leave. Angela came to the door and thanked them and said:

"It is very difficult to find out exactly what goes on in the Valentine's minds. I try to keep out of it. Best thing is not to take any notice." They grinned and left.

When Angela returned into the kitchen Ross said:

"You left no note to say what happened, the flat is ruined with all the blood everywhere. What were we to think when we came home from work?" Angela couldn't give a damn. She said:

"It is high time you all went home and left me alone. I am sick and tired of all the theatrical upheavals you lot cause me. I want my peace. I have had it with you Valentines and the less I see of you the better. Your lives are a mess and they have nothing more to do with me. I am out of it, thank God"

They left not saying another word and Angela closed the door and it felt like a huge load off her mind. She rang Eva and told her all about it. Eva laughed and said if it was not too late, she would come over for a cup of tea. Angela said it was not too late and they sat and chatted until late.

*

Then Chum arrived and lived in Angela's house and took on a job with the Royal Free Hospital in London. He was still registered with the BMA, because as a young doctor he had worked there years ago. Several times a week Angela and Chum went to visit Louise. She abused Chum verbally in a most terrible manner. Angela saw that Chum was very upset and near to tears. She turned to Louise and said:

"If you don't stop this and behave like the nice young lady you once were, we will not come back and as far as I am concerned you can rot in hell." Louise smiled sweetly and just said: "Ok". Angela said sharply:

"Ok, what!"

"Ok, I will respect my father. I have never shouted at you, Angela, even though you locked me up here in this lunatic asylum".

"Carry on; locked you up in this lunatic asylum for what!"

"Ok, ok, I know, for my own good. Can I come out now?"

"No, not until you are off the methadone, and not until you are what you were before Richard got hold of you. "

"You are all wasting your fucking time. As soon as I am out of here, I shall go back and you can't fucking stop me. Richard and I are going to get married, I am an adult and can do what I fucking well want. And you can all fuck off, you fucking fuckers". Angela took no notice and just took Chum's arm and turned to go"

"Fuckers! Yeah, fuck off, fuckers!" She screamed after them.

Angela told Chum that it was her helplessness talking like that. The only weapon she had to get at us.

Chum was a gentle man, quiet and serious and sometimes extremely funny with a straight face. He said:

"She hasn't lost her New Zealand accent at all" and Angela laughed. They discussed the situation and since she had been there 6 weeks already wondered how much longer she would have to stay.

Next day on their visit to the mental home they discussed this with the resident doctor and he thought that 6 month would be the appropriate time for her to be weaned off the methadone, and only then could she be released, but she should be in an environment where she could not get hold of the stuff. Chum told the doctor that he would take his daughter back to New Zealand. Heroin was not yet available there. The doctor sighed:

"I wonder how long you can keep that at bay".

When they told Louise that she was going back to New Zealand around June she flipped.

"You can't make me, fuckers. I shall take the next fucking plane back to England".

On the way home Chum was very quiet. As they got into the house Angela said:

"You could go to the home office and ask for her to be deported and given into your custody, they would take her from the home directly to the airport and that would be that. "Chum looked at her:

"You do that with criminals" and Angela said:

"Or a loving and caring father to his daughter." Chum said he would make inquiries and a week later it was arranged that in June that year, Louise would be deported.

Richard came to the house but Chum did not want to see him. So in future he only phoned and only spoke when Angela was on the phone. He asked her to meet him at a cafe in Epsom and Angela went. He told her he had been arrested and there was to be a court hearing and would she attend. He said he needed somebody who believed in him. Angela told him no, she would not come because she did not believe in him anymore. Whatever he got himself into he would have to go through it by himself. He cried and Angela, still very fond of him, nearly gave in. She knew that the Valentines cry at the drop of a hat. Didn't Ross emotionally blackmail her in this way and she fell for it every time?

"Get yourself admitted, go for help. Get yourself off the stuff and clean and sober; only you can do it. When you are in court, ask for help then, *tell them you need help*. Don't *be arrogant, and don't worry about dad's reputation. Worry about yours."*

They parted and a month later Richard came to the house whilst Chum was working in London and he told her that he had been convicted but got a suspended sentence for two years.

"I am also going to a clinic and can get methadone free and help to get off the heroin. They told me that if I offend again I will be jailed. I don't want that" he said."Will you tell me now where Louise is?"

"No" she told him. "You can make a new start in your life and then we will see. You got two years. Make something off it and if you and Louise really care for one another then you can still marry."

He left and Angela did not see him again for three months. He rang once or twice to have a chat and tell her that he was doing alright. He also told her that he now knew where Louise was, and he was allowed to write to her and tell her what happened to him.

Angela told him that she was pleased. Whichever way he found Louise and the way he accepted that he could only write to her was a sign that he was serious.

Louise got well quickly and began to help in the mental home. She looked after some of the inmates and treated them with respect. She had also refined her language and sounded more like the well-educated Louise Allen, who was actually training to be a radiologist, before she became an addict. As she came off her addiction and could see the world as it really was again, the staff at the hospital began to respect her and treated her like a normal person. She moved to a different room, but she still could not leave the hospital. She had to stay there until the police came to remove her to the airport.

On the first of June Louise and Chum left for New Zealand and Angela felt relieved. Louise had got a wonderful and reassuring farewell from the staff at the home and lovely little gifts from some of the inmates. It had all turned out so well.

*

Angela was working in her workshop without interruptions, the children played in the garden with the neighbour's children. The hole in the fence was a great idea; together they had the biggest garden in Epsom. Angela felt happy, free, and totally in love with her children. She spent a lot of time with her friend Eva up the road in Sunny Bank or Eva and Carl Johann, her husband came to spend the evening with her, since she could not always go up there when she didn't have a baby sitter.

It was a very busy house. Angela had built a Wendy house in the garden in the style of a Finnish log cabin, and at Sarah's birthday party, on the 10th of June it was the centre of delight with all the children. There were two Japanese children in Sarah's class and Angela had a call from one of the mothers, could she come and have a look, her daughter doesn't stop talking about the Wendy House. So Angela invited her and her friend for coffee. As they sat in the kitchen around the table on the benches, they became very interested in her kitchen furniture.They wanted to know if she could make such a table and bench as well and would she teach them how to make one.

Yes, she would teach them and it was arranged that they all came with her to the timber yard and bought their wood with Angela's help. She moved her woodworking bench into the garage and it became a workshop. These Japanese ladies were a wonder in the way they worked. Their husbands worked in London for the Mitsubishi Bank and they had two years before they went back to Japan, but in the meantime they wanted to make this table and bench, which could be flat packed to take home with them. They brought the children when they were not at school and they played with Sarah and Peter and Charlotte's children in the two gardens.

Other neighbours came for advice on how to upholster their chairs and Angela told them to bring them along and they could do it in the garage and Angela would help. The garage became a busy, happy workshop. Angela carried on to do her woodwork while her neighbours came with easy chairs and sofas and lovely material, tacks and brass nails.

They came to have their hair cut by Angela. Angela cut her own and they had asked who her hairdresser was, and when they found out she cut it herself, they asked for her to cut theirs.

Eva's son Freddie, a fifteen year old school boy, came every day after school and made himself at home. Eva and Carl Johann both worked and Ulrika, the eldest sister worked as a model in London and the younger, Christel studied and their house was empty. So he came home to Angela, made tea and a sandwich and did his homework and then played with the children. Sarah was in love with him and told him she would only marry him. These were happy socially fulfilled times. Angela was never on her own and she seemed to have loads of nice friends.

Almost two years of bliss and happiness went by. Ross rarely came and mostly ignored the fact that he also had a son. In letters to and from the solicitors he only talked about the child Sarah and Angela had to remind him of his children Sarah and Peter.

In 1975 the decree nisi had come through, but Ross wanted to come home and stay home and he promised it was all over with the other woman. This time she really had gone to Israel to work in a Kibbutz. He argued that they should try to be a family again before the decree absolute came through.

Angela suggested that they see each other for a few months or so and see how they got on.

He was sweetness himself and Angela slowly began to trust him again. She argued with herself that she must try hard if not for herself but for the children's sake. She found that she loved the man of years ago, not the one he had become. She tried to find that man again.

The children were always so happy to see him and he was so good with them. So they all went off to Mallorca on a wonderful holiday. They stayed with friends and it was blissfully wonderful. Angela was full of hope. Ross moved back in after the holiday.

He went to work every day and came home in the evening. Sarah had started in year two at the primary school and all the friends walked their children to school and it was a happy social walk in the morning and again in the afternoon. Peter wanted to know when he could start. To see all the children go into to school and he had to walk back with the baby sister of one of Sarah's friends was not for him. He could not wait to find out what happened behind those big school doors, but his time came also only too soon.

Then came the day when Angela went to London and unexpectedly arrived at the surgery. She had an appointment with a doctor in Harley Street and thought it would be nice to have lunch with Ross before she went home again. The thought came to her on the spur of the moment. Barbara, the secretary was surprised but told her to go on in because he had no patient at the moment. As she walked in he hastily put down the receiver. Immediately Angela was suspicious, but said nothing. He was innocence himself. They went to a pub in Cavendish Square and had a light meal and then Angela went home.

Two weeks later she rang the surgery to speak to Ross about something and when she said she wanted to speak to Ross, Barbara said:

"Hold on Brenda I get him for you" and then Ross came to the phone and said:

"Hello darling, see you at lunch" and Angela said:

"So this is still going on then" and put down the phone.

He did not ring her and did not come home until late, he had no explanations, no excuses. He did not talk it over. He was found out. Angela waited all afternoon for a call. When the children where in bed and she had had her supper, she went and packed his bags and when he came home at eleven and saw his bags, he quietly took them and left. He said not a word, no apologies, nothing.

Next day when the children wanted to know where dad was, Angela only said he had gone back to his sweetheart. Sarah came to her and hugged her and Angela got Peter as well and the three of them hugged and hugged and Angela tried very hard not to cry. The gardener came at nine o clock and she confided in him. On the way to school she told Charlotte quietly and then they all had coffee in her kitchen and John said:

"He is quite a unique bastard".

Two weeks after that the decree absolute came through. The happy gathering in her garage continued, life went on and the children played happily in the garden or in the playroom above the garage. As long as the children are happy, all is well, Angela thought.

*

Then Angela's mother came to stay and put a stop to it all. It started off with mother being interested in everything and happily provided tea and coffee for the people visiting and praised Angela's haircuts and it all seemed to go so nicely. Then Angela had to go to bed with the summer flu. Her Mother asked her how much she charged for letting her friends use her garage for upholstering and haircutting etc. Angela told her that she did not charge her friends anything.

"No wonder you never have any money!" When Freddie called as usually her mother sent him home and told her friends to go home also.

For the first time in her life, Angela was cross with her mother and they had a terrible row. Her mother left and travelled to Devon to be with Tissi. Her friends were hurt and stayed away. She assured them that she didn't want any money, but it all turned to cold British politeness.

Angela took in three little boys, the same age as her own and since she had so many empty rooms she also took in two lodgers who shared the kitchen and her fridge. One woman was a social worker and the other was a Stewardess with Caledonian Airways and Angela was happy with the rent they paid.

The father of the three little boys worked on the other side of London and had to do a lot of travelling, the mother had gone off with a hippy to live in Bristol. The children missed their mother a lot.

They had a grandmother in Cheam, and Angela often took them all over to use their grandparent's swimming pool in their garden. The children enjoyed the pool but the three little boys were unhappy to have to leave their granny again and come home with Angela. The boys wanted their mum not Angela. The granny gave them each a cake and sweets to take home which they did not share with Sarah and Peter. Angela explained to her two that they are homesick and need something that is totally theirs in this strange home. They understood. And then Peter came and told her that the upstairs loo was blocked. Angela went to investigate with rubber gloves up to her armpits and found the entire fruitcake of the smallest, Tom, in the loo. It would not go round the bend.

Tom, upset that it had not gone down, cried.

"It didn't taste very nice and it was too much, I didn't like it". Angela lifted him up and sat down with him on her lap and told him that next time he should bring it to her and it could be cut into slices and he could put some butter on it and maybe even some honey and it could be shared, and then he would not have the responsibility to have to eat it all by himself. He nodded his head and Angela hugged him and wiped his tears and cleaned his bubble glasses.

On the whole, the children suffered not being able to see their mum. Angela treated them all much like her own children, especially little Tom who was a bit younger than Peter and seemed to be almost blind. John was a few months older than Sarah and Alan was in the middle between Sarah and Peter. Every morning she walked all five of them to school and picked them up again in the afternoon. They enjoyed the garden and Charlotte's children came to play.

Eva and Charlotte were the only people who were still her friends. The Japanese ladies had long since departed with their treasured flat packed tables and benches. When it came to winter she felt that it was just too much. John, the oldest boy became quite unruly and kept saying he didn't want her around. If she asked him to tidy his toys he told her that she could not tell him anything because she was not their mum. She discussed it with their grandmother in Cheam and told her that she could not continue with the children because they were upsetting her own. Alan and little Tom joined their brother and in the end Angela felt she had taken on more than she could handle. Their father was young and terribly immature, and Angela guessed that that was the reason his wife had left him. But she could not understand why she left the children with him. Was she teaching him a lesson? She asked their father to take the children to their Grandmother. Peace returned to her family.

She made inquiries about moving back to Germany and when Ross found out, because Sarah innocently said they were going to live with auntie Bine and their beloved granny, he slammed a court order on Angela so that she could not leave the country without his permission. She was devastated. His selfish excuse was that he needed their "uncritical love". What about the love they needed! Angela was isolated in a foreign country. She had no idea about the school system in England. She knew her way around in Germany and the children could spend time out of school with their cousins and Angela could go back to work and continue to earn money and give the children a secure background. It was then that the last bit of regard she felt for Ross died. She was devastated and lost. Every time Sarah and Peter came back from a visit to their father they were hostile towards her.

*

Ron, Tissi's boss from the time when she first came back to England when Stevie was four years old, had sold his Pub and unsuccessfully ran a hotel in Wales. He sold that and travelled to Germany to persuade Tissi to come and start a business with him somewhere on the south coast in England. Tissi was delighted and left her job in Germany and came back to England in 1970/71 and Ron bought a property in Totnes. Ron obviously had ideas to start a life with Tissi, however Tissi only had the business part on her mind. Ron promised her a 50% partnership if the shop was a success.

Totnes at the time was a quaint little town steeped in history with Dartington Art College and school close by and her third world clothing found happy customers almost immediately. She met Jim very soon after the shop opened and they married within 6 weeks of having met, much to Ron's disappointment. The partnership did not work out and Tissi, with Jims help bought the shop off Ron, and Ron went into retirement.

At first Tissi managed the shop on her own, but soon found that Jim would be an asset if he too helped to manage the business. He gave up his printing business and joined Tissi in Salago. Soon after that Tissi got pregnant.

A year later Angela's mother moved to Totnes permanently to be near Tissi and be a granny to Tissi's Children. When Angela's decree absolute had come through, both Tissi and her mother urged Angela to come to Devon and live in a smaller house and help in the shop. Angela discussed it with Eva and they both decided to leave Epsom. Eva wanted to live nearer Oxford where her older daughter lived and she also suspected that Carl Johann had an affair. So the friends parted. Angela put the house on the market which had meant so much to her and which she thought she would live in forever. All the work she had put into the house now came to her advantage. Her solicitor made sure she got the proceeds of the house and Ross got the mortgage. Since Ross had not contributed anything towards the renovation of the house, and since Angela had spent it all from the meagre housekeeping Ross had given her and her meagre earnings from looking after the boys, she came away with enough money to buy a little cottage in Devon outright.

Charlotte Montgomery, next door also sold her house very quickly and moved to the other side of Epsom. Angela felt very lonely in her big house since she was the last of her friends to find a buyer for her home. It could all have been so nice if only... Epsom was a paradise lost. Angela grieved.

*

Angela was a stranger in a world, she did not know. An England she had not got to know about, working in London for a German firm and then living in Epsom, where people were open, sophisticated and friendly, albeit English friendly, made Angela think erroneously that all England would be the same. She had not travelled greatly in Britain, always abroad or home to Germany.

The village people viewed her with suspicion as a stranger with an even stranger accent, her children were ridiculed in school for their "posh" accent. Peter was asked what it was like to have a Nazi mother, he was shocked. He didn't even know what a Nazi was. Sarah, hurt and lonely, she missed all her school friends from Epsom. The school in Devon was way behind the school in Epsom and both Peter and Sarah were bored. Angela realized she had made a terrible mistake, moving to Devon. Her second terrible mistake in her life; marrying Ross! But it was done and she had to live with the consequences and do battle with herself to get it right for her children. Angela was lonely and depressed. Why had everything fallen apart and why did she not do what Charlotte did and buy a smaller house in Epsom and keep the children at the school they liked. But after her mother told her friends to go home she had received the cold shoulder in Epsom.

The Children loved their Granny. Angela did not show the anger she still felt over what her mother had done to destroy the idyll which had existed in Epsom, even though it was unprofitable for Angela, it was a truly happy time. She often wondered why her best friends had all moved at the same time. Was it for the rude awakening her mother caused? And why did Angela come to Devon? Tissi had not been a friend, quite the opposite. She had caused Angela grief in the past, and also to Ross. Tissi had only ever used her knowingly or unknowingly. Her mother had openly disliked Ross, maybe for a good reason, but it had never helped. For the children's sake Angela had to forgive and forget. She had to find work and at the same time she had to be there for her children.

She unpacked her tools and fitted the garage out into a great little workshop. All her new neighbours viewed her with suspicion but she found that the next door neighbour, Norman, was to become a great friend with his wife, Fay, and all of them became customers after a while.

Angela went to timber yards and came home with all sorts of wonderful off cuts which she purchased cheaply and began to make small chests which she then decorated with continental flower and bird designs. On a Friday, after she had taken the children to school, she went to Totnes Market and sold the things she had made during the week. People asked her what else she could do and she took orders for all sorts of accessories for the kitchen, bathroom and living rooms. Bookshelves, stand-up bookshelves and bookshelves to hang on the wall, loo roll holders, foil dispensers, log baskets, cooking spoons, old fashioned salt dispensers and lavatory seats etc. Her small chests were most popular and of course the most expensive. She could sell them for £40, a small fortune in those days. However, the Totnes Market was exhausted after 2 years and she had no time to find new markets. Trade went down. She stacked shelves at the local Cash and Carry Warehouse and cleaned toilets at two petrol stations. The money Ross gave her to live on was never enough for her growing family, especially after Ross presented Sarah with a horse. He did not provide for stabling, fodder, shoeing, saddles and helmet etc. Angela had to find extra finance to pay for it all.

Then her brother in law, Jim approached her one wet and cold Friday at the market and asked if she was prepared to work in his shop. There would be a regular income. Angela agreed and Jim expanded and had a shop in Newton Abbot and Exeter.

She had to get up early to tend to the horse, then get the children out of bed, always a job. They were Ross's children as well and he had never liked to get up in the morning. They had to practice on their chosen instruments, Sarah piano, Peter violin whilst she prepared breakfast, then Peter went to the village school and Angela took Sarah to Newton Abbot Coombes Head School and then straight to Totnes to work. She had to be back by four in the afternoon when the children came home and to pick up Sarah from town.

Angela worked in the Newton Shop for a while and then she worked in Totnes and Exeter. Later on she did the stocking up of the two away shops and bringing the takings back to Totnes and doing the banking, the books and the wages. Jim and Angela worked out a way of keeping count of the stock, a kind of manual computer before they became a household item, and so Jim always knew what had sold best. Every article, every size got a number and when that item was sold it was recorded and struck off. Everything seemed to thrive and doing well.

In the summer holidays Angela took unpaid leave from the shop. Jim employed students and Tissi and Jim dealt with the work Angela would have done. Angela packed the tent and the children and her mother into the car and for six glorious weeks went to Germany, Switzerland, Austria, France and Hungary, leaving mother with Bine or taking her along. Every year a different destination, looking up the numerous relatives from the North to the South, but mainly to spend as much time with her sister and the children's cousins, so that they might get to know each other and learn German and grow up together. Every year they met and her children got to know most of the relatives who lived in West Germany. Angela introduced them to all of Germany this side of the Iron Curtain. Her children were amazed that there were so many people Angela knew, and that they were all related. In 1980 Angela and her sister Sabine spent 5 weeks in Hungary on Lake Balaton and travelling across the Danube on a prehistoric old and rickety ferry they drove into Bugazc Puzcta. They had an unforgettable time. 4 Days were spent in Budapest, camping on the Romano Campsite.

1981 they went into the mountains and, visited the fairy castle of Neuschwanstein and up the Tegelberg where they watched the kite flyers, jumping into the void and then sailing off into the sky. Angela wanted to join but could not leave the children. They also visited Angela's Grandfather's last wife who still lived in Regensburg.

In 1982 Angela, her children and her mother drove up to Schleswig Holstein and visited cousins of mother's childhood whom she had not seen since her teenage years. Then they visited another cousin in Bad Salzdetfurt and watched Diana's wedding on the German Television. Sarah thought she would like to be a princess. They arrived in Stein, stayed a week and left Granny with Bine and carried on to the Titi See in the Black Forest and stayed two weeks blissfully playing in the water with the children of the campsite. In the past they had visited this campsite many times and the children knew their way around. Peter went off in a dinghy all by himself and when Angela missed him and asked where he was they pointed out into the lake. She could not see him but her mother's heart heard his voice: Maaaammmm!

She borrowed another dinghy and rowed after him. She still could not see him but she distinctly heard him. And then she discovered him. The wind had taken him and he could not row himself back against the strong blast. And there was a storm coming up. When she reached him she lifted him out of his little rubber boat into her own and sheltered him between her legs, tied the other dinghy up and rowed back. She then took him into the tent and rubbed him dry and put him into his sleeping bag and made sure he was comfortable. He was asleep in no time. She was very angry. There were people in little boats all over the lake and they must have heard his cries for help. Nobody seemed to have taken any notice. But there seemed to be no one she could blame. She went back into the tent, looked into the sleeping department and saw that he was still asleep and started cooking. As usual, Sarah came with a string of 'best friends' and Angela put her finger on her lips to tell them not to make too much noise.

After that holiday, Angela bought a small Fiat camper van. They planned a holiday in France, which they had not yet done because Angela had always first gone to her sister and the children's cousins. In 1983 they went from Weymouth to Cherbourg and on to Bordeaux where they stayed near Ares on a wonderful Campsite in their cosy and wonderful little camper. It was such a great experience not to have to put up the tent and battle with the many tubes and pegs but to just open the door, readymade beds and if you opened the back hatch you could attach a tent to it and move out the stove which was tucked into the back and it would make a right wall and the other side would be a worktop with little shelves underneath. The Children were more grown up and helped and Angela could truly relax and enjoy the trip one hundred and fifty percent. It took no time at all to pack up, stake out their spot and go off for the day to be at the Atlantic body boarding. She bought a large bottle of olive oil and rubbed the children up with that and they spent the day in the sea.

After three weeks they packed up and went up the Dordogne spent a few days on the campsite of Rocamadour and then drove slowly up the Loire Valley and finally to the Mont St. Michel. On top of the mount Angela noticed the tide had gone out almost past the horizon and some strange concrete blocks stood out on the sand.

Asking an official what it meant he pointed to the shadow the church tower made and said it was a sundial invented by a French artist. As she watched the pointed spire reached the first block and somebody told her it was eleven o clock. She checked on her wrist watch and found that it was precisely eleven. What an amazing piece of art.

Back home in 1983. Angela learned that Tissi had become unfaithful to Jim and Jim discussed it with Angela. He was shocked and hurt and worried about the boys who were still so small. Angela was speechless. There was nothing she could say.

Jim and Tissi still ran the shop as partners, but as far as Angela was concerned, Tissi had become an unfair boss. Maybe it was jealousy or guilt. The weeks went into months and Tissi's behaviour was embarrassing. Angela tried to talk to her sister and remind her that she had small children who needed her but all she got was abuse. Angela kept quiet and did her job. But then the day came where she could not take it any longer to be told off in front of other staff for nothing else but intrigues. She looked at her sister as she ranted on about something and Angela had no idea what she was talking about, and without another word left her standing, took her handbag and walked out of the shop, thinking to hell with all her bloody relatives in England. She had parked the van at her mother's house and quickly popped in to tell her what had happened when Jim arrived and wanted to talk it over. But Angela had had enough and told him so. He did realize exactly what had happened and was deeply worried. Angela said that he could have stepped in and stop Tissi ages ago from harassing her. He apologized and said he needed Angela to be there. He had relied on Angela a lot, and he would miss her in the office. But he also understood. Angela thought him to be a soft egg.

Angela immediately found a job as manageress in a shop at Dartington trading at Shinners Bridge and earned a lot more money than at Salago.

Jim had to let go of the shops in Newton Abbot and Exeter and Angela thought: "Serves them right" She had done the run-around with her own petrol, and her wages were small. She had used her own car, Jim had never offered to pay for the petrol although Angela had mentioned it a few times, and the little Fiat caravan she had bought had to be sold because it was too expensive to use as a run around.

Jim had offered her a business car but it had never materialized. She would never be beholden to either of them again. Her mother was sad and tried to make peace between them. For the children's and their cousins and of course her mother's sake, Angela pretended that all was well so that the family could gather peacefully, but her heart was cold. She was aware and watchful. Tissi would never hurt her again, of that she was sure.

Jim and Angela often took all the children out at weekends. She would cook a meal and they all sat together. Once they were late and nothing had been cooked beforehand and the children were hungry, so she went to the K F C Place and got a party pack. Then she placed it all on the floor on a blanket and they had a pick nick in her sitting room in front of the open fire. The children never forgot the fun they had.

Peter was now boarding at Buckfast Abbey School. She fetched him home every Sunday after Mass. There was always a roast cooking in the oven and was ready to eat when they got back. After a lovely lunch they spent the afternoon at home as cosily as possible, sometimes with Peter's friends who could not go home every Sunday because they lived too far away. She missed her son very much, but hoped the education would make up for not being in Epsom anymore. Ross paid the fees, but he could not be persuaded to do the same for Sarah. Men! Still thinking women aren't worth it.

She was happy working at Dartington. There were new friends and a completely new world opened up for her. Theatre-and music festivals and special events happening at the Hall and the shopping centre! Her boss was miles away and she could run the shop the way she thought was best. Once a month a supervisor would come from the Bristol or the Bath branch and check what was going on. When Angela needed new stock, she would get her weekend helper to come in and cover whilst she went to South Petherton, where there was an old church converted to be the ware house. She could choose what she thought would sell best. It was all a great success. In the winter when there were few customers, she decorated the entire shop and rearranged the shop and put up more shelves to display things more to their advantage. It all looked festive and wonderful for Christmas and her boss was happy. She got on well with her lunchtime helper and weekend staff. For the Christmas rush she employed an ex-colleague from Salago, who also left because she couldn't get on withthe politics of Salago.

For three happy years she worked for Global Village, then she found that her boss had suddenly changed. She felt he was anxious about something. He came to visit which was rare. He kept telling her she did not meet the targets he had set for her. He wasn't angry, just sort of sad.She argued that she could not sell anything if there were no customers. He understood that. There were dead periods in the winter especially after Christmas when she did not see a single customer all day. She wanted an extra entrance for the shop because she felt the shop entrance was too obscure to attract more customers and she wanted sign posts to point to the shop, but the management of Shinners Bridge at the time would not allow it. It would spoil the entire aspect, they said and anyway the place had a preservation order.

Then all the Global Village Shops in Bristol, Bath, Honiton and Dartington closed their branches. Sadly Angela was unemployed and it was very difficult for her to find work. For the first time in her life she was on the dole. Maggy Thatcher had schemes going for people seeking work and she was sent to learn to use a computer.

Peter had finished his two years at Buckfast Abbey School and had gone to Clifton College in Bristol for a year. But Angela was not happy for him to be there. It had all been arranged behind her back whilst she was working at Dartington, between a man who called himself her friend and her ex-husband Ross.

Why ask the mother, she is after all only a stupid woman!

Peter felt unhappy and out of place. It was the sort of arrangement, that so long as his fee at the school was paid for, he could stay and it did not matter if he coped with the curriculum or not. All he needed at the end of it was the school tie and a certificate that he was a graduate. That wouldn't do for Angela or Peter. He was troubled and unhappy. So, when the first year was over, Angela fetched him back home. She had made inquiries in Teignmouth and he went to Trinity School, also a private school and Ross was happy to pay the fees because it was considerable less than the fee in Bristol.

She had sold the cottage in Abbotskerswell and moved to a beautiful Georgian house in Forde Park, Newton Abbot.

From the house at Forde Park it was only a minute's walk to the station and he took the train every day to Teignmouth and walked up the hill to school. In this school he was much more at home with the curriculum. He had new friends and Angela found that he was relaxed and happy. She got him a cat and the cat went to Peter as if they had been old friends. This cat never let itself be picked up by Angela even though she cleaned the tray and fed the beast.

From Trinity College Peter went to Exeter College.

Sarah was now at the South Devon College in Torquay. She had been telling stories at school that she was having difficulty with her mother and was helped by one of the teachers who found a room right next to the college for her.Sarah told Angela that she would be moving out. There was a heated argument. Her mother told her that she was far too young to leave home.

"I can't study here properly, and I don't want to live at home anymore, and anyway dad thinks it is alright."

Angela was heartbroken. During her daughter's formative years she wanted to have her near. She wanted to teach her to cook and see her grow into a beautiful woman. She wanted her daughter at home, meet her boyfriends, give her backing in everything she did, *and give her a background*. But Sarah had other ideas. She had found a young man and she knew everything better than her mum. Worst of all her father supported her against her mother's wishes. When Angela went to see this teacher at the college, the woman was surprised. She had a completely different picture of Sarah's mother. Angela could only guess what sort of stories Sarah had told this woman. She apologized and promised to keep an eye on Sarah.

However Sarah often came home and always brought her dirty washing. Angela was glad and willing to be there whenever her daughter turned up. She still brought home friends and she came for good meals. In spite of it all they were close. She loved her daughter so deeply and prayed that she would always be safe. That was all she could do. Ross seemed to be satisfied with Sarah's decision to live away from home. Ross never showed a fatherly and family loyalty or concern for his children's welfare. *What was it that made her fall in love with that man?* She shuddered at the thought. That man was a Jekyll and Hide.

She had sold the cottage well and had quite a bit of money left over after she paid for the house in Forde Park. However, since she had no job, she had to use the capital to live on. She also had to put a new roof on the house, a flat roof on the annexe and new windows throughout, the plumbing was dodgy and some rewiring had to be done. . Ross gave her the smallest maintenance he could get away with. After all he had to keep this young woman happy and that cost a lot of money. One day he arrived in a golden Jaguar to visit the children and his number plate showed: Feb 14. Peter proudly advised her that it cost £4500. She was appalled. That was more than their father ever gave her a year for the three of them to live on.

Angela passed her computer course. Soon she was able to handle word processing. She bought herself an Amstrad and started to write. She was also accepted into the computer room at Dartington Hall and was employed to teach other adults to use the word processor. She felt happy and fulfilled. Two of her colleagues lived in Newton Abbot and they shared the driving. It was government funded so that ordinary people would learn how to handle a computer, but after 18 months the funds were stopped. Mrs Thatcher gave and then took it away.

She applied and was accepted into the Access Course for the higher Arts at Dartington and enjoyed a wonderful year. The year was 1988-89. For her graduation she had to produce an installation and decided to break down the Berlin Wall. It took three months to make and she had to do a lot of explaining, because fellow students had little idea of what and where the iron curtain and the Berlin Wall was. English people are strange that way. They imagine that going to Europe you need to know a lot of languages. And since English people rarely learn another language they daren't go to Europe.

They know vaguely where the English colonies are around the globe but are ignorant about Europe. That's abroad, they don't speak

English. All of Europe is foreign, complicated, and too many languages with an even more complicated language system. The colonies were part of the British Empire and the so called Common Wealth. They all speak English

To make it easier for her fellow students and the visitors to understand she divided the little town of Totnes into half. She put the high wall right down Fore Street, High Street through the South Gate past Salago and into the Narrows. It would continue down the bypass, leave the Brutus Bridge to your left, keep the supermarket out and complete the circle on the Planes by the Seven Stars Hotel. That enclosed part of Totnes would then have become the Island inside the land and the Brutus Bridge would have been "Checkpoint Charlie", and the rest of the access roads fenced off with rolls and rolls of barbed wire and beyond that mine fields. Anybody living west of the Wall would never see their relatives living on the other side, never be able to shop in Boots and the East would never be able to come to Somerfield super market. If the Children were on the west side at school while the Wall went up, they could just go home but could not continue at that school and the other way around. Any supplies for the inhabitants of this non-communist island would have to be delivered by helicopters who would have to land on the castle car park, the only place free of houses to deliver food, water, coal, clothing and anything at all which is needed for the population to survive for more than two years.

The Berlin Wall was the cruellest division ever in history, separating loved ones, family and friends from one another for more than 40 years.

Her fellow students were amazed but the most amazing thing of all was that this wall in question actually came down unexpectedly and in reality only 5 months later to everybody's joy and surprize. The greatest miracle since the end of World War II.

The other thing she had to do to graduate was to write her life story. She had three months to do that. She decided to write it in prose form and managed to get it all finished in that short time.

That year Peter left to live and work in Germany and went to Berlin to witness the Happening. He spent 6 years in his mother's homeland. Sarah had gone to London and then to the Film College in Bournemouth. In her holidays she worked for Sam Goldwyn in London, and then after finishing she moved to Los Angeles. She also had a trip around the world to visit New Zealand with her backpack. She came back and finished her relationship with John, whom she had always thought she would marry, but found he was not the right man for her after all.

1990 was the year Angela's mother moved back to Germany. She did not want to die in England.

Angela worked voluntarily at the Devon Guild of Craftsmen in Bovey Tracey and was ready to work every day if and when they needed her. Then in 1993 she got a permanent job with a photograph processing works in Newton Abbot and told the Guild that she could not volunteer any more. By return of post she got the offer of a paid job at the Guild. She accepted because it was a far nicer environment than at the factory. But she was a little bitter too because she now did exactly the same job as before but was paid. They could have made her life just a little easier and given her the job earlier.

She was also head hunted to teach German at various adult education centres, which she did mostly in the evenings. Thursdays was her day off and she taught in the mornings watercolours for beginners and in the afternoon and evening German for beginners and advanced students. It was a fulfilling and busy time and she was tired but happy.

She had started to walk on Dartmoor and spent the time on a free day walking for miles and in her mind wrote poems which she put into her computer in the evening. She had also written a book about the upheaval in her childhood and called it the "Dark Edge of the Rainbow, a children's journey through the War."She used the prose she had written for her graduation.

1994 Sarah came home and together they went to visit Angela's mother in Germany. She had moved into an old people's home and was very unhappy; she missed the family. Peter who lived in Nürnberg at the time came to visit too and they had a sad- happy few days. Angela hugged her mother on that last day of their stay, and as she left the room, looking back at her mother and giving her a last farewell she had a strange foreboding, that she would not see her mother alive again.

She hugged her daughter in the long corridor to the lift. Her mother died 4 weeks later.

As Angela attended a staff meeting at the college where she taught German, she had a premonition and excused herself to have to go home now. At home the answer phone was flashing. She picked up the receiver and was listening to her mother's last words to her. Tissi and Bine were trying to get in touch. Bine's message said that mother was dying. Angela rang Tissi and asked her to book another seat on the same plane where Tissi already had a seat and together they flew to be with their mother. She had died only two hours earlier, knowing they were on their way. She was buried in the Pforzheim municipal cemetery, a beautiful park like area. Both Sarah and Peter made it to the funeral. It was an unbelievably sad farewell.

It was difficult for the family to say good bye to the one person who so lovingly was the centre of the family. Who was there in the difficult times, kept them save in the war, never for one minute complained about the difficult life she had to lead. Always a guide, always loving and caring, so very much missed.

*

On New Year's Day in 1996 she met David, a Dartmoor Guide, who had recently been widowed. They went on many walks together and one day, out of the blue he said: "Well, when will you marry me then?" She said nothing, because she had not thought about it and was not ready for that. She told him that she would have to think it over. She was fond of him and loved the walks they did together. She had friends she saw socially but it never occurred to her to have any intimate relations with any of them. She had been under the impression that as soon as you have intimate relations with anybody, the friendship is over.

They met on a regular basis and David was sweet, attentive and loving and they caught themselves making plans for the future together. Before she realized she said yes to his second request for marriage. She thought it would be nice to have a companion to love and care for and to grow old with. So she decided to start her fifth life. What a life!

*

They married in August of 1997. They bought a Campervan together and after Angela's and David's retirement travelled in Europe far and wide.

In 1999 both Sarah and Peter emigrated to New Zealand. Their father furnished them with a New Zealand Passport each. Angela had known deep in her heart that Ross would do this and only blamed herself for having been so weak as to fall for this man and let herself be manipulated and dominated by him. Looking at her two children, she always thought they would have been born to her even with another man.

Both children asked her repeatedly to come and live in New Zealand, but that was not in Angela's heart. She could not live in New Zealand. It was difficult to live in England but at least it was close to Germany which she loved with all her heart. All her life she suffered with a strange homesickness and always wanted to move back to Germany but it never worked out. Where would home have been anyway? It was now Poland and Russia. There was no home. But Germany was still the place she pined for. The wonderful forests, the will of the Germans to rebuild their beloved homeland, to believe in their land and not to bend and become slaves to or be dominated by a foreign power. For centuries, hostile neighbours have tried to steal bits of Germany all around its borders. The Czechs, the Poles, the French, the Swedes, the Danes and the Russians, all have jealously gnawed on Germany's borders. Britain has tried hard to erase it. In Germany there live many tribes but they have only one language and that keeps them together.

In 1986 the pound lost its value against the mark and the money she would have got for her house would not have been enough to buy the place in Germany she had chosen and she would not live in a

432

flat. So she thought maybe she would move to Germany when she retired, but then David came into her life.

She travelled to New Zealand to visit her children often and by 2004, when Sarah had become pregnant and was preparing to give birth in June, Angela for the 3rd time in two years travelled there to help her daughter. It was a difficult birth, but to Angela's great joy, she was able, with the help of the midwife to deliver her first grandchild, Charlie, who spent his first day on earth on Sarah's birthday. Mother and son share the same day. Isn't that a miracle?

She travelled out again 6 month later and Sarah took her to Fiji to meet the father of her little son. They are good friends, but will not marry.

It was heart-breaking to have to leave the children after every visit, but she belonged to Europe. Her first ten years with David were not easy. She realized after just a few months that David had difficulty to get over the death of his first wife. After some difficult years and a year apart, they became the best of friends and David finally accepted her as an equal and a great love between them developed. He turned out to be a good husband who cooked while she painted. Cooking is his hobby apart from taking beautiful photographs. He is a caring and loving man, albeit stubborn. Aren't all men?

David and Angela travelled in their campervan every summer for 3 to 4 months through Europe and even to the lost parts which once were Germany as well. Angela, like so many other Germans became a "weeping tourist", visiting the lost homeland. The various adventures they had during their times through Europe is another story.

Angela and David now live happily in a tiny house with a tiny but lovely garden on a hill, overlooking Newton Abbot. They still walk, Angela paints and travels to Germany in the summer on her own now. She has a small van. She puts a mattress in the back where she will sleep on her way over.

She is still homesick for Germany, and still cannot understand how it came about that she was unable to go home. She loves the English country side, but Germany is in her heart in this life and the next.

Lightning Source UK Ltd.
Milton Keynes UK
UKHW021848271121
394709UK00005B/484

9 780244 470098